Muhammad:
Son of Abraham, Brother of Moses, Successor of Jesus

Let the noble Seerah inspire you!

Ekram Haque

Muhammad: Son of Abraham, Brother of Moses, Successor of Jesus

FINDING COMMON GROUND WITH PEOPLE OF THE BOOK

Ekram Haque

Printed in the United States.

ISBN: 0692748660
ISBN 13: 9780692748664
Library of Congress Control Number: 2016910565
One Humanity Under God, Murphy, TX

Website: www.onehumanityundergod.com

Table of Contents

Dedication and Acknowledgment

I BEGIN IN THE NAME of Allaah[1], Whose grace and guidance I beseech in all my affairs, and to Whom I remain ever grateful for my spiritual and physical faculties.

This book is dedicated to Him Whose forgiveness knows no bounds and Who sustains even those who belie His existence.

I am thankful to my family for their support and encouragement of this book, and to multitudes of scholars, writers, and speakers for information and inspiration about the Prophet Muhammad, especially to Muhammad ibn Isshaaq, Abdul Malik ibn Hishaam, Muhammad ibn Shihaab Al-Zuhri, Muhammad ibn Sa'ad, Muhammad ibn Umar Al-Waaqidi, Muhammad ibn Ismaa'il Bukhari, Martin Lings, Shams Ad-Deen Muhammad ibn Qayyim Al-Jawziyah, Safiur Rahman Mubarakpuri, Ali Muhammad As-Sallaabee, and Yasir Qadhi, along with too many writers and publications to enumerate in this space.

Throughout this book I have frequently lapsed into my own reflections and invited the readers to do so as well. These reflections provide

1 The proper name for the Only Creator and Supreme Being in the Arabic language is Allaah. Muslims believe that only the word Allaah encompasses the unique qualities of the Creator. Like Muslims, Arab Christians refer to the Creator as Allaah. In this book, the author uses both Allaah and God interchangeably to help the Western readers, mindful that the term "God" is limited in its meaning.

the much-needed pause to ponder over the events that happened fourteen centuries ago and the ways they may relate to our time. My goal is not to simply tell what happened but to explain why it happened and what lessons we may draw from it.

This book would not have been completed without the fine but painstaking editing of Brandy (Noor) Springstubbe, who frequently challenged my ideas, asked probing questions, and kept me on track. I am immensely thankful to Mohammed Younus and Tanweer Akhtar for their sponsorship of this project. Last but not least, I am indebted to Fr. Joshua Whitfield, Omar Suleiman, and Ian Mevorach respectively for writing the Foreword and testimonials.

I pray that God accepts from all of us this humble effort. I hope that this book promotes appreciation for the illustrious life of the Prophet Muhammad, removes misconception, and fosters cordial relations among the peoples of faith.

Preface

THIS BIOGRAPHY OF THE PROPHET Muhammad (may Allaah's peace and blessings be upon him)[2] is as much for Christians and Jews as it is for Muslims. From my study of the *Seerah* (biography) of the Prophet, I am convinced that no Christian or Jew who studies the Prophet Muhammad's life without preconceived notions would fail to notice the nobility of his character, the holiness of his mission, and the reaffirmation of their own scriptures in his message.

I tried not to present the life of the Prophet Muhammad as merely some important historical events that occurred in sixth- and seventh-century Arabia, but rather I tried to find some meaning behind them and how they relate to our time. I will be gratified if this book can help bring the people of the world's three monotheistic religions closer.

Muslims, Christians, and Jews make up more than half of the world's population. The world would immensely benefit if the people of these three Abrahamic faiths could unite on some basic principles. If Christians and Jews delve into their own scriptures and history and do so with open minds, they will realize that they have so much in common with Muslims and with one another.

---

2 Allaah commands the believers to say *Sallallaahu Alayhi WaSallam* after the Prophet Muhammad's name is mentioned. *Sallallaahu Alayhi WaSallam* roughly translates to "may Allaah's peace and blessings be upon him." For the sake of flow, the salutations will be omitted in subsequent mentions of the Prophet's name. Some scholars consider this to be permissible.

Muslims believe that the Prophet Muhammad, like the prophets Moses and Jesus, came to unite the believers under God's divine laws. Part of Islam's mission is to confirm and complement the message of Moses and Jesus. The Qur'aan tells us that the Prophet Muhammad preached the religion of his forefathers: Abraham, Ishmael, Isaac, and other messengers who followed them like Moses and Jesus. May God's peace be upon them all! Islam is the only religion that recognizes all prophets. Jews believe in all the prophets from Adam through the end of the Old Testament, but not Jesus. Christians recognize all previously known prophets and of course Jesus, but not the Prophet Muhammad.

The Prophet Muhammad said, "My parable among the Prophets is that of a man who built a house and did an excellent and complete job, except for the space of one brick which he left unfilled. People began to go around the building, admiring it and saying, 'If only that brick were put in its place.' Among the Prophets, I am like that brick and the prophets end with me."[3]

The prophets Moses and Jesus are beloved and revered figures in Islam and an integral part of the Muslim faith. No Muslim can ever say something disrespectful about Moses, Jesus, or any of the biblical prophets. It would be akin to heresy. To Muslims, Jesus has a unique significance for a number of reasons. Jesus is the prophet immediately before the Prophet Muhammad. According to a number of prophetic traditions (*Hadith*), Jesus will return to the earth toward the end of time, and Muslims will be his helpers against the Antichrist, called *Al-Maseeh Ad-Dajjaal* in Arabic. Muslims believe that then Jesus will rectify Christian belief and say that there is only One God, Allaah, that God does not have a son, and that he is not divine. This, of course, is the central belief of the vast majority of Christians, yet it is precisely where theological conversations between Christians and Muslims should

---

3 A *Hadith* is a saying of the Prophet Muhammad. This *Hadith* was narrated by Ubayy bin Ka'ab, a close companion of the Prophet, and collected by Hadith scholars Bukhari, Muslim, Ahmad, and Tirmidhi.

begin—the question of Jesus as either divine and human as Christians believe, or simply human and prophetic as Muslims believe.

The Prophet Muhammad emphasized his special relationship to Jesus, saying in a Hadith, "I am closest to Jesus, son of Mary, among the whole of mankind in this world and the Hereafter. Prophets are brothers in faith, having different mothers. Their religion is, however, one, and there is no Apostle between Jesus and me." (Muslim, Book 30, Hadith #5836).

Like Jesus, his mother, Mary, occupies a special place in Islam. Mary (Maryam) is mentioned thirty-four times in the Qur'aan, with her genealogy and childhood described in greater detail than in the four Gospels, and the language and way of narration are seen to be particularly significant.[4]

It is generally thought that only those who follow the Prophet Muhammad are Muslim. However, the Qur'aan calls all prophets and their followers Muslim. It says that the prophet Abraham, the patriarch of all three Abrahamic faiths, was "neither a Jew nor a Christian, but he was an upright Muslim; and he was not one of the polytheists" (Aal Imraan 3:67).

In another chapter, the Qur'aan tells us that when Jacob was dying, he verified from his sons that they would worship none other than Allaah and that they were "Muslims":

> *Or were you witnesses when death approached Jacob and he asked his sons, 'Whom will you worship after me?' They said, 'We will worship your God and the God of your fathers, Abraham, Ishmael and Isaac—One True God. And we are Muslims (in submission) to Him.*[5]

---

4 Giancarlo Finazzo, "The Virgin Mary in the Qur'an," *L'Osservatore Romano*, weekly edition in English, April 13, 1978.

5 Baqarah 2:133.

Our world today is mired in violence due to hatred and misunderstanding among the people of the world's three great religions—Islam, Christianity, and Judaism. It is not to say that this is the only cause of violence in the world, but certainly it's one of the most significant. How long can we go on living like this? What legacy are we going to bequeath to our children and their children?

In 2007, a group of Muslim scholars published an open letter to the People of the Book calling it "A Common Word between Us and You." The letter sprang from a verse in the Qur'aan, wherein God commanded the Prophet Muhammad to say to the Christians and Jews:

> *O People of the Scripture! Come to a common word between us and you: that we shall worship none but God, and that we shall ascribe no partner unto Him, and that none of us shall take others for lords beside God." And if they turn away, then say: "Bear witness that we are they who have submitted (unto Him)."*[6]

The letter says, "Muslims and Christians together make up well over half of the world's population. Without peace and justice between these two religious communities, there can be no meaningful peace in the world. The future of the world depends on peace between Muslims and Christians." It further states:

> "The basis for this peace and understanding already exists. It is part of the very foundational principles of both faiths: love of the One God, and love of the neighbor. These principles are found over and over again in the sacred texts of Islam and Christianity. The Unity of God, the necessity of love for Him, and the necessity of love of the neighbor is thus the common ground between Islam and Christianity."

The Prophet Muhammad said, "None of you will have true faith until you love for your neighbor what you love for yourself."[7]

---

6 Aal Imraan 3:64

7 Muslim, Hadith #45

In the New Testament, Jesus Christ says,

> *Hear, O Israel; The Lord our God is one Lord: And thou shalt love the Lord thy God with all thy heart, and with all thy soul, and with all thy mind, and with all thy strength: this is the first commandment. And the second is like, namely this, Thou shalt love thy neighbor as thyself. There is none other commandment greater than these.*[8]

When the Prophet arrived in Madinah, he wrote a charter in which he made the Jews part of "One *Ummah*" (nation) with rights and responsibilities. He recognized that the Jews were the chosen people of their time, and, as fellow monotheists, they were his natural allies against the polytheists. The Qur'aan confirms the Jews' status as the "chosen people": "O Children of Israel! Remember My favors which I bestowed upon you, and that I exalted you above all the nations of the time."[9]

I encourage my Jewish and Christian brethren to reflect on the similarities among the three Abrahamic faiths and ask, Could they be mere coincidences of history? Muslims believe in the miracles that the prophets Moses, Jesus, and others performed with God's permission. If Jews and Christians were to study the life of the Prophet Muhammad from the authentic sources, as this book strives to present, they would realize that he could not possibly have been a "false prophet," as some allege. The People of the Book should ask, Could a false prophet command such an abiding respect from his followers consistently for nearly a millennia and a half? Has a false prophet ever stood the scrutiny of time and inspired great civilizations and enlightenment? Could the ranks of his followers keep growing if he were not a true messenger of God? And finally, is it a mere coincidence that the innumerable Jews and Christians who accepted Islam over the last 1,447 years found in it a reaffirmation of their former faith?

---

8 Mark 12:29–31 King James Version (KJV)

9 Baqarah 2:122

An open and honest look at his life, the miracles he performed, and the certainty of knowledge he exhibited will inextricably lead to one conclusion: that the Prophet Muhammad was God's true Messenger to mankind.

Now, let us look at some of the relevant verses from all three holy books to reflect on the unmistakable similarities. The Qur'aan says that God had given clear signs of His Last Messenger in earlier scriptures. Those signs were so clear that a denial of the Prophet Muhammad would be unimaginable:

> *Those to whom We gave the Scripture (Jews and Christians) recognize him (Muhammad) as they recognize their sons. But verily, a party of them conceals the truth while they know it.*[10]

By citing verses from the Torah and Gospels to draw parallels with Islam, I have opened myself to criticism from Muslims who might ask, Why am I using scriptures that have undergone several revisions over the centuries? To that I would say that although the Torah and Gospels have not been preserved in the same way the Qur'aan was, there are many verses in the ancient scriptures that bear strikingly close resemblance to the verses in the Muslim holy book and therefore can be assumed to have come from the same source.

In the Torah, God said to the Prophet Moses,

> *I will raise them up a Prophet from among their brethren, like unto thee, and will put my words in his mouth; and he shall speak unto them all that I shall command him. And it shall come to pass, that whosoever will not hearken unto my words which he shall speak in my name, I will require it of him.*[11]

While Christians believe the above passage is talking about Jesus, the Muslims see it as referring to the Prophet Muhammad, as the latter was

---

10 Baqarah 2:146

11 Deuteronomy 18: 18–19 KJV

the only prophet from the progeny of Ishmael, who was an older brother of Isaac from a different mother. The Prophet Muhammad was like Moses in that he also received a new canonical law and fought against those who showed enmity to God's commands. For them there was no other prophet like Moses among the children of Israel. Jesus was different from the prophet Moses in that he was born without a father and raised up alive when the Romans tried to crucify him, while Moses had a normal birth and died.[12] In his first coming, Jesus did not establish political authority while the Prophet Muhammad and Moses did.

Jews might say that Deuteronomy 18:17–19 refers to the whole line of prophets God would send after Moses to preach His truth and guide His people, and they would be only from the children of Israel. However, a famous rabbi in Madinah, Abdullaah bin Salaam, had no problem accepting the Prophet Muhammad as the prophet foretold in the Jewish scriptures. Since then, many other Jews have accepted the Prophet Muhammad and embraced Islam, recognizing it as the continuation of the religion of Moses.

According to Jewish tradition, the religion that Noah[13] taught consisted of seven laws:

Do not deny God
Do not blaspheme God
Do not commit murder
Do not engage in illicit sexual relations
Do not steal
Do not eat of a live animal
Establish courts/legal systems to ensure obedience to the law

---

12 Muslims believe that Allaah raised Jesus unto Himself when the Romans tried to crucify him and that he will return to complete his mission and then die. The Romans did crucify someone but that was not Jesus.

13 Noah came before Moses and he is considered by both Muslims and Jews to be a prophet.

Rabbinic tradition holds that while the Jews are obligated to keep all 613 commandments in the Torah, all non-Jews, regardless of religion, are subject to these seven laws in order to be considered righteous people. Any future religion claiming to be of divine origin had to, at minimum, adhere to them. All seven of those principles are found in Islam.

The Qur'aan says that the religion of the Prophet Muhammad is the same as those of God's other prophets. In the following verse, some of God's prophets are mentioned, while all are implied:

> *He has ordained for you the same religion which He ordained for Noah, and that which We have revealed to you, and that which We ordained for Abraham, Moses and Jesus saying you should establish religion and make no divisions in it.*[14]

The Qur'aan says,

> *And remember, Jesus, the son of Mary, said, 'O Children of Israel! I am the Messenger of Allaah (sent) to you, confirming the Law (which came) before me and giving glad tidings of a Messenger to come after me, whose name shall be Ahmed.' But when he came to them with clear signs, they said, 'This is evident sorcery!'*[15]

Ahmed and *Muhammad* are derived from the same Arabic root that means *praised*, so the Prophet's two names mean *The Praised One*. In the Qur'aan Ahmed has been mentioned once to refer to the Prophet Muhammad from the blessed tongue of Jesus.

> Jesus said, *"And I will pray to the Father, and he shall give you another Comforter, that he may abide with you forever."*[16]

---

14 Shoora 42:13

15 Saff 61:6

16 John: 14:16

Parakletos, the Greek term used here for *comforter*, means "called to one's side, called to one's aid." Other translations are *advocate* and *helper*.

> *I have yet many things to say unto you," Jesus said, "but ye cannot bear them now. Howbeit when he, the Spirit of truth, is come, he will guide you into all truth: for he shall not speak of himself; but whatsoever he shall hear, that shall he speak: and he will shew you things to come. He shall glorify me: for he shall receive of mine, and shall shew it unto you."* [17]

> Jesus further said, *"Nevertheless I tell you the truth; It is expedient for you that I go away: for if I go not away, the Comforter will not come unto you; but if I depart, I will send him unto you."* [18]

Christians normally read the above verses from the Gospel of John as referring to the Holy Spirit. However, according to Luke 1:15 and 1:41, the Holy Spirit was already present in the world prior to Jesus's birth.[19]

Judaism, Christianity, and Islam emphasize the unity of God. For example, the Torah says, "Hear, O Israel: The Lord our God, the Lord is one!"[20] As we saw in Mark 12:29–30, Jesus affirmed that "the Lord is One God. And the Qur'aan said, "And your God is one God; there is no God but He! He is the Beneficent, the Merciful."[21]

In their open letter to the Christian world, the Muslim scholars write:

> "If Muslims and Christians are not at peace, the world cannot be at peace. With the terrible weaponry of the modern world; with

17 John 16:12–14 KJV

18 John 16:7 KJV

19 Abu Ameenah Bilal Philips, *The True Message of Jesus Christ* (Riyadh: International Islamic Publishing House, 2002)

20 Deuteronomy 6:4 KJV

21 Baqarah 2:163

> Muslims and Christians intertwined everywhere as never before, no side can unilaterally win a conflict between more than half of the world's inhabitants. Thus our common future is at stake. The very survival of the world itself is perhaps at stake."

On a side note, but an important one, more than 120 Muslim scholars have issued a point-by-point denunciation of ISIS and its claim to Islamic caliphate. Yet, much of the mainstream US media have not found this newsworthy.

Muslims are not at war with Christians or Jews, nor should they be so long as the latter do not wage war against Muslims on account of their religion, oppress them, or drive them out of their homes. The Qur'aan says:

> *Allaah does not forbid you respecting those who have not made war against you on account of (your) religion, and have not driven you forth from your homes, that you show them kindness and deal with them justly; surely Allah loves the doers of justice.*[22]

On the other hand, the Qur'aan praises the righteous among the Jews and Christians, saying:

> *They are not all alike. Among the People of the Book there is a party who stand by their covenant; they recite the word of Allaah in the hours of night and prostrate themselves before Him. They believe in Allaah and the Last Day, and enjoin what is good and forbid evil, and hasten, vying with one another, in good works. And these are among the righteous.*[23]

In his thought-provoking article in *The Huffington Post*, Ian Mevorach writes:

> *Historically, most Christian theologians—including John of Damascus, Thomas Aquinas, Dante, Nicholas of Cusa, and Martin Luther—have*

---

22 Mumtahanah 60:8

23 Aal Imraan 3:114-115

seen Muhammad not as a "Spirit of Truth" but as a "Spirit of Error," a false prophet or heretic. There are many Christians today who respect the Islamic tradition and would never make such an offensive statement about Muhammad.

However, the majority of Christians still maintain a fundamentally Islamophobic position on Muhammad. So I believe that the time has come for peacemaking Christians to contradict this position directly. Changing our view of Muhammad—so that we recognize him as a true prophet rather than discredit him as a false prophet—would effectively inoculate Christians against Islamophobia and would help to establish a new paradigm of cooperative Christian-Muslim relations.

There is no better candidate than Muhammad, no one in fact that comes even close, in terms of fulfilling Jesus's promise of the Spirit of Truth who would bring forth a new revelation from God.[24]

In conclusion, I invite our brethren from the Jewish and Christian faiths to read this biography of the Prophet Muhammad with open minds and decide for themselves if the noble life described herein could in fact be that of a true prophet of God. His triumphs and tragedies, prophecies and conduct, miracles and spirituality, his public and private life, and the revelations he recited deserve an open exploration. The truth emancipates us from irrational fear. Let us seek it without fetters. I believe that religious creed is too serious a matter to be left to chance, and it must be based on analysis, comparison, verification, and reflection.

Ekram Haque
August 2016
Dallas, TX

---

24 Ian Mevorach, "Did Jesus Predict Muhammad? A Biblical Portal Between Christianity and Islam," *Huffington Post*, April 25, 2016, http://www.huffingtonpost.com/ian-mevorach/did-jesus-predict-muhammad_b_9762934.html.

Foreword

"UNITY OF MANKIND, UNITY OF religions, unity of Christians—we ought to search for these unities again, so that a more positive epoch may really begin." These are the words of Cardinal Joseph Ratzinger, later Pope Benedict XVI, and they are words worthy of our age.

In 2006 at the end of his papal visit to Turkey, Pope Benedict made an unscheduled visit to the beautiful Blue Mosque in Istanbul. There he was moved and drawn to pray. He later described the moment in sacred and spiritual terms:

> *[D]ivine Providence granted me, almost at the end of my journey, an unscheduled visit which proved rather important: my visit to Istanbul's famous Blue Mosque. Pausing for a few minutes of recollection in that place of prayer, I addressed the one Lord of Heaven and earth, the Merciful Father of all humanity. May all believers recognize that they are his creatures and witness to true brotherhood!*

A pope paying a sudden visit to a famous mosque, suddenly moved to pray, praying that "all believers recognize that they are his creatures and witness to true brotherhood!" This, I suggest, is the moment, the spiritual moment open to all of us—Christians, Jews, Muslims, all humanity—an opportunity given by God. It's a moment meant for unity, for fellowship and solidarity, for mutual understanding and peace—under God and in His light.

And it's the spiritual moment in which this book has come to be, as a gift for all of us.

All believers in God hope for unity in God because we believe God to be one. Fundamental to Christian, Jewish, and Islamic belief is the yearning for unity—the communion and brotherhood of man. Although of different faiths, this desire is common to us all, and it's a desire all of us must more pressingly pursue in this modern era of secularism and sectarian violence, when all religions are so clearly misused and so falsely blamed. Unity should be a priority for all of us who believe in God.

But what sort of unity? Indeed, it is good for people of every faith to cooperate and stand in solidarity with one another for our common earthly good. We should remain committed (as most people of faith have clearly been) to caring for one another, protecting one another, feeding one another, and speaking up for one another. We should remain partners for a better world, witnesses to the sort of love God's children ought to have for one another.

But there is obviously a deeper unity meant for us too. And that's a theological and spiritual unity had in the light of God. This is the deeper sort of unity that every believer knows is the will of God, the sort of unity all of us ought to seek. A unity not only of this world, but a unity that will bear fruit even in the next.

That's why this book is a gift—because it takes us to the very ground of the debates necessary if Christians, Jews, and Muslims are to find that truly more divine unity. This book invites us to consider the Prophet as prophet. It's a biography that invites theological reflection and not just cultural and sociological reflection. If Christians are to engage seriously with Islam, they must wrestle with the claims Muslims make about Muhammad. And likewise if Muslims are to engage seriously with Christianity, they must wrestle with the claims Christians make about Jesus. That's where the dialogue must begin and end if we are serious about seeking the unity God wills. That's why this is a good book—because it brings us to the place we need to be if we're to talk about any of this seriously.

Now, Christians and Muslims have "engaged" with one another since the seventh century, since Saint John Damascene at least. Sometimes that engagement was beautiful, brilliant, and fruitful, at other times squalid and sinful. Today, however, Christians and Muslims must make a renewed effort toward a common cause for unity, neither shying away from hard theological differences nor trying simply to defeat the other by mere arguments. Rather, standing at the end of so many centuries, we owe it to our forebears and ourselves to speak to one another peacefully but also with the integrity of belief. That's what this book is about, and that's why it's welcome.

As a Christian, I remain convinced of the divinity of Jesus Christ and of the divinity of the Holy Spirit, as well as the triunity of the one God. John's Gospel, the Acts of the Apostles, Saint Irenaeus, the Councils of Nicaea and Constantinople, and so on are all pretty stalwart ancient witnesses to this fundamental creed of Christians. Nonetheless, we must still debate, argue even, charitably and peacefully—even about these first order matters. Again, because the God whom we both worship demands we seek a unity that is more than earthly, a unity rooted in our worship of God together, all of us, as brothers and sisters.

So this is a welcome book. I received it as a gift and recommend it as a gift. It is a book of spiritual moment. We should read it, then look at one another and extend hands of peace. And then we should open our hearts and minds and mouths and speak to one another as brothers—until God in His mercy makes us so forever. *InshaAllaah* (God Willing).

— **Father Joshua J. Whitfield**
Dallas, Texas
August 2016

Pronunciation and Terminologies

THE SPELLING OF ARABIC NAMES and terminologies used in this book is based on the actual sound of that word in the Arabic language. Therefore, diacritical marks have not been used to elongate the sound. For example, instead of using the common spelling for *Allāh*, the book spells it as *Allaah*; similarly, instead of *Qur'ān*, *Qur'aan.* Also, any Arabic word ending in *Taa Marbutah* (ـة) is represented in the English transliteration by an *h* (for example, *Madinah* instead of *Medina*).

Arabic	English
Aadam	Adam
Aayah	Verse
Abu	Father
Allaah	God
Ansaar	Helpers
Ansaari	Helper
Bin	Son
Bint	Daughter
Eesa	Jesus
Fir'awn	Pharaoh
Hijrah	Migration
Iblees	Devil
Ibn	Son
Ibraahim	Abraham
Injeel	Gospel
Ismaa'il	Ishmael
Israa	Night Journey
Jacob	Yaaqub
Jibreel	Gabriel
Madinah	Medina
Mai'raaj	Ascension
Makkah	Mecca
Maryam	Mary
Masjid Al-Aqsa	Mosque in Jerusalem
Masjid Al-Haraam	Sacred Mosque in Makkah
Mikaa'il	Michael
Muhaajir	Emigrant
Muhaajireen	Emigrants
Musa	Moses
Mushrik	Polytheist/Pagan
Nabi	Prophet
Nuh	Noah
Rasul	Messenger
Sahaabah	Companions
Sahaabi	Companion
Shaam	Syria
Shaytaan	Devil
Surah	Chapter
Tawraat	Torah
Umm	Mother
Yahya	John the Baptist
Yusuf	Josef
Zakaat	Mandatory Alms

Who Was This Man?

It is difficult to aptly describe someone who was both an ordinary man and a Messenger of God; who commanded spiritual and worldly authority like no one ever did; and who is loved by 1.8 billion inhabitants of the earth.

No doubt we are living in a time of great political and religious turmoil, a time in which fringe groups of Muslims and non-Muslims are pushing for a clash of civilizations. It is therefore imperative that the life story—the *Seerah*—of Muhammad the Messenger of God be retold so Muslims can be reminded about his noble legacy and non-Muslims informed thereof.

One may ask, what is the need for another book on Seerah when so many by men of renown are available? A simple answer is that books on the Seerah of the Prophet have been written in every era in order to convey his message to the people of that time, in the vernacular of that time, and in a way that it can relate to the people of that time. Many of the Seerah books of the past have been academic in approach or have merely described what happened. This book aims to analyze the significance of these historical events and apply the lessons drawn from them in order to promote mutual respect and peaceful coexistence among all people.

In our time, the voices of extremism on both sides of the divide are winning. Extremist groups among Muslims are bent on fighting the disbelievers, and those in the opposite camp are portraying Islam as evil. Neither side shows any interest in a sincere, honest, and respectful dialogue. If voices of reason remain silent, the extremists and hatemongers on both sides will set the course of interhuman relations, and the world will continue to suffer from unnecessary misunderstanding and senseless violence.

The Prophet followed a path of moderation and mercy in all his affairs, having been sent by God, according to the Qur'aan, as a "Mercy to the Worlds." God called Muslims a "justly balanced nation" that should avoid all extremes. Therefore, extremism of any sort is antithetical to Islam, and many of the things that the extremist Muslims are doing in the name of Islam are the exact opposite of what the Messenger of Mercy preached and lived by. Historically Muslims and Christians enjoyed a peaceful and mutually beneficial coexistence, even offering one another help in times of need. For example, when the early believers faced persecution in Makkah (Mecca), the Christian King Negus offered them refuge in Abyssinia. The Prophet Muhammad advised the early group of Muslims to migrate to Abyssinia because Negus was a just ruler who would not persecute them for their belief. Thus these early Muslims enjoyed a period of peaceful refuge under the protection of a Christian king.

Muslims, Christians, Jews, Hindus, and others could greatly benefit from understanding the wisdom behind God creating us to be different. Had we not looked different, spoken different languages, believed in different religions, how would we ever stand out? Out of their sincere convictions, people will continue to invite others to their own faiths, believing that theirs is the only true religion. And they should have the freedom to do so, without coercing or compelling others. However, in the end only God will judge them and tell them if they hit the goal or missed the mark. The Qur'aan says:

> *To each of you We prescribed a law and a path. Had Allaah willed, He would have made you one nation (united in religion), but He intended to test you in what He has given you; so race to all that is good. You will all return to Allaah, Who will then inform you concerning that over which you differed.*[25]

Muslims believe the Prophet Muhammad is the greatest in the long line of God's prophets and messengers, which began with Adam and continued through Noah, Abraham, Moses, and Jesus and culminated in Muhammad. There were thousands in between, although the Qur'aan mentions only twenty-five of them by name, may God's peace and blessings be upon them all! However, when a Muslim extols the virtues of the Prophet Muhammad, others might see it as self-serving. Therefore, it is important to look at what some influential non-Muslims have to say about him.

The renowned French writer, poet, and politician Alphonse de Lamartine[26] said of the Prophet Muhammad, "As regards all standards by which human greatness may be measured, we may well ask, is there any man greater than he?"

When American writer Michael Hart[27] compiled a list of the history's most influential people, he put the Prophet Muhammad at the top. In explaining his decision, Hart said, "My choice of Muhammad to lead the list of the world's most influential persons may surprise some readers and may be questioned by others, but he was the only man in history who was supremely successful on both the religious and secular level."

---

25 Maa'idah 5:48.

26 Alphonse Marie Louis de Prat de Lamartine (Oct 21, 1790–Feb 28, 1869) was instrumental in founding the Second Republic and the continuation of the Tricolor as the flag of France.

27 Michael H. Hart (born 1932) is an American astrophysicist and author, most notably of *The 100: A Ranking of the Most Influential Persons in History*. He has described himself as a white separatist and is active in white separatist causes.

What Is Seerah?

The word *Seerah* comes from the Arabic language and means a journey. When Muslims use it in a religious context, it typically means the journey through the life of the Prophet Muhammad.

Why Should We Learn About Muhammad?

There are numerous reasons. The early generation of Muslims taught the Seerah to their children like they taught them the Qur'aan. There are about fifty verses in the Qur'aan that command the Muslims to know the Prophet, to follow him, to respect and obey him, to support him, and to send peace and blessings upon him.

For instance, the Qur'aan says:

- *"The Prophet is closer to the believers than themselves."* (Ahzaab 33:6)
- *"Indeed in the Messenger of Allaah you have a good example to follow for him who hopes in Allaah and the Last Day, and remembers Allaah much."* (Ahzaab 33:21)
- *"He who obeys the Messenger, has indeed obeyed Allaah."* (Nisaa 4:80)
- *"O you who believe! Raise not your voices above the voice of the Prophet, nor speak aloud to him as you speak to one another, lest your deeds should be wasted while you perceive not."*[28]

Muslims cannot achieve the excellence of faith until they love the Prophet Muhammad more than their own selves. The Prophet said, "None of you will be a true believer until I am more beloved to you than yourself" (Al-Bukhari).

Once Umar bin Al-Khattaab, one of the closest Companions of the Prophet and the second rightly guided caliph, said to the Prophet, "By Allaah, I love you more than everything except myself."

28 Hujuraat 49:2.

The Prophet replied, "No, O Umar, your faith will not be complete until you love me more than yourself." After some soul searching, Umar professed that now he loved the Prophet more than himself.

Allaah mandates loving the Prophet more than oneself in several places in the Qur'aan, and the wisdom behind it is quite evident. Without an abiding love (and allegiance) to the Prophet, believers would have defied his authority and indirectly Allaah's. One should also love the Prophet more because he was a mercy for us in this life and a source of salvation in the Hereafter with his intercession with Allaah on our behalf.

Reflections: People of other faiths are not obligated to love the Prophet Muhammad as Muslims do, but knowledge of Muslim sentiments toward the Prophet should help during interfaith dialogue. Drawing cartoons of the Prophet or insulting him surely hurts Muslim feelings. To the contrary, no Muslim will ever insult Jesus, whom the Qur'aan refers to as Eesa. Jesus and his mother, Mary, are towering figures in Islam, and the chapter in the Qur'aan called "Maryam" is named after Mary.

The Prophet once said, "I will be the leader of the children of Adam on the Day of Judgment, without boasting."

He has been given many honorary names and attributes, such as:

- Muhammad and Ahmad—These are his proper names. *Muhammad* means the "praised one." The Prophet Muhammad is constantly praised around the world by Muslims in their prayers. And in the Hereafter he will be praised by the entirety of humanity when he is the only one who intercedes with Allaah (God) on behalf of the people. Ahmad means the "one who is highly praised." This name is mentioned in the Qur'aan from the tongue of Jesus.

- He is Al-Maahi, someone who eradicates paganism. Within a short span of time, in his own lifetime, the idol worship was wiped out from the Arabian Peninsula.
- He is Al-Haashir, "the gatherer" around whom people will assemble on Judgment Day.
- He is Al-Aaqib, the last of God's messengers and prophets.
- He is the Prophet of Mercy for all of humankind.

A Muslim's life is intertwined with the Prophet's quite literally from the cradle to the grave. When a Muslim is born, the Adhaan (call to prayer) is said in his or her ears, and it includes the phrase, "I bear witness that Muhammad is the Messenger of Allaah."[29] Similarly, this phrase is used in the Adhaan for every mandatory prayer. A Muslim prayer is not complete without asking for Allaah's blessings on the Prophet and his family. When a dead Muslim is being carried to the grave, people say, "*BismiAllaah wa Alaa Sunnati Rasul Allaah*"[30] (in the name of Allaah and according to the way of the Messenger of Allaah). And finally, when a deceased is questioned in the grave soon after the burial, one of the questions he or she is asked is about who the Prophet Muhammad is.

The Prophet was extremely concerned about his followers, which is confirmed by God himself:

> *Verily, there has come unto you a Messenger from among yourselves. It grieves him that you should receive any injury or difficulty. He is eager for you; for the believers he is kind, merciful, and full of pity.*[31]

Once the Prophet said to his *Sahaabah* (Companions) that he wanted to meet with his brothers. Surprised, the Companions asked, "Aren't we your brothers?"

---

29 Some scholars say this practice is based on a weak Hadith.

30 According to another version, *BismiAllaah wa Alaa Millati Rasul Allaah*

31 Tawbah 9:128.

"No," he said, "my brothers are those who will come after me and believe in me without having seen me." He would pray for his yet-to-come brothers and seek God's forgiveness for them.

By studying his noble life, Muslims can revive his Sunnah and defend him against smears.

A Muslim should study the Seerah to know the morals and manners of the Prophet, to discover how he acted in peace and war, with his family and friends, and with the masses and his adversaries. The Prophet said that one of his greatest missions other than conveying God's message was to perfect the good manners of the people. He promised, "The most beloved and nearest to me on the Day of Judgment will be one with the best character."[32]

Studying the life of the Prophet Muhammad is essential for the learning of the Qur'aan. The text of the Qur'aan cannot be truly understood without the context that only the Prophet's Seerah provides. Much of the Qur'aan was revealed in response to events that happened in his life or those of the people around him.

His was a miraculous life. He was sent to a backward, illiterate people whom the Romans and the Persians held in low esteem. But within a span of twenty-three years, he transformed the Arab society into the world's best and most progressive.

He is among the most celebrated of Allaah's creations. He was praised in the scriptures of previous nations before he was born. He himself said, "Allaah had decreed me when Aadam (Adam) was between the mud and spirit," meaning the soul had not yet been breathed into the body of Aadam.

---

32 Sunan At-Tirmidhi, Hadith #2018.

He is praised in the heavens by Allaah and His angels. And Allaah makes it an obligation for Muslims to invoke His peace and blessings upon the Prophet.

> *Indeed, Allaah confers blessing upon the Prophet, and His angels (ask Him to do so). O you who have believed, ask (Allaah to confer) blessing upon him and salute him with a worthy salutation.*[33]

Sources of the Seerah

Teaching the Seerah or writing about it has its challenges. The Prophet Muhammad did not have an official biographer who shadowed him, pen in hand, to record the events of his life. That is especially true of his life before the Prophethood. He was born an orphan, his father having died a few months before his birth. By the time he was six, his mother had died, and he was transferred into the care of his grandfather. By the time he was eight, the grandfather had also passed away. From then onward until he was married at age twenty-five, he lived under the care of one of his uncles. The Prophethood did not come until age forty; before that time people had no clue that an orphan of yesteryear would become a mighty messenger of God. Only his truthfulness and trustworthiness marked him as different from his peers; hence they called him Al-Saadiq (the truthful) and Al-Ameen (the trustworthy).

The first people to compile anecdotes about the Prophet's life were the sons of his Companions. Many of them had not seen the Prophet or had not been old enough to record anything during his lifetime. In most cases, they wrote down the stories their parents had told them about the Prophet. And these stories were more about wars than about the everyday life of the Prophet.

---

33 Ahzaab 33:56.

The earliest of these writers was Abaan bin Uthmaan[34]— the son of Uthmaan bin Affaan, who was the son-in-law of the Prophet. Abaan compiled a short history of the Seerah.

Then there was Urwah bin Al-Zubayr bin Awwaam. Zubayr was a cousin and close Companion of the Prophet. Urwah's mother was Asmaa bint Abi Bakr, and his aunt was Aayeshah, the wife of the Prophet. Urwah was one of the primary narrators of Hadith[35], Tafseer, and Seerah, as he had easy access to Aayeshah.

Abaan bin Affaan—the son of Uthmaan, who was the son-in-law of the Prophet—compiled a short history of the Seerah. These early writings are not available, perhaps because they were incorporated in the works of later generations of Seerah scholars.

One of the earliest compilers of the Seerah was Ibn Shihaab Az-Zuhri. His work was among the first compilations that were done formally and systematically.

Muhammad ibn Isshaaq, born in Madinah around 85 AH (704/705 CE)[36], is the foremost scholar of the Seerah. He grew up around the children and grandchildren of the Sahaabah. Ibn Isshaaq began writing everything that he heard about the Prophet in chronological order. He was known for routinely citing the chain of narrators for the information he collected, including their lineage. The chain of narration is something unique to Islamic scholarship. Collectors ask the people they are collecting from, "Who told you, and who told that person?" until they can trace it back to the Prophet Muhammad. (It is to be kept in mind, though, that the Seerah historians

---

34 *Bin* means the son of (and *bint* means the daughter of) the person whose name follows. Another word interchangeably used for the son is *ibn*.

35 Hadith are sayings of the Prophet Muhammad. They are the Prophet's own words but based on God's revelations to him outside of the Qur'aan.

36 AH stands for Al Hijrah, the year the Prophet Muhammad migrated from Makkah to Madinah. CE stands for the Common Era.

have not used the same strict standards of authentication as Hadith collectors.) In order to collect the information on the Prophet's life Ibn Isshaaq traveled to Basrah and Kufah, where many of the Companions' children lived. Before he died in 150 AH (767/768 CE), Ibn Isshaaq had penned a massive book on the Seerah, called *Sirat Rasul Allah* (*Path of the Messenger of Allaah*).

Another indispensable name in the genre of the Seerah is that of Abdul Malik ibn Hishaam, who was a student of Ibn Isshaaq. Ibn Hishaam was mindful that his teacher's work on the Seerah was too voluminous for the masses, and so he decided to abridge it by trimming the chains and lineages and eliminating repetitions. He also removed a long chapter called "The History of Humanity."

While much of Ibn Isshaaq's work is lost, abridged versions are available, including one translated into English by A. Gillaume. However, what Ibn Hishaam put together is more widely available under the title *Seerat ibn Hishaam*.

Other than books, the collections of Hadith are another great source of information on the Seerah of the Prophet Muhammad. Although collected somewhat later, the Hadith follows a stricter standard for fact-checking than the Seerah books. One of the earliest was Imam Maalik bin Anas's *Al-Mu'atta*. At the top of the Hadith books is Imam Al-Bukhari's *Saheeh Al-Bukhari*, followed by *Muslim*, *Tirmidhi*, *Sunan Abu Dawud*, *Nasaa'i*, and *Ibn Maajah*. Collectively they are called "the Six Authentic Books of Hadith" (As-Sihaah As-Sittah).

Books on *Shamaa'il* (traits) of the Prophet were written by Imam Muhammad ibn Esa Al-Tirmidhi and others.

Books on *Dalaa'il* (miracles) of the Prophet include *Ad-Dalaa'il An-Nabuwwah* by Abu Bakr Ahmad ibn Husayn Al-Bayhaqi.

What the Prophet Said

The Prophet Muhammad's sayings (Hadith) are in thousands. Here I quote a selected few.

On Human Equality

"All mankind is from Adam and Eve; an Arab has no superiority over a non-Arab or a non-Arab over an Arab; similarly, a white person has no superiority over a black person or a black person over a white person, except by piety and good action." [37]

On Forgiveness

"When Allah created His creation, He wrote in a Book which is with Him, above the Throne: 'My Mercy prevails over My wrath.'" [38]

The Prophet quoted Allaah as saying: *"O son of Adam, so long as you call upon Me, and put your hope in Me, I shall forgive you for what you have done, and I shall not mind. O son of Adam, were your sins to reach the clouds in the sky and were you then to ask forgiveness of Me, I shall forgive you. O son of Adam, were you to come to Me with an earthful of sins and were you then to face Me, without having worshiped anyone other than Me, I shall forgive you."* [39]

When someone asked him to invoke God's curse on his enemies who were persecuting him, the Prophet: "God did not send me to curse people; I have been sent as mercy." [40]

God said about the Prophet in the Qur'aan: *"And We have not sent you except as a mercy to the worlds."* [41]

37 Tirmidhi

38 Bukhari and Muslim

39 Tirmidhi

40 Muslim

41 Ambiyaa 21:107

On Reliance on God

The Prophet said to Companion Abdullaah bin Abbaas: *"O young man, let me teach you some words. Be mindful of Allaah and Allaah will protect you. Be mindful of Allaah and you will find Him in front of you. If you ask, ask of Allaah. If you seek help, seek help from Allaah. Know that if the nations were to gather to benefit you with something, they would not be able to benefit you except with what Allaah has already decreed for you. And if they were to gather to harm you with something, they would not be able to harm you except with what Allaah has already decreed for you. The pens have been lifted and the pages have dried."* [42]

"Know Allaah during times of prosperity, He will know you in times of adversity. Know that what has passed you by was never to befall you. And know that what has befallen you was never to have passed you by. And know that victory accompanies perseverance, relief accompanies affliction, and ease accompanies hardship." [43]

On Love and Kindness

"None of you truly believes (in Allaah and in His religion) until he loves for his brother what he loves for himself." [44]

"Let whosoever believes in Allaah and in the Last Day either speak good or be silent. Let whosoever believes in Allaah and in the Last Day honor his neighbor. Let whosoever believes in Allaah and in the Last Day honor his guest." [45]

42 Tirmidhi

43 ibid

44 Bukhari and Muslim

45 ibid

On Avoiding Doubtful Things

"Truly, what is lawful is clear, and what is unlawful is clear, and between them are doubtful matters which many people do not know about. He who guards against doubtful things keeps his religion and honor blameless, and he who indulges in doubtful things indulges in fact in unlawful things, just as a shepherd who pastures his flock round a preserve will soon pasture them in it. Beware! every king has a preserve, and the things Allaah has declared unlawful are His preserves. Beware! in the body there is a flesh; if it is sound, the whole body is sound, and if it is corrupt, the whole body is corrupt, and behold! It is the heart." [46]

On Worship

The Prophet quoted Allaah as saying: *"Nothing endears My servant to Me than doing what I have made obligatory upon him to do. And My servant continues to draw nearer to Me with extra prayers so that I shall love him. When I love him, I shall become his hearing with which he shall hear, his sight with which he shall see, his hands with which he shall hold, and his feet with which he shall walk. And if he asks Me for something, I shall surely give it to him, and if he takes refuge in Me, I shall certainly grant him it."* [47]

"Everyone who dies will regret. The one who did well will regret for not having done more, and the one who did evil, he will regret for not having restrained himself." [48]

On Charitable Deeds

"Charity is due upon every joint of the body for every day upon which the sun rises. Being just between two people is charity. Helping a man with his animal and lifting his luggage upon it is charity. A kind word is charity. Every step that

46 ibid

47 Bukhari

48 Tirmidhi

you take towards the mosque is charity, and removing harmful things from the road is charity."[49]

A man asked: *"O Messenger of Allaah, who is most deserving of kind treatment and good companionship?" The Prophet answered, "Your mother." The man asked: "And then?" He said, "Your mother". The man asked again: "And then?" The Prophet repeated, "Your mother." When asked the fourth time, the Prophet said, "Your father."*[50]

On Moderation

"Be moderate in your religious practices and do deeds that are within your ability." Bukhari

"Ruined are those who insist on hardship in matters of religion." The Prophet repeated this three times.[51]

"The religion (of Islam) is easy, and whoever makes the religion a hardship it will overpower him. So follow a middle course (in worship)."[52]

On Accountability

"A servant of Allaah will remain standing on the Day of Judgment till he is questioned about four things: his life on earth and how he spent it, his knowledge and how he used it, his wealth and how he acquired and spent it, and his body and how he wore it out."[53]

49 Bukhari and Muslim
50 ibid
51 Muslim
52 Bukhari
53 Tirmidhi

The Prophet's Lineage

A biography of the Prophet Muhammad cannot be complete without information about his ancestors. Nearly half of humanity traces its religious beliefs to the same ancestors as the Prophet Muhammad. Jews, Christians, and Muslims find a common link in the Prophet Abraham (Ibraahim). Arabs and Jews are Semitic people through their bloodline with the Prophet Ibraahim. The Arab branch descends from Ishmael (Ismaa'il), the Prophet Abraham's son with Hagar (Haajar), while the Jewish and Christian lines descend from Isaac (Isshaaq), the son of Abraham and Sarah (Saarah).

The Arabs can be divided into two broad categories: Arab Al-Baa'idah (the extinct Arabs, such as the People of Aad and Thamud) and Arab Al-Baaqiyyah (the surviving Arabs).

Of the second category, there are two groups: Al-Arab Al-Aaribah (those who descended from Qahtaan, particularly from his son Yaa'rub) and Al-Arab al-Mustaaribah (those who came from Adnaan some twenty generations after Ismaa'il and whose original language was not Arabic although they later acquired it).

The Prophet Muhammad is from Adnaan, who is his twentieth-great-grandfather. The original language of Prophet Ismaa'il was not Arabic, but he grew up among the Arabic-speaking people of Jurhum, who were from Qahtaan in Yemen but had settled in Makkah to be near the blessed Zamzam well. Ismaa'il later married into the Jurhum tribe. As such he was both an Adnaani and a Qahtaani.

The Prophet's genealogy as recorded by earliest historians is as follows:

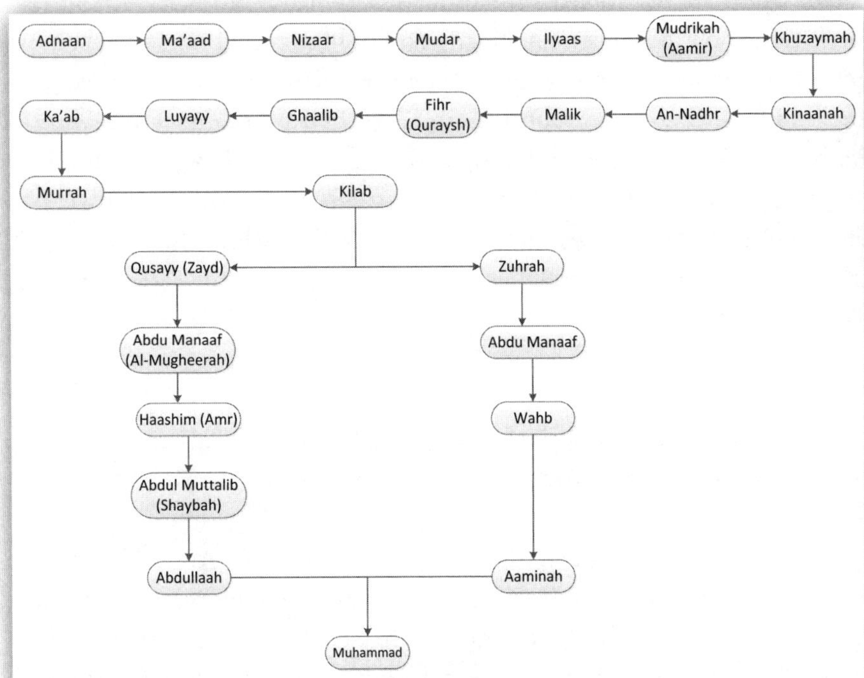

The Prophet's mother was Aaminah bint Wahb, bin Abdu Manaaf, bin Zuhrah, bin Kilaab, bin Murrah, bin Ka'ab, bin Luyayy, bin Ghaalib, bin Fihr, bin Maalik, bin An-Nadhr. The Prophet's parents shared some common ancestors.

The Jurhum became the custodians of the Ka'bah (the cube-shaped building in Makkah), but over time they began to commit evil acts, such as exploiting the pilgrims, cheating them, and using the gifts given to the House of Allaah for personal benefits. Eventually they were forced out from their prestigious position by the tribe of Al-Khuza'ah.

Years passed, and Al-Khuza'ah did something far worse. Their leader, Amr bin Luhayy Al-Khuzaa'i, for the first time introduced idol worship in a house that Prophets Ibraahim and Ismaa'il had consecrated for the worship of the one true God, Allaah. Amr brought an original idol of Hubal from Syria, which at the time was a major idol-worshipping society. Soon there were other idols, such as Laat, Uzzah, and Manaat. So many were added over the years that by the time the Prophet Muhammad appeared on the scene, there were 360 large and small idols inside the House of Allaah. Among them were also Wadd, Su'aa, Yaguth, Ya'uq, and Nasr, the idols that were worshipped in the time of Prophet Noah (Nuh).

The Quraysh, were still not seen as a major player, until one of the ancestors of the Prophet, Qusayy bin Kilaab, married the daughter of Hulayl bin Hubshiyah, the chieftain of Khuza'ah, and eventually became its de facto leader. Qusayy lived five generations before the Prophet and was his great-great-grandfather.

Qusayy's son was Abdu Manaaf, and his son was Haashim (Amr), the Prophet's great-grandfather. He was called Haashim, which means bread masher, because he mashed bread and made some kind of porridge from it for the pilgrims. Haashim had married a smart and independent-minded lady named Salma bint Amr in Yathrib, whom the Prophet later renamed Madinah. Salma was from the tribe of Banu Najjaar. Fate had created a bond for the would-be Prophet with a city that he would one day migrate to.

After Qusayy, and after much wrangling among the various tribes, the mantle of leadership was passed on to Haashim. Haashim is known to have started the tradition of the winter trade journeys to Yemen and the summer trade journeys to Syria (*Rihlaat Ash-Shitaai was-Saif*). These two trade journeys were the economic lifelines for the Quraysh and are famously mentioned in the Qur'aan, chapter 106.

Haashim's wife, Salma, gave birth to a boy who was named Shaybah,[54] which means gray-haired, because he had streaks of white hair on his head.

54 His full name was Shaybah Al-Hamd.

However, to the world he became known as Abdul Muttalib. There is an interesting story regarding how he came to be known as Abdul Muttalib.

When Haashim died, Salma and Shaybah continued to live in Yathrib. Shaybah's paternal family in Makkah did not know Haashim had left a son. When Haashim's brother, Muttalib, discovered he had a nephew in Yathrib, he came and somehow convinced the young man (and perhaps his mother) that a great future awaited him in Makkah. As the two entered Makkah, Shaybah was walking behind Muttalib, giving the impression to some that he was a slave, so they called him Abdul Muttalib (Slave of Muttalib). That name stuck with him the rest of his life, and few, if any, addressed him as Shaybah after that.

Abdul Muttalib was a smart, handsome, and wise young man. Because of these qualities, the leadership of the Quraysh was passed on to him a few years after Haashim's death. Abdul Muttalib was well liked by his people.

One of the momentous contributions of Abdul Muttalib was the rediscovery of Zamzam, the well of blessed water that God had given to Ismaa'il when he was a baby crying of thirst in the arid valley of Makkah, between the hills Safaa and Marwah. Muhammad Ibn Isshaaq reported that when the Jurhum were forced out of Makkah, they filled in the Zamzam well, and over time it was forgotten.

It is said that one night when Abdul Muttalib was sleeping in the Hijr near the graves of Ismaa'il and his mother, Haajar (Hagar), a voice ordered him to dig Zamzam, the well of blessed water that had been lost over time.

When Abdul Muttalib and his son Al-Haarith, who was his only son at the time, found the opening of the well, they felt immense joy and cried out *Allaahu Akbar* (God is greater). The news about this huge find spread quickly, and the rest of the Qurayshi clan demanded their share of the water, saying they were his cousins and their sons. For a desert people, water is one of the most precious commodities. And Zamzam was no ordinary water.

Abdul Muttalib refused, saying the well had been shown to him and not to them. They continued to dispute with him about Zamzam, so he agreed to go to a female diviner from Banu Sa'ad Hudhaym in the Syrian uplands to settle the matter. On the way to Syria, Abdul Muttalib, his group, and those contesting his exclusive right to Zamzam ran out of their water supply. The situation became so hopeless that Abdul Muttalib said every man should dig a grave for himself while he had the strength, so if one of them died, the others would throw his body in it.

After some time had passed, Abdul Muttalib decided that it was not right to just wait for death. So he got up and rode his mount. As he proceeded, water gushed out from his camel's knees. When the Quraysh saw the unnatural phenomenon, they took it as a sign that Abdul Muttalib had the right claim to Zamzam, and they acquiesced.

The Zamzam incident served to remind Abdul Muttalib that he had fewer sons than his cousins had. So he vowed that if Allaah gave him ten sons, he would sacrifice one of them. The prayer was heard. Abdul Muttalib was blessed with nine other sons and six daughters. His sons were Haarith (the first one), Abbaas, Hamzah, Abu Taalib, Zubayr, Hajla, Muqawwim, Dhirar, Abu Lahab (Abdul Uzzah), and Abdullaah.

His daughters were Safiyyah, Umm Al-Hakim, Aatikah, Umaymah, Arwa, and Barrah. Of these children, Abu Taalib, Zubayr, and Abdullaah, as well as all thc daughters except Safiyyah, were from Abdul Muttalib's wife Faatimah. Therefore, they, except for Abdullaah, were full uncles and aunts of the Prophet Muhammad. Abdullaah was the youngest of those sons and was the Prophet's father.

After Abdul Muttalib was endowed with ten sons, he proceeded to fulfill his vow. He gave an arrow to each of his sons and asked each to write his name on it. He stood near the idol Hubal, gave the arrows to a man there, and told him, "Cast the lots of my sons with these arrows." When the man drew the lot, it indicated Abdullaah, Abdul Muttalib's favorite son.

So the father took Abdullaah by the hand and brought him up to Isaaf and Naailah, two idols to which the Quraysh offered their sacrifices. When the clan saw Abdul Muttalib with a large knife, they inquired about his intentions, and when told what he intended to do, they vehemently disagreed. They said he could not do so until he tried to ransom his son through some huge expiatory sacrifice. Abdullaah was most well-liked in the clan, and they would not let him be sacrificed like that.

Finally, one of the people in the crowd suggested he go to a sorceress in the Madinah area who was in contact with a spirit and who could help decide. Abdul Muttalib found her in Khayber. She told him to go home and draw a lot between Abdullaah and ten camels. If Abdullaah's arrow was drawn, then he should add ten more camels and draw again until the camels' arrow was drawn. He did what the sorceress said, but Abdullaah's name came up each time until on the tenth attempt the camels' arrow was drawn. Thus Abdullaah was saved, and Abdul Muttalib sacrificed the camels instead.

The Prophet Muhammad once said, "I am the son of two sacrificed ones," meaning Ismaa'il and Abdullaah.

Abrahah and His Elephant

The story of Abrahah is an important milestone in the life of the Prophet Muhammad. A chapter of the Qur'aan, called "Al-Feel" (The Elephant), describes Abrahah's attempt to destroy the Ka'bah (the cube-shaped building in Makkah), and many scholars believe this attempt took place the year the Messenger of God was born.

Abrahah was a general in the Abyssinian army, which the king had deployed in Yemen. He served under the leadership of Aryat, whom the Abyssinian king had appointed governor of the area. Abrahah killed Aryat treacherously and installed himself as the governor. The king became furious and wanted to punish Abrahah, but the latter's cunning and tact persuaded the king to spare his life. Abrahah was allowed to remain as governor.

Abrahah was given to grandiose ideas. He had built a massive Christian church to rival the House of God in Makkah. He wanted the pilgrims to come to his church and abandon the Ka'bah. This made some Arabs unhappy. The Ka'bah had for years enjoyed unsurpassed reverence, and they would allow nothing to challenge that reverence. One of the Arabs, in his envious rage, defiled Abrahah's church by defecating in it. This vile action brought the ire of Abrahah, who, instead of catching and punishing the culprit, decided to destroy the Ka'bah itself.

Abrahah prepared a large army that also included an elephant named Mahmood. The news of Abrahah's march sent fear and panic among the Arabs. Along his route to Makkah, Abrahah overpowered several Arab tribes. Some became so fearful of Abrahah that they offered to act as travel guides to help him reach Makkah by the best route.

When Abrahah finally arrived near Makkah, he began to plunder the villages. His army also confiscated some two hundred camels that belonged to Abdul Muttalib, the chief of the Quraysh and the grandfather of the Prophet Muhammad. As a leader of his people, Abdul Muttalib became very worried and ordered them to move up to the mountains to avoid being harmed by Abrahah's forces. However, Abdul Muttalib decided that he would go and meet with Abrahah.

Abdul Muttalib was a man with extraordinarily good looks and an impressive personality, which allowed him to pass through checkpoints and reach Abrahah. Seeing a man of uncommon dignity, Abrahah left his throne, sat next to Abdul Muttalib, and asked what had brought him there. Abdul Muttalib said he wanted the governor to release his camels.

Abrahah was visibly surprised. “Here I am, ready to destroy your house of worship, and all you care about is your camels!” he exclaimed.

Abdul Muttalib said, “I am the lord of these camels, and the House also has a Lord who will protect it.”

Abrahah responded, “He will not be able to protect it from me.”

Abdul Muttalib said, “We shall see.”

So the troops marched into Makkah, and Abrahah ordered Mahmood, the elephant, to destroy the Ka’bah. But the outcome was very different from what he had anticipated. The elephant sat down and refused to move every time it was made to face the Ka’bah, and it got up and ran when it was faced away from the Ka’bah. Many years later, at the time of the incident of Hudaybiyah, the Prophet’s camel Qaswa refused to move, and some Companions called it stubborn; the Prophet said, “The same Lord who stopped the elephant has stopped Qaswa.”

Abdul Muttalib took back his camels, and he prayed to Allaah to protect the Ka’bah. It was then that the sky became filled with small birds, which some say were either starlings or swallows. Each bird carried three pebbles of baked clay, one in the mouth and one in each claw, and threw them at the army of Abrahah. The powerful forces that Abrahah had arrayed against the House of God were soon decimated. Abrahah himself was gravely wounded, and he died upon returning home in a deplorable condition.

More than forty years later, Allaah revealed the Surah Al-Feel (The Elephant), which captured the incident and the ignominious end of Abrahah and his army. In the next chapter, "Quraysh," Allaah made it clear that He had destroyed Abrahah not only to protect His House but also to safeguard the Quraysh from hunger and fear and to keep open their trade journeys to Yemen and Syria.

In the classic brevity of the Qur'aan, "Quraysh," with just four verses, summed up the reason for Abrahah's destruction:

> *For the uniting of the Quraysh; and their caravans, in winter and in summer. So, let them worship the Lord of this House. Who has fed them against hunger, and has made them safe from fear.*[55]

It was clearly an abnormal event. The small pebbles these birds carried did not have the power to wreak such havoc on an army, but this was an act of God. It was similar to what happened when the Prophet Muhammad threw a fistful of pellets at the Quraysh at the outset of the Battle of Badr. While throwing, he said, *"shaahatil wujuh"* (may the faces be disfigured), and the pebbles hit the enemy forces so hard that for a moment they were taken aback. In chapter 8 (Anfaal), verse 17, Allaah called the Prophet's actions His own. The event was also similar to the parting of the Red Sea when the Prophet Moses struck it with his staff.

When the birds dropped the little stones on Abrahah's army, they killed the people they hit. Abrahah was smote in his body, and as they carried him away, his fingers fell off one by one. Pus and blood began to flow from their places. It is said that he died when his heart burst out from his chest.

This incident raised the stature of the Quraysh. They appeared to be people Allaah wanted to preserve. Other tribes began to say the Quraysh were "*Ahl Allaah*," the People of God.

---

55 Quraysh 106:1–4.

The Prophet's Birth

Around the same time as Abrahah's attack on the Ka'bah, or a little before that, Abdul Muttalib was seeking a wife for his most beloved son, Abdullaah. He was relieved that Abdullaah had been saved from the ceremonial sacrifice through the ransom of one hundred camels. After some searching, Abdul Muttalib decided upon Aaminah, the daughter of Wahb.

As Abdul Muttalib was walking toward Aaminah's house, holding his son's hand as if in a gesture of solidarity, they met a woman named Qutaylah, a sister of Waraqah bin Nawfal. She looked at Abdullaah and said that if he were to marry her, she would give him one hundred camels, which would compensate Abdul Muttalib for the one hundred he had given in ransom for his son. Abdullaah said he was going with his father to get married and would not disobey him.

Abdullaah married Aaminah bint Wahb. Perhaps a few days later, when he was returning home, he saw Qutaylah again and mentioned her marriage proposal. Qutaylah said she no longer wished to marry him. It is said that when Abdullaah was going to Aaminah's house, Qutaylah saw a white blaze of light in Abdullaah's eyes, but when he was returning, after Aaminah had conceived, the blaze was no more.

Qutaylah had probably learned from her brother, Waraqah, who had knowledge of the Gospel (*Injeel*), that the time for the birth of a prophet had come. Forty years later, Waraqah, who had become a Christian, was the first person after Khadijah to testify that the one who had come to the Prophet Muhammad in the Cave of Hira was the Angel Gabriel (Jibreel) and that the Prophet had been chosen to be God's Messenger.

Soon after returning home, Abdullaah left on a trade journey to Syria. He did not know that Aaminah was pregnant. On the way back from Syria, he fell seriously ill and rested in Yathrib at his grandmother's house. When Abdul Muttalib found out about the grave condition of his most beloved son, he sent someone on a fast horse from Makkah to bring Abdullaah back. But it was too late. Abdullaah had passed away.

The loss of his favorite son devastated Abdul Muttalib, so when Aaminah bore him a grandson a few months later, he became ecstatic. He thought it was a compensation for the loss of his son. He named his grandson Muhammad and took him to the Ka'bah and celebrated.

The signs of the Prophet's birth were in the air. The Jews were waiting for their Messiah. Waraqah bin Nawfal, the Christian, and Salmaan Al-Farisi, the Persian who had made a long trek to Madinah in search of a prophet, were also expecting this prophet to appear.

There is not much authentically known about the early childhood of the Prophet. The reason for that is simple. Who would be sitting in the house of Aaminah to chronicle the beautiful childhood moments of baby Muhammad? After all, this was a normal family, and people went about their business without noticing anything extraordinary.

The only exception is what the Apostle of God himself confirmed after he became a Prophet or what others observed because of personal contact with him. He said, "I am the prayer of my father Ibraahim and the glad tiding of my brother Eesa; when my mother conceived me she saw a light issue from her and illuminate the palaces of Syria."[56]

Aaminah, his mother, is reported to have said that she saw a light coming from her and illuminating the palaces of Bosra in Shaam. The land of Shaam was one of the first places that came under Islamic rule during the caliphate of Umar. Today, Shaam is Syria, but in the time of the Prophet Muhammad, the land of Shaam encompassed present-day Syria, Palestine, Jordan, and Lebanon.

---

56 Mustadrak Al-Haakim, 2:418; Ibn Hibbaan, Hadith #6404.

Some of the early books report that Aaminah heard a voice telling her that she was carrying the lord of his people and that she was to name him Muhammad. Stories that claim that the Prophet was born circumcised and that he prostrated to Allaah after birth are just part of the legend, but there is no authentic narration to support them. The early books did report that Abdul Muttalib had had his grandson circumcised on the seventh day. Muslims would do better not to create stories out of nowhere when trying to honor the Prophet Muhammad. The Qur'aan and Hadith have already provided ample proof of his stature in this world and the Hereafter, and they should suffice. In fact, the Prophet Muhammad has warned his followers not to exaggerate in respecting him.

When Was He Born?

Although the majority of Muslims believe that the Prophet was born on the twelfth day of the Islamic month of Rabi Al-Awwal, scholars have offered more than ten opinions concerning his date of birth. Some said the Prophet was born on the twelfth of Rabi al-Awwal; others said the third, eighth, or tenth. Some even said he was born in Ramadan. Even the year of his birth is subject to differences of opinion. A general consensus is that the Prophet was born in the Year of the Elephant *(Al-Aam Al-Feel)*, meaning the year in which Abrahah came to destroy the Ka'bah, 570 or 571 CE. However, some scholars place his birth a few years away from the Year of the Elephant.

The only thing we know from the Messenger of Allaah himself is the day of his birth. When asked why he fasted on Mondays, he said, "This is the day I was born." So he fasted on Mondays to thank Allaah for his birth. On another occasion he also said that deeds were taken up to Allaah on Mondays and Thursdays, so he wanted his deeds to be presented to his Creator when he was fasting. Therefore he fasted on Thursdays as well.

The difference of opinion about the Prophet's date of birth is quite understandable. More than fourteen centuries ago, it was not an Arab practice to record exact dates of birth. A person's birth would be tied to something remarkable that happened around the time of his birth. In the Prophet's case, many historians and chroniclers have opined that he was born the same year as Abrahah's invasion of Makkah. Even if somehow the Prophet's birth had been accurately recorded, fourteen centuries later there would be a difference of forty-two years due to the difference between the lunar and solar calendars.

Reflections: The discussion of the Prophet's date of birth inevitably leads us to the subject of his birthday celebrations, called *Mawlid* in Arabic. In the Muslim world today, the birth of the Prophet is celebrated by a large number of people. In some countries it is an extravaganza. But from the study of historical records, we find that the practice of celebrating *Mawlid* did not gain ground until five hundred years after the passing of the Prophet. This means that the Prophet's Companions, who learned his traditions firsthand, did not celebrate it, nor did many generations after them.

Yasir Qadhi, a contemporary American scholar, in a three-part article on muslimmatters.org,[57] wrote that it was not until the turn of the sixth century Hijri (1200 CE) that a Fatimid ruler celebrated the Prophet's birthday. The Fatimids ruled over Egypt, and today's Ismaa'ili and Bohra communities come from this Shi'ah group. Mawlid came into Sunni practice in the latter half of the sixth century AH, during the reign of Nuruddin Al-Zangi. It was popularized by a Sufi named Umar Al-Mulla.

As to why the twelfth of Rabi al-Awwal became more famous as the Prophet's birthdate, it may be because Ibn Isshaaq mentioned it and also because a Sunni ruler chose this date.

Even though the Mawlid entered Muslim celebrations half a millennium after the Prophet's death, it has become an entrenched tradition

57 The first part of this article was published 3/11/2009.

in our time, with millions celebrating it, some of whom are people of knowledge. And we leave this subject as one on which Muslims may continue to passionately disagree.

The Fostering of the Prophet

The year the Prophet was born, a number of foster families from the Banu Sa'ad bin Banu Bakr came to pick up newborns from the elite families of the Quraysh for suckling and rearing.

It was a common practice of the rich families of the Quraysh to send their newborns to a wet nurse to raise them for a couple of years. And they did so for multiple reasons. First, the newborns would spend their early years in the pure, pollution-free environment of the desert. Second, they would learn the classical Arabic language of the Bedouins (and Banu Sa'ad were famous for their literary qualities). Third, they would grow up strong, having been raised in the harsh desert climate. Finally, fostering was simply a status symbol in those days.

The women of the Banu Sa'ad passed over baby Muhammad because they did not expect much reward from an orphan's family. Halimah bint Dhu'yaib Al-Saa'diyah was one of those who passed over the orphan child. But when other women chose babies to take home and she had none, Halimah felt embarrassed. At that point, her husband, Haarith, said, "Take Muhammad. It may be that Allaah will bless us through this child."

Halimah's family was extremely poor, especially that year, as they had been struck by a severe drought. She had come to Makkah riding on a lean mount, and her herd did not produce much milk. Because of the effects of starvation, she herself could not generate enough milk for her own children.

But soon her husband's hopes and prayers were to be realized. No sooner had they picked up baby Muhammad than their condition began to change. Her riding animal suddenly became the fastest in the group, and milk started to flow both in herself and her herd. People were shocked. Halimah said that her herd would return home in the evening with their udders filled with milk, even though there was still no vegetation in the area. The blessings were all too evident for people to see.

More than forty years later, when chapter 93 was revealed, Allaah informed the Prophet how he was helped in childhood, as well as in later years:

> *By the forenoon. By the night when it darkens. Your Lord has neither forsaken you nor hates you. And indeed the Hereafter is better for you than the present. And verily, your Lord will give you so that you shall be well-pleased. Did He not find you an orphan and gave you a refuge? And He found you unaware and guided you? And He found you poor and made you rich? Therefore, treat not the orphan with oppression. And repulse not the one who asks. And proclaim the grace of your Lord.*[58]

Although Ibn Isshaaq did not mention it in his biography of the Prophet, there are reports that two other women besides Halimah also suckled baby Muhammad. One was Thuwaybah Al-Aslamiyah, a maidservant of Abu Lahab, the Prophet's uncle. She was the first to suckle but did so only briefly. Then there was also a woman named Khawlah bint Al-Mundhir bin An-Najjaar.

Yet another woman who played a crucial role in the life of the Prophet was Umm Ayman, also referred to as Barakah. She was not a foster mother but the right hand of the Prophet's mother, Aaminah. She took care of baby Muhammad when Aaminah passed away. She was first married to Ubayd bin Zayd, from the Khazraj tribe, from whom she had a son named Ayman. After Ubayd's death she married Zayd bin Haarithah,

58 Duha 93:1–11.

the Prophet's so-called adopted son, from whom she had Usaamah. She was a freed Abyssinian slave, but the Prophet treated her like a member of his family, in complete rejection of the society's treatment of slaves. The Prophet once said, "Umm Ayman is the last of my family, and she was to me a mother after my mother had passed away."[59]

Foster Siblings and a Terrifying Incident

Halimah and Haarith had several children of their own: Abdullaah, Aniyah, Hudhaafah, and Hadh-dhaaqah, popularly known as Ash-Shaymaa. It seems Abdullaah was approximately the same age as the Prophet.

Shaymaa used to help her mother in taking care of baby Muhammad. She bathed him, took him for walks, and always embraced him with love. When it came time for him to return to his mother, she was very sad to see him leave. Her story came to light after the Battle of Hunayn, which will be told in detail in another chapter. The Prophet's encounter with his long-lost foster sister after the Battle of Hunayn showed his sense of gratitude for those who did a favor for him. He told his followers that thanking people was akin to showing gratitude to God: "He who does not thank people does not thank Allaah."[60]

For Halimah, the time to part with this blessed baby came too soon. But the fact was that two years or so had passed like a fleeting moment, and it was the agreed-upon time to return the baby Muhammad to his mother. Grudgingly, Halimah took the baby back to Aaminah, all the while wishing she could find a way to keep him for a little longer. Upon arrival in Makkah, Halimah begged Aaminah to let her keep the baby for a few more months. Aaminah, noticing Halimah's love for and bond with her son, agreed, although it was hard on her.

---

59 Ahmad Khaleel Jumaah, Nisaa Min Asr Al-Nabiy, Damascus, Daar Ibn Kathir (2003), 23.

60 Abu Daawood, Hadith # 4177; At-Tirmidhi, Hadith #1877.

It was during this second fostering period that one day Halimah's children came running to her, scared and shouting that their Qurayshi brother had been murdered. Halimah and her husband, Haarith, ran out, only to find the child Muhammad sitting pale-faced. When asked, the child said, "Two men in white dress came and threw me down and opened up my belly and searched inside for something." Halimah and Haarith looked at his chest, but there was nothing except a scar.

Later on, after he had become a Prophet, he told his Companions what had happened.

Anas bin Maalik, a servant of the Prophet, narrated that "Jibreel came to the Messenger of Allaah when he was playing with the other boys. He took hold of him and threw him to the ground, and then he opened his chest and took out his heart, from which he took a clot of blood and said, 'This was the Shaytaan's share of you.' Then he washed it in a vessel of gold that was filled with Zamzam water. Then he put it back together and returned it to its place. The boys went running to Halimah and said, 'Muhammad has been killed!' They went to him and his color had changed. Anas said, 'I used to see the mark of that stitching on his chest.'"[61]

The first incident scared Halimah and her husband, who said, "Let us return this boy back to his mother before something happens to him." So they took the child back to Makkah and hesitatingly told Aaminah what had happened. To their surprise, Aaminah, unlike most mothers, did not show a sudden anxiety but instead said that she believed great things were in store for her son. She took this incident as a sign of the miraculous things to come.

When the Prophet was six years old, Aaminah went to Yathrib (later to be called Madinah) to visit her husband's grave or perhaps to visit the Prophet's great-grandmother's family, who were from the tribe of Banu

61 Muslim, Hadith #162.

Najjaar. Destiny had brought her to Yathrib. She fell ill on the way back to Makkah and died in a place called Al-Abwaa. Just six years earlier, the Prophet's father, Abdullaah, had also died in Madinah. Now the young child had neither father nor mother.

It has been recorded that once while the Prophet was traveling with his Companions, he left the main road and kept walking until he reached a grave. The Companions simply followed, not knowing why he had done so. Then they saw the Prophet crying until his thick beard became wet. They also began to cry at the Prophet's unexplained sorrow.

Then he turned to them and said, "This is my mother's grave. Before I had asked you not to visit the graves, but I asked Allaah to allow me to visit my mother's grave and my request was granted, so I am permitting you now to visit graves."[62] Then he told them the reason for his tears: Allaah had not permitted him to pray for his mother.

Reflections: A Muslim can and should pray for his non-Muslim parents while they are alive. But if they die in disbelief, God does not permit believers to pray for them after their deaths. Islam's approach in all matters reflects God's wisdom, knowledge, mercy, and justice. In Surah Luqmaan (chapter 31), God tells mankind to be kind to their parents and, if the latter invite them to believe in many gods, not to obey them but still maintain good relations with them. The Prophet had to live with a similar situation when dealing with Abu Taalib, his uncle who was his greatest benefactor yet who did not accept Islam. When the Prophet tried to pray for Abu Taalib after his death, Allaah sent verses to stop him from doing this.

The Grandfather Becomes Guardian

Abdul Muttalib was in awe of his grandson. He loved him so much that he went beyond normal conventions to accommodate him. Abdul Muttalib

62 Muslim, Janaa'iz, Hadith #36.

had a raised platform adjacent to the Ka'bah where he would sit and hold court. Nobody else was allowed to sit there. Once when his beloved grandson ran onto the stage, the boy's uncle Zubayr quickly tried to pull him back, but Abdul Muttalib said, "Let him be."

Another time the uncles sent young Muhammad to look for a lost camel when he may have been seven or eight years old. Abdul Muttalib became upset that they had sent the young grandson out of his sight. They said they had dispatched him only because they had noticed that whatever their nephew did, he was successful at it. People couldn't help but observe that this boy was different from his peers.

Another Trauma Afflicts the Prophet

While life was passing comfortably for the young Muhammad in the company of his grandfather, this era also was soon to come to an end. Abdul Muttalib was becoming weak with old age, and shortly he, too, died. The future Prophet was 8 years old. In human history few children have been tried with such traumas as the Prophet Muhammad. And there clearly seems to be a divine wisdom behind these frequent tragedies: Allaah wanted His Messenger to be prepared for the hardships that were to be put on him. Surely, one of the Makki (Makkan) revelations makes this clear: "Verily, We shall send down to you a heavy word (Qur'aan)."[63]

The Messengerhood was still thirty-two years away, and Muhammad the child needed yet another caretaker. So one of his full uncles, Abu Taalib, took the young nephew under his wings. Abu Taalib was poor and had a large family himself, but in young Muhammad he saw a calling. Historians have not recorded much about the Prophet's childhood days in the household of Abu Taalib; however, enough has been documented of the relationship between the nephew and his uncle after the former was conferred Prophethood. Abu Taalib went through severe challenges from those who

63 Qiyamah 75:5.

opposed his nephew's message, demanding that he either disown his nephew or hand him to them. Abu Taalib resolutely refused, and the strength of character and resolve he exhibited will be discussed in a later chapter.

Baheera Incident: Did It Really Happen?

Some of the books of Seerah have reported that when the Prophet was about eleven years old, Abu Taalib went on a trade journey to Syria, and the Prophet implored his uncle to take him along. Young children would not normally undertake long desert journeys, but his nephew's pleas compelled Abu Taalib to go against convention and take him on the journey. So the story goes like this…

When the Qurayshi caravan passed by a Christian monastery on the way to Syria, a monk named Baheera[64] came out and invited all of them for a meal, although he had never done so on their previous journeys. Included in this group were Abu Bakr and Bilaal, who were later to become respectively the Prophet's friend and servant. Reportedly, Baheera saw a patch of cloud shading the Prophet from the sun's heat and a tree bowing to him. When the caravan had sat down for a meal, Baheera asked if everyone had joined. He was informed that everyone had except a young boy named Muhammad, whom they had left to look after the herd. He insisted that the boy should be invited too.

When the young Muhammad joined them, Baheera observed his manners and asked some questions. He even managed to check the Seal of the Prophethood that was on the boy's back between his shoulder blades.[65] At one point, before asking a question, Baheera swore by the Qurayshi idols Al-Laat and Al-Uzzah to see the young boy's reaction.

64 Some have called him Buhayrah.

65 The Seal of the Prophethood was a raised area of flesh the size of a pigeon's egg in the Prophet's back, between the two shoulders.

"There is nothing more hateful to me than these," the young boy said, referring to the idols.

Baheera became convinced that the boy was indeed the Prophet who had been mentioned in his scriptures. To convince himself even more, he asked Abu Taalib, "What is your relationship with him?"

Out of affection or cultural norm, Abu Taalib said, "He is my son." Baheera replied that it could not be, as the boy's father was supposed to have died before his birth. Abu Taalib finally admitted the boy was his nephew.

In a rather serious tone, Baheera advised Abu Taalib to immediately send the boy back to Makkah, for if the Romans or the Jews were to find out who he was, they would harm him.

Imam Muhammad bin Ahmad Adh-Dhahabi and others have found many holes in this story, including the following:

a. If the Prophet was eleven years old, Abu Bakr should have been nine. He was not from the Quraysh, so what was he doing in the Qurayshi caravan? Also, it is not known if Abu Bakr was a childhood friend of the Prophet.
b. Bilaal, much younger than the two, should not even have been born at this time. It was not until much later that Abu Bakr purchased Bilaal from Umayyah bin Khalaf and freed him.
c. Why was only Baheera able to notice the cloud and tree cover?
d. Most importantly, if Baheera had already told Abu Taalib that the young Muhammad would be the Prophet of his people, why was Abu Taalib, along with others, surprised twenty-nine years later, when his nephew announced that Gabriel had come to him and told him he was a Prophet of Allaah? Is it not strange that, instead of celebrating what they had already been told, the Makkans belied and opposed the Prophet?

Because of Baheera's critical role in this story, some Orientalist historians had a field day, saying, "Aha, we told you that Muhammad first learned about prophethood from the Christians and then, twenty-nine years later, simply repeated what he had learned."

Manhood and Livelihood

Life went on in the house of Abu Taalib, and the Prophet followed the daily routine of the family. He was by no means alone there. Abu Taalib had a large family, and his sons Taalib and Aqeel were like younger brothers to young Muhammad. Ali had yet to be born. Except for a few unusual things that people observed about him, the Prophet went through his teen years and finally entered adulthood without standing out too much. However, he was definitely very different from others in that he did not worship idols. He was what was known as a *Hanif*, meaning he believed that there was a Creator but did not know how to worship Him until Allaah showed him the way. So until the first revelation came to him, the Prophet was longing for the truth, and while the truth was hidden from him, he still followed his pure natural instincts.

Abu Taalib went out of his way to take care of his nephew. Abu Taalib's wife, Faatimah bint As'ad,[66] was also very kind and caring to the young Muhammad. When she died some fifty years later, the Prophet attended her funeral and said, "May God shower his mercy on you, mother. You were to me a mother after I had lost my mother; you went hungry so I could have enough to eat; you gave me clothes that you were in more need of; you denied yourself the good things of life so that I could enjoy them; and you sought only God's reward for all that."[67]

Later on, the Prophet returned the favor by adopting Ali, Abu Taalib's youngest son, to whom he also married his beloved daughter Faatimah.

---

66 While Abu Taalib did not embrace Islam, his wife Faatimah did.

67 Ahmad Khaleel Jumaah, Nisaa Min Asr Al-Nabiy, Damascus, Daar Ibn Kathir (2003), 23.

However, when the Prophet reached adolescence, he began to shepherd the herds of other people. He did so in order to ease the financial burden on Abu Taalib. Being a shepherd was not a lucrative profession, and the Prophet was paid just a few *Qarareet* (pennies). The *Qarareet* were made of simple stones, whereas more expensive currencies were made of gold and silver.

In later years, the Prophet lauded the job of shepherding, saying in a Hadith collected by Bukhari, "Allaah never sent a prophet except that he was a shepherd."

The Companions asked, "And even you, O Messenger of Allaah?"

The Prophet said, "Even I," and told them he used to graze his herd in Ajyad, a valley near the Ka'bah.

Why Did Allaah Make All Prophets Shepherds?

With so many professions in the world, one wonders why Allaah decreed that His prophets and messengers at some point in their lives would work as shepherds. After some contemplation we may understand the divine wisdom.

1) A shepherd grows up cut off from the material world.
2) A shepherd knows the character of each sheep in the flock and deals with them accordingly. As the personalities of the sheep differ, so do the personalities of people; a messenger needs to know how to deal with each person. It is well known that the Prophet dealt with people at their level and picked them for tasks that were most suitable for them.
3) A shepherd has more chance to reflect on the purpose of life.
4) Perhaps it was this training, among other things, that taught the Prophet to treat each person as if that person was most important

to him. When the Prophet greeted a man, he brought his whole body to face the person, shook his hand while smiling, and did not pull his hand away until he felt that the other man wanted to pull his away. The Prophet greeted women with the same kindness but without shaking their hands.

The Prophet could have been given the keys to the treasures of this world, but Allaah made him earn his livelihood as a shepherd. He lived shunning the glitters of this temporary life while setting his gaze on the eternal and better life of the Hereafter.

The fact that, moneywise, the Prophet was at the bottom rung of his society helped him treat the poor and the destitute with great empathy when he became their spiritual and political leader. It is because of this sympathy, compassion, and humility that his Companions loved him rather than feared him.

Reflections: In reference to the Hadith that all prophets were shepherds, we must note here that, although some prophets may have adopted other professions, all of them had tended to their herds as shepherds, either for money or to help their families at some point in time. The fact that Prophet Solomon (Sulaymaan) was given the greatest kingdom later in life does not contradict the general meaning of the Hadith.

The Sacrilegious War

When the Prophet was at the age of puberty, he lived in a society where the powerful could exploit and oppress the weak with impunity. Every day he felt great revulsion as he saw the atrocities being committed against the lowest class of society.

It was around this time that a significant event occurred, leading to a revolutionary change in the Arab society a few years later. The event was the so-called Sacrilegious War (*Al-Harb al-Fujaar*). It was called so because it occurred during a sacred month.

It so happened that a man from the Kinaanah treacherously killed a man of the Banu Aamir, a subtribe of the Hawaazin, who were a subtribe of the Qays Aylaan. Because the Quraysh were a subtribe of the Kinaanah, according to the pre-Islamic customs, the Quraysh had to come to the Kinaanah's defense. The Kinaani man ran to the Ka'bah knowing that he would be protected there because of the long-held belief that whoever entered the sacred precincts would be saved. In fact it was God's command, in response to Prophet Abraham's supplication, that no blood could be spilled in the Ka'abah and its immediate surroundings, called *Al-Meqaat*.

But the Qays Aylaan pursued and killed the Kinaani man inside the sanctuary. Although they had a right to retaliate for the killing of their tribesman, it was not their right to shed blood in the Ka'bah. The Qays Aylaan's action was even more serious because it occurred in a sacred month, during which all fighting had been prohibited from Prophet Abraham's time. The Quraysh had abided by this prohibition for the most part. Clearly, they had transgressed.

So the Kinaanah and the Quraysh decided to fight back. The Prophet was about fourteen years of age at the time. He did not directly participate in the war but helped his uncles by collecting arrows for them. His role was minor, as he had not yet attained adulthood, which in those days was fifteen at the earliest. However, on one of the worst days of the war, the Quraysh allowed him to actually shoot arrows.

Eventually, the Quraysh won the war. Abu Taalib had noticed that on the days his nephew Muhammad joined the war, they would win, so he asked his nephew to join them every day. The Prophet said that he did not regret participating in that war because it had been waged to defend the sanctity of the Ka'bah. After prolonged fighting and some loss of life, both sides were exhausted, and they realized the futility of the conflict.

We should note that in those days there was no government or political authority that would give people their rights back when they were wronged. Therefore, the only way to protect oneself or one's family was to live as a tribe. Outsiders knew that if they harmed anyone from another tribe, that person's entire tribe would come to his or her defense. For injustices committed within the same tribe, the tribal leader or the council would dispense justice. The problem with the tribal system was that people would support their fellow tribesmen whether they were right or wrong.

After he received the Prophethood, the Apostle of God changed that. He famously said to his Companions, "Help your brother whether he is oppressed or an oppressor."[68]

Surprised, the Companions asked, "O Messenger of God, we understand helping our brother when he is oppressed, but how can we help him when he is an oppressor?"

The Prophet replied, "By preventing him from oppression."

A Revolutionary Pact

Six years had passed since the Sacrilegious War, and when people remembered it, they felt a sense of remorse and disgust. The Prophet was now twenty years old. People were unhappy about their situation, for although major wars were not being fought, small squabbles were happening frequently, and the strong still treated the weak unjustly. Creating another impetus for change, the elites who had the means to travel to Syria, Yemen, and Abyssinia had returned impressed with the working examples of relative justice and civil society they had seen in those lands.

While feelings of discontent with the status quo were gaining strength, and desire for change was on people's minds, a man from Yemen's Zubayd

68 Bukhari, vol. 3, Hadith #624.

tribe came to Makkah for Hajj and also to buy and sell. He sold something to Al-Aas bin Waa'il As-Sahmy, the chief of the Banu Sahm, who told him that he would pay after the pilgrimage. When the man was done with his rites and went to collect the money, Al-Aas to him come back tomorrow, and when he went next day, the same thing happened, until the man realized that Al-Aas was not going to pay him for his merchandise. Frustrated, he went to some of the tribes, including the Quraysh, but nobody wanted to help him against the chieftain of a tribe.

So the Zubaydi man composed a poem and went to the top of a hill called Al-Qubays near the Ka'bah. People used to stand on this hill when they had an important announcement to make. The man denounced Al-Aas in his poem without naming him.

> O family of Fihr (Quraysh), I have been wronged
>
> In the valley of Makkah far from home and my helpers
>
> I am still in *ihraam*,[69] my hair is still dusty and uncombed and have not yet completed my Umrah
>
> O my men, where are you to help me between *Hijr* (the half circle) and *Hajr Aswad* (the Black Stone)
>
> Indeed the Haram[70] belongs to those whose manners are perfect
>
> And there is no sanctity for the one who wears a dress while he is a dissolute person and fraud

Composing poems came naturally to the people of Arabia back then, even though most did not know how to read or write. Arabic was an oral tradition

69 Dress for male pilgrims

70 The Grand Mosque including Ka'bah in Makkah

for them passed on from father to son. Their poems were known for literary beauty, and they artfully used them to express their feelings and emotions. Poetry was also more effective than prose in catching people's imagination. If one reads Ibn Isshaaq's biography of the Messenger of Allaah, one will notice that after every few pages there is poetry about an important event. For example, upon the death of Abdul Muttalib, six of his daughters wrote poems to express their loss.

The poem of the Yemeni visitor touched a raw nerve and appealed to the sense of justice of the nobles of the Quraysh. Some hearts were already yearning for justice after the Sacrilegious War, so this proved to be the last straw. The elder uncle of the Messenger of Allaah, Zubayr bin Abdul Muttalib, and others said they must do something about this injustice.

So the leaders of the tribes met in the house of Abdullaah bin Jud'aan, the chief of the Banu Taym. Among the participants was the young Muhammad, still twenty years away from the Prophethood, who went with his uncle Zubayr. Another person who participated was Abu Bakr, who came with his father, Abu Quhaafah. Abu Bakr was around eighteen at that time. The people decided that from then on they would stand for justice and oppose oppression against the weak, whether it was against one of their own or an outsider. They forced Al-Aas bin Waa'il to pay for the merchandise. Those who supported this pact also dipped their hands in perfume as a way of attesting to the treaty, so it was called the Treaty of the Perfumed Ones (*Hilf Al-Mutayyibeen*) or the Treaty of No Business (*Hilf Al-Fudhool*). The latter designation came from Al-Aas's remarks that the people who were trying to intervene had no business getting into his business. However, the justice-inclined people decided that it was their business to redress the wrong done to the Zubaydi man and to set a better standard for their society.

Years later, the Prophet Muhammad fondly remembered the treaty: "I was present in the house of Abdullaah bin Jud'aan (to support the pact). And if now, in Islam, I were called to join it, I would gladly do so."

Abdullaah bin Jud'aan was among the most noble of his society. His generosity, his sense of justice, and his kindness were legendary. He was a distant great-uncle of Aayeshah. He died before the Prophetic da'wah (missionary call) began.

Aayeshah once asked, "O Messenger of Allaah, what will be the status of Abdullaah bin Jud'aan in the Hereafter?"

The Prophet said, "He will be in the fire."

She said, "But why?"

The Prophet said, "Because not once in his life did he say, 'O Allaah, forgive me!'"

Reflections: Lest people misunderstand, the Prophet was not denying the goodness of Abdullaah bin Jud'aan. He was simply conveying God's command that good actions in themselves cannot save a person in the Hereafter, unless he has faith in God in this life and performs those actions to please Him. Islam teaches that a nonbeliever will be rewarded for his good actions in this world but that there will be no reward in the afterlife. Even a Muslim's good actions will be rejected in the Hereafter if the Muslim did them to seek the praise of people or to show off, rather than to earn the pleasure of Allaah. Another point that needs elaboration is that before the coming of the Prophet Muhammad, the people who followed the teachings of Jesus, Moses, and other prophets of God were Muslim because in doing so they submitted themselves to the will of God.

There are many precious lessons that can be derived from *Hilf Al-Fudhool.* Muslims should become involved in acts of common good, even if they are living as a minority. Muslims in the United States, Europe, and wherever else they may be living as a religious minority should lend their voices to fight against racism, child abuse, homelessness, drugs, and violence. These issues have nothing to do with religion, and they affect all of humanity. The Prophet Muhammad joined this pact before he had been given the divine mission, and even after he became a Prophet, he would have been willing to join it. When we do something about the problems of the society we live in, we appear sincere in the eyes of that society. Imagine if a Muslim man or woman were shown on prime-time evening news helping a local or national cause. How powerful a message would that be? If Muslims do not become involved in the societies where they live, then they will be seen as outsiders. Some of the Muslims who migrated to this country of ours still think that this is not home. This is simply wrong. A Muslim does not only take from the society but when possible also gives back, whether it is by donating to worthy causes, volunteering one's time, or simply greeting people with a smile.

On the positive side, many Muslims have become involved today. They are helping society at many levels. The biggest responsibility is on the shoulders of the American-born Muslims, for whom America is the only home, whose native tongue is English, and who understand the American society better than the immigrant Muslims can. We need to encourage some of our children to go into social sciences, public advocacy, law, and education. Frankly, medicine and engineering have become far too saturated. Muslims are underrepresented in other vital fields. Unfortunately, the American media has for too long engaged in negative reporting about the Muslim community. The positive portrayal of American Muslims is so rare that most people cannot remember when they have seen or read or heard something positive about the American Muslims or their overseas counterparts. Muslims have a long history in America. For those who see Islam and Muslims as foreign, it may be apt to point out that a Muslim country, Morocco, was the first nation to recognize the newly born United States of America.

Khadijah in Awe of the Prophet

When the Prophet was about twenty-three or twenty-four years old, he was hired along with another young man to graze the camel herd of Haalah, the sister of Khadijah. This was more than a coincidence. This was destiny. After they were finished with the job, the other man asked his fellow shepherd, Muhammad, to go with him to Haalah to collect the wages, but Muhammad declined, saying he was too shy to go ask a woman for wages. He suggested that the other man go instead. So he did.

But seeing him alone, Haalah asked, "Where is Muhammad?"

The man said, "Muhammad is too shy to come, but I can collect his wages."

Khadijah, the younger sister of Haalah, happened to be there and was impressed to hear about the modesty of a man in her community. In pre-Islamic Arabia, modesty and moral uprightness were rare commodities.

"Who is Muhammad?" Khadijah asked her sister, upon which Haalah went on and on, praising the good character of the shepherd Muhammad, saying how noble, honest, and trustworthy he was. Khadijah was even more impressed. She was the richest woman among the Quraysh, having inherited a fortune from her second husband, who did not have any heirs. (Otherwise, women in pre-Islamic Arabia did not inherit anything from their families.) She was a smart business woman who had invested that money in trade caravans and was quite successful at it.

The praise she heard of the shepherd Muhammad from her own sister prompted Khadijah to hire him to go on business travels on her behalf. So much was she impressed that she overlooked the fact that young Muhammad had no experience of this kind; he had never engaged in business or gone on trade journeys.[71] She even offered him a bigger profit from the business than she gave others.

The Prophet agreed to Khadijah's generous offer. As he left on his first trade journey, Khadijah sent along her servant, Maysarah, perhaps because

71 According to a popular but questionable account, the Prophet did go on a trade journey with his uncle Abu Taalib when he was eleven.

of the Prophet's inexperience with trading. Upon return, Maysarah praised the conduct of his noble Companion and even reported seeing angels shading him from the sun. Some have viewed these reports with skepticism, but others do not think there is anything surprising about them since a diverse group of people has reported a large number of narrations about miraculous events in the Prophet's life.

Khadijah began to notice that, since young Muhammad had started managing her business, her profit had tripled. This confirmed once again that whatever the Prophet put his hand into, God blessed it. While his honesty was legendary and people saw it, only people of reflection could notice the blessing the Prophet Muhammad was endowed with throughout his life. Khadijah was a wealthy widow, and in the Prophet Muhammad she started to see a future beyond an employer-employee relationship. After she became convinced that there was no one nobler she could marry than her own employee, she confided this to her friend, Nafisah.

"Do not worry," said Nafisah. "I will take care of it."

Nafisah wasted no time and went straight to the Prophet Muhammad. "Why do you not get married?" she asked the Prophet. Perhaps the Prophet was surprised by such a direct question.

"And who will want to marry me?" said he, adding, "I am an orphan and from the poor of the Quraysh."

Nafisah said, "What if Khadijah wanted to marry you?"

The Prophet replied, "Why would Khadijah want to marry me?"

At that point Nafisah left, convinced that the Prophet was not opposed to the idea of marrying Khadijah, just that he did not see why a rich widow who was also his boss would marry a poor employee.

Khadijah sent a formal proposal to the Prophet, now twenty-five. He consulted his uncle, Abu Taalib, who wholeheartedly supported accepting the proposal. On the day of the wedding, Abu Taalib gave a sermon in which he recounted Allaah's blessings upon the Quraysh, extolling the lineage of his nephew and the status of the Quraysh.

Khadijah's uncle Amr bin As'ad acted as the guardian and accepted the matrimony. Khadijah's *mahr* (dowry) was twelve *uqyyah* of silver, which some estimates put at about $400 of our time. The Prophet also gave her twenty camels. She gave him a slave-servant named Zayd bin Haarithah, whom the Prophet later freed and adopted as a son.

It is generally believed that at the time of her marriage with the Prophet, Khadijah was forty years old. However, some of the other scholars, like Abdullaah bin Abbaas, Al-Bayhaqi, and Ibn Isshaaq, said she was younger. This marriage shattered many taboos of the Qurayshi society. A young and most-eligible bachelor married a twice-widowed lady older than he was, and they lived happily ever after. Khadijah was a blessing from the heavens for the Prophet. She was his advisor-in-chief and an exceptionally loving and caring wife. She bore the Prophet six children, four daughters and two sons despite her middle age. The only other child of the Prophet, a boy, was born of Maariyah Qibtiyah. The Prophet remained happily married to Khadijah until she died in advanced years.

Reflections: The Prophet Muhammad said: "Modesty (*Al-Hayaa*) is part of faith." God commands believing men and women to lower their gaze when talking to someone of the opposite sex who is not a close family member like a parent, sibling, aunt, or niece. Christians and Jews may find similar commandments in their own scriptures (for example, 1 Timothy 2:8–10). However, in the Western context, a man who does not look in the eyes of the woman he is talking to will usually be considered rude. That, obviously, creates a dilemma for the Muslim man: should he follow the dictates of his faith or adhere to the local customs? Often with education one can avoid such awkward situations. The desire to commit

a sin often enters a person's heart through the eyes. It is easier to protect the chastity of the heart when the eyes are guarded.

The Rebuilding of the Ka'bah

The Ka'bah that Prophets Abraham and Ishmael had built was a rectangular structure, and it had been damaged by the elements, especially floods. A few years before the revelation started to come to the Prophet Muhammad, the tribes that were assigned various responsibilities for the maintenance of the Ka'bah decided to rebuild it.

According to Muhammad ibn Isshaaq,

> *When the Messenger of Allaah reached 35, the Quraysh gathered to rebuild the Ka'bah, which included covering it with a roof. However, they were afraid to demolish it lest the wrath of Allaah befall them. They were also hesitant because every day a large snake came out of the vault to sunbathe against the wall of the Ka'bah. One day, Allaah sent an eagle which seized the snake and took it away. They thought this was sign from Allaah to begin the work. Through a divine plan something else was happening nearby that would be part of the rebuilding. A Roman ship laden with expensive wood and ceramic tiles was headed somewhere to build a church. The ship ran into a fierce storm near Jeddah (also called Juddah) and broke up. The Qurayshi leaders heard about it and went there to salvage and purchase the expensive material to rebuild the Ka'bah. There was also an expert carpenter and architect on the ship whom they hired. When they decided to begin the demolition to rebuild the House of God, Abu Wahb bin Amr bin A'idh from the Banu Makhzum pulled out a stone from the Ka'bah; the stone slipped from his hand and went back to where it was before. He said, "O people of Quraysh! Do not spend on rebuilding the House, except from what was earned from pure sources. No money earned from a prostitute, usury or injustice should be included."*

Ibn Isshaaq said that some have attributed these words to Waleed bin Al-Mugheerah. There is another report that it was Abu Jahl who said this.

Ibn Isshaaq continued,

> *The Quraysh began to organize their efforts to rebuild the Ka'bah, each subtribe taking the responsibility of rebuilding a designated part of it. However, they were still wary about bringing down the Ka'bah. Waleed bin Al-Mugheerah said, "I will start to bring it down." He held an ax and stood by the Ka'bah and said, "O Allaah! No harm is meant. O Allaah! We only seek to do a good service." He then started to chop the House's stones. The people waited that night and said, "We will wait and see. If something strikes him, we will not bring it down and instead rebuild it the way it was. If nothing happens to him, then Allaah will have agreed to what we are doing." The next morning, Waleed went to work on the Ka'bah, and the people started bringing the Ka'bah down with him. When they reached the foundations that Ibraahim built, they uncovered green stones that were above each other, just like a pile of spears. A man from the Quraysh, who was helping rebuild the Ka'bah, placed the shovel between two of these stones to pull them up; when one of the stones was moved, all of Makkah shook, so they did not dig up these stones.*

The rebuilding began in earnest, and when the Ka'bah was two-thirds done, the construction material ran out, so they built the Ka'bah in a square shape and cordoned off the uncovered area with signage showing the boundaries of the original building. That uncovered area is now called *Hateem* or *Hijr Ismaa'il*, the semicircular structure in front of the Ka'bah.

Many years later, when Aayeshah had asked the Messenger of Allaah if it was possible to pray inside the Ka'bah, he said, "Yes, pray in the Hijr." And that is because the Hijr is part of the original Ka'bah.

A Dispute over the Black Stone

Ibn Isshaaq said,

> *The tribes of Quraysh collected stones to rebuild the House, each tribe collecting on their own. They started rebuilding it, until the rebuilding of the Ka'bah reached the point where the Black Stone was to be placed in its designated site and a dispute erupted between the various tribes of Quraysh, each seeking the honor of placing the Black Stone for their own tribe. The dispute almost led to violence between the leaders of the Quraysh in the area of the Sacred House. Banu Abd Ad-Dar and Banu Adiy bin Ka'ab bin Lu'ay, gave their mutual pledge to fight until death. However, four or five days later, Abu Umayyah bin Al-Mugheerah bin Abdullaah bin Amr bin Makhzum, the oldest man from the Quraysh, intervened at the right moment. Abu Umayyah suggested that the Quraysh should appoint the first man to enter the House from its entrance to be a mediator between them. They agreed. The Messenger—Muhammad—was the first person to enter the House. When the various leaders of the Quraysh realized who the first one was, they all proclaimed, "This is Al-Amin (the honest one). We all accept him; this is Muhammad." When the Prophet reached the area where the leaders were gathering and they had informed him about their dispute, he asked them to bring a garment and place it on the ground. He placed the Black Stone on it. He then requested that each of the leaders of the Quraysh hold the garment from one side and all participate in lifting the Black Stone, moving it to its designated area. Next, the Prophet carried the Black Stone by himself and placed it in its designated position.*

Reflections: From this incident it is evident that the Quraysh looked to the Prophet Muhammad (who was not yet a prophet) as a unifier and peacemaker. They unanimously agreed to his mediation in their dispute. The Prophet also showed wisdom by including representatives of the disputing tribes when placing the Black Stone. But just five years later, the same Quraysh forgot everything and turned against him when,

as a Prophet, he invited them to the worship of Allaah alone. They called him a madman, a poet, a person who was creating a rift in their families. And eventually they conspired to kill him.

Before the Revelation

By the time the Prophet Muhammad was thirty-nine and a half years old, he had begun to experience some unusual things. Every night he saw dreams that were very vivid and clear. His wife Khadijah said whatever he dreamed would come true the next day. He did not understand why it was happening, but he found consolation in the words of Khadijah, who said something big would soon happen to her husband.

Some years later, the Prophet said, "True dreams are one forty-sixth part of Prophethood."[72] We understand his statement about his dreams to mean that they began six months before the Prophethood, and his mission lasted 23 years. If we divide 23 years by 2, we get 46 six-month periods.

In a long Hadith in Bukhari, Aayeshah described what happened in the days immediately before the Prophethood and what followed it. She had not been born at this time, but the Prophet himself informed her years later. She said:

> *The first form in which revelation to the Messenger of Allaah started was the true vision in sleep. And he would not see any vision but it came true like the bright gleam of dawn. Then solitude became dear to him and he used to seclude himself in the cave of Hira, where he would engage in tahannuth (worship for a number of nights) before returning to his family and getting provisions to go back. He would then return again and take provisions for a like period, till the Truth came upon him while he was in the cave of Hira.*[73]

---

72 Bukhari, Hadith #6472; Muslim, Hadith #42.

73 Bukhari, vol. 3, book 1, Hadith #3.

The Prophet Muhammad said it was during the dream period that he noticed stones and trees saying "As-Salaamu Alaykum" (peace be upon you) to him. He would turn around but not see anyone. Then he realized that one stone in particular always said salaam. Some years later, he said he still remembered which stone used to say salaam.

Three Days before the Revelation

The Prophet was now into a deeper meditative trance, and the solitary confines of a small cave on *Jabal Al-Noor* (Mountain of Light) seemed dearer to him than anything else. He would take a small supply of dates and water and isolate himself from the people in that cave, which was more than an hour's trek up the mountain. After a few days had passed, Khadijah herself would undertake the arduous climb to check on her husband and replenish his food and water. He was delving into big questions: Who is the Creator of life, and what is life's purpose? Why is there suffering in the world?

On a Friday night, while in the mountain, the Prophet heard a loud sound and saw a light in the sky; he looked around but did not find anything or anyone. The incident was repeated on Saturday and Sunday. One has to admire the bravery of the Prophet Muhammad that he did not run home scared when he experienced the unexplained phenomenon all alone on a mountain.

On Monday (some say it was the twenty-first night of Ramadan), suddenly Angel Gabriel (Jibreel) appeared to him and ordered, "*Iqra*" (Read). The Prophet was terrified to see someone the like of whom he had never seen and who had entered the cave without the minutest sound.

Shaken, he said to the angel, *"Ma Ana Bi Qaari"* (I am not a reader). The Prophet Muhammad understood this command to mean he should read or recite from a book.

Aayeshah narrated the whole incident thus:

The angel came to him and asked him to read. The Prophet replied, "I do not know how to read." The Prophet added, "The angel caught me and pressed me so hard that I could not bear it any more. He then released me and again asked me to read, and I replied: I do not know how to read; thereupon he caught me again and pressed me a second time until I could not bear it any more. He then released me and again asked me to read but I replied: I do not know how to read; thereupon he caught me for the third time and pressed me, and then released me and said:

"Read! In the Name of your Lord Who created. Created man from a clot. Read! And your Lord is the Most Generous. Who has taught by the pen. He has taught man that which he knew not."[74]

When Allaah's Apostle returned home with the revelation, his heart was beating severely. Then he went to Khadijah and said, "Cover me! Cover me!" She covered him until his fear subsided, and then he told her everything that had happened. He said, "Indeed, I fear that something may happen to me."

Khadijah replied, "Never! By Allaah, Allaah will never disgrace you. You keep good relations with your family, you help the poor and the destitute, you serve your guests generously, and you assist those afflicted by calamities. I swear you are going to be a Prophet of Allaah." With these five verses, Muhammad the man became Muhammad the Prophet of Allaah.

Some of the scholars say that Gabriel squeezed the Prophet hard to show him that he was not dreaming and that he would have difficulties ahead

74 Alaq 96:1–5.

after that night. Perhaps one reason also was to "show the weightiness and great import of the message he was being inspired with…"[75]

The verses show that Allaah created man and taught him how to read and write, and they indicate that the Prophet's job would be to keep on reciting. They explain the importance of knowledge for an unlettered people, who rose to great heights by the Qur'aanic commandments.

Seeing how shaken the Prophet was with his encounter with Gabriel, Khadijah went to a Christian slave of one of the Prophet's uncles. His name was Addaas. When Addaas heard about what had happened, he became excited and said, "Did the angel of Allaah come to this heathen place Makkah?"

Next, Khadijah took the Prophet to her cousin Waraqah bin Nawfal, an elderly blind man who had become a Christian in the pre-Islamic days and who knew the scriptures and the Hebrew. Khadijah said to Waraqah, "Listen to the story of your nephew, O my cousin!"

When the Prophet described his experience to Waraqah, the elderly man exclaimed, "This is Naamoos (Gabriel), the same one who keeps the secrets and whom Allaah sent to Moses. I wish I were young and could live up to the time when your people will turn you out."

The Prophet was astonished to hear the last part. "Will they drive me out?" he asked.

Waraqah replied, "Anyone who came with the message that you have brought would be treated with hostility, and if I should remain alive till the day when you will be turned out, then I would support you strongly."

75 Ali Muhammad As-Sallaabee, *The Noble Life of the Prophet* (Riyadh: Darussalam, 2005), 1:136. Translated by Faisal Shafeeq.

But soon thereafter Waraqah died. Waraqah's statement reminds us of what Jesus is reported to have said: "No prophet is acceptable in his hometown."[76]

Reflections: Who was the first person to believe in Islam? Scholars have differed on this. Was it Ali, or Abu Bakr, or Khadijah? Some have tried to reconcile the matter by saying that the first to embrace Islam among the men was Abu Bakr, among the women was Khadijah, and among the children was Ali. However, if we look at the chronology of events, it seems that the very first person to accept Islam was Khadijah, since the Prophet directly came to her after his encounter with Gabriel, and the words she spoke clearly indicated that she believed that her husband was chosen to be a Prophet of God. The second person appears to be Waraqah because he confirmed the Prophet's experience in Hira, believed that he was a Prophet, and offered him support. The third person could be Ali, since he was under the care of the Prophet and the Prophet first invited his family to Islam. Zayd bin Haarithah could be the fourth person, since he was a servant at the Prophet's house. The fifth person could be Abu Bakr, who was a friend of the Prophet but who was not part of his family. And Allaah knows best.

The Prophet confirmed Waraqah's Islam when he said, "I saw Waraqah in a white garment in *Jannah* (Paradise), and Allaah had given him gardens." This statement also confirms that the true religion before the advent of the Prophet Muhammad was to follow the teachings of the Prophet Jesus, and when the new messenger came, as had been foretold in the earlier scriptures, people were required to follow him. From this we deduce that Prophets Jesus and Muhammad did not bring a new religion with them; rather they conveyed the same basic message that started with the first Prophet, Adam (Aadam).

76 Luke 4:24, ESV.

Soon after the First Revelation

Indeed the appearance of Gabriel in the cave was unlike anything the Prophet had ever experienced. And it seems the dreams he had been seeing in the preceding six months had been meant to prepare him to handle the out-of-this-world experience. Yet when it actually happened, the Prophet was shaken. Who was this creature? Could he be a jinn (spirit) who came to possess him? And why had he not appeared again? These thoughts continued to occupy the Prophet. Although the first encounter with Gabriel was frightening, the Prophet still longed to see him again and would become distressed when Gabriel did not come.

After the first meeting with Gabriel and before the second revelation, the Prophet saw the angel several times on the horizon, each time assuring him that he was indeed the Messenger of Allaah. At least once the Prophet saw him sitting on a chair stretching between heaven and earth. The Prophet heard a sound, and when he lifted his gaze, he saw Gabriel, who had filled up the whole horizon. The Prophet was overwhelmed by this vision, like he had been by the first, and he hurried to his house. "Wrap me up! Wrap me up!" he told Khadijah. That was when the second revelation came down:

> *"O you who are enveloped in garments! Arise and warn! And magnify your Lord! And purify your garments! And keep away from the idols!"*[77]

Scholars agree that the first revelation comprised the five verses of Surah Al-Alaq (chapter 96), but there is a difference of opinion on which were the next three. Looking at the events in the Prophet's life, it seems that the second revelation comprised five verses of Muddassir (chapter 74), followed by Qalam (68) and Muzzammil (73).[78]

---

77 Muddassir 74:1–5.

78 The chapters of the Qur'aan are not listed in the same order in which they were revealed.

The second revelation made it clear that the Prophet had been assigned the monumental task of inviting his people to the worship of the One and Only Creator and warning them of destruction if they persisted in worshipping the idols. To comfort him against the insults that were bound to follow his call, God revealed the following verses:

> *Noon. By the pen, and by that which they write, by the grace of your Lord you are not a madman, and for you is a reward without measure, and you are upon an exalted character.*[79]

It is no coincidence that the pen has been mentioned in the first two revelations. The Prophet said: "Verily, the first of what Allaah created was the Pen, and He said to it: 'Write.' The Pen said: 'O my Lord, what shall I write?' He said: 'Write the decree and whatever will happen throughout eternity.'"[80]

So Allaah gave the pen knowledge of events, and it wrote them. When the Prophet went to the heavens during the Ascension (A*l-Mai'raaj*), he heard the sound of pens writing.[81]

Receiving the Revelation

How did the Prophet Muhammad receive the revelations? Perhaps this question was on the mind of many of his Companions until one day someone asked, "O Messenger of God, how does revelation come to you?" The Prophet's answer and explanation can be summed up thus:

---

79 Qalam 68:1–4. *Noon* in the beginning of the chapter is a letter of the Arabic language, and no one knows its meaning. There are some other chapters in the Qur'aan that likewise begin with single, double, or multiple letters. They are called *Al-Muqatti'aat* (the standalone) letters.

80 Sunan Ahmad, At-Tirmidhi.

81 There is no contradiction between the mentions of the pen's writing and of the angels' writing. The incident of the pen's writing refers to the recording of the decree of Allaah on *Al-Lawh Al-Mahfouzh* (the Preserved Tablet) in heaven, whereas the writing of the angels means their recording of the deeds of the people.

1) A True Dream—Inspiration first came to him in the form of true dreams. He said that dreams are of three kinds: a good and truthful dream that comes from Allaah; a meaningless dream that comes from ourselves and that relates to things we have been thinking about; and a scary and confused dream that comes from Satan. Six months before the coming of Gabriel, the Prophet had started seeing dreams that would come true the next day. At one point he said, "Visions of the prophets are revelation." It was in a dream that the Prophet Abraham was commanded to sacrifice his son, to whom he said, "O my son, indeed I have seen in a dream that I am slaughtering you."[82]
2) Inspiration—In another form of revelation, the angel would breathe the message into the heart of the Prophet, without being seen. The Prophet said, "The Holy Spirit, Gabriel (Jibreel) has inspired me that no soul will die until it has completed its appointed term and received its provision in full, so fear Allaah and seek provision moderately."
3) Ringing of a Bell—Sometimes it came when he heard a bell-like sound while others around him did not hear it. This form was most difficult for him. The Prophet said, "Sometimes it is like the ringing of a bell, and this is the most difficult. When it stops, I have grasped what is said. Other times the angel comes in the form of a man and speaks to me and I grasp whatever he says."[83]
4) Without Gabriel—At times the Prophet would be directly inspired without the involvement of an angel.
5) Gabriel's True Form—The Prophet would see Gabriel in his original form, and Gabriel would convey the divine revelation to him.
6) Gabriel in the Form of a Man—Gabriel would appear as a man named Dihya Al-Kalbi, a Companion of the Prophet, to convey the message, as in the famous incident known as *Hadith Jibreel.*

82 Saaffaat 37:102.

83 Bukhari vol. 1, Hadith #2.

The Prophet said that after his death Allaah's revelations would cease except for true dreams (*Al-Mubash-shiraat*).

More on Khadijah

It is said that behind every great man there is a great woman, whether a mother or a wife. Indeed, in the case of the Prophet Muhammad, it was Khadijah, his first wife. Therefore it is important that we mention a few things about the virtues of Khadijah. God had bestowed on her an immensely intelligent mind and an equally noble heart. The Prophet vouched for her status when he said that among women four had perfected their faith: Maryam bint Imraan, the mother of Jesus; Khadijah bint Khuwaylid, the Prophet's wife who was also known as *Al-Kubraa* (the Great) and *Al-Taahirah* (the Pure);

Faatimah bint Muhammad, the Prophet's and Khadijah's daughter; and Aasiyah, the Pharaoh's wife.

Khadijah was the first person to attest to her husband's Prophethood. Her intelligence and natural faith that good could only beget good told her that what her husband had encountered in the cave of Hira could not have been an evil spirit, given Muhammad's exalted character. Thereafter, she spent her entire wealth in the service of Islam.

Her status reached such heights that Allaah sent greetings of peace on her with Gabriel when he visited the Prophet.

Abu Hurayrah narrated,

Gabriel (Jibreel) came to the Prophet and said: "O Allaah's Messenger! Khadijah is coming to you with a dish of meat soup. When she reaches you, greet her on behalf of her Lord and on my behalf, and give her the glad tidings of a palace in Paradise made of Qasab,[84] *wherein she will neither hear any noise nor (experience) toil."*[85]

Khadijah was thrilled, and she responded, "Allaah is As-Salaam (the source of peace); upon Jibreel be Salaam, and upon you, O Messenger of Allaah, be salaam." Her response showed the gems of her understanding about matters of faith. While she returned the greeting of peace to Gabriel, she did not return Allaah's greetings the same way; she did not say, "Peace on You too, O Allaah," but rather she said, "God Himself is peace."

The Prophet lived a happy life with Khadijah and did not marry any other wife in her lifetime. He would mention her with such admiration that it stoked jealousy in Aayeshah, who later became his wife. She said she was never more jealous of any of the Prophet's wives than she was of Khadijah, even though she had never met her.

Some months after the Migration to Madinah, Khadijah's older sister Haalah came to visit the Prophet; she knocked at the door and sought permission to enter as Khadijah used to. The Prophet's face changed with anticipation, and he said, "O Allaah, Haalah."

Haalah reminded him of Khadijah and the old days. The Prophet treated Haalah with the utmost kindness and hospitality. She was also the mother-in-law of his daughter, Zaynab, but there is no doubt that the Prophet's extra kindness toward Haalah was to honor the memory of Khadijah.

After Haalah was gone, Aayeshah burst out, saying, "What makes you remember an old woman among the old women of the Quraysh who

84 Qasab was a kind of precious wood, and here it could mean a palace made of the finest material.

85 Bukhari, #3820; Muslim, #2432.

died long ago and in whose place Allaah has given you somebody better than her?"

This proved too much for the Messenger of Allaah, who said, "Indeed Allaah did not grant me better than her; she accepted me when people rejected me, she believed in me when people doubted me, she shared her wealth with me when people deprived me, and Allaah granted me children only through her."

Aayeshah said that after this incident she "learnt to keep quiet whenever Khadijah's name was mentioned by the Prophet." This incident must have happened before the Prophet married Maariyah Qibtiyah, from whom he had a son named Ibraahim.

The Prophet's honoring of Khadijah was not limited to her relatives. When he slaughtered sheep or had food, he would send a share to Khadijah's friends.

The Prayer

Around this time, another revelation came that emphasized the role of prayer.

> *O you who are wrapped up (in clothing)! Stand to pray all night, except a little. Half of it or less than that; Or a little more. And recite the Qur'aan in a slow, rhythmic way.*[86]

In this early Makki (Makkan) era, the prayer was not mandatory, but in these verses, God seems to be readying the people for what was to come in a few years. One day, Gabriel came to the Prophet on a hill above Makkah and struck the turf of the hillside with his heel, whereupon a spring gushed forth from it. Then he performed the ritual ablution to show the Prophet

86 Muzzammil 73:1–4.

how to purify himself for worship. Then he showed him the postures and movements of the prayer—the standing, the bowing, the prostrating, and the sitting—as well as the words that should be recited in each posture. The Prophet taught the prayer to Khadijah, who again seems to have been the first person after the Prophet to learn how to pray.

The prayer was made obligatory on the night of Ascension, which happened after the death of Khadijah. However, under concession from God, people prayed only two units of prayers in Makkah. The four units of midday and late-afternoon prayers became mandatory after the migration to Madinah.

The Mission Begins

The Prophet understood that his days of living a normal and inconspicuous life had come to an end. The stage was now set for him to begin his mission to invite others to the worship of Allaah, the only true Creator. But how should he begin a task that had been so difficult for the prophets before him—Jesus, Moses, and others? Prophet Nuh (Noah) had preached for over nine hundred years, and only a handful had embraced his call. He knew well that the Makkans were steeped in idolatry and could violently oppose his message. The Prophet decided, either of his own accord or because of inspiration from heaven, to invite people privately. So at this stage the call was private in nature, limited to those with whom the Prophet had a certain level of comfort. He would talk to them and invite them to Islam. Those who accepted the message would invite their friends on the Prophet's behalf. So the one-on-one approach kept on going, and the message slowly spread.

The handful of people who embraced the new faith at this early stage and against heavy odds deserve brief mentioning, as they made a huge impact on the history of Islam, and their sincerity and sacrifices continue to inspire Muslims today.

Ali bin Abi Taalib—After Khadijah and Waraqah bin Nawfal, Ali seems to be the next convert.[87] At age ten, he was also the youngest to accept Islam. He was raised in the house of the Messenger of Allaah. His father, Abu Taalib, was dearest and closest to the Prophet from among his elders. The Prophet later married his beloved daughter, Faatimah, to Ali. He called Ali *Baab al-Ilm and Asadullaah* (respectively the Door of Knowledge and the Lion of Allaah). Ali proved to be among the bravest soldiers of Islam, from the first battle to the last. He died as a martyr at the hands of a rebellious group of Muslims.

Zayd bin Haarithah—The Prophet freed him from bondage and adopted him as a son. He was so beloved that when the Prophet sent an expedition, he generally made Zayd its leader. Zayd died as a martyr in the Battle of Mu'tah. Aayeshah is reported to have said that had Zayd been alive at the time of succession, there was no way people would have chosen her father as the first caliph. Zayd's son, Usaamah, was also very beloved by the Prophet. In his caliphate, Umar gave Usaamah a higher stipend from the government treasury than he gave his own son, Abdullaah, because of Usaamah's and his father's closeness to the Messenger of Allaah. When Abdullaah complained, Umar said, "O my son, Usaamah was dearer to the Prophet than you, and his father (Zayd) was dearer to him than your father (meaning himself)."

Abu Bakr—His given name was Abdullaah, but he was better known as Abu Bakr. His father, Uthmaan bin Abu Quhaafah, also called him Ateeq. No Sahaabi (Companion) of the Prophet surpasses the virtues of Abu Bakr. He is the only one whom the Prophet called *As-Siddeeq* (the most truthful and foremost in religion). A *Siddeeq* is the highest rank a believer can achieve with Allaah. The Prophet said everyone among the adults he invited to Islam hesitated for a moment before accepting, except for Abu Bakr. It should be noted that Ali had not reached the age of consent when he

87 Some Muslims prefer to use the term "revert" instead of "convert" due to a saying of the Prophet that people are born on their pure nature, meaning Islam, but they choose another religion because of their non-Muslim parents. Hence by accepting Islam they are deemed to have reverted to the original religion.

accepted Islam. Allaah called Abu Bakr "Second of the Two"[88] in the cave with the Prophet when they were secretly migrating to Madinah. A few days before his death, the Prophet said, "Allaah has taken me as a close friend (*Khaleel*) as He took Ibraahim as a close friend. If I were to take anyone from among my *Ummah* as a close friend, I would have taken Abu Bakr as a close friend."[89]

Abdullaah bin Mas'ud—He was an early convert who came from the servant class, but he was quickly recognized for his zeal for the religion. He was considered an accomplished Qur'aan reciter among the Sahaabah, having learned seventy surahs directly from the Prophet. About him the Prophet said, "If someone wants to hear the Qur'aan as fresh as when it was revealed, let him hear from Abdullaah bin Mas'ud." Ibn Mas'ud was severely beaten by the polytheists for openly reciting the Qur'aan in front of the Ka'bah in the early days when the persecution was most intense.

Sa'ad bin Abi Waqqaas—He accepted Islam at the invitation of Abu Bakr. His bravery during the Battle of Uhud prompted the Prophet to say, "May my mother and father be ransom for you," a kind of exaggerated praise for someone who excelled in virtuous deed. According to some reports, Sa'ad traveled to present-day China to spread the message, and he built a mosque in Guangzhou called the Huaisheng Mosque, which exists to this day. He is buried in China.

Uthmaan bin Affaan—Uthmaan was an extremely modest person who accepted Islam in his youthful years. The Prophet gave his daughter Ruqayyah into marriage to Uthmaan, and when she died the Prophet married another daughter, Umm Kulthoom, to him. When she also died, the Prophet said that if he'd had more daughters, he would have married them to Uthmaan one after another. Uthmaan's generosity for Islam became legendary. To support the Tabuk expedition against the Romans, he single-handedly

88 Tawbah 9:40.

89 Muslim, Al-Janaa'iz, Hadith #970.

equipped one-third of the army. Seeing his large-heartedness, the Prophet said, "Nothing will harm Uthmaan after this day."

Zubayr bin Al-Awwaam bin Khuwaylid—His father was Al-Awwaam bin Khuwaylid of the As'ad clan of the Quraysh tribe, making Al-Zubayr a nephew of Khadijah. His mother was the Prophet Muhammad's aunt, Safiyyah bint Abdul Muttalib. The Prophet called him his disciple, saying, "Every Prophet has a disciple, and Al-Zubayr is my disciple." He was one of those ten Companions whom the Prophet had said would be an inhabitant of Paradise. Asmaa, the older daughter of Abu Bakr, was married to Al-Zubayr, and thus he was a brother-in-law of the Prophet.

Abdur Rahmaan bin Awf—He was a wealthy businessman who left everything for Islam. He arrived in Madinah with just the clothes on his back. When the Prophet created *Al-Muwaakhaah* (brotherhood) between the Emigrants and Helpers, he joined Abdur Rahmaan with Sa'ad bin Ar-Rabi', a rich man of Madinah. Sa'ad is famous for saying to Abdur Rahmaan that he would give half his wealth to his brother-in-faith and divorce one of his wives so Abdur Rahmaan could marry her. Abdur Rahmaan thanked the generosity of Sa'ad, prayed that Allaah would bless his wealth and family, and simply asked to be shown the marketplace. Abdur Rahmaan soon became a wealthy man in his own right, and he spent much of it helping the Islamic cause. Sa'ad's statement about divorcing his wife should not be taken literally. In every era and society, people say things to emphasize a point, and those around them understand the context. In Islam, a woman cannot simply be divorced to be married off to another man. Her consent is essential for her marriage.

Abu Ubaydah bin Al-Jarraah—The Prophet called him the "trustee" of his *Ummah* (nation). Abu Ubaydah lost some of his teeth pulling out the iron that had pierced the cheeks of the Prophet in the Battle of Uhud. He was one of the two (the other being Umar) whom Abu Bakr had proposed to succeed the Prophet. Umar appointed him commander of the Muslim forces in his caliphate. He died in a plague in Balqaa (Shaam) and refused to leave his troops to save himself.

The people mentioned above were well to do, except for Abdullaah bin Mas'ud, who was from a servant class. But in an act of great courage, many slaves and poor people also embraced Islam. The Qurayshi polytheists had dehumanized the slaves so that anything could be done to them with impunity. Accepting Islam meant they would earn the wrath of their masters, and for sure many were severely punished.

Sumayyah bint Khayyaat—She was brutally tortured for accepting Islam, as were her husband, Yaasir, and sons, Ammaar, Horayth, and Abdullaah. The persecution of the weak, dispossessed, and slaves was especially harsh in the pagan society. Abu Jahl, whom the Prophet had called the Pharaoh of this *Ummah* (nation), kept torturing her until she died. She is considered the first martyr in Islam.

Yaasir bin Amir—He was also brutally killed like his wife, Sumayyah. It is said ropes were tied to his legs, and horses pulled him apart. Abu Jahl and his cohorts derived sadistic pleasure in this torture. The Prophet Muhammad was unable to help Yaasir and his family, but when he passed by, he would say, "Patience, O family of Yaasir! Your meeting place will be Paradise."

Ammaar bin Yaasir—Because his mother was the first martyr, the Prophet Muhammad called him Ibn Sumayyah (Son of Sumayyah) to honor her, instead of calling him Ibn Yaasir (Son of Yaasir), which was the norm. His brother was also tortured and thrown into a ditch. One day Ammaar came to the Prophet and said he had committed words of disbelief under torture. The Prophet asked him, "How did you find your heart when you said those words?" Ammaar said that his heart was firm on faith. The Prophet said, "When they do the same to you again, you do the same."

Then Allaah revealed in the Qur'aan a verse to soothe the heart of Ammaar and others who had said words of disbelief under torture:

> *Whoever disbelieves in Allaah after his belief, except (one) who is forced while his heart is content with the faith. But rather one who opens his chest to disbelief, then upon them is the wrath of Allaah and for them is a great punishment.*[90]

Reflections: The story of Ammaar holds a practical lesson for us. In recent times, we have learned with horror about the incidents of torture against scores of Muslims in the secret prisons of the world. Many of them were suspected of wrongdoing, but they were never tried, much less convicted, of any crimes. Under extreme torture they said something their captors wanted to hear, and now they live with a sense of guilt. Like Ammaar, those who have said regretful things under torture should know that God looks at their hearts, and He alone knows what resides in them. Allaah said in the Qur'aan:

> *"And indeed We have created man, and We know what his self whispers to him. And We are nearer to him than his jugular vein."*[91]

Because of chapter 16, verse 106, as quoted earlier, the scholars agree that people undergoing oppression are permitted to proclaim disbelief in order to protect their lives. This cannot be called treachery. Laws of nations today distinguish between freely obtained evidence and that obtained through coercion.

Bilaal bin Rabaah—He was a slave of Umayyah bin Khalaf, who would torture Bilaal to force him to renounce Islam. Umayyah would put an iron ring around Bilaal's neck and leave him in the sun with a rock on his chest.

90 Nahl 16:106.

91 Qaaf 50:16.

He would let loose the ruffians of the society on Bilaal. The more evil among them put a rope around Bilaal's neck and dragged him. The other poor and weak converts were also punished, and under extreme torture they were forced to say something against Islam. Bilaal was the only one who never gave in. As for those who said a word or two critical of Islam under torture, the Prophet exonerated them from responsibility as long as their hearts were steadfast upon faith. Seeing Bilaal tortured so viciously, Abu Bakr purchased him from Umayyah and freed him.

To insult Bilaal even more, Umayyah said, "Take him, for he is not worth much."

To honor Bilaal, Abu Bakr responded, "I would have paid even a higher price if you had asked for it."

The Prophet appointed Bilaal the official *Mu'adhdhin* (caller to prayer) because he had the best and strongest voice. For more than ten years in Madinah, Bilaal's beautiful voice announced the call to prayer five times a day. At the Conquest of Makkah, the Prophet asked Bilaal to climb up on the roof of the Ka'bah and call the *Adhaan*. When the Prophet went to *Mai'raaj*, he heard the sound of some footsteps in Paradise and asked Gabriel about it. Gabriel said they were the footsteps of Bilaal.

Khabbaab bin Aratt—He was an Arab slave whose owner was a woman named Umm Anmaar. She used to brand Khabbaab with a heated iron, and his cries could be heard from far away. When the Prophet passed by him, it grieved him, and he prayed, "O Allaah, help Khabbaab. O Allaah, protect him." Soon thereafter Umm Anmaar fell severely ill, panting, twisting, and turning. The doctors of Makkah prescribed that the only treatment that would help her would be cauterization (branding) on the head and the back. It was God's will that Umm Anmaar should taste her own punishment. Years later, Umar, when he was khalifah, asked Khabbaab, "What did Umm Anmaar do to you?" Khabbaab simply lifted his shirt up and showed his back. Umar cried, “By Allaah, I have not seen anything like this.” Then he sat Khabbaab beside him and honored him.

Suhayb bin Sinaan Ar-Rumi (the Roman)—He was not really Roman but an Arab who had been captured at a young age and sold into slavery to the Romans. Later he was able to buy his freedom back and return to his hometown of Makkah. He had learned Latin and forgotten much of his Arabic. He was an indentured servant of Abdullaah bin Jud'aan, the noble Qurayshi, who, although not a Muslim, was just and compassionate. Seeing Suhayb's intelligence and the fact that he was among the few in Makkah who could read and write, Abdullaah bin Jud'aan made Suhayb his business manager and wrote in his will that Suhayb would be freed after his death. So when Abdullaah passed away, Suhayb became a free man. With his business acumen he earned a sizeable amount of wealth. Perhaps he received the least amount of torture because of whom he worked for.

Bilaal, Ammaar, and Suhayb were close friends who hung out together. One time Abu Jahl came to the Prophet and said, “If Islam is the true religion, how is it that people like Bilaal, Ammaar, and Suhayb are in it before us?” The pagan leaders said to the Prophet that they would come and listen to him if he removed the slaves and the poor from his gathering.

To chastise Abu Jahl and his ilk and to elevate the status of these three believers and others like them, Allaah revealed in the Qur'aan:

> *And turn not away those who invoke their Lord, morning and evening seeking His Face. You are accountable for them in nothing, and they are accountable for you in nothing, that you may turn them away and thus become of the wrongdoers.*[92]

The Prophet took special care of the destitute Companions, at times giving them precedence over his own family's needs. The idea of sacrificing one's own needs or those of one's family for others might appear strange to some

92 An'aam 6:52.

people, but the Christians and Jews will find many such stories in their own faith traditions.

A Pause in Revelation

After the first ten revelations, there was suddenly a period of silence, until the Prophet began to fear that he may have unintentionally done something that had displeased Allaah. Revelations were his lifeline; they had given his life direction and purpose. When Khadijah saw him depressed, she comforted him by saying that Allaah was not angry with him, given his devotion to Him.

One of the incidents that really hurt the Prophet was when an old woman, probably Abu Lahab's wife, who had come to know about the pause in revelation, taunted, "Your devil has now left you." To console the Prophet and admonish this woman and those like her, Allaah revealed a short chapter called *Duha* (The Forenoon):

> *By the morning brightness, and by the night when it is still, your Lord has not forsaken you nor does He hate you, and the Hereafter will be better for you than this world, and your Lord shall give His bounty that will please you. Did he not find you an orphan and gave shelter, and find you unaware (of the right path) and guided you, and find you needy and enriched you? Therefore, do not oppress the orphan, or repel the beggar, and the bounty of your Lord.*[93]

These verses greatly pleased the Prophet, and Muslims recite them to this day.

In this phase of the private missionary call (*da'wah*), the Prophet recognized the perils that Muslims faced for saying *La Ilaaha Illallaah* (there is no god but Allaah). Therefore, he remained discreet in his approach and advised his followers to do the same. In one interesting incident, he even

93 Duha 93.

discouraged a foreigner from embracing Islam because the Prophet feared that pagans would kill this man.

The story goes like this: A man named Amr bin Abdullaah bin Abasi came to the Prophet to profess faith. A citizen of Yemen, Abdullaah had heard about the coming of a new Prophet, and so when the news reached him that someone named Muhammad was privately calling people to the worship of One God in Makkah, then a den of idolatry, he became excited. Amr had become convinced that what the Prophet Muhammad was inviting people to was the true religion.

Amr met with the Prophet in a secret place and said he wanted to declare his faith in Allaah. Surprisingly, the Prophet told him, "Not now, but come back to me when you hear that my mission has triumphed." Amr returned to Yemen, but being true in his conviction, he waited for the Prophet's message to succeed. Years passed, and the news from Makkah continued to be grim. If anything, the persecution of the Prophet and his Companions had intensified. The pagans had even tried to assassinate the Prophet.

Finally, when Amr heard that the Prophet and his Companions had migrated to Madinah and established an Islamic society, he went there and recited the Islamic profession of faith: "I bear witness that there is no god except Allaah, and I bear witness that Muhammad is the Messenger of Allaah." Subsequent to his declaration, Amr returned to his homeland. Al-Waaqidi in his *Kitab Al-Maghazi* said that Amr moved back to Madinah during the caliphate of Umar bin Al-Khattaab.

Calling the Family to Islam

While the Prophet was occupied with the selective *da'wah*, a verse came down that commanded him to invite his kith and kin. This was something he had avoided so far out of expediency. The command was clear: "And warn your tribe of near kindred."[94]

---

94 Shu'araa 26:214.

The verse had a certain sternness to it, and it came after the mention of Pharaoh's rebelliousness against another of God's messengers, Musa (Moses). Pharaoh (Fir'awn) and his people were eventually drowned for their persistence in disbelief.

When the verse came down, the Prophet called Ali and said to him, "Allaah has commanded me to warn my family, my nearest of kin, and the task is beyond my strength." He told Ali to prepare a leg of lamb, fill a cup with milk, and assemble all of the Bani Abdul Muttalib so that he may tell them what Allaah had ordered him to say. Ali did exactly as instructed, and about forty men from the clan of Banu Haashim came to the meal. There was no way one leg and a cup of milk would have sufficed for forty people. The Prophet took a piece of the meat, bit upon it, and put it back into the dish, saying, "Eat it in the Name of God." The men ate to their fill until they could not eat any more. Ali reported that, despite the fact that so many men had eaten the food, its quantity did not appear to have diminished. Then the cup of milk was brought forth, and they all drank from it without any decrease in the quantity. This was the first of many such miracles, where a small quantity of food or water sufficed for a large number of people, that the Prophet was to perform in the years ahead. It was a blessing that God had bestowed upon him.

After the meal was over, the Prophet thought that the time was right to invite his kinsmen to Islam, but as he prepared to address them, Abu Lahab, his oldest uncle, preempted him, saying to the clan, "Your host has placed a spell upon you," which caused them to disperse before the Prophet could say a word.

The Prophet ordered Ali to prepare the meal again the next day. So as not to be forestalled again, the Prophet said, "O sons of Abdul Muttalib, I know of no Arab who has come to his people with a nobler message than mine. I bring you the best of this world and the next. Allaah has commanded me to call you unto Him. Which of you, then, will help me in this and be my brother, my executor, and my successor among you?"

Suddenly there was silence, as if the audience had been made speechless. Jaa'far bin Abu Taalib and Zayd bin Haarithah could have come forth, but they knew the Prophet was not asking them, since they already believed in the message. When nobody else spoke, Ali felt he needed to say something, so he broke the silence. "O Prophet of Allaah, I will be your helper in this."

The Prophet said, "This is my brother, my executor and my successor among you. Hearken unto him, and obey him."[95]

The men got up laughing and saying to Abu Taalib, "He has ordered us to listen to your son and to obey him."

Public Outreach

When the family did not respond positively to the invitation, the Prophet climbed a hill and called out: "O Bani Abdul Muttalib; O Bani Fihr; O Bani Lu'ayy; O Bani Abdu Manaaf; O Faatimah, daughter of Muhammad; O Safiyyah, daughter of Abdul Muttalib, I cannot help you before Allaah. What do you think if I told you that there was a cavalry at the foot of this mountain coming to attack you—would you believe me?"

They said, "Yes."

The Prophet then told them, "Then I warn you of a great punishment that is close at hand."

Abu Lahab said, "May you perish for the rest of the day! You only called us to tell us this!"

Allaah's wrath against Abu Lahab was swift. The following chapter came down, forever damning Abu Lahab and his wife, Arwah bint Harb

95 Martin Lings, *Muhammad: His Life Based on the Earliest Sources* (Rochester, VT: Inner Traditions, 2006), 53.

bin Umayyah, who was a sister of Abu Sufiyan and who was also very vile toward the Prophet:

> *Perish the two hands of Abu Lahab and perish he! His wealth and his children will not benefit him! He will enter a blazing fire! And his wife too, who carries wood (spreads calumny). In her neck is a twisted rope of palm fiber.*[96]

Reflections: This chapter leaves no doubt that Abu Lahab is destined for Hell. It also points to a very important Islamic principle that only Allaah decides who goes to Paradise or Hell. No Muslim should judge anyone concerning a matter over which that person has no authority. The only exceptions to this rule are cases in which Allaah has issued a verdict and has informed us about it.

The Campaign to Discredit the Prophet

The Prophet's call began to worry the leaders of Makkah. They realized that it was a revolutionary message that threatened the existing world order. If this religion were to succeed, their claim to greatness, power, and glory would be a thing of the past. A slave would have the same rights as they; therefore, this message and its bearer needed to be stopped. So they came up with a multipronged approach to discredit the Prophet. They called him *Saahir* (magician) and told people to avoid talking to him if they wanted to maintain their sanity. When that did not work, they called him *Mas-hoor* (possessed). When that did not work, they accused him of being insane. When even that did not work, they called him *Kaahin* (sorcerer) and *Shaa'ir* (poet).[97] Allaah defended the Prophet against all this slander and declared that the Qur'aan was not poetry.[98]

96 Masad 111:1–5.

97 Poets can make up tales and exaggerate things. They can also be the conscience of a society in opposing injustice. The Prophet allowed poetry that advanced the cause of the truth.

98 Two of these accusations are mentioned in verses 41 and 42 of chapter 69, and the rest are scattered across various others chapters of the Qur'aan.

Without saying anything to anyone, the Prophet would at times stand in front of the Ka'bah and recite those parts of the Qur'aan that had already been revealed. Because the Qur'aan was in their language and its words were extremely powerful, the leaders ordered people to put cotton in their ears or make noise to drown out the Prophet's voice. The Prophet sometimes would raise his voice so the Qur'aan could be heard over the noise of the Quraysh.

As if to assure the Prophet that his message would succeed whether he raised his voice or not, and to teach him the right pitch of voice when reading the Qur'aan, Allaah sent down the following verse:

> *And offer your prayer (recite) neither aloud nor in a low voice, but follow a way between.*[99]

One day, some of the Companions asked who would like to recite the Qur'aan in the Ka'bah the next day. Abdullaah bin Mas'ud, a young, petite convert originally from Yemen with no tribal support in Makkah, volunteered. Fearing for his safety, the Companions tried to dissuade him, but Ibn Mas'ud remained insistent. So he went and recited Surah Ar-Rahmaan, an especially beautiful surah about the mercies of God.

The Quraysh started listening, thinking maybe it was some poetry, but soon they realized from the style of recitation that it was the Qur'aan. So the ruffians pounced on Ibn Mas'ud and beat him until he was bloodied. Despite his injuries, Ibn Mas'ud wanted to go out again the next day and recite the Qur'aan, but the other Muslims stopped him.

It was about this Companion that the Prophet said, "If someone wants to listen to the Qur'aan as fresh as when it was revealed, let him hear it from Ibn Mas'ud."

---

99 Israa 17:110.

In the Madani period, some Companions once joked about Ibn Mas'ud's skinny legs. When the Prophet heard about it, he said Ibn Mas'ud's legs were stronger than Mount Uhud. This was a way to acknowledge the young Companion's steadfastness and resolve in the path of Allaah.

Secret Admirers of the Qur'aan

Interestingly, some of the Qurayshi leaders who publicly forbade others from listening to the Qur'aan did not follow their own advice. Seerah books have recorded that for three consecutive nights Abu Sufiyan, Akhnas Al-Shareef, and Abu Jahl sneaked out of their houses in the middle of the night and secretly listened to the Prophet when he recited the Qur'aan in Khadijah's house. Every night they somehow ran into each other and felt mutually embarrassed at their self-contradiction. On the third night they promised to stop listening.

A day or two after this incident, Akhnas went to Abu Sufiyan and asked him what he thought of the Qur'aan. Abu Sufiyan said, "You tell me your opinion first."

So Akhnas told him, "By Allaah, it is the truth."

When it was Abu Sufiyan's turn, he gave a diplomatic statement, saying, "I understood some things but did not understand others."

Akhnas then went to Abu Jahl to ask the same question. Abu Jahl, the Fir'awn of the Quraysh, said, "We Banu Makhzum (his clan) used to compete with the Banu Abdu Manaaf (the Prophet's clan) neck and neck, so much so that if they fed the pilgrims, we fed the pilgrims, but now one of them has claimed to be a Prophet. How can we compete with that?" Then he swore that he would oppose the Prophet Muhammad as long as he lived.

Waleed bin Al-Mugheerah's Ploy

Despite a well-organized campaign to prevent people from listening to the Qur'aan, the speech of Allaah reached some ears, even if only by a sentence or two at a time. Those who heard felt overpowered by the truth and eloquence of the Qur'aan. Some accepted Islam, while others tried to find an excuse to reject it.

One such person who listened to the Qur'aan was Waleed bin Al-Mugheerah, a chief of the Banu Makhzum. He had heard Abu Bakr recite the Qur'aan in his house and had been captivated by it. One day he went to Abu Bakr's house and asked him to describe the Qur'aan. Abu Bakr's description further stirred his heart.

Waleed wasted no time and went straight to the Quraysh, saying, "What a great thing this is that Ibn Abi Kabsha (meaning the Prophet)[100] has brought. I swear by Allaah that it is neither poetry nor magic nor the prattling of insanity. Verily, his speech is from Allaah!" It is also said that Waleed muttered something to himself in praise of the Qur'aan, and he was overheard by some.

Waleed was an accomplished poet and therefore could easily recognize poetry. Waleed's praise of the Qur'aan caused quite a stir, and people began to talk about it. They worried that if Waleed accepted Islam, all the Quraysh would follow suit. When Abu Jahl, a fellow Makhzumi chief, heard about Waleed's utterances and the people's concerns, he tried to calm them, saying, "Do not worry; I will take care of the matter."

---

100 Ibn Abi Kabsha was a derogatory term that the pagans used for the Prophet. Among ancient Arabs, a man named Ibn Abi Kabsha had traveled to parts of the world and found a people who believed in astrology and worshipped a star called Shiyara. Upon return he suggested to the Arabs that they leave the idols and worship Shiyara, but they rejected the advice. So when the Prophet told the pagans to stop worshipping idols and to worship Allaah alone, they called him Ibn Abi Kabsha.

Armed with a deceitful strategy, Abu Jahl went to Waleed's house and said, "O Waleed, don't you see that your people are collecting charity for you?"

Waleed shot back, "Don't I have more wealth and children than they do?"

Abu Jahl answered, "They are saying that you only went to Ibn Abi Quhaafah's house so that you can get some of his food."

That upset Waleed. "Is this what my tribe is saying? Nay, by Allaah, I am not seeking to be close to Ibn Abi Quhaafah (Abu Bakr), nor Umar, nor Ibn Abi Kabsha. And his speech is only inherited magic of old."

Abu Jahl and his ilk worried about the coming Hajj and the annual fair, among other things. Large numbers of people would visit the Holy Sanctuary and might hear the message of the Prophet. How could they be inoculated against that message? What could they possibly say about the Prophet?

Waleed, who had been won over by Abu Jahl, said, "If you said contradictory things about Muhammad, we all would lose our trust among the people. Therefore, let us agree upon one opinion, which we should all say without dispute."

Some said that they would call the Prophet Muhammad a soothsayer. Waleed said, "No, by God, he is not a soothsayer. We have seen the soothsayers and heard their murmur and rhymed speech."

Other people said, "He is possessed."

Waleed responded, "He is not possessed. We have seen possessed people, and here is no choking, spasmodic movement, or whispering."

Yet others said, "Then we say he is a poet."

Waleed said, "No, he is not a poet, for we know poetry in all its forms, and what he presents conforms to none."

The people said, "Then he is a sorcerer."

Waleed said, "He is no sorcerer either, for here is no spitting or knots."

At this Abu Jahl kept pressing Waleed. "Your people will never be pleased with you unless you say something about Muhammad."

Then, after prolonged thought and consideration, Waleed said, "The nearest thing to the truth is that you tell the Arabs that he is a sorcerer who has brought a message by which he separates a man from his father, from his brother, from his wife and children, and from his family." They all agreed.

It is also said Waleed began to tensely pace back and forth in his house, wondering how he should craft his refutation of the Qur'aan and the Prophet Muhammad. Despite the fact that Waleed was thinking to himself in his house in the middle of the night, he did not escape the knowledge of Allaah, who revealed the following stern verses about him:

> *Leave Me alone (to deal) with whom I created lonely. And then granted him resources in abundance. And children attending. And made life smooth and comfortable for him. After all that he desires that I should give more. Nay! Verily, he has been opposing Our verses. I shall force him to flat-faced in Hell! Verily, he thought and plotted. So let him be cursed, how he plotted! And once more let him be cursed, how he plotted! Then he thought. Then he frowned and he looked in a bad tempered way. Then he turned back, and was proud. Then he said: "This is nothing but magic from that of old. This is nothing but the*

word of a human being!" I will cast him into Saqar. And what will make you know (exactly) what Saqar is. It (is fire that) spares not, nor does it leave (anything)! [101]

Ridicule of the Prophet

Once someone came to Abu Jahl to ask for the money he owed him. Instead of returning what he owed the man, Abu Jahl told him, "Go to Muhammad; he will pay you back." The Prophet had nothing to do with it, but that was Abu Jahl's way of making fun of him. The man went to the Prophet, thinking perhaps the latter owed money to Abu Jahl. The Prophet asked the man to follow him to Abu Jahl's house.

When Abu Jahl answered the knock and came out, the Prophet told him in a commanding tone to return the man's money. Suddenly, Abu Jahl's face became pale, and he immediately ran inside the house and brought a pouch of money, which he gave to the man. Some people saw this incident and reproached Abu Jahl for being such a coward, to which he said, "You did not see what I saw standing behind Muhammad. I saw some angry camels that were ready to pounce at me."

One day Abu Jahl vowed that if he were to see the Prophet Muhammad praying in front of the Ka'bah, he would step on his neck while he was in prostration. As the Prophet lay prostrate, Abu Jahl came close, and as he was about to carry out his dastardly act, he moved his hands as if to push something away and then came back.

People asked, "What happened to you?"

He said, "As I got close to Muhammad, I saw a pit of fire and wings."

101 Muddassir 74:11–28.

The Prophet said, "Had Abu Jahl come one step closer, the angels would have torn him into pieces."

Uqbah bin Abi Mu'yait, the Meanest

While Abu Jahl was an implacable enemy, in Makkah there was someone meaner than he was: Uqbah bin Abi Mu'yait. Al-Bukhari narrated that Abdullaah bin Amr bin Al-Aas said, "While the Messenger of Allaah was praying in the courtyard of the Ka'bah, Uqbah bin Abi Mu'yait came and grabbed the shoulder of the Messenger of Allaah and started twisting his garment so that it strangled him. Abu Bakr came and grabbed Uqbah's shoulder and pushed him away from the Prophet. Then he said, 'Would you kill a man because he says: My Lord is Allaah?'"

Some other ruffians were cheering at Uqbah, and when Abu Bakr confronted them, they beat him so severely that his mother thought he would not survive. As if to support Abu Bakr, Allaah repeated the former's statement verbatim in the Qur'aan through the tongue of another pious person:

> *And a believing man of Pharaoh's family, who hid his Faith said: "Would you kill a man because he says: My Lord is Allaah?"*[102]

On another occasion, Abu Jahl asked who could throw the gut of a recently slaughtered camel on the Prophet Muhammad while he went into prostration. Uqbah rose to his feet and said he would. Even though he was from the elite of the Quraysh, he did not mind personally carrying the rotting entrails of the camel and throwing them on the Messenger of God. When he was done committing the heinous act, the evil people in the crowd began to cheer.

---

102 Ghaafir 40:28.

Because of the weight of the camel's intestines, the Prophet could not get up. However, a good-hearted person went to Faatimah, the Prophet's daughter, who was around nine at the time, and said, "Your father needs help."

Faatimah came crying and removed the entrails from her father's head. The Prophet got up and raised his index finger toward the heaven as if to invoke Allaah's help against Uqbah and his gang. When they saw him in this state, they became quiet and fearful. The Prophet called out Allaah's wrath against Abu Jahl, Uqbah bin Abi Muyait, his son Waleed, Umayyah bin Khalaf, Shaybah bin Rabi'ah, and Utbah bin Rabi'ah. All whom the Prophet had prayed against were eventually killed in the Battle of Badr.

Then Allaah revealed verses against Abu Jahl and perhaps Uqbah:

> *Have you seen him who prevents. A servant when he prays. Have you seen if he is on the guidance Or enjoins Piety. Have you seen if he denies and turns away. Knows he not that Allaah sees. Nay! If he ceases not, We will scorch his forehead. A lying, sinful forehead! Then let him call upon his council. We will call out the guards of Hell!*[103]

Choosing of the House of Arqam

The public and private da'wah had resulted in almost forty people becoming Muslim, and the community now needed a bigger place to congregate. The Prophet chose the house of Arqam bin Abi Arqam, which was behind Mount Safa. This was a brilliantly strategic decision because people were always coming to the Ka'bah in large numbers, so a few Muslims seen in that area would not arouse suspicion. Moreover, Arqam bin Abi Arqam was from the Bani Makhzum, the same tribe that Abu Jahl belonged to. The Banu Makhzum had always had a rivalry with the Banu Haashim. It would

103 Alaq 96:9–18.

be considered very unlikely that a person of the Banu Makhzum would help the Prophet Muhammad.

The new believers secretly gathered in this house and learned their religion from the Prophet. They offered prayers behind the Prophet and learned to read the Qur'aan. Many of them were young people who left the hustle and bustle of Makkah to quietly worship Allaah. This house was a safe haven in a den of hostility.

The First Emigration to Abyssinia

In the fifth year of his Prophethood, as the torture became intense, the Prophet allowed a group of people to migrate to Abyssinia. He said, "Go to Najaashi (Negus); he is a just king and does not persecute people for their beliefs." Najaashi (Negus) was the title of the Abyssinian kings, but the real name of the king at the time was said to be As-huma bin Abjar.

Although the most severe torture was reserved for the slaves and the poor who had embraced Islam, most of those who emigrated were the nobles of the Quraysh. Among them were Uthmaan bin Affaan and his wife Ruqayyah bint Muhammad, the Prophet's son-in-law and daughter. The simple reason for this apparent paradox was that the slaves and the poor either could not leave without the permission of their masters or did not have the financial means to travel. The irony of the situation could not be missed, as those who really needed to escape the persecution could not do so.

Even for those who could migrate, it was a hard decision. Migration caused dislocation and disruption, especially in seventh-century Arabia, where people lived within their tribes for protection. In those days moving away from one's tribe could lead to enslavement. Those who could migrate had to leave most of their wealth, which meant sure poverty in the new land. Added to that was the prospect of dealing with a new culture and language.

The First Emigrants

In the first wave of migration were fifteen men and women and some children. They were the following:

1. Uthman bin Affaan (son-in-law of the Prophet Muhammad)
2. Ruqayyah bint Muhammad (daughter of the Prophet)
3. Abu Hudhayfah bin Utbah
4. Sahla bint Suhayl (wife of Abu Hudhayfah)
5. Zubayr bin Al-Awwaam (a nephew of Khadijah bint Khuwaylid and a cousin of the Prophet)
6. Mus'ab bin Umayr Abdari
7. Abdur Rahmaan bin Awf
8. Abu Salamah (Abdullaah) bin Abdul Asad Al-Makhzumi (who died in Abyssinia)
9. Umm Salamah (Hind) bint Abi Umayyah Al-Makhzumiyah (wife of Abu Salamah who later married the Prophet Muhammad)
10. Uthmaan bin Maz'oon Al-Jumi
11. Aamir bin Rabi'ah (an ally of the Adiy clan)
12. Layla bint Abi Hathamah (wife of Aamir)
13. Abu Sabra bin Abi Ruhm
14. Abu Haatib bin Amr bin Abd Ash-Shams
15. Suhayl bin Bayda (from the Al-Haarith clan)

Note: It is said that Jaa'far bin Abi Taalib and his wife, Asmaa bint Umays, migrated to Abyssinia on their own.

Umar's Dialogue with Layla

An interesting incident took place as the emigrants were getting ready to leave. While Layla bint Abi Hathamah was loading her bags, Umar happened to pass by.

"Where are you going?" he asked her.

Layla was already upset because the pagans were making life unbearable for the Muslims, and when Umar, who tormented the believers, asked this question, she snapped. "This is all because of you that we have to leave our home to worship Allaah. You have terrorized us and left us with no choice."

That hit Umar hard, and he replied, "Has the matter reached this level? May Allaah be with you!" She was shocked to hear this, as Umar was not known for softness. Indeed this was the first time Islam made a small dent in Umar's heart.

Reflections: Muslims living in the West have debated whether it is permissible for them to live in a land whose laws are not based on the Islam. Such a land is one where they are in the minority and the laws are made by a group of politicians. Some scholars have opined that people may visit such lands for business, education, and missionary work but may not live there. However, the fact that the Prophet sent a group of Muslims to Abyssinia to live clearly demonstrates that as long as Muslims can practice their faith freely, they can live anywhere in the world. In fact, Muslims today generally find more religious freedom in the West than in Muslim countries.

The Muslims lived in Abyssinia for fourteen years, and the last group left seven years after an Islamic government had been founded in Madinah. Moreover, as long as the Muslims lived in Abyssinia, they abided by local laws and never once tried to subvert or overthrow the government of their adopted country. Muslims should remember that their first land of refuge was a Christian country and therefore be thankful to Christians. The multitudes of Muslims who have moved to the West in the last few decades have found there to be more religious freedom and safety here than in the countries they left behind.

Why Did the Prophet Choose Abyssinia?

One wonders why, of all the places, the Prophet sent the oppressed Muslims to a land whose language and culture were different from theirs. The main reason was the freedom of religion that existed under the king of Abyssinia at the time. But there could have been secondary reasons as well; for instance, Abyssinians knew about the Quraysh and Makkah, and their land was relatively close.

It seems that Najaashi followed a version of Christianity that was different from that of the masses, and his beliefs were very similar to those of Muslims. For example, Muslims believe that the Prophet Jesus (*Eesa*) was a Messenger of God, and that is what Najaashi believed. Muslims believe that Allaah raised Jesus up to Himself when the Romans tried to crucify him. From many accounts, it seems as if someone resembling Jesus was crucified on the cross. The disappearance of Jesus created a big trial for his followers, who debated where he had gone. While Jesus was living among them, they did not claim that he was the Son of God. However, in the confusion that followed his absence, people became divided. Joseph Barnabas, for one, preached that Jesus was a Prophet of God. The Gospel of Saint Barnabas stated that Jesus had told his followers that a Prophet named Ahmad (Muhammad) would come after him to carry on his work, which is exactly what the Qur'aan says.

> *And (remember) when Eesa, son of Maryam, said: "O Children of Israel! I am the Messenger of Allaah unto you, confirming the Torah which came before me, and giving glad tidings of a Messenger to come after me, whose name shall be Ahmad." But when he came to them with clear proofs, they said: "This is plain magic."*[104]

While Barnabas's teachings about Jesus are very close to the Islamic viewpoint, his gospel is not included in the New Testament, and orthodox

104 Saff 61:6.

Christian scholars and theologians do not recognize his version as accurate or authoritative.

On the other hand, Paul, who is believed to have authored much of the New Testament, started preaching a very different version of Christianity from that taught by Jesus and recorded in the four New Testament Gospels. For over three hundred years, the controversy continued. The Roman Emperor Constantine, who claimed to believe in the Trinity for political expediency, supported this Pauline version of Christianity. He had no real interest in religious doctrine and was only baptized a Christian on his deathbed, but a unified Christian church was best for the social and political stability of his empire. In 325 CE he convened the Council of Nicaea and invited all Christian scholars to put forward their understandings of the nature of Jesus to further define and unify Christianity. One of the scholars, named Arius, disagreed with most of the other scholars, saying that Jesus was a Son of God but that he had a beginning; therefore, he was subordinate to God. The majority view was that Jesus was the Son of God and was of one substance with God. The emperor, who wanted one version of Christianity as suited his empire, ordered Arius and two of his most ardent supporters exiled and his writings destroyed.

An official decree said:

> *In addition, if any writing composed by Arius should be found, it should be handed over to the flames, so that not only will the wickedness of his teaching be obliterated, but nothing will be left even to remind anyone of him. And I hereby make a public order, that if someone should be discovered to have hidden a writing composed by Arius, and not to have immediately brought it forward and destroyed it by fire, his penalty shall be death. As soon as he is discovered in this offense, he shall be submitted for capital punishment.*[105]

105 Athanasius, "Edict by Emperor Constantine against the Arians," *Fourth Century Christianity*, Wisconsin Lutheran College (23 January 2010).

The council composed the trinitarian Nicene Creed, and Constantine declared the Trinity as the official creed of his court. Because it was backed up by the throne, this belief became the accepted dogma in the Christian church. Today, all three main branches of Christianity—Orthodox, Catholic, and Protestant—believe in the Trinity. But to this day, there are some, like Jewish Christians or Messianic Christians and other sects, who do not believe in the Trinity. Some of those who did not believe in the Trinity may still have had access to some of the original scriptures and may have believed Jesus was a prophet who would be followed by another prophet. That is why when Najaashi, Salmaan Al-Farisi, and Waraqah bin Nawfal heard of a man named Muhammad who claimed to be a Prophet, they believed in him.

On to Abyssinia

When the emigrants had packed up, they headed to the port of Juddah (now Jeddah) and boarded a ship for Abyssinia. Although their migration was not secret, for some unexplained reason the Quraysh did not try to prevent them. Only after they were gone did the Quraysh realize that it had been a mistake to let them go. On top of that, the word came that the emigrants had been well received by Najaashi. That was a little too much for the Qurayshi leaders to digest, so they sent Amr bin Al-Aas and Abdullaah bin Abi Rabi'ah with valuable gifts to the court of Najaashi. They first bribed the ministers and the generals of Najaashi's court, asking them to support the expulsion or deportation of the immigrants. Having earned their gratitude, they went to Najaashi and told him that some misguided Makkan lads had fled town and taken refuge in his land. They told the king that these young men were neither following the religion of their forefathers (paganism) nor following his (Christianity) but rather were following a new faith. The Qurayshi delegates asked that Najaashi hand over the Muslims to them. Seeing this as an opportune time, Najaashi's ministers warmly supported the idea of expulsion.

"Not so fast," said Najaashi. "These people have come to seek refuge in my land, and I cannot return them unless I ask them some questions."

So Najaashi summoned the Muslims to the court and asked them to explain the teachings of their religion. The Muslim immigrants were put on the spot, but they consulted among themselves and decided to tell the truth no matter the consequences.

Ibn Isshaaq said their leader, Jaa'far bin Abu Taalib, an older brother of Ali, spoke.

> *O King! we were plunged in the depths of ignorance and barbarism; we worshipped idols, we lived unchastely, we ate the dead animals, and we spoke abominations; we disregarded every feeling of humanity and the duties of hospitality and neighborhood; we knew no law but that of the strong. Then Allaah raised among us a man of whose birth, truthfulness, honesty, and purity we were aware, and he called us to the* Oneness of God *and taught us not to associate anything with Him. He forbade us the worship of idols; he enjoined us to speak the truth, to be faithful to our trusts, to be merciful, and to take care of the rights of the neighbors and kith and kin; he forbade us to speak evil of women or to eat the wealth of orphans; he ordered us to abstain from evil, to offer prayers, to pay alms, and to observe fast. We have believed in him; we have accepted his teachings and his injunctions to worship God and not to associate anything with Him; and we have* allowed what He has allowed, and prohibited what He has prohibited. *For this reason, our people have risen against us, have persecuted us in order to make us forsake the worship of God and return to the worship of idols and other abominations. They have tortured and injured us, until, finding no safety among them, we have come to your country, and we hope you will protect us from oppression.*

Najaashi was impressed by what he heard and the eloquent way in which it was said. So he asked Jaa'far if God had revealed anything to his Prophet. From divine wisdom, a portion of Surah Maryam (Mary) that dealt with Jesus and his mother had come down recently. One may think of it as a provision for the journey that God had bestowed upon Jaa'far and his Companions. Jaa'far recited the opening verses of Surah Maryam, chapter 19, verses 16–36:

> *And mention in the Qur'aan Mary, when she secluded herself from her family to a place facing east.*
>
> *She placed a screen from them; then We sent to her Our Spirit (Gabriel), and he appeared before her in the form of a man in all respects.*
>
> *She said: "Verily! I seek refuge with Allaah from you, if you do fear Allaah."*
>
> *The angel said: "I am only a Messenger from your Lord to announce to you the gift of a righteous son."*
>
> *She said: "How can I have a son, when no man has touched me, nor am I unchaste?"*
>
> *The angel said: "So it will be, your Lord has said: That is easy for Me, and I wish to appoint him as a sign to mankind and a mercy from Me. And it is a matter already decreed."*
>
> *So Mary conceived him and withdrew with him to a far place (Bethlehem).*
>
> *And the pains of childbirth drove her to the trunk of a date-palm tree. She said: "Would that I had died before this and had been forgotten and out of sight!"*
>
> *Then a voice cried out from below her, saying: "Grieve not! Your Lord has provided a water stream under you.*

> *"And shake the trunk of the date-palm tree towards you, it will let fresh-ripe dates fall upon you.*
>
> *"So eat and drink and be glad, and if you see any human being, say: 'Verily! I have vowed a fast unto the Most Beneficent Allaah so I shall not speak to any human being today.'"*
>
> *Then she carried the baby to her people. They said: "O Mary! Indeed you have brought a mighty thing. O sister of Aaron, Your father was not an adulterer, nor was your mother an unchaste woman."*
>
> *Then she pointed to Jesus. They said: "How can we talk to someone in the cradle?"*
>
> *Jesus said: "Verily! I am a servant of Allaah, He has given me the Scripture and made me a Prophet. And He has blessed me wherever I may be, and has enjoined on me prayer, and alms, as long as I live. And made me dutiful to my mother, and made me not arrogant, unblessed. And peace be upon me the day I was born, and the day I die, and the day I shall be resurrected."*
>
> *Such is Jesus, son of Mary. It is a statement of truth about which people dispute. It befits not the Majesty of God that He should beget a son. Glorified be He. When He decrees a thing, He only says to it, "Be!" and it is.*
>
> *Jesus said: "And verily Allaah is my Lord and your Lord. So worship Him (alone). That is the Straight Path."*

The verses, when translated, moved Najaashi and his bishops to tears, and the king exclaimed, "It seems as if these words and those that were revealed to Jesus have come from the same source." Turning to the envoys of the

Quraysh, he said, "I am afraid I cannot give you back these asylum seekers. They are free to live and worship in my country as they please."

Given the warm reception Najaashi gave the Muslims and the similarity between Christianity and Islam, it is not a surprise that Allaah praised Christians in the Qur'aan:

> *And you will find the nearest in love to the believers those who say: "We are Christians." That is because among them are priests and monks, and they are not proud. And when they listen to what has been sent down to the Messenger, you see their eyes overflowing with tears because of the truth they have recognized. They say: "Our Lord! We believe; so write us down among the witnesses. And why should we not believe in Allaah and in that which has come to us of the truth. And we wish that our Lord will admit us along with the righteous people." So because of what they said, Allaah awarded them with Gardens under which rivers flow, they will abide therein forever. Such is the reward of good-doers.*[106]

There is an opinion that the above verses were revealed about a delegation of Najaashi that came to the Prophet in Makkah, heard the Qur'aan, and accepted Islam.

A Second Meeting with Najaashi

Amr bin Al-Aas and Abdullaah bin Abi Rabi'ah were not quite ready to give up, especially Amr, who had qualities of a politician. So the next day they went back to Najaashi and said the man who claimed to be the Prophet and his followers were blaspheming Jesus.

"Ask the immigrants what they say about Jesus," Amr said.

106 Maa'idah 5:82–85.

Hearing that, Najaashi became upset and ordered that the Muslims be brought back right away. When they arrived in the court, Najaashi sharply asked, "What is your belief about Jesus?"

This was a more difficult challenge than the first one, but Jaa'far decided that no matter what he would say exactly what Muslims believed about Jesus. So he stood up and said, "We will speak about Jesus as we have been taught by our Prophet, that he is the servant of Allaah, His Messenger, His spirit, and His word breathed into Virgin Mary."

The king replied, "Even so do we believe. Blessed be you, and blessed be your master." The king turned to the two frowning Makkan envoys and to his bishops who were visibly angry and said, "You may fret and fume as you like, but Jesus was nothing more than what Jaa'far has said about him."

The King assured the Muslims full protection, returned the gifts to the envoys of the Quraysh, and sent them away.

Najaashi's White Lie

Najaashi's endorsement of the Muslim position concerning Jesus had made the bishops very upset. They accused him of leaving the Christian religion. Najaashi foresaw a coming rebellion against him. So the first thing he did was call Jaa'far privately and tell him that he had prepared two ships for him and his party. "If I am defeated, go where you please; if I am victorious, stay where you are."

Then Najaashi came up with an idea that can be described as a white lie. He wrote on a piece of paper, "I testify that there is no God but Allaah and that Muhammad is His slave and apostle; and I testify that Jesus, Son of Mary, is His slave, His apostle, His spirit, and His word, which He cast into Mary." He put that paper securely inside his chest pocket near the heart. He then called his people and asked, "What is your problem concerning me?"

They said, "You have left our religion, and you claim that Jesus is a slave of Allaah."

Najaashi said, "And then what do you say about Jesus?"

"We say that he is the Son of God."

Najaashi then put his hand on the chest pocket and said, "I testify that Jesus, the Son of Mary, was no more than *this*." They thought he was agreeing to their position and went away content.

Najaashi died a Muslim, but his Islam was not known to his people; therefore, no funeral prayer was offered for him in Abyssinia. When Gabriel (Jibreel) informed the Prophet of Najaashi's death, he informed the Companions, "Your brother has died," and led a funeral prayer in Madinah.

The So-Called Satanic Verses

In the fifth year of the mission, the Prophet received Surah Najm (chapter 53) and recited it near the Ka'bah as some of the pagan leaders and their people listened. It was a very powerful chapter, and when it came from the clear tongue of the Prophet, people were rendered speechless. At the end of the surah was a verse that required the Prophet to prostrate himself on the ground, and as he did so, everyone around him, including the pagans, prostrated themselves too.

Imam Bukhari recorded these words from Abdullaah bin Mas'ud: "Surah Najm was the first surah in which a prostration was revealed. The Prophet recited it in Makkah and prostrated. Those who were with him did the same, except an old man who took a handful of soil and prostrated on it. Later on, I saw him killed as a disbeliever; he was Umayyah bin Khalaf." Bukhari recorded this Hadith in several places of his *Saheeh* (authentic collection of Hadith), as did other collectors, such as Muslim, Abu Dawud, and An-Nasaa'i, using various chains of narration. In another version, the person who took a handful of dust was Waleed bin Al-Mugheerah.

After the polytheists fell prostrate, they felt embarrassed and badly needed a story to save face. Some began to taunt others for prostrating themselves. So they invented a story, saying that the only reason they fell in prostration was that they heard the Prophet Muhammad praise their goddesses, Al-Laat, Al-Uzzah, and Al-Manaat.

They claimed that after the Prophet recited verses 19 and 20 of Surah Najm, "Have you then considered Al-Laat, and Al-Uzzah. And Manaat, the other third," he added, "These are the high-flying ones, whose intercession is to be hoped for!"

This was a ludicrous claim and is not supported by either the text of the Qur'aan or the events that happened afterward. The books of Seerah do not mention this claim being made by the Quraysh ever again, neither in peace nor in war. Unfortunately, some Muslim scholars of a later generation opined that Satan had shouted those additional words, thereby confusing the Prophet. Many centuries later some non-Muslim historians used this alleged incident to cast doubt on the authenticity of the Qur'aan. The allegation of Satanic verses (actually it is just a single line) mixing with the Speech of God does not pass scrutiny for several reasons.

The eyewitness account of Abdullaah bin Mas'ud as recorded by Bukhari simply states that the Prophet recited Surah Najm, and at the end of it he prostrated himself and the polytheists followed him in prostration. There is no mention of any additional incident. Also, verse 23 of Surah Najm emphatically rejects any claim that these idols have power: "They are but names which you have named—you and your fathers—for which Allaah has sent down no authority."[107]

107 Najm 53:23

Allaah has categorically stated in the Qur'aan that the revelation is protected against every kind of tampering: "Falsehood cannot come to it from before it or behind it, (it is) sent down by the All-Wise, Worthy of all praise."[108]

The preservation of Qur'aan is guaranteed. Allaah said: "Indeed We have sent down this reminder (the Qur'aan) and surely We will preserve it."[109]

The term *Satanic Verses* was coined by an Orientalist named William Muir (27 April 1819–11 July 1905) centuries after the Surah Najm was revealed. In 1988, Salman Rushdie, a British author, repackaged historical controversies in his book, *The Satanic Verses*, which caused a furor in the Muslim world. Rushdie mocked the Prophet and Islam through fictional characters in his book.

The Second Emigration

When it became clear that the news of reconciliation between the pagans and the Muslims was false, some went back to Abyssinia. And this time a large new group decided to migrate. In hindsight it seems that the controversy surrounding Surah Najm paved the way for greater migration. Just about every Qurayshi family was affected. It was a slap in the face of the evil leadership of Makkah that their own relatives were leaving.

According to Ibn Isshaaq, there were 101 adults (83 men and 18 women), plus their children, in the second migration to Abyssinia. Some of the notables of this migration follow:

1. Jaa'far ibn Abi Taalib (second migration)
2. Asmaa bint Umays Al-Hilaaliyah (wife of Jaa'far, first migration). Their sons Abdullaah, Muhammad, and Awn were born in Abyssinia.

108 Fussilat 41:42.

109 Hijr 15:9.

3. Ubaydullaah bin Jahsh. He later became a Christian in Abyssinia.
4. Umm Habibah (Ramlah) bint Abi Sufyan (daughter of Abu Sufiyan and wife of Ubaydullaah). She later married the Prophet Muhammad after her husband adopted Christianity.
5. Abdullaah bin Jahsh (brother of Ubaydullaah)

Hamzah's Conversion to Islam

The city of Makkah had considerably changed since the Prophet began preaching the message. The Prophet's patient perseverance over the previous five or so years had paid rich dividends, to the point that there was hardly any house where someone had not become a Muslim. Many of the early converts were young people, and their decision to adopt the new faith had created much strife in their families. The more the pagan leadership had tried to suppress Islam, the more resilient it had become. Some were slowly resigning themselves to the situation, but others, such as Abu Jahl, were becoming more desperate and vile.

One day Abu Jahl found the Messenger of Allaah sitting alone near the Ka'bah and went into a frenzied tirade of insults against him. The Prophet left the place without saying a word, but one or more of the women of the Banu Haashim saw how viciously their most gentle-mannered tribesman was insulted.

Soon thereafter Hamzah, one of the Prophet's uncles, returned from a hunting trip, and before he could go to make the Tawaaf (circumambulation) of the Ka'bah, as was his habit, the women told him all that had happened. Hamzah was not yet a Muslim, but he could not accept that his beloved nephew was treated in that manner. With his blood boiling, Hamzah went straight to Abu Jahl and, without asking anything, hit him with his bow across his face.

"How dare you treat my nephew like that and know that I also am of his religion?" Hamzah thundered. Some people from Abu Jahl's

Makhzum tribe got up to help him, but he motioned them to stay away and said, "Abu Ummaarah, yes, I insulted your nephew like never before, and you have the right to be angry." Ummaarah was Hamzah's daughter, and to calm him down, Abu Jahl had addressed him as "father of Ummaarah," using his *Kunniyah*.[110] This is the most polite form of address in the Arab society.

When Hamzah told Abu Jahl that he had become a Muslim, faith had not yet entered his heart. His tongue had preceded his heart. So at night he began to ponder over what he had publicly said. He did not want to go back on his word, but what should he do about a heart that had not yet become a believer?

After much contemplation, he prayed: "O Allaah, you know I am a leader of the Quraysh, and I cannot take it back. So if this matter is true, guide my heart to it; otherwise let me die right now."

He spent the night twisting and turning in his house. By the morning his prayer had been answered. Feeling content with how his heart was inspired, he went to the Prophet and told him, "O my nephew, this is what has happened; tell me what I should do."

The Prophet got up and advised him with the words of Allaah, reminding him of the reality of this world and the Hereafter. It was at that point that Hamzah recited the declaration of faith and formally became a Muslim. The Prophet now had the support of a senior-most person of the Quraysh as a believer.

110 Kunniyah is a genitive form in which a father or mother is called by the name of their eldest male child (or if there is no male child, then by the name of the eldest daughter).

Umar's Conversion

It was not that long ago that Umar bin Al-Khattaab had received a sharp rebuke from Layla bint Abi Hathamah when she was preparing to migrate to Abyssinia. She had told Umar that he, along with other disbelieving leaders of the Quraysh, bore responsibility for her plight, and Umar for the first time had felt some sympathy for what the Muslims were going through. In fact he had for the first time prayed for her success when he said, "May Allaah be with you!"

In the meantime, the Prophet had beseeched his Lord to guide Umar or Abu Jahl to Islam. The Seerah and Hadith books have recorded that the Prophet prayed: "O Allaah, give honor to Islam through the one who is more beloved of the two to You, Umar bin Al-Khattaab or Abul Hakam (Abu Jahl bin Hishaam)."

The prayer was answered in favor of Umar, who embraced Islam only three days after Hamzah's conversion. But it happened gradually.

One night in the sixth year of the Prophethood, Umar craved wine and went to the winemaker to drink and socialize, but the place was closed. Perhaps destiny brought him from there to the Ka'bah. Lo and behold, there Umar found the Prophet Muhammad reciting the Qur'aan all by himself in the stillness of the night. Umar himself narrated the entire incident after he became a Muslim.

Seeing the Prophet all alone, Umar thought this might be the ideal time to get rid of him. He crept up quietly and began to listen to the recitation of the Prophet, who was reciting Surah Al-Haaqqah (chapter 69). Umar began to listen intently and was amazed at its rhythm. He thought it must be the work of a poet, but the next verse said, "It is not the word of a poet, little is that you believe!" He thought it might be the work of a soothsayer, but the next verse said, "Nor is it the word of a soothsayer, little is that you remember!"

Puzzled, Umar thought, "Who is this from, then?"

And the next verse directly answered his question: "This is the revelation sent down by the Lord of the worlds."

Still not fully convinced, Umar thought, "What if Muhammad made it all up on his own?"

The next verse answered him again: "And if he had forged a false saying concerning Us, We surely would have seized him by his right hand and then We certainly would have cut off the artery of his heart."

Allaah seemed to be talking to Umar through the Qur'aan without his realizing it. Omar knew only that the Prophet's recitation was overpowering in its beauty, its eloquence, and its truthfulness. Umar said that this was the first time Islam entered his heart, although he did not accept it quite yet.

Reflections: The story of Umar is not an isolated one by any means. Millions throughout history have embraced Islam simply by listening to the Qur'aan or reading its translation in another language. The stories of people like Cat Stevens, H. Rap Brown, Malcolm X, and Yusuf Estes abound. They came to Islam through an encounter with the Qur'aan, realizing that it was actually addressing their doubts and confusion.

Every year, hundreds of thousands of people around the world enter Islam convinced of the irrefutable truth of the Qur'aan, often through translation. One can only imagine how much more powerful the Qur'aan must have been for those Arabs in whose language it was revealed. No wonder the pagan leaders asked their people to plug their ears with cotton or make noise so as to avoid listening to the Qur'aan.

One particular verse in the Qur'aan explains that people will continue to recognize the truth of the Book of Allaah through His signs.

Addressing all of mankind, Allaah says: "We will show them Our signs in the horizons and within themselves until it becomes clear to them that it (the Qur'aan) is the truth."[111]

Umar Finally Accepts Islam

While Umar was feeling the stirrings of the new message within him, Abu Jahl had remained defiant and ever hostile. One day, in a particularly bad mood, he went on his tirade against the Prophet, claiming that he was insulting their forefathers and their gods. He offered a bounty of one hundred of the best camels on the head of the Prophet. It was a large sum of money that Abu Jahl had pledged, something akin to giving away one hundred of the finest cars as a prize. So Umar became tempted. He unsheathed his sword and headed out to kill the Prophet.

On his way, Umar heard some voices telling him not to do it, but he pressed on until he ran into a Muslim named Nuyaim bin Abdullaah bin Nahhaam. Nuyaim became quite nervous upon seeing Umar like that. Hiding his faith from Umar, he asked him what he was up to. When Umar told him about his intention, Nayaim panicked. Umar was known for his harshness and bravery.

Nuyaim desperately wanted to stop Umar, so he said, "Umar, do you think you will live if you do this? Will Abdu Manaaf leave you alone if you kill him?" Without waiting for Umar's response, he fired the final shot. "Why don't you fix your own family first? Your own sister (Faatimah bint Khattaab) and her husband (Sa'eed bin Zayd) have accepted Islam."

Umar was shocked to hear this, and he straightaway rushed to his sister's house. When he reached the house, he heard somebody reading the Qur'aan. Khabbaab bin Aratt, a young Muslim, was teaching them the

111 Fussilat 41:53.

verses of Surah Ta Ha. Umar violently knocked at the door of his sister's house. She panicked and hid the parchment on which the verses were written. Khabbaab hid in a closet. Umar stormed the house and demanded to know what she was listening to, and when she did not tell him, he began to beat her and his brother-in-law until blood started to gush forth from his sister's face. Seeing his sister's blood made Umar remorseful, and he started to calm down. On the other hand, his sister went on the offensive.

"Do what you want, but we are not going to leave this religion," she said.

Umar's heart began to race, and he politely said, "Show me what you were reading."

His sister said, "Not until you take a bath."

When Umar had cleansed himself, he read what was on the parchment. It blew him away. The faith had finally penetrated his heart. He asked where the Prophet was, and Sa'eed informed him that the Prophet was in the house of Al-Arqam.

Umar sprinted to Al-Arqam's house behind Mount Safa, and when one of the Muslims looked through an opening in the door, he saw Umar with an unsheathed sword. He alerted others inside, but Hamzah said, "Let him in, for if Allaah wants good, he will accept Islam, and if Allaah wants other than this, then we will take care of him with his own sword."

When Umar entered, two people held his arms and brought him to the Prophet. The Prophet grabbed Umar's shirt and pulled him closer.

"O son of Khattaab, what brings you here? By Allaah, if you continue on this (idolatrous) path, Allaah will destroy you."

In a respectful tone, Umar said, "O Messenger of Allaah, I have come to accept Islam."

Hearing this, the Prophet cried out *Allaahu Akbar* (God is Greater) so loudly that everyone in Dar Al-Arqam knew Umar had accepted Islam.

After he became a Muslim, Umar narrated that when the Messenger of God had seized his shirt, he had begun to shake in awe of him. This was not the case just with Umar. Many others reported being unable to stare at the Prophet because of the overpowering respect they felt for him. The Prophet himself said, "I have been given superiority over the other prophets in six respects: I have been given words which are concise but comprehensive in meaning; I have been helped by terror (in the hearts of enemies); spoils have been made lawful to me; the earth has been made for me clean and a place of worship; I have been sent to all mankind; and the line of prophets is closed with me."[112]

Now Umar and Hamzah, two of the greatest men of Makkah, had become Muslim, and for the first time they led about forty Muslims to the Ka'bah to openly pray there. Nobody dared to insult or prevent them. This was the first example of Allaah honoring Islam through Umar. Many more were to come.

Umar said he thought his maternal uncle Abu Jahl would be most annoyed by his Islam. So he knocked at Abu Jahl's house, and when he came out, Umar said, "I have come to inform you that I have become a Muslim." Hearing that, Abu Jahl cursed Umar and slammed the door on him.

Abu Taalib's Courage

When the da'wah (call) became public and the number of people entering Islam kept increasing, the pagan leaders like Abu Jahl started to panic. After

112 Muslim, Hadith #1062.

consultation with one another, they decided to complain to Abu Taalib and demand that he stop his nephew one way or another. They resolved to persist in their demand until Abu Taalib relented.

First, they went to Abu Taalib and said, "Your nephew is cursing our idols and asking people to leave the religion of their forefathers."

Abu Taalib managed to send them away. He knew that was a blatant lie. The Prophet had already received a command from Allaah not to curse the idols lest the pagans insult Allaah in their ignorance.

> *And insult not those whom they worship besides Allaah, lest they insult Allaah wrongfully without knowledge.*[113]

Second, they came back to Abu Taalib and said, "Look, you'd better take care of your nephew or let us take care of him. Enough is enough."

Abu Taalib felt the heat and sensed a coming rebellion against his leadership. So he went to the Prophet and said, "O son of my brother, have mercy on me and yourself. Lay not upon me a burden greater than I can bear."

The Prophet of God loved Abu Taalib more than he loved anyone. He was the father figure who had raised him from age eight, and without his uncle's protection, the Prophet could not have lived in Makkah relatively unscathed. But at the same time, the Messenger could not disobey Allaah, so he respectfully said to Abu Taalib, "O my uncle, I swear by Allaah that if they put the sun in my right hand and the moon in my left and asked me to abandon this message, I will not do so until He has made me victorious or I have perished trying."

113 An'aam 6:108.

Abu Taalib had never heard his nephew speak like that, and when he saw the Prophet's resolve, he said, "Do as you please; I will never again ask you to stop preaching, or forsake you on account of this."

Abu Taalib strictly adhered to this promise as long as he lived, and as a result he endured severe hardships.

When Abu Taalib could not persuade the Prophet to quit preaching and Islam continued to progress, the Quraysh approached Abu Taalib again. This time they brought some of the family members of the Prophet and a son of Waleed bin Al-Mugheerah. They said to Abu Taalib, "We have brought to you one of the most handsome young men and one of the best in lineage in all of the Quraysh. Take this young man and hand over your nephew."

Abu Taalib snapped at them. "What an evil bargain; you want me to keep your son and fatten him while I give you my nephew so that you may kill him! Do what you can, but I will never hand Muhammad to you."

This was an amazing feat of bravery, as Abu Taalib was now politically weakened and stood to lose much from this stance. The whole of Quraysh, even some of his family members, had turned against him, but he did not waver in his promise to the Prophet. Abu Taalib, who was one of the finest poets, wrote some poems to chastise his own relatives for falling into the trap of the evilmongers.

The Boycott

Finally, when the Quraysh realized they could not break Abu Taalib's resolve concerning the Prophet, they came to him for the last time and said they would not buy from, sell to, or socially deal with the Muslims until he disowned his nephew. Abu Taalib, instead of caving in to threats, decided to seclude himself with Muslims and the clans of Banu Haashim and Banu

Al-Muttalib in a narrow pass commonly known as Shi'b Abi Taalib. It is said that the Banu Haashim owned some valleys in or around Makkah.

The boycott lasted for approximately two years, although some say longer. The Muslims and the non-Muslim members of the Banu Haashim clan who were confined there suffered physical, financial, and emotional harm. The only exception was Abu Lahab, who, although from the Banu Haashim, stayed in town and therefore did not become the target of the boycott. These were extremely difficult times for Muslims, and they endured the suffering with dignity. To their credit, even the non-Muslim Hashemites did not rebel against Abu Taalib or ask him to disown the Prophet Muhammad. The boycott was something like the modern-day sanctions that nations slam against their adversaries to make them compliant.

There were some good people in Makkah, however, who would sneak in some food and supplies to the Muslims. Among them was Mut'im bin Adiyy. He at times sent a camel loaded with supplies. The boycotted community used the supplies he sent as well as slaughtered the camel to consume its meat. People like Khadijah and Abu Bakr spent much of their wealth to secretly buy the essentials at exorbitant prices from those who wanted to profit from the Muslims' misery.

Hakeem bin Hizaam, a nephew of Khadijah, would clandestinely bring in some supplies. During one of these attempts, Abu Jahl intercepted him, and only after an influential person named Abul Bukhtari intervened was Hakeem allowed to deliver his aid.

Another person who tried to help the besieged people was Hishaam bin Amr. Hisham was one of the most compassionate to the Muslims in their tragedy. He used to load his camel with food and other supplies, take it during the night, and pass by the entrance to the quarter where the Muslims were isolated. He would detach the reins of the camel and let it go free, whipping it on the sides so that the camel would enter into the quarter and be seized by the Muslims.

One day Hishaam was so disgusted by the injustice that he went to Zuhayr bin Abu Umayyah, whose mother was Aatikah, daughter of Abdul Muttalib, and said, "O Zuhayr, how could you eat and wear new clothes and marry and enjoy life when your uncles are locked up and isolated, unable to buy anything, to give or to take anyone in marriage? By God I swear that if the Muslims were the uncles of Abul Hakam bin Hishaam (Abu Jahl) and you had asked him to boycott them as he asked you to boycott the Muslims, he would have never fulfilled your request."

It was a stifling siege, and cries of starving children carried from the camp. People resorted to eating leaves and dried animal skins in order to survive. The author of the boycott document was a pagan named Bagheed bin Aamir bin Haashim. To publicize the banning, the document was hung from the door of the Ka'bah. Because the whole matter was orchestrated to show hostility to Allaah's religion and to punish His Messenger, the Prophet invoked Allaah against Bagheed. It is said that soon Bagheed's hands were paralyzed.

Abu Taalib was most concerned about his nephew, the Prophet Muhammad, since he was the Quraysh's main target. Fearing that they might try to assassinate his nephew, Abu Taalib would insist that the Prophet swap places with him at night. Despite heavy odds, the Prophet kept preaching, especially to outsiders who came to Makkah, and to the chagrin of the pagans, there were positive responses.

A Collective Resolve against Injustice

The evil and unjust treatment of the Muslims and their supporters was also taking a different kind of toll on the Quraysh. Their collective conscience was shaming them. And the fair-minded among them were greatly troubled by it. How could they treat a group of people like this for believing in God? How could the pagans have the freedom to worship stones but deny the Muslims the freedom to worship Allaah? The injustice eventually began to create dissension in their ranks. After all, many of the boycotted people were their own relatives, an uncle, a brother, a cousin.

Fed up with the status quo, Hishaam bin Amr asked Zuhayr to do something about it. Zuhayr said he was helpless against the chieftains but agreed to help form a pressure group to dismantle the boycott. Besides them, three other people—Mut'im bin Adiyy, Abul Bukhtari, and Zam'ah bin Al-Aswad—joined this pact.

According to the plan, Zuhayr first circumambulated the Ka'bah seven times and then chastised the people, asking how they could enjoy the amenities of life while their kith and kin of the Banu Haashim faced death due to starvation! Zuhayr swore he would never relent until the boycott document was torn to pieces.

Abu Jahl, standing nearby, challenged him, saying that it would never be torn. Zam'ah became furious and accused Abu Jahl of lying, adding that the decision to boycott had been made without his consent. At that point Abul Bukhtari intervened and backed Zam'ah and Mut'im, while Hishaam attested to the truthfulness of their two Companions. Abu Jahl was shocked and defensive. He left saying that they had hatched a conspiracy against the boycott.

A Sign from Heaven

In the meantime, through a revelation God informed the Prophet that termites had eaten the text of the boycott except for the name of Allaah. When the Prophet told Abu Taalib about it, the latter suddenly became imbued with an idea. "Why don't I go to the chieftains armed with this information and impress upon them that this was a sign from Allaah that this boycott is now null and void?"

The document had been hanging from the door of the Ka'bah since the day the boycott was decided, and nobody had looked inside to check its condition. There was no need for it. In order to make the news credible, Abu Taalib wanted to tell the Quraysh that his nephew had received a revelation that the document had been eaten away by the termites and bet that if that was not true, he would hand over his nephew to them. But Abu Taalib hesitated. What if his nephew's information was wrong? He did not want to take such a gamble with the Prophet's life. But the Prophet assured Abu Taalib that the revelation was from Allaah and that it could not be wrong.

Subsequently, Abu Taalib went to the chieftains and said that his nephew had received a revelation from God that termites had eaten away the document except for Allaah's name. He told them that, if the information turned out to be untrue, he would hand over the Prophet to them. He demanded that, if the news did turn out to be true, the boycott would have to be repealed. The Makkans agreed to Abu Taalib's proposition, as it seemed reasonable to them.

Mut'im climbed up the steps of the Ka'bah to look at the parchment on which the boycott was written, and he confirmed exactly what the Prophet had said. The pagan leaders were now put on the defensive. They grudgingly annulled the boycott but still insisted on their idolatry.

The Death of Abu Taalib

Abu Taalib was the greatest benefactor of the Messenger of Allaah among non-Muslims. He did not cave in to threats and pressures to disown the Prophet, his nephew. So when death approached Abu Taalib in the tenth year of the Prophethood, the big leaders of the Quraysh came to him. People like Waleed bin Al-Mugheerah, Umayyah bin Khalaf, Utbah and Shaybah bin Rabi'ah, Abu Sufiyan, Abu Jahl, and some others said, "Now that you are ready to depart, we are very concerned about the state of the relationship between us and your nephew. We want to make a deal with him so that he leaves us alone and we leave him alone."

Abu Taalib sent for the Prophet and told him, "O my nephew, these nobles of the Quraysh want to give you something and want something in return."

The Prophet said, "Then ask them to give me one word, a word whereby they will rule over the Arabs, and the Persians will become their subjects."

Hearing this, Abu Jahl became excited. "We will give you that and ten more words."

The Prophet said, "Then say, 'There is no god but Allaah,' and renounce the worship of idols." They clapped their hands in frustration, said they could not accept the proposal, and went their way.

As signs of death appeared on Abu Taalib, the Prophet drew near his bed and said to him, "O my uncle, say 'There is no god but Allaah,' and I will plead with Allaah for you on the Day of Resurrection."

Abu Taalib replied, "O son of my brother, I would say these words if I did not fear that the Quraysh would think I said them only because of the fear of death."

It is also reported that the Qurayshi leaders had earlier questioned him rhetorically, asking, "Will you leave the religion of your father?" and reminding Abu Taalib of the esteem in which his father, Abdul Muttalib, was held.

Just before he passed away, Abu Taalib moved his lips as if to say something. Abbaas, his brother, drew closer to him and told the Prophet that he heard Abu Taalib recite the declaration of faith. However, the Prophet replied that he had not heard what his uncle had tried to say.

In Abu Taalib's death, the Prophet had lost not only an uncle but his greatest supporter among his relatives. The Prophet loved him immensely, and his death as a non-Muslim grieved the Prophet much. The Prophet had been sent as a Mercy to Mankind. Allaah says in the Qur'aan: "And We have not sent you (O Muhammad) except as a mercy for the worlds."[114]

114 Ambiyaa 21:107.

Therefore, it was especially hard for the Prophet that his own uncle was deprived of the mercy he was trying to spread to the masses.

Allaah revealed some verses to console His Prophet, saying: "Verily, you cannot guide whom you love, but Allaah guides whom He wills."[115]

After Abu Taalib died, the Prophet said he would continue to pray for his forgiveness until Allaah stopped him. Then Allaah revealed: "It is not for the Prophet and those who believe to ask Allaah's forgiveness for the polytheists, even if they be of kin, after it has become clear to them that they are the dwellers of the Fire."[116] It was at that point that the Prophet stopped supplicating for Abu Taalib.

Was the Prophet Able to Help Abu Taalib?

One day after Abu Taalib had died, Abbaas went to the Prophet and said, "O Messenger of Allaah, my brother (Abu Taalib) helped you so much. Were you able to help him?"

The Prophet replied, "Yes, I was able to help him. Because of my supplication for him, Allaah has moved him to the outskirts of the fire, where he will receive the least amount of punishment of all people."

People knew how heartbroken the Prophet was about his beloved uncle's failure to accept Islam, so when Abu Bakr's father, Abu Quhaafah, accepted Islam at the conquest of Makkah and put his hand in the hand of the Prophet, Abu Bakr said, "How I wish that it was your uncle Abu Taalib's hand in your hand, O Messenger of Allaah." Abu Bakr was keenly aware of how earnestly the Prophet had wished for his uncle to become a Muslim.

---

115 Qasas 28:56.

116 Tawbah 9:113.

Understanding Abu Taalib's Refusal

Without reflection, it may not be possible to understand all the reasons that Abu Taalib refused to accept Islam. Granted, one reason was his concern for the pagan chiefs' taunts. But was it all? One may ask, "Why does Allaah guide some people to Islam and not others?" One might argue that Abu Taalib seemed to be a prime candidate for conversion. One piece of the wisdom we can derive is that, had Abu Taalib become a Muslim, he could not have helped the Prophet as he did. The pagan chieftains would have treated him with the same disdain that they had reserved for other Muslims. They also would have rejected his leadership and opinion in any matter. But some might say, "Why couldn't Abu Taalib accept Islam on his deathbed?" No one can answer this question with certitude. Indeed it is one of those matters whose reality only Allaah will reveal on the Day of Judgment.

The scholars are unanimous that supplication (du'a) may be made for the guidance of nonbelievers while they are alive. But if they die in disbelief, the matter rests with Allaah, Who will judge them.

Reflections: We take away several points from Abu Taalib's story. One, salvation does not come from one's lineage. God judges people by their own actions. Two, good actions alone are not enough for success in the Hereafter. They must stem from faith in God and a desire to please Him. Three, Allaah rewards the good deeds of nonbelievers in this life, but the everlasting reward of the Hereafter is for those who performed good actions as believers in God and with sincerity.

Allaah has said: "And whoever seeks a religion other than Islam, it will never be accepted of him, and in the Hereafter he will be among the losers."[117]

It must be noted that Muslims are not just those who follow the Prophet Muhammad. Muslims are also all those who believed in Prophets Moses and Jesus as well as other prophets of God. The Prophet Muhammad did

117 Aal Imraan 3:85.

not bring a new religion, but rather followed and preached the same religion as all of God's prophets before him.

The Year of Sorrow

While the Prophet was still reeling from the effects of Abu Taalib's death, another tragedy struck him. Khadijah, his beloved wife, fell ill and died in the tenth year of the Prophet's mission (620 CE). Khadijah's health had been severely impaired by the stress and starvation brought on by the boycott. Her death created a vacuum in the life of the Prophet, who suddenly found himself a single parent who must now care for young children. He had once said about Khadijah, "Indeed, her love had been nurtured in my heart by Allaah Himself."[118]

Some reports say that the interval between the two tragedies was forty days. Both Abu Taalib and Khadijah were mighty pillars of support, the former outside the religion and house and the latter inside. These losses took a personal toll on the Prophet. The Sahaabah reported that, for months after the death of Khadijah, they did not see a smile on the face of the Messenger of Allaah. Because of these two huge tragedies, this year was called the Year of Sorrow.

The Prophet himself lowered Khadijah's body into the grave. She was buried in Jannatul Mu'alla Cemetery, also called Al-Hajun, in Makkah.

Reflections: Some Muslims believe that after a woman dies, her relationship is cut off from her husband, and the husband may not even touch her body. So this incident tells us that the Prophet had no problem with burying his wife, Khadijah, with his own hands. We also know from the Seerah that close to his own death, when the Prophet complained of a headache and when Aayeshah also complained of it, he said to her that her headache would not kill her and joked that if she were to die before

118 Muslim, Hadith #2435.

him, he would wash her body and bury her. There are also reports that when Abu Bakr died, his wife washed his body, and when the Prophet's daughter Faatimah died, Ali, her husband, washed her body.

Abu Lahab Offers Protection to the Prophet

The Prophet understood the severity of the situation in a world without Abu Taalib and Khadijah. Suddenly he had become politically vulnerable. In the meantime, word came out that another Qurayshi had severely insulted the Prophet. Abu Lahab, the Prophet's uncle who had now assumed the chieftaincy of the Banu Haashim, felt that it was his responsibility to protect the members of his tribe, even those he did not see eye to eye with. So, in an about-face, he told the Prophet that he could do whatever he had done during the lifetime of Abu Taalib. Abu Lahab's protection was not to support the religion of God but to protect his nephew against attacks in keeping with the tribal laws.

When Abu Jahl, the chief antagonist, found out that Abu Lahab had extended the same protection to the Prophet as Abu Taalib had offered, he became upset. He consulted his friend Waleed bin Al-Mugheerah, and together they devised a plot. Together they went to Abu Lahab, but Abu Jahl led the conversation.

"How can you provide protection to your nephew when he insults your father? Go and ask Muhammad what he thinks of Abdul Muttalib."

So Abu Lahab put this question to the Prophet: "What is the status of my father after death?"

The Prophet understood that it was a loaded question and gave a response that could be understood in more than one way. "He is with his people," the Prophet said. Abu Lahab came back satisfied, thinking that the Prophet said something positive about his own grandfather.

When Abu Lahab told Abu Jahl, he said, "Are you a fool? Your nephew is saying that, like the rest of his non-Muslim people, Abdul Muttalib will also be in the fire." Upon hearing that, Abu Lahab withdrew his protection from the Prophet, leaving him open to verbal and physical attacks.

A Fateful Trip to Taa'if

Recognizing the political climate and seeing the writing on the wall, the Prophet decided to travel to Taa'if to invite the leaders of the Banu Thaqif to Islam. He took Zayd bin Haarithah with him. Taa'if is about sixty-six miles east of Makkah. It was known for the Banu Thaqif's fortresses and the idol named Al-Laat. The rulers of Taa'if considered their city a sister city of Makkah and to some extent its rival. However, no city could reach the stature of Makkah, the only city that housed the Ka'bah.

The leaders of the Banu Thaqif were three brothers—Abdul Yaalayl, Mas'ud, and Habib—who had decided to share authority among them. They rejected the Prophet in a most arrogant and vile manner. One of them said, "I would tear up the cover of the Ka'bah if Allaah had truly sent Muhammad as a Prophet."

Another said, "Could Allaah not find someone better than him to send as a Prophet?"

Yet another said he would not talk to the Prophet Muhammad, for if he was indeed a Prophet of Allaah, he was too high to speak to, and if he was lying, then it would be no use talking to him.

With his invitation thoroughly rejected, the Prophet left the brothers, but before departing, he asked them to keep the matter secret, for he was concerned that the news of rejection would further embolden the Quraysh in Makkah.

The Prophet, however, did not give up. He stayed in Taa'if for about a week in hopes that the common folk might embrace his message. When the rulers found out that the Prophet was preaching to the masses, they let loose the ruffians and young boys of the society, who began to pelt rocks at the Prophet and Zayd. Both suffered cuts and bruises. Bloodied and dazed, the Prophet and his Companion ran for cover. Finally, when they were beyond the reach of the stone throwers, they stopped at Qarn Ath-Tha'alabah. There they sat outside the wall of an orchard that belonged to one of the distant relatives of the Prophet.

This was undoubtedly one of the most difficult and humiliating experiences of his life, yet the Prophet's concern was not for his or Zayd's injuries, or thirst and hunger, but for the possibility that Allaah was displeased with him.

Immersed in self-reflection, he poured his heart out. "O Allaah, to You do I complain of the weakening of my strength, of my few options, of the way people humiliate me; O Most Merciful of the merciful ones, You are the Lord of the weak ones, and You are my Lord. To whom will You entrust me? To a distant (stranger) who will show me an unwelcoming face, or to an enemy, whom You have given control over my situation? If You are not angry with me, then I do not care. I seek refuge with the light of Your Face, which removes darkness, and upon which the affairs of the world and the Hereafter become right—from Your anger descending upon me, or Your displeasure befalling me. I will continue to seek Your pleasure, until You become pleased (with me). And there is neither might nor power except with You."

No sooner had he finished his supplication than Allaah responded. Gabriel came down with the angel of mountains, *Malakul Jibaal*. He said to the Prophet, "I am at your command. If you tell me, I will turn the mountains on the people of Taa'if." But the Prophet, who was sent as a mercy unto the world, declined and expressed hope that the progeny of those people would one day embrace Islam. Barely fifteen years later, what the Prophet had hoped for came true. Not just Taa'if but almost all of the Arabian Peninsula had embraced Islam.

An Amazing Encounter with a Christian

The garden whose outer walls the Prophet and Zayd were resting against belonged to two Makkan nobles—Utbah and Shaybah bin Rabi'ah—who were watching the cruel episode from behind. Pitying the plight of the two men, one of whom was a relative, they instructed their Christian slave Addaas to take a tray of grapes to the Prophet and his Companion. The Prophet took the grapes with his right hand, said, "BismiAllaah" (in the name of Allaah), and began to eat.

Addaas was surprised. "The people of these lands don't say these words!" he said.

"And where are you from, and what is your religion?" the Prophet asked him.

"I am a Christian from Ninewah (Iraq)," replied Addaas.

"From the town of the righteous man, Yunus bin Mattah (Jonah)?" the Prophet asked.

Addaas burst out in excitement, "And what makes you know about Yunus bin Mattah?"

The Prophet replied, "He is my brother. He was a Prophet, and so am I."

Addaas kissed the Prophet's forehead, hands, and feet while his two masters stared in disbelief. When reprimanded by his masters for what he did, Addaas said to them, "O my masters, there is nothing on earth that is better than him; he has indeed informed me about a matter that only a

Prophet could know about." How amazing that, while the Prophet's own people had rejected and attacked him, a foreigner had acknowledged his Prophethood.

After a seemingly unsuccessful mission, the Prophet and Zayd left Taa'if for Makkah. When they reached Nakhlah, an oasis near Makkah, by dusk, they decided to camp out. While their wounds were still fresh and the dried blood still on their skin, the Prophet rose to his feet to pray Qiyam al-Layl (late-night prayer) and began to recite the Qur'aan. A number of the *jinn* listened to his recitation and believed in the Qur'aan.[119]

While the Prophet was unaware of the jinn's conversation, Allaah informed him in a surah by the same name:

> *It has been revealed to me that a group of Jinn listened. They said: "Verily, we have heard a wonderful Recitation! It guides to the right path, and we have believed therein, and we shall never join anything with our Lord."*[120]

The story of the jinn's embrace of Islam is also mentioned twice in Surah Al-Ahqaaf.

> *And (remember) when We sent toward you a group of the Jinn, to listen to the Qur'aan. When they attended it, they said: "Listen quietly!" And when it was concluded, they returned to their people, as warners.*[121]

This was a very symbolic incident and by inference a criticism of the people of Taa'if: "Look, while you rejected the Prophet's message, another creation of God accepted it."

119 In Islamic theology, the jinn is a separate creature that Allaah created from smokeless fire. Like humans, they are capable of doing good and evil, but they are hidden from the human view.

120 Jinn 72:1–2.

121 Ahqaaf 46:29.

Seeking Adoption or Asylum

The next day, the Prophet and Zayd proceeded to Makkah. The Prophet was fully aware that he could not enter the city of his birth unless somebody vouched for his safety. Ibn Isshaaq said in his Seerah book that when the Prophet Muhammad came close to Makkah, he met a Makkan whom he asked to take his message to Al-Akhnas bin Shariq. When the latter agreed, the Prophet told him to convey this on his behalf to Al-Akhnas: "Will you give me protection so I may convey the message of my Lord?" Some say the Prophet sent Zayd with this message.

Al-Akhnas bin Shariq was living in Makkah as an ally of the Quraysh, but he was not a Qurayshi. When he received the Prophet's request, he responded, "Since I am an ally of the Quraysh, I cannot give protection to somebody who is from the tribe I am allied with." He thought doing so would displease the Quraysh.

Then the Prophet sent the request to Suhayl bin Amr. Suhayl replied that he could not give protection against the Banu Ka'ab.

While these exchanges were taking place, the Prophet was stranded on the outskirts of Makkah. Finally, he sent the request to Mut'im bin Adiyy, who agreed to protect them. Mut'im put on his weapons, as did his sons and nephews, and together they escorted the Messenger of Allaah to the Ka'bah.

In a strong voice Mut'im announced, "Everybody should know that I am giving protection to Muhammad!"

When Abu Jahl heard this, he asked, "Are you only giving protection, or are you following him?"

Mut'im said, "Giving protection."

Abu Jahl responded, "We give protection to whom you protect."

Spreading the Message during Hajj

Mut'im's support provided the Prophet the basic protective cover he needed to spread his call. Every year, Arabs from far and wide would throng to Makkah to perform the annual pilgrimage. The Prophet Abraham started this tradition. The Prophet Muhammad found the Hajj to be a golden opportunity to tell people about God's true religion, which the Prophet Abraham had also preached, a faith that the people had corrupted over time.

On this occasion, the Prophet took with him his close friend Abu Bakr, who had a deep knowledge of the Arab tribal lineage. It is reported that an old man would sometimes follow the Prophet Muhammad as he visited the pilgrims, and after he was done talking to them, the man would tell them, "O men, do not listen to Muhammad; he is crazy, a liar. If you listen to any of his words, you will go astray." This man was his own uncle, Abu Lahab.

The Prophet visited the tribes of Kindah, Banu Hanifah, Banu Amr bin Sa'saa, and others. They neither accepted his message nor gave him asylum.

The Banu Amr's leader, Bayhara bin Faraas, was actually impressed by the Prophet, and he said, "I swear, if I were to have this brave man of the Quraysh, I could eat up the Arabs with his support." Bayhara was thinking how he could use the Prophet's genius to extend and strengthen his authority. He was considering the long-term goals, so he tried to bargain with the Prophet, saying, "If we were to follow your orders and then Allaah gave you victory against those opposing you, would we have power after you?"

The Prophet responded, "The earth belongs to Allaah, and He may give power to whomever He wishes."

Bayhara said, "Are we to present our throats to the Arabs for your defense? And then if God gives you victory, we see power go to someone other than to us?" He declined the Prophet's request.

A Journey to Jerusalem and the Heavens

There is a saying in the Arabic language that means a reward is proportionate to the action. The recent deaths of Abu Taalib and Khadijah and the rejection at Taa'if had left the Prophet emotionally wounded and politically weakened. He was living in his own city under the protection of a non-Muslim named Mut'im bin Adiyy and was being verbally abused by the ignorant of the society. It was during this time that Allaah chose to reward him with what is known as *Al-Israa* and *Al-Mai'raaj* (the miraculous Night Journey to Jerusalem and Ascension to the Heavens). The two events served to uplift him at a time when his sufferings and worries had mounted.

When Did It Really Happen?

There are five different opinions among scholars about the date of *Al-Israa* and *Al-Mai'raaj*, and the most popular among them is that it happened on the twenty-seventh of the Islamic month of Rajab. However, an authentic Hadith from Aayeshah indirectly points to an approximate date. Aayeshah said that Khadijah died before the prayers became obligatory. Since prayer was made obligatory in *Mai'raaj* (Ascension), we deduce that this event took place a year to a year and a half before the migration to Madinah. There is no record in the Seerah that the early generations of Muslims celebrated *Al-Israa* and *Mai'raaj*; however, some Muslims do celebrate them today.

Was It a Physical Journey or a Dream?

Muslim scholars have differed over this question. Some say it was a spiritual event, while others say it was a physical experience.

Allaah said in the Qur'aan: "Glorified is He Who took His servant for a Journey by Night from Grand Mosque (in Makkah) to Al-Aqsa Mosque (in Jerusalem), the neighborhood whereof We have blessed, in order that We might show him of Our Signs. Verily, He is the All-Hearer, the All-Seer."[122]

122 Israa 17:1.

There are many clues that clearly show that it was a physical experience; among them is that Allaah has praised Himself because of this extraordinary event. He said, "Glory be to Him Who one night took His slave from the Grand Mosque in Makkah to the Farthest Mosque (Al-Aqsa) in Jerusalem…in order to show him some of His Signs." In the Qur'aan, Allaah has praised Himself by some of His major signs. After the Qur'aan, the Night Journey to Jerusalem and Ascension was the greatest miracle Allaah gave to the Prophet. The Prophet was shown things that no eyes had seen. He was taken higher than even Gabriel had ever been and ushered into the presence of God, which no soul before him had experienced.

Also, Allaah used the word *Abd*, which means Slave, in the first verse to describe the Prophet, which denoted the highest honor for him as well as to showed that he was taken on this journey in body and soul. In the Arabic language, the word *Abd* can be used to mean either the body only or the body and soul together. It is not used to mean soul only. This word challenged the opinion that the Prophet was taken in a dream.

The other word that was used in verse 1 was *asraa*, which also means a night journey of body and soul in the state of consciousness. This same verb is used in two other places in the Qur'aan to denote a live night journey. God ordered Moses to take the Children of Israel by night: "Depart you with My servants by night. Surely, you will be pursued."[123] This could not have meant that Moses should take them by their souls. In the second example of the use of the word *asraa*, Allaah said to Lot: "They (angels) said: 'O Lot! Verily, we are the messengers from your Lord! They shall not reach you! So travel with your family in a part of the night, and let not any of you look back.'"[124]

123 Dukhaan 44:23.

124 Hud 11:81.

In the verse that directly mentions the Night Journey, Allaah says: "We appointed the vision which we showed thee as an ordeal for mankind."[125]

Those imbued with faith and correct knowledge understood this verse to mean a physical journey in body and soul. The event of *Al-Israa* and *Al-Mai'raaj* cannot be understood any other way if we look at the context and the linguistic meaning. Ibn Abbaas, a Companion of the Prophet and the greatest commentator of the Qur'aan, explained that "the Messenger of Allaah saw this vision with his own eyes."[126]

Perhaps the greatest logical argument in favor of a physical journey was the objection of the disbelievers. Had it been in a dream, why would they have made such an issue about it? A dream after all is a dream, and no one is ever criticized for seeing a dream. But they were shocked because they understood it to be a physical event and found it beyond comprehension. However, this event strengthened the faith of others, like Abu Bakr, who testified to the Prophet's truthfulness and God's Almightiness, which earned him the title of *As-Siddeeq* (roughly translated, it means someone foremost in testifying to the truth).

How Did the Journey Begin?

The story of these profound events has been pieced together from the reports of various Companions of the Prophet, including his wife, Aayeshah. There are many scattered reports of *Al-Israa* and *Al-Mai'raaj*, and piecing them together has been a scholarly challenge.

For example, there is a report that on the night of Al-Israa, Gabriel came to the Prophet by opening the roof of the house where he was sleeping. From another report we learn that this was actually the house of Umm Hani (sister of Ali, daughter of Abu Taalib). We know it was Umm Hani's

125 Israa 17:60.

126 Bukhari, 6:204.

house because after his return from the trip, the Prophet told her, "Do you remember I prayed last night with you? And now I am praying this morning with you, and I went in *Israa* and *Mai'raaj* and have returned from it." Then the Prophet got up to go, and Umm Hani cautioned him not to tell people about his experience because they would make fun of him. The Prophet responded that indeed he was going to inform them about it.

There is another report that said that the Prophet was sleeping in the Hijr (part of the Ka'bah), and Gabriel came and woke him up thrice. He had a vessel filled with Zamzam water. Then Gabriel opened the Prophet's chest and washed his heart with Zamzam. It seems that all of this was being done to strengthen the Prophet and prepare him for what he was about to see. Some of the scholars said that if an ordinary man had seen what the Prophet was shown, he would have gone mad.

Behind the Washing of the Heart

Why did Gabriel take out the Prophet's heart and wash it? In Islam, the heart has a spiritual dimension much more important than its physiological character. For example, the heart is the place of all our intentions. A heart has feelings; it cries and feels happy. It fears Allaah and fights off evil inclinations. On this special night, God willed that His Prophet's heart be ritually cleansed before meeting. About the heart Allaah said, "In their hearts is a disease and Allaah has increased their disease. A painful torment is theirs because they used to tell lies."[127]

And the Prophet used to pray, "O the turner-over of the heart, keep my heart firm on your religion."

Gabriel offered the Prophet milk and wine. The Prophet chose milk, prompting Gabriel to remark, "You have chosen the *Fitrah* (pure nature),

127 Baqarah 2:10.

and your *Ummah* (nation) will be safe. Had you chosen wine, your Ummah would have been corrupted."[128]

Reflections: From Hadith we know that *Fitrah* is original and pure, and Allaah has created mankind upon it. Similarly, milk comes directly from the animal. It is pure; it strengthens the body and gives pleasure to its drinker. On the other hand, wine, while coming from pure juices, is corrupted during processing. And when it is ready, it smells foul, and when consumed, it intoxicates and impairs one's mind and sometimes causes headaches. Wine does have some benefits, but its harm is greater than the benefit. Wine is also addictive, and therefore when Allaah prohibited it, He did so in stages.

In the Hereafter, those who shun the wine of this world, which God has made unlawful, will be given the pure wine that will neither cause headaches nor intoxicate. Allaah says in the Qur'aan: "Immortal boys will go around them (serving) with cups, of flowing wine, from which they will neither get headache nor intoxication."[129] Rather, this wine will have a delightful taste. Ibn Abbaas, the famous commentator of the Qur'aan, said, "The wine (of this life) has four side effects: it intoxicates, gives headaches, induces vomiting, and causes excessive urination. So Allaah mentioned that the wine of Paradise will be free from these characteristics."

In Surah Al-Mutaffifeen, Allaah says, "They (the pious) will be given to drink of pure sealed wine. Sealed with musk, and for this let those strive who want to strive. It will be mixed with Tasneem. A spring from which those nearest to Allaah will drink."[130]

128 Wine was not forbidden at this time, yet the Prophet chose milk.

129 Waaqiyah 57:17–19.

130 Mutaffifeen 83:25–28.

The Journey Begins

After the Prophet was physically and spiritually readied, Gabriel brought a riding animal called *Buraaq* that he had never seen before. Its name may have come from the Arabic word for lightning, *barq*. The Prophet described it as larger than a donkey, smaller than a mule. When the Prophet tried to climb the animal, it became uncooperative. Gabriel placed his hand on its mane and admonished it, saying, "Are you not ashamed, O *Buraaq*, to behave this way? By God, no one more honorable than Muhammad has ever ridden you." The animal became calm and broke into a sweat. From this we may infer that some others may have ridden this animal, but we do not know their identity. The Prophet said the beast galloped as far as his eyes could see.

The Prophet said Gabriel's first stop was in a land with date-palm trees. He was asked to dismount and pray. When he was done praying two units of prayer, Gabriel asked him, "Do you know where you prayed?"

The Prophet answered, "Allaah knows best."

Gabriel said, "This is Yathrib; this is Taybah."[131]

The *Buraaq* continued until it reached Mount Sinai. The Prophet was again told to dismount and pray. Perhaps this was done to honor Prophet Moses. The next stop of the *Buraaq* was *Bayt Lahm* (Bethlehem), where the Prophet Jesus (Eesa) was born. After the Prophet Muhammad had offered yet another prayer, the journey resumed until they reached Jerusalem. Outside was an iron ring, to which he tied *Buraaq* and then entered the mosque. According to one Hadith, the Al-Aqsa Mosque in Jerusalem was built forty years after the Prophets Abraham and Ishmael built the Ka'bah in Makkah. This is where Allaah gathered all the prophets and

131 The first was the city's name before Islam and the second after the Prophet's migration to it.

messengers, and the Prophet Muhammad led them in prayer. This goes back to one of the Prophet's sayings: "I will be the leader of the children of Adam on the Day of Judgment, without boasting."

The Prophet said that on the way to Jerusalem he saw Prophets Abraham and Moses praying in their graves. He also saw Prophet Jesus praying.

During his journey, the Prophet smelled a pleasing fragrance, about which he asked Gabriel. The latter said this pleasant scent was coming from the grave of the woman who used to comb the hair of Pharaoh's daughter. One day, as she was combing Pharaoh's daughter's hair, the comb fell from her hand. She picked it up, saying, "In the name of Allaah."

Pharaoh's daughter was surprised. "Do you have a god other than my father?"

The woman said, "Yes. My Lord and the Lord of your father is Allaah."

Pharaoh's daughter told him what had happened. Pharaoh demanded that the lady renounce her belief, but she refused. So he ordered that water should be boiled in a huge pot. When the water came to a boil, Pharaoh ordered that her children be thrown into it. The woman remained steadfast throughout this heart-wrenching situation, until Pharaoh reached for her youngest child—a baby boy still breastfeeding. She felt a burst of pity for him.

Allaah enabled the infant to speak. He said to his mother, "O Mother, be patient. The torture of the Hereafter is far worse than the torturc of this life, and do not be sad, because you are right." At this the woman asked Pharaoh if he would collect the bones of her and her child after they died and bury them in the same grave. Pharaoh agreed.

Al-Mai'raaj (The Ascension)

When the Prophet had finished what God had commanded him to do in Jerusalem, Gabriel told him that he would be taken to the heavens. Since the *Buraaq* was an earthly transport, it was replaced with another vehicle that could ascend toward the heavens, past outer space. Some say it was a type of lift or ladder called *Al-Mirqaat*. This new transport was a manifestation of God's power, and therefore it was not bound by the limitations of heavenward travel known to man.

When the Prophet and Gabriel arrived at the first heaven, the latter requested that the gate be opened. The angel assigned to the gate asked, "Who is with you?"

Gabriel answered, "It is Muhammad."

The angel asked, "Was he sent for?"

Gabriel affirmed that it was so, and the gate was opened for him. The Prophet Muhammad entered the first heaven. There he saw a tall and handsome man with people on both sides of him. When the man looked to his right, he would rejoice, and when he looked to his left, he would cry. The Prophet asked Gabriel who this man was. Gabriel said, "This is your father Aadam; give him *salaam* (salutation)."

The Prophet Aadam returned the salaam, saying, "Welcome, righteous Prophet, righteous son." Aadam was seeing the souls of his descendants. Those on his right were his descendants who had died as believers, and those on his left were his descendants who had died as nonbelievers.

The Prophet moved to the next heaven until he reached the seventh, and in each the same questions were asked and the same answers provided.

In the second heaven, he met the Prophet John the Baptist (Yahya) and Prophet Jesus (Eesa). They were cousins in the world. The Prophet was instructed to give them salaam.

In the third, he met the Prophet Joseph (Yusuf). The Prophet described Joseph as if Allaah had given him half of the beauty of the world. Joseph's extraordinary good looks have been amply described in a chapter in the Qur'aan called Yusuf.

In the fourth, he met Enoch (Idrees), in the fifth Aaron (Haaroon), and in the sixth Moses. The Prophet described Moses as looking like a person from the people of Shenu'ah, who were known to be dark skinned. Moses addressed the Prophet Muhammad as "Ya Ghulaam" (O young man). Moses had died long ago at the age of 130, whereas the Prophet was in his early fifties. Moses cried that a much greater number of the people from the *Ummah* of Prophet Muhammad would go to Paradise than his own.

Finally, in the seventh heaven he met Prophet Abraham (Ibraahim), who returned the Prophet Muhammad's salutation, saying, "Welcome, righteous Prophet, righteous son." He described Prophet Abraham as closest in looks to him. He was sitting, leaning against *Al-Bayt Al-Ma'moor* (literally, the most-frequented house), which was above the Ka'bah. Every day, seventy thousand angels entered this house and never came out. It is impossible to do the math since seventy thousand times eternity is not a number any computer can fathom. Hence Allaah has said: "No one knows the hosts of your Lord except He."[132]

In a Hadith narrated by Abdullaah bin Mas'ud, the Prophet said, "I met Ibraahim on the night of my ascent, and he said: 'O Muhammad, say my salaam to your *Ummah*, and inform them that Paradise has luscious soil and delicious water, and that it is a flat treeless plain, and that its seeds

132 Muddassir 74:31.

are: *Subhaan Allaah, Al-Hamdulillaah, Wa La Ilaha Illallaah, Wa Allaahu Akbar*'" (Glory be to Allaah, Praise be to Allaah, and there is no God but He, and He is Greater). Abraham meant that when a believer praised God on earth, it resulted in a tree being planted in Paradise.

The Prophet asked Abraham, Moses, and Jesus what they knew about the Day of Judgment. Abraham and Moses said they knew nothing about it. On the other hand, Jesus said the only thing he knew was that he would be sent back to the earth before the Day of Judgment, would kill the Antichrist (*Dajjaal*), and would pray against Gog and Magog (*Ya'jooj wa Ma'jooj*). Jesus said his second coming would be so close to the Day of Judgment that it would be like a pregnant lady of full term who might give birth at any time.

Finally, Gabriel brought the Prophet Muhammad face-to-face with *Sidratul Muntaha*, that majestic Lote Tree in the seventh heaven beyond which nobody is allowed, not even Gabriel. All things that rise to the heaven end at this tree, and all things that descend from the heaven come down from it. One may call it a point of origination and termination.

The Prophet described its fruits as large like big jars, and its leaves like the ears of elephants. It was an exceptionally beautiful tree. Butterflies of gold fluttered around it, and the colors that shone on it were numerous and hitherto unseen. A Hadith says that Allaah's light, the angels, and spectacular colors covered this tree. Some of the scholars say that the *Sidratul Muntaha* starts in the sixth heaven and ends in the seventh. Allaah said that on this night "indeed he (the Prophet Muhammad) saw some of the greatest signs of his Lord."[133]

---

133 Najm 53:18.

What Was the Prophet Shown?

The Prophet was escorted on this trip by the greatest angel of God, Gabriel, whom other angels obey. And Gabriel introduced his honored guest to some of the highest inhabitants of Paradise.

The first of the great signs that were shown to the Prophet were the Lote Tree and the bedazzling lights and butterflies. Another sign he saw was Gabriel, who appeared in his real form. He said Gabriel had six hundred wings, and pearls and rubies were dripping from them. He saw Gabriel at the distance of two bow lengths or even closer. The first sighting of Gabriel's real form had been in the early days of the revelation.

The Prophet was shown four mighty rivers flowing out from the base of the Lote Tree, two hidden and two visible. He asked Gabriel what they were. Gabriel told him: "As for the two hidden rivers, they are rivers of Paradise—*Al-Salsabeel* and *Al-Kawthar*, and as for the two visible rivers, they are the Nile and the Euphrates."

The Qur'aan has mentioned both Al-Salsabeel and Al-Kawthar. Allaah has gifted the entire Al-Kawthar to the Prophet, as mentioned in Surah Al-Kawthar. As for the Nile and Euphrates, we know they have been the cradles of human civilization. In a Hadith Allaah's Apostle said, "Soon the river Euphrates will uncover a mountain of gold, so whoever will be present at that time should not take anything of it."[134]

Abu Hurayrah reported that Allaah's Messenger said, "The Last Hour will not come before the Euphrates uncovers a mountain of gold, for which people would fight. Ninety-nine out of each one hundred would die, but every man among them would say that perhaps he would be the one to succeed."

The Prophet said, "While I was walking in Paradise, I saw a river whose banks were domes of hollow pearls, and I asked, 'What is this, O Gabriel

---

134 Muslim, book 41, Hadith #6918.

(Jibreel)?' He said, 'This is Al-Kawthar, which your Lord has given to you.' And its scent—or its mud—was of fragrant musk."

The pious will drink from Al-Kawthar from the hands of the Prophet. They will also be served pure wine from Al-Salsabeel. The Qur'aan says: "And they will be given to drink there a cup (of wine) mixed with Zanjabeel (ginger) from a spring there called Salsabeel."[135]

Understanding Heaven and Paradise

In this chapter, the words *heaven* and *Paradise* have been used frequently, and it is important to distinguish between them. In Islamic terminology, the heaven is *Samaa* (sky), and Paradise is the eternal abode of the pious, called *Jannah*. In the English language, the word *heaven* is used for Paradise. Many Christians use *Paradise* to refer to the Garden of Eden (which they believe to have been a place on earth) instead of to the eternal bode of the pious.

Samaa

The *Samaa*, or skies, are seven. Allaah says in the Qur'aan that it is He Who has "created seven heavens one above the other."[136]

Linguistically, the Arabic word *Samaa* means the uppermost part of something. It refers to the sky and any part of the wider expanse of the universe. Many surahs of the Qur'aan refer to *Samaa* (often using its plural form, *Samawaat*); for example, see 10:101; 11:108; 12:101; 14:19; 15:85; 16:49; 17:102; and 18:51.

The word *Samawaat* is usually accompanied by *Ard* (Earth), signifying its opposite (meaning *low*). So the lowest heaven is called *As-Samaa*

135 Insaan 76:17–18.

136 Mulk 67:3.

Ad-Duniya. The word *Duniya* means something close and low. God has beautified the lowest heaven with stars. We the earthlings can only see the ceiling of the lowest heaven and marvel at its beauty and the way it is standing in its place without pillars. What lies on the other side of the first sky is concealed from our view. Allaah has put immense beauty in the lowest sky, and those who live in rural areas can truly attest to that beauty in a star-studded night. Allaah says, "And indeed We have adorned the lowest heaven with lamps."[137]

Paradise

In the Qur'aan the word used for Paradise is *Jannah*, and heaven. *Jannah* means garden as well as something hidden. Both meanings are applicable to Paradise. They are gardens of perpetual bliss reserved for the pious servants of God. While the *Samawaat* are only seven, *Jannaat* are many. For example, for the martyrs alone there are one hundred levels of Paradise or *Jannaat*.

Abu Hurayrah narrated that the Messenger of Allaah said, "In Paradise there are one hundred degrees which Allaah has prepared for those who strive in jihad for the sake of Allaah. The distance between each two degrees is like the distance between the heavens and the earth."[138]

The Prophet said, "The one who was devoted to the Qur'aan will be told on the Day of Resurrection: 'Recite and ascend (in ranks) as you used to recite when you were in the world. Your rank will be at the last verse you recite.'"[139]

Based on this Hadith, Aayeshah said, "There are 6,236 levels (of Paradise), as the number of verses in the Qur'aan."

---

137 Mulk 67:5.

138 Bukhari, Hadith #2637.

139 Abu Dawud.

The Qur'aan has mentioned at least eight types of Paradise:

1. *Jannatul Adn* (Garden of Eden)
2. *Jannatul Firdaws* (the best Paradise, in the middle and at the highest)
3. *Jannatun Na'eem* (Garden of Delight)
4. *Jannatul Ma'wa* (Garden of Abode)
5. *Dar Al-Khuld* (House of Eternity)
6. *Dar Al-Maqaam* (House of Everlasting Stay)
7. *Dar As-Salaam* (House of Peace)
8. *Jannatul Aaliyah* (Lofty Garden)

Seeing some of the delights of *Jannah*, the Prophet said, "A piece of Paradise the size of a bow is better than all that the sun rises and sets upon."

The Prophet said that Allaah told him, "I have prepared for My slaves what no eye has seen, no ear has heard, and no human heart can imagine." Then he said, "Recite if you wish, 'No person knows what is kept hidden for them of the joy (that is prepared) as a reward for what they used to do.'"[140]

"In Jannah there is a tree called Tooba," said the Prophet, "so big that it will take a rider one hundred years to cover its shade, and the clothes of the people of Paradise will come from the outer parts of its flowers."

While touring Paradise, the Prophet heard some footsteps and enquired of Gabriel about them. Gabriel said, "That is Bilaal." Apart from this being the most uplifting news for Bilaal, an Abyssinian freed slave, it also confirmed once again that Allaah does not look at the color or status of people; he looks at their faith and action.

140 Sajdah 32:17.

A Glimpse of Hell

While the Prophet was in the heavens, Gabriel told him, "O Muhammad, this is Maalik, the keeper of Hell." The Prophet turned toward this stern-looking angel to greet him, but Maalik greeted him first. When Maalik had taken leave of them, the Prophet told Gabriel that, in contrast to the cheerful disposition of the other inhabitants of the heavens, Maalik had no smile on his face. To that Gabriel replied, "He has not smiled since he was created, and if he were to smile at anyone, he would have smiled at you."

The Prophet was then shown a glimpse of the people in Hellfire. People were being punished for fornication, backbiting, slander, suicide, and so forth. He saw the ferociousness of the fire. Allaah has said in the Qur'aan that on the Day of Judgment, the fire will speak: "On the Day when We will say to Hell: 'Are you filled?' It will say: 'Are there more?'"[141]

Perhaps it was after seeing a glimpse of Hell that the Prophet told the Sahaabah, "If you knew what I know, you would laugh little and cry much."

When the Prophet recited verses about Hell and its punishment, he was deeply anguished by them. Once he told Abu Bakr that some of his hair had turned gray because of the description of Hell in surahs Hud, Al-Waaqiyah, Al-Mursalaat, An-Naba', and Al-Takweer.

Beyond the Farthest Lote Tree

Allaah had chosen the Prophet Muhammad for a very special honor that He had not bestowed upon anyone before. The Prophet was called into God's presence, which meant ascending beyond the Farthest Lote Tree (*Sidratul Muntaha*). Gabriel told the Prophet that he would have to go alone, as the angel was not allowed beyond this point.

---

141 Qaaf 50:30.

When Allaah caused the Prophet to ascend above the Lote Tree, he heard the scratching of the pens. A number of questions come to mind. Who was writing with these pens, if nothing went beyond the Lote Tree? Were the pens writing by themselves, or were there angels writing? Also, what was being written about, since all that is to ever happen is already recorded on the Preserved Tablet (Al-*Lawh Al-Mahfoozh*)? Perhaps this statement of Allaah provides some clue: "And with Him is the Mother of the Book."[142]

The Prophet said about this Book that "when Allaah decreed the creation, He wrote in His Book which is with Him above His Throne: 'My mercy prevails over My wrath.'"[143]

The Prophet said that he saw the Throne (*Arsh*) of Allaah, which is above the highest Paradise. The Arsh is like a dome stretching over the entire universe. We may call it the ceiling of the universe. Below the Paradise are the seven heavens. Allaah's Throne is His greatest creation, and it encompasses everything, but even that cannot encompass Allaah's Being (*Wujood*) because the creation cannot contain the Creator. There are four angels who carry the Throne, and on the Day of Judgment, eight angels will carry it.

Gifts for the Traveler

When the Prophet was alone in Allaah's presence in one of the most sacred and exclusive places, above the reach of Gabriel, Allaah decreed fifty units of daily prayers for his *Ummah* (nation). No one knows how this communication took place, and the Prophet is not known to have disclosed the means. The Prophet was also given the last two verses of Surah Al-Baqarah:

> *The Messenger believes in what has been sent down to him from his Lord and (so do) the believers. Each one believes in Allaah, His*

142 Ra'd 13:39.

143 Sahih Bukhari, Hadith #3022; Sahih Muslim, Hadith #2751.

> *Angels, His Books, and His Messengers. (They say) "We make no distinction between one another of His Messengers. We hear, and we obey. We seek Your forgiveness, our Lord, and to You is our return)." Allaah does not burden a person beyond his scope. He gets reward for that (good) which he has earned, and he is punished for that (evil) which he has earned. "Our Lord, Punish us not if we forget or fall into error! Our Lord, lay not on us a burden like that which You laid on those before us; our Lord, put not on us a burden greater than we can bear. Pardon us and grant us forgiveness. Have mercy on us. You are our Mawla (Protector) and give us victory over the disbelieving people."*[144]

The Prophet said, "Whoever recites the last two verses of Surah Al-Baqarah at night, it will suffice for him." It means Allaah will protect him and reward him immensely. It is from God's mercy that He picked only two verses from the longest chapter in the Qur'aan for this blessing. The commentators of the Qur'aan have written extensively about these verses, noting that Allaah promised in them to forgive the unintentional and forgetful mistakes of the Prophet Muhammad's followers.

And finally, the Prophet was told that those of his *Ummah* who committed serious sins would be forgiven eventually, as long as they did not associate partners with Allaah.

On the way down, the Prophet Muhammad passed by Moses, who was eager to know what Allaah had given him. The Prophet said, "Fifty prayers a day."

The Prophet Moses said, "Go back to your Lord. I have experience with the Children of Israel; your nation will not be able to handle it." It is said that the Prophet looked at Gabriel as if asking for a second opinion, and Gabriel concurred. So the Prophet went back and asked Allaah for

144 Baqarah 2:285–286.

a reduction, and He reduced it to forty-five units of prayer. Moses said that was still too great a responsibility and kept insisting that the Prophet Muhammad seek more reduction until it was reduced to five. Moses yet again asked the Prophet Muhammad to go back, but he said he felt too shy to ask for further reduction. Out of His generosity, Allaah said that whoever offered these five daily prayers would be rewarded as if they had prayed fifty.

Did the Prophet Muhammad See Allaah?

In order to understand this, we have to go back to the Qur'aan and Sunnah because there is controversy among Muslims on the subject of whether or not the Prophet Muhammad saw Allaah during the Ascension.

Most of the Prophet's Companions were of the view that he did not see Allaah on the night of the *Mai'raaj* (Ascension). The Qur'aan and Hadith both contain evidence supporting this view. From this evidence it becomes clear that human eyes are incapable of seeing Allaah, the Creator, in the earthly life. However, the people of Paradise will be able to see Him because God will resurrect them with the ability to encompass His vision.

When the people of Paradise enter it, Allaah will ask them if they want anything more, and they will say, "Have You not admitted us into Paradise and saved us from Hell?" People will praise Allaah and say they could not think of asking for anything else. Then Allaah will remove the veil from His face, and the people of Paradise will be delighted, and nothing will be more ecstatic for them than looking at their Lord. Allaah's veil should not be equated with the veil that some women wear. Allaah's veil is more like a screen of light, but its true reality is only known to Him.

The Qur'aan says that when Prophet Moses pleaded with Allaah at Mount Sinai to let him see Him, Allaah said that he would not be able to encompass His vision.

> *And when Musa came at the time and place appointed by Us, and his Lord (Allaah) spoke to him; he said: "O my Lord! Show me (Yourself), that I may look upon You." Allaah said: "You cannot see Me, but look upon the mountain; if it stands still in its place then you shall see Me." So when his Lord appeared to the mountain, He made it collapse to dust, and Musa fell down unconscious. Then when he recovered his senses he said: "Glory be to You, I turn to You in repentance and I am the first of the believers."*[145]

In another place Allaah says: "No vision can grasp Him, but His Grasp is over all visions."[146]

The Companion Abu Dharr said, "I asked the Messenger of Allaah, 'Did you see your Lord?' He said, 'He is veiled by light; how could I see Him?'"[147] The Qur'aan says that in the Hereafter the righteous will have no problem seeing Allaah. "Some faces that Day shall be shining and radiant, looking at their Lord."[148]

And in Surah Qaaf, Allaah says that in Paradise they will get whatever they desire, and "We (will) have something more for them."[149]

Why did the Prophet not see Allaah in *Mai'raaj*? Most likely because he was still in his earthly body, and Allaah has decreed that only the people of Paradise in the Hereafter will be able to see Him.

---

145 Aa'raaf 7:143.

146 An'aam 6:103.

147 Muslim, Hadith #261.

148 Qiyamah 75:22–23.

149 Qaaf 50:35. Commentators have described the word *more* (*mazeed*) in this verse as Allaah allowing Himself to be seen by the people of Paradise.

What is Masjid Al-Aqsa?

The *Masjid Al-Aqsa* today is frequently a scene of violence between Israeli forces and Palestinian youth. It is built on what is known as *Al-Haram Al-Shareef* (the Noble Sanctuary). When the Prophet was taken to Jerusalem in his miraculous Night Journey, there was no Al-Aqsa Mosque as we know of today. It was built by Umar bin Al-Khattaab and later caliphs. At the time there were only the remnants of the house of worship the Prophet Solomon had built. The Muslims initially faced toward Jerusalem in prayers; only later was the focal point changed to Makkah. From a Hadith we learn that Masjid Al-Aqsa was built before Solomon, around the time of Prophet Abraham.

Abu Dharr said, "I asked, 'O Messenger of Allaah, which mosque was built on the earth first?' He said, 'Al-Masjid Al-Haraam (in Makkah).' I asked, 'Then which?' He said, 'Al-Masjid Al-Aqsa.' I said, 'How much time was there between them?' He said, 'Forty years.'"[150]

The Dome of the Rock, the building with the golden dome often plastered on Israeli tourism literature, is not Al-Aqsa Mosque. The Dome of the Rock was built by Caliph Abdul Maalik bin Marwaan in 72 AH (691/–692 CE), and it encompasses the rock from where the Prophet Muhammad is said to have ascended to the heavens.

Return to Makkah and a Storm of Controversy

The Prophet returned to Makkah the same night. The next morning when he told Abu Jahl about his Night Journey, Abu Jahl could not believe his ears. "Will you say to the people what you have told me?" Abu Jahl asked. The Prophet said yes.

Abu Jahl quickly gathered a crowd there, hoping to prove to them that there was definitely something wrong with the Prophet. Abu Jahl also ran

150 Bukhari, Hadith #3366; Muslim, Hadith #520.

to Abu Bakr and told him, "Your Companion thinks he went to Bayt Al-Maqdis (Jerusalem) last night, performed prayer there, and then returned here to Makkah in the morning."

Abu Bakr said, "If he said it, I believe in it. By Allaah! I believe in something more amazing than that. He informs me that revelation comes to him from the sky to the earth during the day and night." Thus Abu Bakr earned the title of *As-Siddeeq* (foremost believer in the truth), a title greater than that of a martyr. It is reported that the Prophet did not tell the Quraysh about Mai'raaj (the Ascension), thinking that that would be even more unbelievable for them.

When the Prophet told the public about Israa (the Night Journey to Jerusalem), the disbelievers laughed at him and refused to believe anything he had said. They asked him to describe Masjid Al-Aqsa for them. The Prophet said that Gabriel brought the Noble Sanctuary in front of him, and he told his detractors the minutest details of the place. The Prophet also told them that he saw a caravan headed toward Makkah that had lost a camel. Several days later the caravan arrived and confirmed what the Prophet had said. Even then the heedless among them refused to believe in his message.

The Case of a Blind Companion

The Prophet strove hard to invite the leaders of the Quraysh to Islam, knowing that if they accepted the message, their tribesmen would follow suit. On one such occasion when he was in a deep conversation with Utbah bin Rabi'ah, Shaybah bin Rabi'ah, Abu Jahl, Umayyah bin Khalaf, Ubayy bin Khalaf, Al-Waleed bin Al-Mugheerah, and a Companion who had been blind since birth interrupted the Prophet.

"O Messenger of Allaah, teach me what Allaah has taught you," said Abdullaah bin Umm Maktoom, the blind Companion, who was completely unaware of what was going on. The Prophet politely told Abdullaah that he would teach him later. He simply did not want any distraction from his outreach to the Qurayshi leadership. But Abdullaah was insistent, repeating his request until the Prophet became annoyed and turned away from him.

Allaah disapproved of the Prophet's treatment of the blind Companion's request, and revealed verses to rebuke His Messenger.

> *He frowned and turned away. Because there came to him the blind man. And how can you know that he might become pure. Or he might receive admonition, and the admonition might profit him. As for him who thinks himself self-sufficient. To him you attend; What does it matter to you if he will not become pure? But as for him who came to you running. And fears (Allaah). Of him you are neglectful and divert your attention to another.*[151]

The Prophet's reaction to Abdullaah's interruption of his meeting was based on his *Ijtihaad* (reasoning). In the absence of divine guidance, he did what he thought was right. On the other hand, Allaah's command reflected His infinite knowledge, including the knowledge of the future. As it turned out, those the Prophet was trying so hard to invite to Islam died opposing it. From another point of view, Allaah's seeming rebuke of the Prophet was actually directed at the leaders of the Quraysh, whose end was already known to Allaah.

The Prophet loved Ibn Umm Maktoom. He appointed Ibn Umm Maktoom second *mu'adhdhin* (one who issues the call for daily prayers), after Bilaal bin Rabaah, and more than once he appointed the blind Companion his deputy in Madinah during his absence. Sometimes when Ibn Umm Maktoom visited the Prophet, the Prophet would affectionately say, "Welcome to him on whose account my Sustainer has rebuked me."

---

151 Abasa 80:1–10.

The Story of Al-Tufayl Al-Dawsi

The Prophet had continued to diligently approach visitors to Makkah with his message, and the Quraysh tried their best to intercept them before the Prophet had a chance to talk to them. The Qurayshi would repeat to the strangers their well-rehearsed lines, like, "Do not ever listen to this man. He is insane, a magician, a soothsayer." One such visitor was Al-Tufayl Al-Dawsi, leader of the Al-Daws tribe in Yemen.

Tufayl was a very smart man, but initially he fell victim to the Quraysh's propaganda. Historians have recorded Tufayl's story in his own words:

> *The next morning I went to make Tawaaf (circumambulation) around the Ka'bah to glorify the idols we used to worship. I put cotton in my ears so that not a word of Muhammad's teachings would reach my hearing. But as soon as I got into the sacred area, I found the Prophet standing in front of the Ka'bah, making a prayer that didn't look like the ways of our traditions. I was much taken by this scene. I found myself walking nearer and nearer to him until I was quite close to him, despite my will. It was the will of Allaah that I should hear some of what he was saying. It was so beautiful that I told myself, "Woe to you, Tufayl! You are an intelligent poet; you are able to differentiate the good from the bad. Why don't you listen to the man? If what he says is good, accept it, and if it's bad, reject it!"*
>
> *I stood there until the Prophet left for his house. I followed him, and when he entered the house, I said, "Muhammad, your people told me many bad things about you. They scared me so much that I put cotton in my ears to prevent myself from hearing you. But Allaah let me hear your speech, and I found it good. So please explain to me what this is all about."*
>
> *He (the Prophet) explained it to me and read Surah Al-Ikhlaas and Surah Al-Falaq (chapters 112 and 113). I swear, I had never heard*

anything better than that, nor had I met someone more fair on this earth. On the spot, I gave him my hand and pronounced the Shahaadah (Testimony of Faith) that "There is no god but Allaah" and that "Muhammad is His messenger," and I became a Muslim.

I stayed in Makkah for a while to learn the teachings of Islam and to memorize what I could of the Qur'aan. When I decided to go back to my people, I said, "0 Messenger of Allaah, I have influence upon my people. I am going back to them and I shall invite them to Islam. Pray to Allaah that He gives me a sign to help me invite them." So he (the Prophet) prayed, "O Allaah, give him a sign." I went back to my people.

When I was about to reach my land, I felt a light falling between my eyes just like a lamp. I said, "O Allaah, put it somewhere else but not my face, for I am afraid my tribe might think it is a punishment for leaving their religion." So the light moved to the tip of my whip, and it shone on the people as if it were a suspended lamp.

When I saw my elderly father, I said, "Don't approach me, Father. I am no longer from you, and you're not from me."

He said, "Why, son?"

I said, "I have become Muslim and I follow the religion of Muhammad ibn Abdullaah of Makkah."

He said softly, "Son, your religion is my religion!"

Delighted at these words I said, "Go, wash yourself, put on clean clothes, then come to me so I may teach you what I have been taught!"

So he went and did so. Then he came back, I explained Islam to him and he became a Muslim.

> *Then my wife came to me and I said, "Be off with you, for I have nothing to do with you or you with me." "Why?" she said, "my father and be your ransom!" I said, "Islam has divided us and I follow the religion of Muhammad." She said, "Then my religion is your religion."*[152]

However, Tufayl's people were slow to embrace Islam, except for one very special person named Abdush-Shams, who later became known as Abu Hurayrah and who has collected the largest number of Hadith from the Prophet.

Abyssinian Christians Accept Islam

Some twenty Abyssinian Christians visited the Prophet in Makkah to inquire about the faith he was preaching. The Prophet explained to them and recited some verses of the Qur'aan. When they heard the Qur'aan, they began to cry because it sounded so much like the teachings of Prophet Jesus (Eesa). Without delay, they accepted Islam.

Allaah has mentioned those Christians' positive attitude toward the Qur'aan in two places.

> *And when they listen to what has been sent down to the Messenger, you see their eyes overflowing with tears because of the truth they have recognized. They say: "Our Lord! We believe; so write us down among the witnesses."*[153]

Another verse:

> *Those to whom We gave the Scripture before it, they believe in it. And when it is recited to them, they say: "We believe in it. Verily,*

152 Muhammad Ibn Isshaaq, *Sirat Rasul Allah*, trans. A. Guillaume as *The Life of Muhammad*, 27th Ed. (Karachi: Oxford University Press, 2014).

153 Maa'idah 5:83.

it is the truth from our Lord. Indeed even before it we have been from Muslims."[154]

Ibn Isshaaq reported that many among the early scholars believed that these verses had been revealed about Najaashi and his Companions. But both opinions could be true. Moreover, these Christians were from Abyssinia, and Najaashi was their king who had also given shelter to the Muslim immigrants. It is possible that these Christians had come to verify the message directly from the Prophet.

As the Christians were leaving, the Quraysh started to verbally abuse them, saying, "What a wretched people you are, that the moment you heard this man, you renounced your religion."

The Christians said, "Peace be upon you. We are not going to engage in any foolish conversation with you."

Not only was the Abyssinian delegation's response profound; it also showed that as former Christians they had access to the original teachings of the Prophet Jesus. How else could their statement to the Quraysh be so similar to the teachings of the Qur'aan?

For example, the Qur'aan says:

When the ignorant address them (in a rude, disrespectful manner) they say, "peace."[155]

In another place the Qur'aan exhorts Muslims to respond kindly to unkindness:

154 Qasas 28:52–53.

155 Furqaan 25:63.

The good deed and the evil deed are not equal. Repel (the evil) with something better. Then verily! He, between whom and you there was enmity, (will become) as though he was a warm friend.[156] (Fussilat 41:34)

Revelation of Surah Al-Kawthar

A personal tragedy struck the Prophet again. His first son, Qaasim, had died sometime earlier. From the birth of his first son, he had been called Abul Qaasim (father of Qaasim). It was an Arab tradition to call someone "father of so-and-so" to show respect. This time Abdullaah, his second son, died of illness. Abdullaah was born after his father had been conferred Prophethood. Some say that because of this Abdullaah was also called Taahir and Tayyab (meaning pure), although others say they were the Prophet's other sons. But the latter seems to be a weak opinion.

The Prophet felt much grief at Abdullaah's death. His grief was compounded when Abu Jahl (although some say it was Al-Aas bin Waa'il) remarked that "Muhammad has been cut off from all good (meaning lineage)." In the pagan society, where many buried their infant daughters alive on the presumption that they might bring the family shame, lineage could only continue from male children. The insensitive remark rubbed salt on the Prophet's wounds, and Allaah consoled His Prophet by revealing Surah Al-Kawthar:

Verily, We have granted you Al-Kawthar. Therefore turn in prayer to your Lord and offer sacrifice. For he who hates you, he will be cut off.[157]

Anas bin Maalik, a Companion, provided the background of the revelation. He said, "While we were with the Messenger of Allaah in the mosque, he dozed off. Then he lifted his head, smiling. We said, 'O Messenger of Allaah! What has caused you to laugh?' He said, 'Verily, a surah was just

156 Fussilat 41:34.

157 Kawthar 108:1–3.

revealed to me.' Then he said (about Al-Kawthar), 'It is a river in Paradise that my Lord has given me. It is whiter than milk and sweeter than honey. There are birds in it whose necks are (long) like carrots.' Umar said, 'O Messenger of Allaah! Verily, they (the birds) will be beautiful.' The Prophet replied, 'The one who eats them (i.e., the people of Paradise) will be more beautiful than them, O Umar.'"

First Signs Pointing to Madinah

In the eleventh year of the Prophethood when the Prophet was visiting the pilgrims to convey the message, as was his habit, he came across a group of six from Yathrib (later to be called Madinah). Some say they had come to one of the fairs. He had not seen them before, so he asked, "Who are you?"

They said they were from the tribe of Al-Khazraj and were allies of the Jews of their town. Their alliance with the Jews was an uneasy one, for they would sometime attack the Jews when they felt angry with them. The Jews would say to them, "A prophet will be sent soon. His day is at hand. We shall follow him and kill you by his aid." So when the news of a man in Makkah claiming to be the Prophet reached Yathrib, the Al-Khazraj, along with their rival tribe Al-Aws, and of course the Jews, became curious.

The Prophet sat with the six Khazrajites, explained Islam to them, and recited some verses of the Qur'aan. The visitors accepted Islam or accepted it in principle and returned home with fond memories of their encounter with the Prophet. Among them were As'ad bin Zuraarah, Awf bin Al-Haarith, Raafi bin Maalik, Qutbah bin Aamir, Uqbah bin Aamir, and Jaabir bin Abdullaah.

The First Pledge of Al-Aqabah

The following year, a group of twelve men from Yathrib came to Makkah, and they included some who had already accepted Islam at their first meeting with the Prophet. This time there were three pilgrims from the tribe of Aws as well. The message of the Prophet Muhammad had started to resonate in small circles of Aws and Khazraj. Because they had often heard from the Jews that the time for the appearance of the Messiah (a new prophet) had come, they wanted to be the first ones to accept his message and be saved. Among this group were As'ad bin Zuraarah, Awf bin Al-Haarith, his brother Mu'aadh, Raafi bin Maalik, Dhakwaan bin Abdu Qays, Ubaadah bin Al-Saamit, Yazid bin Tha'alabah, Al-Abbaas bin Ubaadah, Qutbah bin Aamir, Uqbah bin Aamir, Uwaym bin Saa'idah, and Abul Haytham bin Al-Tayhaan. They all gave a pledge of allegiance to the Prophet that they would follow Islam and obey him.

According to another narration, the names of these twelve were as follows:

From Banu Khazraj:

1. Abdullaah bin Rawaahah
2. Sa'ad ibn Ubaadah
3. As'ad bin Zuraarah
4. Sa'ad bin Ar-Rabi' bin Amr
5. Raafi' bin Malik
6. Al-Bara' bin Maa'rur bin Sakhr
7. Abdullaah bin Amr bin Haraam
8. Ubaadah bin Saamit
9. Al-Mundhir bin 'Amr bin Khunais

From Banu Aws:

1. Usayd bin Hudhayr bin Sammaak
2. Sa'ad bin Khaythamah bin Al-Haarith
3. Rifa'a bin 'Abdul Mundhir

Ubaadah bin Saamit, who attended this pledge of allegiance, said that the Prophet asked them not to enjoin partners with Allaah, nor steal, nor commit fornication, nor kill their children, nor slander their neighbors, nor disobey the Messenger in what was right. And if they obeyed him in these, Allaah would reward them with Paradise, and if they committed any of the major sins and did not repent, Allaah may punish them or forgive them as He pleased.

This pledge was also called the Pledge of the Women because it did not impose any political or military obligations on the participants. Before returning to Yathrib, the new Muslims asked for a teacher to be sent to them to recite the Qur'aan and teach them the tenets of faith. The Prophet chose Mus'ab bin Umayr, a learned, pious young man.

The Story of Mus'ab bin Umayr Abdari

Mus'ab was an inspiring man even for other Companions. He had lived a princely life before Islam. His clothing came from Yemen, costing in today's money probably tens of thousands of dollars apiece. He perfumed himself generously and had a very handsome, elegant look. Some say physically he resembled the Prophet. He was so mature for his age that the Quraysh used to let him sit in their inner circle, where they made important decisions.

When he was twenty-four, the Prophet's message reached Mus'ab, and he accepted Islam. Soon his world changed profoundly. His mother, who loved him dearly, became furious and expelled him from her house. One report says he was even imprisoned in his own house. When he was finally allowed to leave, his stepfather stripped him of the clothes that he had on, saying he did not deserve them because they had been purchased with the money of his deceased biological father, whose religion he had forsaken.

In this state Mus'ab went to the Messenger of Allaah, who clothed and sheltered him. Mus'ab was passionate about learning the teachings of Islam, so he immediately busied himself with it and excelled.

These were the days of persecution of the Muslims, and seeing the intensity of oppression, the Prophet gave permission to a handful of people to migrate to Abyssinia (Habashah). Mus'ab was one of them. Soon the rumor spread that the Quraysh had reconciled with the Muslims, and Mus'ab, like some other emigrants, returned to Makkah, only to discover that the persecution had actually become more intense.

Historians say that Mus'ab went through extreme hardships and hunger. From a handsome, well-nourished, and expensively clothed young man, Mus'ab became a malnourished person who wore coarse and ragged clothes. The Messenger of Allaah used to be sad to see Mus'ab that way, and the Sahaabah shed tears looking at him. It is said that the Sahaabah's tears were not the warm tears of sorrow but the cool tears of joy, as Mus'ab's strong faith was an inspiration to them.

As the persecution became unbearable, the Prophet allowed a second migration to Abyssinia. This time a much larger group migrated, with Mus'ab joining them as a returnee. However, Mus'ab's heart was in Makkah. He sorely missed the company of Rasul Allaah, so he returned to Makkah. It was then that the Prophet commanded him to move to Madinah to teach the new Muslims and invite others to Islam.

In Madinah, Mus'ab stayed in the house of Companion Usayd bin Hudhayr and started teaching Islam and making da'wah (calling people to Islam). Allaah gave him great success in his work. People like Sa'ad bin Mu'aadh accepted Islam at Mus'ab's invitation. There was not a single clan or family among the Ansaar (Helpers) where someone had not embraced the new faith. Delighted by the sight of so many faithful, Mus'ab one day sent a message to the Prophet seeking his permission to address all the people of Ansaar in a single gathering. The Prophet granted the request and ordered him to gather the Muslims on a Friday at noon, address them, and lead them in prayer. Because of this incident, some scholars say that Mus'ab was the first person in Islam to pray Jumu'ah (the Friday congregational prayer).

Many of the Ansaar who came to Makkah a year or so later and entered into the Second Pledge of Al-Aqabah were those who had accepted Islam at Mus'ab's hands. Mus'ab valiantly fought in the Battle of Badr in 2 AH (625 CE) and died a martyr next year in the Battle of Uhud.

The Second Pledge of Al-Aqabah

Mus'ab's missionary work was so successful that within a short time almost 250 people had accepted Islam in Madinah, closely rivaling the number of believers in Makkah. There were several reasons for this spectacular success. First, in Madinah there was no persecution for believing in One God. Second, the old leadership of Madinah had been almost wiped out in the Wars of Bu'aath between Aws and Khazraj. The town's young people were tired of their leaders fighting useless wars on frivolous grounds. Third, the young people, like the young everywhere, were open to trying new ideas. They also saw in the Prophet a person who could unify their tribes.

Some years later Allaah revealed verses reminding the Helpers about the unity He had bestowed upon them:

> *O you who believe! Have consciousness of Allaah as He deserves, and die not except as (true) Muslims. And hold fast, all of you together, to the Rope of Allaah, and be not divided among yourselves, and remember Allaah's favor on you, for you were enemies of one another but He joined your hearts together, so that, by His grace, you became brethren, and you were on the brink of a pit of Fire, and He saved you from it. Thus Allaah makes His Ayat clear to you, that you may be guided.*[158]

The above verses can also be applied to all the other Arabs of that time who were given to fighting senseless wars.

158 Aal Imraan 3:102–103.

The following year, the largest group of Helpers as yet—seventy-three men and two women—came to Makkah. They were all eager for the Prophet to migrate to their city and leave Makkah's oppressive and hostile environment. And Jaabir bin Abdullaah, an early Muslim from among the Ansaar, seems to have spoken for everyone when he said, "How long will we leave Rasul Allaah circling the mountains of Makkah and being fearful?"

The Madinah Muslims wanted to meet with the Prophet and make entreaties of him to move to their city. Sensing the criticality of the moment, the Prophet instructed the Muslim pilgrims from Madinah to meet him on the last night of the Hajj in the last third of the night on the Plains of Aqabah. He appointed Abu Bakr and Ali as lookouts. One challenge in meeting with the Muslim pilgrims from Madinah was that among them were also pagan pilgrims. It is important to note that even non-Muslims performed Hajj; however, some of their rituals were opposed to the teachings of Prophet Abraham, and the Prophet Muhammad abolished those rituals when Allaah gave him control of Makkah some ten years later.

When the appointed time came, the people of Khazraj and Aws sneaked out of their tents, leaving their pagan Companions sleeping, and headed to the meeting place. The Prophet came with his uncle Al-Abbaas, who was not a Muslim yet but who spoke first. Abbaas looked at the Muslims from Madinah and said, "I do not know any of these people." He was clearly worried. Ibn Isshaaq reported that Abbaas said out loud, "O people of Khazraj, you know what position Muhammad holds among us. We have protected him from our own people. He lives in honor and safety among his people, but he will turn to you and join you. If you think you can be faithful to what you have promised him and protect him from his opponents, then assume the burden you have undertaken. But if you think you will betray and abandon him, then leave him now."

Abbaas had clearly embellished his speech to make a point, because after the death of Abu Taalib, none of the Prophet's family members had been able to protect him. It was Mut'im bin Adiyy, an unrelated pagan, who had offered protection to the Prophet. Abbaas had addressed Khazraj, but he also meant Aws. He simply wanted to show that the former was a bigger tribe and that more of their people were in the group than from Aws.

The Muslims of Madinah were growing anxious, and they said to Abbaas, "We have heard you. You speak, O Apostle of Allaah, and choose for yourself and your Lord what you wish."

It was at that point that the Messenger of Allaah spoke. He first praised Allaah and recited the Qur'aan, and then he said, "I invite your allegiance on the basis that you will protect me as you protect your women and children."

At that, Al-Baraa bin Maa'rur got hold of the hand of the Prophet and said, "By Him Who sent you with the truth, we will protect you as we protect our women. We give you our allegiance, and we are men of war."

While Al-Baraa was speaking, Abul Haytham bin Tayhaan interrupted him and said, "O Messenger of Allaah, we have ties with other men (meaning Jews) that will be broken. And if Allaah gives you victory, will you then return to your people and leave us?"

The Prophet smiled and said something historic that was tested after the Conquest of Makkah: "No, your blood is my blood; I am of you and you are of me. I will wage war against those you go to war with and will be at peace with those you have peace with."

Then the Prophet asked that they bring twelve leaders from among them who could take charge. When they did so, he said, "You are responsible over your people, just as the disciples of Jesus (Eesa), son of Mary, were responsible to him, while I am responsible for all Muslims."

At that point Abbaas bin Ubaadah got up and said, "O men of Khazraj, do you realize what you are committing yourself to in pledging your support to this man? It is to go to war against all. If you think that you will give him up when you lose your property and your nobles are killed, then do so now, for now it will bring you shame only in this world, but you will face shame in both worlds if you betray him later. But if you think you will be loyal, then take him, for, by Allaah, it will profit you in this world and the next."

Given what was requested of them, some people asked the Prophet frankly, "What would we get in return for our loyalty?"

The Prophet replied, "Paradise."

Allaah revealed a verse in the Qur'aan to confirm His Prophet's promise:

> *Indeed, Allaah has purchased from the believers their lives and their properties (in exchange) for Paradise.*[159] (Tawbah 9:111)

People put their hands on the Prophet's hand to pledge fealty, except for the two women, who swore verbally. (The Prophet never touched a woman who was not a close relative.) Unlike the First Pledge of Al-Aqabah, this one clearly included both political and military support. Inviting the Prophet to live in Madinah under an all-out protection was akin to declaring war against the Quraysh, and the Helpers soon found this out in a very real way.

The Devil Tries to Expose the Pledge

After the pilgrims had made the pledge, *Shaytaan* (the devil) shouted in a piercing voice, "O people of Mina, wake up while you are sleeping; this Sabi and the apostate (meaning the Prophet) has come to wage war against you."

159 Tawbah 9:111.

The Prophet told the Muslims, "This is Izb, the Shaytaan of this valley, the son of Azyab." Then, addressing the Shaytaan, he said, "Do you hear, O enemy of Allaah? I swear I will take care of you."

The next morning, an alarmed Quraysh went from the tents of the pilgrims to find out if they had had a meeting with the Prophet the night before. One by one, they said no. Finally, they came to the tents of the Ansaar. Before the Muslims could speak, the pagan Yathribites in their group said they knew nothing about this meeting. The Muslims simply kept quiet. The pagans were correct because Allaah had willed that they sleep soundly while their Muslim townspeople had quietly stepped out of the tent to meet with the Prophet.

It was only after the Helpers had left for Madinah that the Makkan leadership found out that what they had feared had indeed happened. They quickly sent some people in pursuit. The only person they could overtake was Sa'ad bin Ubaadah. They tied him up and beat him on the way. Sa'ad said to them that he used to protect the merchants of Jubayr bin Mut'im as well as Al-Haarith bin Harb and asked for leniency in return. People went to Jubayr (the son of the Prophet's protector, Mut'im bin Adiyy) and Al-Haarith. When both confirmed that Sa'ad was telling the truth, he was released. Jubayr became a Muslim a few years later in Madinah.

Nusaybah bint Ka'ab's Pledge

Among the pledgers were two women: Nusaybah bint Ka'ab and Asmaa bint Amr. The Prophet's biographers have not collected much information on Asmaa, except that she was known as Umm Manee and was the mother of a well-known Companion named Mu'aadh bin Jabal.

As for Nusaybah bint Ka'ab, also known as Umm Umaarah, volumes have been written. She was from the Banu Najjaar tribe of Madinah, the tribe of the Prophet's paternal great-grandmother. Nusaybah was the sister of Abdullaah bin Ka'ab, and the mother of Abdullaah and Habib bin Zayd Al-Ansaari.

Nusaybah, like other women, attended the Battle of Uhud to bring water to the soldiers, while her husband and two sons fought. But after the Muslim archers ignored the Prophet's orders and left their assigned stations, causing the tide of battle to turn against Muslims, Nusaybah entered the fray, carrying a sword and shield. She felt an abiding call to protect the Prophet Muhammad from the enemies, and she was wounded while answering that call.

When a horse-mounted Qurayshi attacked her, she pulled on his horse's bridle and plunged her sword into its neck, toppling the horse on top of its rider. The Prophet saw this and called Abdullaah, Nusaybah's son, to help his mother.

Umar ibn Al-Khattaab reported that the Prophet said, "Whenever I turned left or right on the Day of Uhud, I saw her (Umm Umaarah) fighting in my defense." So he prayed, "O Allaah, make Umm Umaarah and her family my Companion in Jannah (Paradise)."

Ibn Hajar Al-Asqalaani, who wrote the famous explanation of Saheeh Al-Bukhari, said, "She (Nusaybah) participated in the battles of Uhud, Hudaybiyah, and Khayber. She also witnessed the victory of Makkah and participated in the battles of Hunayn and Yamamah, in which she lost one of her hands."

The Migration to Madinah

When it became clear that a peaceful coexistence was no longer possible in Makkah and that the Muslims of Madinah were eager to receive their brethren from the Sacred City, in the eleventh year of his mission the Prophet gave the people permission to migrate to Madinah. However, the migration did not happen at once. The biggest reason for the delay was that the Quraysh were bent on stopping people from migrating, even by force if needed. Also, the Prophet himself may have been waiting for Allaah's command.

The first one to migrate to Madinah was Abdullaah bin Abdul Asad, better known in the Islamic history as Abu Salamah. It is said that he migrated even before the Pledge of Aqabah. The story of his migration is both sad and inspiring. When he and his wife Umm Salamah (real name Hind bint Abu Umayyah) returned from their previous migration to Abyssinia, the Quraysh mistreated him. Since he was not a Qurayshi, he had lesser claim to protection in that society. Fed up, Abu Salamah packed up and decided to leave in daylight. He thought the Quraysh wouldn't care if he left, but it was not so.

As he and his family were leaving, some of the people from Banu Al-Mugheerah surrounded them. They said to Abu Salamah, "As for you, you may leave, but as for your wife, she is from our tribe." So they pulled away Umm Salamah and her young son.

To make matters more heartbreaking, the men from Abdul Asad (to which Abu Salamah belonged) became angry and said, "We will not leave our son with her (meaning Umm Salamah), seeing that you have torn us from our tribesman." So a tug of war ensued between the Quraysh and the Banu Abdul Asad, during which the hand of the young child was dislocated. The Banu Abdul Asad took the boy away, while the Quraysh kept Umm Salamah. Abu Salamah left for Madinah alone.

Umm Salamah was devastated, for now she had neither her husband nor her son. She narrated, "I used to go out every morning and sit in the valley weeping continuously until a year or so had passed, when one of my cousins from the Banu Al-Mugheerah passed and saw my plight and took pity on me. He said to his tribesmen, 'Why don't you let this poor woman go?' So they said to me, 'You can join your husband if you like,' and then the Abdul Asad restored my son to me. So I saddled my camel, placed my son on my lap, and set out in the direction of Madinah. When I reached Tan'eem (three miles from Makkah), I met Uthmaan bin Talhah."

Uthmaan and his family were the keepers of the key of the Ka'bah, but he had not yet embraced Islam. Surprised to see Umm Salamah that way, Uthmaan asked, "Where do you think you are going?"

"I am going to my husband in Madinah," she replied.

"And isn't there anyone going with you?"

Umm Salamah answered, "None except Allaah and my little boy here."

Uthmaan's good character shone through. "By Allaah," he said, "I will not leave you until you reach Madinah."

Umm Salamah continued: "He then took the reins of my camel and led us on our way. By Allaah, I have never met an Arab more generous and noble than he. Whenever we reached a resting-place, he would make my camel kneel down, wait until I had dismounted, and then lead the camel to a tree and tether it. Then he would go and rest in the shade of a different tree. When we had rested, he would get the camel ready again and then lead us on our way. This he did every day until we reached Madinah. When we reached a village near Quba (about two miles from Madinah), belonging to the Banu Amr bin Awf, he said, 'Your husband is in this village. Enter it with the blessings of Allaah.' Then he turned around and headed back to Mecca."

Allaah honored Uthmaan for his nobility in more than one way. He guided Uthmaan to Islam, and after the Conquest of Makkah, the Prophet called him and said that until the Last Day the keys of the Ka'bah would remain with Uthmaan and his family. Fourteen centuries later, Uthmaan's descendants are still the keepers of the keys of the Ka'bah.

The Story of Umar's Migration

Soon to follow Abu Salamah in migration were Bilaal and Ammaar. However, the migration that really made headlines was that of Umar. While most of the other Muslims left Makkah discreetly, even secretly, Umar declared publicly that he was migrating. Not only that, but he dared the Quraysh to stop him.

Ali bin Abi Taalib said, "I never knew anyone to migrate openly except Umar, for he girt on his sword and slung over his bow, grasping the arrows in his hand. He went to the Ka'bah, where the chiefs of the Quraysh were sitting, went around it seven times, then prayed two raka'ats (units) at the Station of Abraham, and went to each one of them saying, 'Whoever wants that his mother bereave for him and his child be left an orphan and his wife a widow, let him meet me behind this valley,' but no one followed him."

Twenty other Muslims joined Umar in his migration; among them were Ayyaash bin Abu Rabi'ah Al-Makhzumi and Hishaam bin Al-Aas bin Waa'il Al-Sahmi. They made an appointment to meet at the thorn tree of Adat of Banu Ghifaar about ten miles outside of Makkah. It was decided that if any one of them failed to turn up at the appointed place by sunrise on the day of departure, it would be construed that he was not coming and had been held back by force.

Umar and his Companions, including Ayyaash, arrived at the appointed meeting place. However, Hishaam did not turn up and was considered held back by the Quraysh. After days of arduous journey, the party arrived in Quba on the outskirts of Madinah. There they stayed with Banu Amr bin Awf.

Back in Makkah, Abu Jahl and Al-Haarith were particularly upset at the migration of Ayyaash, who was their cousin. Some weeks later they went to Madinah to bring Ayyaash back. They told Ayyaash that his mother had vowed she would neither comb her hair nor take shelter from the sun until she saw Ayyaash.

Umar told Ayyaash that this was nothing but a trick, and added that if the lice disturbed his mother, she would comb her hair, and if the heat of Makkah oppressed her, she would take shelter. But Ayyaash felt inclined to go. He said, "I may go for a short while. I will clear my mother of her vow. I also have some money to recover from the people in Makkah that I would like to get."

Umar said, "I am one of the richest of the Quraysh, and if you do not go with them, you may have one-half of my money." Ayyaash, however, persisted in his wish to go to Makkah. Umar offered more advice: "If you must go, then take this camel of mine. She is well bred and easy to ride. Don't dismount, and if at any stage you suspect them of treachery, you may well escape on this camel." Then Ayyaash left for Makkah on Umar's camel.

After they had proceeded some distance, Abu Jahl said to Ayyaash, "Nephew, I find my beast hard to ride. Will you not mount me behind you?" Ayyaash agreed, and when they made their camels kneel to make the change, Abu Jahl and Al-Haarith fell on Ayyaash and bound him securely.

They brought him to Makkah and said, "O men of Makkah, deal with your fools as we have dealt with this fool of ours."

When the Prophet, who by now had migrated, came to know how Hishaam had been held back and how Ayyaash had been abducted, he said, "Who will bring me Ayyaash and Hishaam?"

Al-Waleed bin Al-Mugheerah volunteered to undertake the mission. When Al-Waleed reached Makkah, he found out that Hishaam and Ayyaash were imprisoned in a house that had no roof. One night, Al-Waleed climbed the wall and cut the prisoners' chains with the strokes of his sword. The two men rode to freedom with Al-Waleed. Going to Makkah to free the two Muslim prisoners was like entering the den of a lion. Had the Quraysh found out, they would have captured and even harmed Al-Waleed. When the three returned to Madinah, the Prophet was relieved. He welcomed Hishaam and Ayyaash and praised Al-Waleed for his valor.

Suhayb Ar-Rumi Migrates

Like other Muslims, Suhayb also decided to leave. The day he set out for Madinah, the Quraysh surrounded him and said there was no way they would allow him to leave. Suhayb, who was one of the finest sharpshooters, said, "You will not be able to touch me until every one of my arrows has touched your flesh and my sword has struck you." They backed off but said there was no way he could take all that money he had earned in Makkah. Suhayb was carrying with him only a fraction of the wealth he had, and the rest he had concealed in Makkah. His greatest goal was to get to Madinah, so he said, "Will you let me go if tell you where I have hidden my money?" They consented but also wanted the camel he was riding on. Suhayb agreed and walked toward Madinah.

Suhayb was perhaps the only person who traveled to Madinah on foot. By the time he reached Madinah, he was emaciated and disheveled. The Prophet personally removed dust from his clothes and said, "O Suhayb, your trade has been successful."

Suhayb understood that the Prophet knew what happened to him in Makkah, so he said, "I swear by the One Who has sent you with the truth that no one knew about this matter." God indeed had informed His Prophet.

Then Allaah revealed the following aayah to praise Suhayb:

And of mankind is he who would sell himself, seeking the pleasure of Allaah. And Allaah is full of kindness to (His) servants.)[160]

The Prophet's Migration

After the Prophet had given Muslims permission to migrate, people were leaving however they could. But he himself waited for Allaah's order to migrate. His closest friend and confidant, Abu Bakr, had asked him for permission to leave, but the Prophet had told him, "Do not be hasty; it may be that Allaah will give you a traveling Companion." Hearing that, Abu Bakr began to prepare two camels.

What does it mean to prepare a camel? When people were faced with a long desert journey, they would overfeed their camel to fatten it, and mix salt in the food to make it drink extra water, which it would store in its belly. Camels were and continue to be the ships of the desert. Abu Bakr was trying to fortify his ship.

A Plan of Assassination

With the migration of so many Muslims, Makkah was turning into a desolate city. There was hardly a house that had not been affected by the exodus. The success of the new faith and the resolve of its adherents had clearly become a mortal threat to the pagan way of life. People like Abu Jahl were seething with anger and despair, for they knew that the Prophet now had support in another city. What if the Prophet also left and Madinah became a bastion of Islam?

Occupied with these thoughts, the Quraysh convened a top-secret leadership meeting in their *Daar An-Nadwah* (the Consultative Council). Their

160 Baqarah 2:207.

only focus was what to do with the Prophet Muhammad. The who's who of the Qurayshi elite were invited to this meeting, except for two very prominent people: Abu Lahab and Mut'im bin Adiyy. This shows both tribal honor and shrewdness on their part. As for Abu Lahab, they did not want him to be part of a plot against his own nephew, which would be shameful in the tribal society. And as for Mut'im, they knew he had pledged protection to the Prophet, and it would make no sense to ask him to harm the very person he had sworn to protect.

Ibn Isshaaq wrote that as the Quraysh were about to begin their meeting, they found a handsome old man at the door. Ibn Abbaas, the famous commentator of the Qur'aan, said it was Iblees (Satan). Surprised, the Quraysh asked him who he was. He said he was a sheikh (learned man) from Najd in the north and wanted to attend their meeting so that he might help or advise them. They thought he looked like a wise man, so they invited him in.

People began to lay out their case against the Prophet, accusing him of dividing their society, insulting their idols, and posing a threat to their way of life. They noted that the threat from the new religion was increasing by the day and said the Prophet Muhammad had to be stopped somehow.

At that point, someone suggested they imprison the Prophet. Iblees interjected, saying his people would eventually free him. Another person recommended exiling him, but Iblees again objected. He said if they exiled the Prophet, he would join his followers.

It was then that Abu Jahl said, "Let me say what is on the mind of everyone but what nobody has the guts to say. Why do we not kill him?"

Iblees said, "That man is right; in my opinion it is the only thing to do!"

Abu Jahl jumped to his feet and quickly proposed a plan: "Let every tribe put forward one of its strongest warriors with a sword. All of them should attack Muhammad at once. Then there is no way the Banu Haashim will be able to fight back all the tribes, and they will be forced to accept Diya (blood money)."

Allaah Sends Gabriel to Expose the Plot

While they were hatching their dark plot, Allaah sent Gabriel to the Prophet to inform him of the plan. "Do not sleep in your bed tonight," Gabriel told him. Some years later, when Surah Anfaal was revealed, it contained a verse about this plot. Allaah says:

> *And (remember) when the disbelievers plotted against you to imprison you, or to kill you, or to expel you (from your home, Makkah); they were plotting and Allaah too was planning; and Allaah is the best of planners.*[161]

Aayeshah narrated that the Prophet used to visit Abu Bakr every day, but one day he came at high noon, when nobody visited anyone because of the intense heat. He had covered his face, but from his gait and his walking style, they recognized him. Abu Bakr said, "By Allaah, he has not come at this hour except for something important."

The Prophet asked permission to enter, and he came inside. He said to Abu Bakr, "Tell everyone who is present with you to leave."

Abu Bakr replied, "There is no one here but your family, may my father be sacrificed for you, O Messenger of Allaah!" By saying *your family*, Abu Bakr was showing respect and closeness to the Prophet. Abu Bakr had already given the Prophet his younger daughter, Aayeshah, in marriage, and he was the Prophet's closest friend.

---

161 Anfaal 8:30.

Satisfied that there was no outsider in the house, the Prophet broke the news: "I have been given permission to migrate."

Suddenly charged with expectation, Abu Bakr asked, "Companionship, O Messenger of Allaah?"

The Prophet replied, "Yes, Companionship."

Upon hearing this, Abu Bakr began to cry, and Aayeshah said, "I did not know that someone could cry out of happiness until I saw Abu Bakr crying on that day." Allaah had chosen Abu Bakr to be the only person to accompany the Prophet on this blessed migration, a fact Allaah mentioned in chapter 9, verse 40 of the Qur'aan. This special status was cited by Umar when he proposed Abu Bakr as the successor to the Prophet after his death.

Abu Bakr said, "O Messenger of Allaah, may my father be sacrificed for you; take one of these two she-camels of mine."

The Prophet said, "Only for a price." The Prophet made sure that he was making the *Hijrah* (migration) purely on his own.

Abu Bakr took some five thousand dirham, a large sum at that time, for the journey. This was all that he had left. Asmaa, Abu Bakr's older daughter, quickly prepared the baggage and put some food in a leather bag for them. Then she cut a piece from her waist belt and tied the mouth of the leather bag with it. For this reason she was nicknamed *Dhaat-un-Nitaaqayn* (the owner of the two belts).

When they were gone, Abu Quhaafah, Abu Bakr's father, turned toward Asmaa and Aayeshah and angrily complained about his son, "What kind of a father is he that he left you without money?"

Asmaa quickly put some pebbles in the money sack and jingled it in the face of her grandfather, saying, "Look, our father has left all this money for us."

Abu Quhaafah, who was a blind old man, said, "Then it is fine." He accepted Islam after the Conquest of Makkah.

With the coming of darkness, the young men of the Quraysh gathered outside the Prophet's house, lying in ambush. The Prophet had asked Ali to sleep in his bed that night, perhaps informed through revelation that the latter would be safe. True to his title of *Al-Ameen* (the Trustworthy), the Prophet had instructed Ali to return the valuables that the Makkans had deposited with him for safekeeping.

While his enemies surveilled his house, the Prophet came out and went right past them without a single one of them noticing him. The Prophet picked up a fistful of dust as he passed by and threw it at them while reciting, "And We have put a barrier before them, and a barrier behind them, and We have covered them up, so that they cannot see."[162]

From the above verse it becomes evident Allaah had momentarily taken away the sight of the ambush party.

The young men waited the whole night and were furious when, in the morning, they saw Ali emerging from the house. They realized that they had been outsmarted. The Prophet was one step ahead of them.

When Abu Jahl understood he had been outwitted, he panicked and offered a prize of one hundred of the best camels for anyone who would bring the Prophet and Abu Bakr, dead or alive. In a fit of rage, he went to Abu Bakr's house and asked Asmaa, his eldest daughter, about the whereabouts of the Prophet and her father. When told she did not know, Abu

162 Ya-Seen 36:9.

Jahl slapped her so hard across her face that her earring fell off. The man whom the Prophet had called "the Pharaoh of my nation" had no civility even toward women.

The Escape Plan

After quietly leaving his house, the Prophet and Abu Bakr went to Ghaar Thawr, a cave south of Makkah. This was exactly in the opposite direction from Madinah, but the Prophet did not want to take the well-traveled road. Abu Bakr had hired a man named Abdullaah bin Arqat as the guide because he was exceptionally knowledgeable about the "highways" and unfamiliar pathways of the time. Abdullaah was instructed to bring the two she-camels to the cave after the third night had passed. The plan was to stay in the cave for three days and nights to allow for the commotion to die down and the frantic search to end.

The Prophet and Abu Bakr kept passing by the houses of Makkah, and when they were past the city's boundaries, the Prophet turned back and said wistfully, "You are the most beloved city to me, and had my people not expelled me, I would not have left you." In another narration, he said, "Of all Allaah's earth, you are the dearest place to Allaah and to me, and if my people had not driven me out, I would never have left you."

There were other people who were part of the Hijrah plan, each with a specific job:

Abdullaah, the son of Abu Bakr, was to walk around in the streets of Makkah during the day, training his ears on what people were talking about, and he would provide the news to the Prophet and Abu Bakr at night in the cave.

Aamir bin Fuhayrah, Abu Bakr's freed slave, was to graze the flock of sheep with other shepherds by day, and when night fell he was to bring them to the cave so they could be milked for drink and so their hoofprints would erase Abdullaah's footsteps and his own.

Asmaa, Abu Bakr's daughter, was to bring them food.

Reflections: Even though Abdullaah bin Arqat was a pagan, the Prophet and Abu Bakr trusted him in this critical time. This showed once again that a Muslim can ask a non-Muslim for help if the non-Muslim is trustworthy. There was a bounty of one hundred red camels for someone who would help capture the Prophet and Abu Bakr, yet they trusted that Abdullaah would not betray them for the huge reward. What they were going to pay him for his service was a fraction of that amount.

While the Prophet and Abu Bakr were in the cave, some of the bounty hunters came right by them, and Abu Bakr panicked. "O Messenger of Allaah, if they look at their feet, they will see us."

The Prophet comforted him, saying, "What do you think of the two whose third is Allaah?"

Allaah mentions this incident in the Qur'aan, as quoted earlier:

When they were both in the cave, he said to his Companion: "Do not be sad, surely, Allaah is with us."[163]

After the search had subsided and Abu Jahl and his ilk had been thrown into despair, the Prophet and Abu Bakr came out of the cave on the third day, corresponding to the Second of Rabi' Al-Awwal (the third month in the Islamic calendar). Abdullaah bin Arqat led the way, accompanied by Aamir bin Fuhayrah. They first went south, away from Madinah, only to turn around and head north. Amazingly, the modern highway that connects

163 Tawbah 9:40.

Makkah to Madinah follows the same route and is called *Tareeq Al-Hijrah* (Path of Migration).

Not everyone in Makkah had given up hope of capturing the Prophet. Suraaqah bin Maalik, from the Bani Mudlij, thought he could achieve this feat. He had heard from a man who had just returned from the shores of the Red Sea that he had seen some people from far away heading toward Madinah. The man said he thought they were the Prophet and his fellow travelers. Suraaqah kept the information to himself because he did not want to share the prize with anyone.

Suraaqah narrated this incident some years later.

"I, too, realized that it must have been they. But I said, 'No, it is not they, but you have seen so-and-so, whom we saw set out.' I stayed in the gathering for a while and then got up and left for my home, and ordered my slave-girl to get my horse, which was behind a hillock, and keep it ready for me.

"Then I took my spear and left by the back door of my house, dragging the lower end of the spear on the ground and keeping it low. Then I reached my horse, mounted it, and made it gallop. When I approached them (the Prophet and Abu Bakr), my horse stumbled, and I fell down from it. Then I stood up, got hold of my quiver, and took out the divining arrows and drew lots as to whether I should harm them or not, and the lot that I disliked came out.

"But I remounted my horse and let it gallop, giving no importance to the divining arrows. When I heard the recitation of the Qur'aan by Allaah's Messenger, who did not look hither and thither, while Abu Bakr was doing it often, suddenly the forelegs of my horse sank into the ground up to the knees, and I fell down from it. Then I rebuked it, and it got up but could hardly take out its forelegs from the ground, and when it stood up straight again, its forelegs caused dust to rise up in the sky like smoke. Then again I drew lots with the divining arrows, and the lot that I disliked came out. So I called upon them to feel secure. They stopped, and I remounted my horse and went to them. When I realized that some unseen power had stopped me from harming them, I became convinced that the cause of Allaah's Messenger (Islam) would become victorious.

"So I said to him, 'Your people have assigned a reward equal to the blood money for your head.' Then I told them all the plans the people of Makkah had made concerning them. Then I offered them some journey food and goods, but they refused to take anything and did not ask for anything, but the Prophet said, 'Do not tell others about us.' Then I requested him to write for me a statement of security and peace. He ordered Aamir bin Fuhayrah, who wrote it for me on a parchment, and then Allaah's Messenger proceeded on his way."

In Ibn Isshaaq's version of the story, it was Abu Bakr whom the Prophet asked to write the note. This story is an integral part of the migration and has been recorded with slightly different wordings by many other Seerah historians.

In another narration, Suraaqah said that as he was returning the Prophet addressed him, "O Suraaqah, how would you be on the day when you will wear the bracelets of Kisra?"

The Arabs knew that Kisra was the emperor of Persia, so Suraaqah was shocked and exclaimed, "Kisra?"

The Prophet repeated, "Yes, Kisra, the son of Hormuz."

When Suraaqah returned to Makkah, he told the Quraysh all that had happened. Abu Jahl mocked him, saying what a fool he was to let the Prophet and Abu Bakr slip out of his hands. Suraaqah became upset and told Abu Jahl, "If you had seen what I saw, you would have realized, but you do not know."

The Persian kings were famous for wearing jewelry, and the Prophet's promise to Suraaqah that one day he would possess Kisra's bracelets seemed unbelievable, especially coming from someone who was fleeing persecution and an assassination plot.

Years later, Suraaqah became a Muslim, and the Muslim forces defeated the Persians in the Battle of Qaadisiyyah during the caliphate of Umar. When the treasures of Persia, which included Kisra's bracelets, were brought to Madinah and piled up in front of Umar, he remembered the Hadith of the Prophet and at once called for Suraaqah. Umar gave the bracelets to Suraaqah, who was overwhelmed at the sight and began to cry.

The Prophet and Abu Bakr pressed on toward Madinah. The two were traveling in different manners. While the Prophet was riding calmly and reciting the Qur'aan, Abu Bakr was tense, frequently going around the Prophet to ensure no enemy could attack him from any side. Somewhat earlier, Aamir bin Fuhayrah, the shepherd, had returned to Makkah. A while later Abdullaah bin Arqat, the guide, also left.

On the way, a traveling party passed by, and one of the members recognized Abu Bakr from years before. "Who is with you?" the man asked, referring to the Prophet.

Abu Bakr said, "He is my guide; he guides me to the path." Abu Bakr exhibited caution and wisdom here. His words could be interpreted in more than one way, a practice called *Tawriyah* that is permitted in Islam.[164] In his heart, Abu Bakr could have meant that this person (the Prophet) guided

164 Tawriyah means that a person is allowed to use a word or expression that is ambiguous and could be understood in different ways. It is used under certain circumstances to avoid lying, but it is not the norm.

him to Paradise, whereas to his acquaintance it may have sounded like he was a traveling guide.

Further along the journey, Zubayr bin Al-Awwaam, the Prophet's cousin, met them. He was part of a Muslim trade caravan that was returning from Syria. Al-Zubayr gave the Prophet and Abu Bakr new white garments, which they put on. According to another version, it was Abu Bakr's cousin Talhah who gave them the garments.

The Story of Umm Ma'bad

Before reaching Quba, the oasis adjacent to Madinah, the Prophet and Abu Bakr stopped at the tent of an elderly lady known as Umm Ma'bad and asked her for some food. She, however, had nothing to offer but a dry, boney she-goat. The Prophet asked her if he could milk the goat. Umm Ma'bad did not think the goat was capable of producing any milk, but she gave her permission anyway. Saying "in the name of Allaah," the Prophet touched its udders, and they miraculously filled up with milk. They all drank to their fill and left plenty for Umm Ma'bad's husband. When the husband came home, he was equally surprised to see the milk, and he asked where it came from.

She said, "By Allaah, a blessed man passed by our way and did so-and-so."

He said, "Describe him to me, O Umm Ma'bad."

In response she read an eloquent poem that has been one of the most important sources of the physical description of the Prophet:

"I saw a man who is handsome, of glowing countenance, and of good proportions, with neither a large stomach nor a small head. He is smart of appearance, with balanced features, deep black eyes, and long eyelashes. His voice is not coarse. He has a long neck, a full rounded beard, and thick eyebrows that meet each other. When he is silent, he is stately and composed, and when he speaks, his appearance is impressive.

"He is the most beautiful and striking man from a distance and the best and most beautiful from close up. He is well spoken, clear in what he says, saying neither too much nor too little, with his words flowing forth like a perfect string of pearls.

"He is neither too tall nor overly short, a stately man in the company of two other stately men, and he is the most prominent among them and the well-respected.

"He has Companions who surround him. If he speaks, they listen to him, and if he commands, they hasten to fulfill his command. He is well served and attended, though he is neither stern nor argumentative."[165]

Arrival in Quba

Most of the emigrants from Makkah had first stayed in Quba, and a group of local Muslims, who had heard about the Prophet's departure, eagerly awaited his arrival. Every morning, they would go to the lava field and look out in the distance, expecting the Prophet and Abu Bakr to emerge, and they would return when the sun became unbearable.

One day, after they had returned home, a loud voice rang out, saying, "O sons of Qaylah, here is your great man you have been waiting for." This was the voice of a Jewish man who was standing on his roof. He knew that the Muslims were waiting for their Prophet, and when he saw the two men emerge from a sand dune, he could not contain his excitement. Interestingly, the Jews were waiting for their Messiah, who was none other than the

165 This was recorded by Al-Haakim in his A*l-Mustadrak* (3/9–10), Al-Tabaraani in A*l-Mu'jam Al-Kabir* (3605), Abu Nu'aym in *Dalaa'il Al-Nubuwwah* (282–278), and Al-Laalikaa'i in *I'tiqaad Ahl As-Sunnah* (1434–1437).

Prophet Muhammad, but they differed, except a few, like Abdullaah bin Salaam, who accepted the Prophet and embraced Islam.

Finally the Prophet and Abu Bakr arrived and sat under a tree for shade. Scholars have differed as to the date of their arrival. According to one opinion, they arrived on 12 Rabi Al-Awwal (27 September 622 CE), exactly twelve days after they had left Makkah.

The people had not seen the Prophet or Abu Bakr, so they did not know who was who until they saw one of them shading the other with his garment when the shade moved away from him. They realized the person being shaded had to be the Prophet and gave him and Abu Bakr greetings of salaam. This incident showed the humility of the Prophet, who, despite being an unquestioned leader, did not exhibit the trappings of leadership that the worldly people do. He used to sit among his Companions so discreetly that strangers had to ask who the Messenger of God was.

The Ansaar (Helpers) were joyous to see the Prophet, whose message and virtues they had come to know from Mus'ab bin Umayr, the Prophet's ambassador to Madinah. Anas bin Maalik, a young Companion, said that "the day the Prophet came to Madinah was the happiest day."

The Prophet stayed in Quba with Kulthoom bin Al-Hadm (some say Al-Hidaam), an elderly chief of the tribe of Amr bin Awf who was known for his hospitality. While in Quba, the Prophet laid the foundation of a simple mosque that was also the first in the new land. The fact that the only thing the Prophet built in Quba was a mosque underscored the importance of people worshipping together; otherwise the believers could have prayed in their own homes.

Ali arrived a few days later and stayed with the Prophet, while Abu Bakr stayed with another host. There are a number of narrations about how many days the Messenger of Allaah stayed in Quba. They range between four and eighteen days, but the majority of scholars take the narration of Imam Bukhari, which said the Prophet stayed in Quba for ten or twelve days.

Why Madinah?

The question may well be asked, "Why did the Prophet choose Madinah, and not Taa'if or Khayber, which were also fertile lands with date-palm trees?"

There were many reasons, and it is important to know them.

The Prophet was shown in a dream that he would move to a land of date-palm trees between two lava rocks. Madinah fit this description, while Taa'if and Khayber did not.

He had blood ties with the Khazraj tribe of Madinah through his great-grandmother, Salma bint Amr, who was married to Haashim. His grandfather, Shaybah (commonly known as Abdul Muttalib), was born in Madinah and had moved to Makkah when he was a young boy. Therefore, the Prophet's leadership of Madinah could not be challenged on the basis of nationality or ethnicity.

The people of Madinah (formerly Yathrib) had become disgusted with the stubborn old leadership, which had embroiled them in needless wars. The Wars of Bu'aath, as they were called, had killed almost the entire cadre of senior leadership. The younger generation had grown tired of the old ways and was ready for fresh ideas under new leadership. When they heard the message of the Prophet, they were naturally drawn to it. Madinah was also a hospitable place and remains so to this day.

The Prophet Prays for Madinah

When the Emigrants came to Madinah, they missed Makkah, and the debilitating fever of their adopted city afflicted them. Abu Bakr's fever was so severe that he thought he would die. Aayeshah said, "When we came to

Madinah, it was among the unhealthiest of Allaah's lands, and it used to flow with impure, colored water."

Concerned about the homesickness and fever of the Emigrants, the Prophet prayed, "O Allaah! Make us love Madinah as we love Makkah or even more than that. O Allaah! Give blessings in our measures and weights, make the climate of Madinah suitable for us, and divert its fever toward Al-Juhfah (an inhabited valley)."

It is said that the tribes of Banu Matraweel and Banu Hauf were the first to inhabit and cultivate the oasis of Madinah. Both were descendants of Shem, the son of Prophet Noah. Many years later, the Yemeni tribes of Banu Aws and Banu Khazraj arrived at Madinah.

Because the Prophet graced Madinah with his presence and the resulting blessing, Madinah came to be known by ninety-five other names, each extolling its virtues. For example, Taybah (Kindness), Al-Mubarakah (the Blessed), Daar Al-Abraar (the Land of the Pious), Daar Al-Akhyaar (the Land of the Good-Doers), Daar Al-Hijrah (the Land of the Migration), and Daar As-Salaam (the Land of Peace).

The Prophet did not like Madinah's old name, Yathrib. This was in keeping with his personality. When he found a name to have a repugnant or bad meaning, he suggested changing it to one with a good meaning. The word *Yathrib* comes from *Tathreeb* (blame) or from *Tharb* (corruption). The Prophet disliked the negative connotations of the name Yathrib and renamed the city Madinah. The name Yathrib appears in the Qur'aan only from the tongues of the pagans.

There are a number of narrations from the Prophet about the superiority of Madinah. He said, "Madinah is a *haram* (sacred sanctuary). Its trees should not be cut, and no heresy should be innovated nor any sin should be committed in it, and whoever innovates in it a heresy or commits sins, then he will incur the curse of Allaah, the angels, and all the people."

Abu Hurayrah narrated, "If I saw deer grazing in Madinah, I would not chase them, for Allaah's Apostle said, 'Madinah is a sanctuary between its two mountains.'"

The Prophet said, "The terror caused by Al-Masih Ad-Dajjaal (the Antichrist) will not enter Madinah, and at that time Madinah will have seven gates, and there will be two angels at each gate guarding them."

The Prophet is reported to have supplicated, "O Allaah! Bestow on Madinah twice the blessings You bestowed on Makkah."

Whenever the Prophet returned from a journey and saw the silhouettes of Madinah, he would make his camel go faster, and if he was on a horse, he would make it gallop because of his love for the city.

More than ten thousand Companions are buried in Madinah, including the Prophet's entire family except his first wife Khadijah and his son Abdullaah.

Which Is Superior, Makkah or Madinah?

Muslim jurists are unanimous that Makkah and Madinah are the two most sacred places on earth, but they have differed as to which is higher in status. The majority of the jurists, including the Hanafis, Shaafa'is, and Hanbalis, as well as some Maalikis, view Makkah as superior to Madinah, for the following reasons:

- Allaah has ordered Muslims to pray in the direction of Makkah.
- The obligatory Hajj can only be performed in Makkah.
- The Prophet stayed in Makkah for fifty-three years, whereas he stayed only ten years in Madinah.
- A large number of prophets and messengers are said to have visited Makkah. Also, more people visit Makkah than Madinah.

- The Black Stone that came from Paradise and that the pilgrims kiss is in Makkah.
- Allaah made Makkah a sanctuary on the day He created the heavens and the earth, and it was not permissible for any of the messengers and prophets to fight therein except our Prophet, and even for him it was permitted for a short time on the day of the Conquest of Makkah.
- Allaah praised the Ka'bah in the Qur'aan, but He did not praise Madinah in this manner: "Verily, the first House (of worship) appointed for mankind was that at Bakkah (Makkah), full of blessing, and a guidance for the worlds."[166]
- One unit of prayer in the Grand Mosque in Makkah is equivalent to one hundred thousand units of prayer offered elsewhere. Comparatively, one unit of prayer in the Prophet's Mosque in Madinah is equivalent only to one thousand units of prayer elsewhere.

The Move to Madinah

After staying in Quba for a little less than two weeks, the Prophet sent for the Banu An-Najjaar, the tribe of his maternal great-grandmother, to come and escort him and his entourage to Madinah. The people of Madinah, the Ansaar (Helpers), lined up to greet him, each vying to host him, but the Prophet was silent. People would hold the halter of Al-Qaswa, the Prophet's she-camel, and plead, "Alight here, O Messenger of Allaah; stay with us," only to be told, "Let her go; she is under the command of Allaah."

After moving through the streets of Madinah, Al-Qaswa left the road and entered a large courtyard that seemed like the ruins of a building. There were a few date-palm trees and an area set aside for drying dates. She slowly moved to a small enclosure, which As'ad bin Zuraarah had set up as a prayer area. As'ad was one of the six people from Madinah who

166 Aal Imraan 3:96.

had accepted Islam in the eleventh year of the Prophethood in Makkah during Hajj. Al-Qaswa knelt for a moment but then got up and began to walk again. Then she turned back to the place of the first kneeling and sat. The Prophet alighted and said, "*InshaAllaah* (God willing), this is my dwelling."

The Prophet asked about the owner of the courtyard. It turned out it belonged to two young orphan brothers, Sahl and Suhayl, who were under the stewardship of As'ad. When the Prophet asked them if they would sell the land to him, they said, "No, but we give it to you as a gift, O Messenger of God." The Prophet nevertheless had a price negotiated with As'ad's help, and he purchased the land. It was on this land that the Prophet's house and the mosque were built some weeks later.

The area was the neighborhood of the Banu An-Najjaar, and the Prophet asked for his closest relatives living there. Abu Ayyub Al-Ansaari came forward and said that he was his closest relative, from his great-grandmother's side, and he quickly carried the Prophet's baggage into his house. Abu Ayyub had already embraced Islam at the Second Pledge of Aqabah. Abu Ayyub was ecstatic that, of all people, the Prophet was going to stay in his house. His was a two-story dwelling, and the Prophet stayed on the first floor while Abu Ayyub and his family moved upstairs. The Prophet's wife Sawdah, an older lady whom he had married after Khadijah's death, and two of his daughters, Faatimah and Umm Kulthoom, joined later.

Disobeying the Prophet Out of Love

Abu Ayyub and his wife were extra hospitable to their honorable guest, cooking the best food they could and making sure his needs were well taken care of. They were in such awe and love of the Prophet that when the food platter they had sent to him came back, they would eat from the very spot where he had eaten. The Prophet ate very little, advising his followers to eat enough to fill one-third of the stomach, drink enough to fill one-third, and leave the last third for air.

One day, the food came back untouched. Abu Ayyub and his wife panicked, wondering what they could have done wrong. The Prophet told them he did not eat the food because there was garlic in it. He did not like the smell of raw garlic and onion, and he told his Companions to avoid coming to the mosque if they smelled of them. Aware that the Prophet's ruling was only about raw garlic and onion, Umar once told the people that if they must eat them, then they had better cook them well.

Love can have a strange effect on people. Abu Ayyub and his wife one day realized that they were sleeping above the Prophet, and they felt that this was not respectful. So the next day they went to the Prophet and said there was no way they would sleep upstairs while he slept downstairs. The Prophet told them he preferred to stay downstairs because people often visited him, but Abu Ayyub did not budge. The Prophet eventually had to move upstairs. This incident showed that a person can feel compelled to disrespect his leader, and not just any leader but a Prophet of God, out of love.

The Prophet's Marriages after Khadijah

Before we continue with life in Madinah, it seems appropriate to discuss the Prophet's marital life, as it has been the subject of intense debate, even criticism, in some circles. Contrary to the negative picture of his personal life his critics have painted, an unbiased study finds nothing reproachable. The suggestion that he was lustful is simply ludicrous in view of the historical truth.

The Prophet had married Khadijah when he was twenty-five, and she was much older and twice widowed. Given that he was the most handsome and noble man, he could have easily married a young virgin. The two remained happily married for over twenty-five years, until Khadijah, who bore him all his children except one, passed away. This cannot be the profile of a man who was driven by lust.

Khadijah's passing had deprived the Prophet of his most loving Companion and trusted advisor. Besides mourning her loss, he was also faced with the difficult task of raising his minor children. It was around the time the Prophet was living as a single parent, looking after his children and conveying God's message, that Khawlah bint Hakeem, the wife of Uthmaan bin Maz'oon, both of whom later migrated to Abyssinia, came to the Messenger of Allaah and said, "Would you not like to remarry?"

The Prophet asked, "Marry whom?"

She said he should marry a virgin, a widow, or a divorcee. When the Prophet asked her who they were, Khawlah said, "As for the virgin, she is Aayeshah, the daughter of a person who is most beloved to you, and as for the widow, she is Sawdah, who believes in you."

The Prophet said, "Go and mention me to them." This incident happened a few months before the migration.

Sawdah, the daughter of Zam'ah, was older and a rather large figure. She had migrated to Abyssinia along with her first husband, Sakran bin Amr. When Sakran died in Abyssinia, Sawdah was left in a precarious condition in a foreign land. The Prophet recognized her sacrifices and honored her by marrying her. She became a foster mother to the Prophet's children. In later years she gave away some of her nights to Aayeshah out of consideration for the Prophet's love for Aayeshah.

The story of the Prophet marrying Aayeshah is quite interesting. In a Hadith that Aayeshah herself narrated, Gabriel had shown her to the Prophet in a dream, saying, "This is your wife."

The Prophet had responded, "If it is from Allaah, then it will be so."

When Khawlah bint Hakeem, the lady who had facilitated the Prophet's marriage to Sawdah, took the proposal to Aayeshah's house, her father, Abu Bakr, was not home. When he was informed, Abu Bakr accepted the proposal but was concerned on two accounts: first, he had already approved an earlier proposal for Aayeshah on behalf of the son of Mut'im bin Adiyy, and second, Abu Bakr considered himself to be like a brother to the Prophet; therefore, it would be odd if the Prophet were to marry his daughter.

As for the first concern, Abu Bakr asked Mut'im if the proposal for his son was still valid. Muti'm's wife responded that she was worried that Abu Bakr's daughter would turn their son away from the religion of their forefathers, meaning polytheism. Mut'im concurred, and the proposal was withdrawn. Abu Bakr felt relieved that he was no longer beholden to that promise.

As for Abu Bakr's other concern, that the Prophet was like a brother to him, the Prophet explained that their brotherhood was Islamic, not biological, and, therefore, there was no problem with him marrying Aayeshah.

Aayeshah and the Age of Marriage in Islam

Aayeshah's young age at the time of her marriage to the Prophet has been one of the favorite talking points by non-Muslims in the last few centuries. However, it was not controversial in those times. In fact, the pagans did not attack the Prophet's character on account of his marriage to Aayeshah.

In Islam, there is no set minimum age for a woman's marriage. However, the consummation of marriage cannot happen until the girl reaches the age of puberty. It is said that girls entered puberty earlier in Arabia because of the climate. Even in the United States, it has been reported that some girls reach puberty at eight or nine years of age.

It is only in our time that people have legislated the minimum age for a woman's marriage to be eighteen, but even then they allow a sixteen-year-old to be married with parental consent.

Today, with greater knowledge of human biology, we can understand that the reason the Creator did not set a specific age for a girl's marriage is that girls reach puberty at different ages.

How Old Was Aayeshah at Marriage?

The majority of Muslim scholars have said that Aayeshah was nine when she was sent off to live with the Prophet. One of the proofs they have used is Aayeshah's own statement, recorded in Bukhari, volume 5, book 58, Hadith #234. However, there is also a strong dissenting opinion that contends that Aayeshah was much older. To support their position, they offer this evidence:

- The opinion that Aayeshah was nine years old is based primarily on the narration of Hishaam bin Urwah, who was a grandson of Asmaa bint Abi Bakr and had never seen the Prophet.
- Ibn Hishaam's narration regarding Aayeshah's age came after he had moved to Iraq, when he was very old and had an unreliable memory.
- The discrepancy in the narrations about the birth of Aayeshah, with some saying she was born in the pre-Islamic days, would put her at fourteen years of age at the time of the Migration.
- According to one opinion of At-Tabari, Aayeshah was betrothed at seven years of age and began to cohabit with the Prophet at the age of nine. However, in another work, At-Tabari says, "All four of

Abu Bakr's children were born in the pre-Islamic period.[167] This puts Aayeshah's marriage contract at fourteen and send-off at sixteen. One opinion even puts her age at nineteen at the time of cohabitation.

- According to Ibn Hajar Al-Asqalaani, the Prophet's daughter Faatimah was five years older than Aayeshah. Faatimah is reported to have been born when the Prophet Muhammad was thirty-five years old, which means Aayeshah was born when he was forty years old, and she was twelve when he married her at fifty-two.[168]
- There are verses in the Qur'aan (such as those below) that state that a girl is considered able to take on responsibility when she is in the age of puberty and mature:

And test orphans until they reach the age of marriage; if then you find sound judgment in them, release their property to them.[169]

And come not near to the orphan's property, except to improve it, until he (or she) attains the age of full strength.[170]

Marriage Age Since 1880

While girls were typically married around the age of puberty over a millennium ago, it is interesting to note that just 150 years ago the marriage age for girls in many of the US states was ten. According to the Center for History and New Media, the minimum marriage age in the US state of

167 *Tarikhul-Umam wal-Mamluk* (Beirut: Daar Al-Fikr, 1979), 4:50.

168 Ibn Hajar Aal-Asqalani, *Al-isabah fi Tamyizi'l-Sahabah* (Riyadh: Maktabatul Riyadh Al-Haditha, 1978), 4:377.

169 Nisaa 4:6.

170 An'aam 6:152.

Delaware was seven for girls. The table below shows the legal age for marriage in 1880 and after:

	1880	1920	2007
Russia	10	14	16
United States			
Alabama	10	16	16
Alaska	-	16	16
Arizona	12	18	18
Arkansas	10	16	16
California	10	18	18
Colorado	10	18	15
Connecticut	10	16	16
District of Columbia	12	16	16
Delaware	7	16	16
Florida	10	18	18
Georgia	10	14	16
Idaho	10	18	18
Illinois	10	16	17
Indiana	12	16	16
Iowa	10	16	16
Kansas	10	18	16
Kentucky	12	16	16
Louisiana	12	18	17
Maine	10	16	16
Maryland	10	16	16
Massachusetts	10	16	16
Michigan	10	16	16
Minnesota	10	18	16
Mississippi	10	18	16
Missouri	12	18	17
Montana	10	18	16
Nebraska	10	18	17
Nevada	12	18	16
New Hampshire	10	16	16
New Jersey	10	16	16
New Mexico	10	16	17
New York	10	18	17
North Carolina	10	16	16
North Dakota	10	18	18
Ohio	10	16	16

The Status of Aayeshah

Muslims have debated who was the Prophet's most beloved wife, Khadijah or Aayeshah. The fact is that both Khadijah and Aayeshah enjoyed a superior status among the Prophet's wives, and they had some things that were unique about them.

Aayeshah herself said she had been given special honors over the Prophet's other wives in the following things:

- The Prophet did not marry any virgin other than her.
- He did not marry a woman whose parents were both Emigrants except her.
- Allaah revealed several verses of the Qur'aan from the heavens regarding her innocence (Nur, chapter 24).
- Gabriel brought her picture from the heaven in silk and said to the Prophet, "Marry her; she is your wife."
- He and she used to bathe from the same vessel, and he did not do that with any of his wives except her.
- The revelation would come to him while he was with her, and it did not come down when he was with any of his wives except her.
- Allaah took his soul while he was propped up against her chest.
- He died on the night when it was her turn.
- And he was buried in her room.[171]

The Prophet's Mosque

The Prophet ordered his followers to build a mosque where the courtyard of the orphan brothers, Sahl and Suhayl, was located, and the work began in earnest. As in Quba, the Prophet made it clear that a place of communal worship was to be the centerpiece of a Muslim community's life. Everything needed to revolve around that focal point. The mosque was a simple structure built with bricks, stones, mud, and the trunks of date-palm trees.

171 Tabaqaat Ibn Sa'ad, 8:88.

The mosque had three doors: *Baab Ar-Rahmah* (the Door of Mercy) to the south, *Baab Al-Jibreel* (the Door of Gabriel) to the west, and *Baab Al-Nisaa* (the Door of Women) to the east. The niche where the Prophet stood to lead people in prayer was to the north, facing Jerusalem. When the qiblah (prayer direction) was changed to Makkah, the mosque was reoriented to the south. In just a few years, the mosque had to be doubled in size to accommodate the increasing number of Muslims.

The Prophet's Mosque was the nerve center of Muslim life. It was from here that armies were sent for *Jihaad* (fighting),[172] and scholars were trained under the direct guidance of the Prophet himself. The apartments of the Prophet's wives were built next to the mosque, and their doors opened into the courtyard. Some other people, including Abu Bakr, had also built dwellings adjacent to the mosque. Among the last instructions the Prophet gave before his death was that all the doors that opened into the mosque should be shut except the door of Abu Bakr. This, in the view of some, was to signify Abu Bakr's status.

The Story of the Adhaan

The Muslims prayed in Madinah without fear of being attacked, and the community kept growing. With the growth came new challenges, one of which was how to inform Muslims about the prayer time. There were no clocks or alarms back then. People would gather and guess that it was time for prayer based on the time of the day or night. They began to discuss a way to come up with an effective method to determine the prayer time and inform others of it. Some suggested using a bell like the Christians did, while others proposed blowing a horn (trumpet) like the Jews, yet others suggested lighting a fire. The Prophet did not approve any of those suggestions.

172 The Arabic term *Jihaad* means to strive. It can also mean to fight in the path of God. However, Jihaad never means *holy war*, as it is popularly translated by non-Muslims or portrayed in the media.

One day, a Sahaabi named Abdullaah bin Zayd came to Prophet Muhammad and said that the night before he had had a dream in which a man wearing green garments taught him words by which to call people to prayer. When the Prophet asked him what those words were, Abdullaah said:

Allaahu Akbar
God is greater

Ash-hadu An La Ilaaha illa Allaah
I bear witness that there is no god except the One God

Ash-hadu Anna Muhammadan Rasul Allaah
I bear witness that Muhammad is the Messenger of God

Hayya Alas-Salaah
Come to prayer

Hayya Alal-Falaah
Come to success (Rise up for Salvation)

Allaahu Akbar
God is greater

La Ilaaha Illa Allaah
There is no god except the One God

The Prophet approved Abdullaah's dream as God-inspired and announced that henceforth the *Adhaan* (call to prayer) would be issued in those words. Not long after that, Umar bin Al-Khattaab came running and said he, too, had seen the exact same dream, but Abdullaah bin Zayd had already beaten him to it.

The Prophet asked Abdullaah to teach Bilaal bin Rabaah the words of the Adhaan. Bilaal was known for his powerful voice. From then onward

Bilaal became one of the two *Mu'adhdhins* (callers) of the Prophet, the other being Abdullaah bin Umm Maktoom.

Reflections: One might say that the dream of a *Sahaabi* (Companion) became a source of religious injunction for Muslims for all time to come. However, it should be noted that this dream became legislation only after the Prophet approved its message. As to why two Companions were chosen for this dream instead of the Prophet, that is something whose reality is known only to Allaah. In another interesting incident related to the Adhaan, Bilaal one morning came to the Prophet to see if he was ready for the dawn prayer. When Bilaal saw that the Prophet was sleeping, he said, "As-salaatu khayrum-minan-nawm" (prayer is better than sleep). The Prophet woke up and approved of what Bilaal had said. The Prophet ordered this phrase to be added to the call of the dawn prayer, and it has been used ever since.

The Madinah Charter

As soon as the Prophet set foot in Madinah, he approved a simple but profound charter that affirmed the brotherhood of faith among Muslims and a universal brotherhood among all citizens of the city-state. It affirmed the rights and duties of Muslims, as well as Jews, Christians, and pagans, and proclaimed freedom of religion for everyone. It was the best example of a pluralistic society coexisting in peace and harmony. The Prophet called the signatories of the charter one *Ummah* (one nation).

As the undisputed leader of Madinah, the Prophet Muhammad exercised jurisdiction over non-Muslims as well as Muslims. A greater legitimacy to his rule came from his status as the Prophet of Allaah. The charter was signed by the *Muhaajireen* (Muslim immigrants from Makkah), the *Ansaar* (indigenous Muslims of Madinah), and the *Yahud* (Jews). It is interesting to note that the Jews were constitutional partners in the making of the first Islamic government.

In the Western parlance, the agreement of the Messenger of God with the inhabitants of the city was akin to a social contract that, centuries later, Western political thinkers like Jean-Jacques Rousseau and John Locke expounded and the American Mayflower Compact offered. But the Madinah Charter was different from them in that it was both a social contract and a blueprint of an elementary constitution. It should be noted, however, that the Madinah Charter by itself cannot be compared to a modern constitution since it was quite limited in its scope.

Attesting to its brilliance, the Madinah Charter illustrated a successful model of relationship between the divine revelation and a covenant, incorporating opinions of the constituents. In his great wisdom, the Prophet demonstrated a democratic spirit. He chose to empower people as long as they did not contradict the fundamental laws of their Creator. This was exhibited in articles of the charter. (See Appendix for articles of the Madinah Charter.)

Although Madinah was just a city-state, its charter lasted until the beginning of the Umayyad Dynasty in 1661. It inspired the enlightened Muslim rule in southern Spain, called Andalusia, and the Ottoman Empire, the last Muslim caliphate, whose seat was in Turkey and which ended in 1924.

Some think that the Madinah Charter was the first written constitution in the world. They say that Aristotle's treatise known as the Constitution of Athens was actually an account of the constitution of the city-state of Athens and not the constitution itself. In any event, the world does not know much about the Athenian document. Other legal writings on the conduct of ancient societies have been found, but none can be described as a constitution. In our modern time, the US Constitution of 1787 is a landmark document, but it came one thousand years after the Madinah Charter.

Upon a close examination of the US Constitution, we find that it contains many of the core values embodied in the Madinah Charter. The

God-inspired ideals of governance epitomized by the Madinah Charter influenced many intellectuals around the world, including the framers of the US Constitution. More importantly, Muslim progress resulting from critical thinking, research and development, and reliance on God helped usher in the European Renaissance.

Amid the tumult of today, Muslims should take heart in the fact that what gave them glory in the past can certainly make them ascendant again. God gave us victory and honor as long as we followed His prescription for success. Pursuing any other means to rebound from the current state will only lead to more disarray and dejection. Can a people with the best roadmap be lost while they follow it?

Jewish-Muslim Relations in the New Land

When the Prophet arrived in Madinah, he learned firsthand about the existence of a several-thousand-strong Jewish community. Given that the Jews believed in One God and were People of the Book, the Prophet felt a natural affinity toward them. He extended a hand of friendship to the Jews and called them "one community" along with Muslims. When he found Jews fasting on the Day of Aashoora, he asked why they did so. They told him that it was to commemorate the fasting of the Prophet Moses (Musa) at the freeing of the Children of Israel from Pharaoh. To show respect to Prophet Moses, the Prophet fasted on Aashoora and ordered his followers to do so as well. Since then many Muslims have fasted on this day as a voluntary fast.[173]

The Jews of Madinah were waiting for their Messiah before the Prophet Muhammad's arrival. And so, when the Prophet came to Madinah, it was easy for them to verify the signs he came with as foretold in their book.

The Qur'aan leaves no doubt that the Jews and Christians were informed with certainty about the coming of the Prophet Muhammad.

---

173 Aashoora is the tenth day in the Islamic month of Muharram.

> *Those to whom We gave the Scripture (Jews and Christians) recognize him as they recognize their sons. But verily, a party of them conceal the truth while they know it.*[174]

However, the Jewish response was not positive. Their main problem was that the Prophet Muhammad was not a descendant of Isaac (Isshaaq) but of Ishmael (Ismaa'il), Prophet Abraham's first son. This feeling was so strong among them that it did not matter that their book had already foretold that the Prophet Muhammad would be from the brothers of the Children of Israel, meaning the Arabs.

One of the interesting examples of Jewish recognition of the Prophet Muhammad as a prophet of God and of their outward rejection of him is found in an incident that Safiyyah bint Huyayy narrated. Safiyyah was daughter of the Huyayy bin Akhtab, leader of the Jewish tribe of Banu Nadheer. The Prophet married her after the Battle of Khayber.

After the marriage Safiyyah narrated a childhood story that showed that the Jews' outward attitude toward the Prophet stood in conflict with their inner belief. She said:

> *I was my father's favorite and also a favorite with my uncle Yaasir. They could never see me with one of their children without picking me up. When the Messenger of Allaah came to Madinah, my father and my uncle went to see him. It was very early in the morning, between dawn and sunrise. They did not return until the sun was setting. They came back worn out and depressed, walking with slow, heavy steps. I smiled to them as I always did, but neither of them took any notice of me because they were so miserable. I heard my uncle ask my father, 'Is it him?' My father said, 'No doubt, it is him.' My uncle asked, 'What should we do now?' My father responded, 'I will oppose him as long as I live.'"*[175]

---

174 Baqarah 2:146.

175 Safiur-Rahman Mubarakpuri, *The Sealed Nectar*. Riyadh: Darussalam

Against this backdrop, the Prophet's rapprochement with the Jews did not flourish. Frictions began to appear. That they had rejected the Prophet as a true prophet of God in defiance of their own belief was one problem. But a bigger problem was that some of the Jewish leadership tried to kill him.

Abdullaah bin Salaam, the Jewish Rabbi

While the overall state of Jewish-Muslim relations had turned sour, there were some hopeful moments, one of which was the story of Abdullaah bin Salaam, the Jewish rabbi.

Abdullaah was the leader of his people as well as their scholar. When he learned that a man in Makkah had announced he was a prophet of God, Abdullaah quickly realized that he was indeed the Prophet foretold in the Tawraat (Torah). And as soon as the Prophet came to Madinah, Abdullaah embraced Islam. His coming into Islam was a promising sign, but with some twists. Abdullaah narrated his own story thus:

"When I heard about the Prophet, I knew from his description, his name, and the time at which he appeared that he was the one we were waiting for, and rejoiced greatly at that, although I kept silent until the Prophet came to Madinah. When he came to Quba, a man came with the news while I was working at the top of a palm tree and my aunt Khaalidah bint Al-Haarith was sitting below. When I heard the news, I cried, 'Allaahu Akbar,' and my aunt said, 'Good gracious, if Musa (Moses) bin Imraan had come, you would not have shown such excitement.' I said, 'He is the brother of Musa and follows his religion.' Straightway I went to the Prophet and became a Muslim."

In another narration, Abdullaah said, "When the Messenger of Allaah came to Madinah, the people rushed toward him and said, 'The Messenger of Allaah has come!' I came along with the people to see him, and when I looked at the face of the Messenger of Allaah, I realized that his face was not the face of a liar. The first thing he said was, 'O people, spread (the greeting of) Salaam, offer food to people, join the ties of kinship, and pray at night when people are sleeping, you will enter Paradise in peace.'"[176]

However, Abdullaah knew full well that his people would despise him for his decision to leave Judaism for Islam. He told the Prophet about his apprehensions, and when the Jews came to meet with the Prophet, Abdullaah hid behind a curtain.

The Prophet asked the Jewish visitors what they thought about Abdullaah. They heaped their praises on him, saying, "He is our chief, the son of our chief, our rabbi, and our learned man."

Then Abdullaah bin Salaam came out, announced that he had become a Muslim, and admonished his people, "O Jews, fear God and accept what He has sent you. For by God, you know that he is the Prophet of God. You will find him described in your Torah and even named."

The Jewish delegates became furious at Abdullaah and cursed him, calling him a liar.

The Best of Jews

Another inspiring incident came a couple of years later when Mukhayriq, a leader of the Jewish tribe of Bani Tha'alabah, came to defend the Prophet at the Battle of Uhud in 3 AH (624/625 CE). Like Abdullaah bin Salaam, Mukhayriq was also a rabbi and wealthy. On the Day of Uhud, Mukhayriq urged his people to support Muhammad against the pagan army from Makkah. He reminded them that, being the signatories of the Madinah Charter, they had no choice but to defend the city against external threat.

176 Sunan Ibn Maajah, 1334.

But the Jewish leaders excused themselves, saying it was Sabbath and they would not fight on this day. Mukhayriq rejected their excuse. Saying, "May you not have a Sabbath," he plunged into the battle and died fighting on the side of the Muslims. Before going into the fight, he had made a last will that specified that, if he died, all his wealth should go to the Prophet Muhammad. When Mukhayriq died in the battle, the Prophet praised him, saying, "Mukhayriq was the best of Jews."

Muwaakhaah—An Exemplary Brotherhood

Barring exceptions, the Emigrants from Makkah were destitute. In most cases they had come to Madinah with the clothes on their back. The Prophet was deeply concerned about their well-being and felt sad at their plight. Realizing that something practical needed to be done to help the Emigrants, the Prophet announced that he would personally join an Emigrant in brotherhood with a local Muslim. These were some examples of the pairings:

Bilaal bin Rabaah with Abdullaah bin Abdur Rahmaan
Ammaar bin Yaasir with Hudhayfah Al-Yamaan
Abu Bakr with Khaarijah bin Zayd
Umar bin Al-Khattaab with Utbaan bin Maalik
Uthmaan bin Affaan with Aws bin Thaabit
Abu Dharr Al-Ghifaari with Al-Mundhir bin Amr
Mus'ab bin Umayr with Abu Ayyub Al-Ansaari
Abu Ubaydah bin Al-Jarraah with Sa'ad bin Mu'aadh
Zubayr bin Al-Awwaam with Salaamah bin Waqsh
Abdur Rahmaan bin Awf with Sa'ad bin Rabi'ah
Talhah bin Ubaydullaah with Ka'ab bin Maalik

Ali bin Abi Taalib alone was left without a brother. When he expressed unease at his situation, the Apostle of God held him by his arms and said to him, "You are my brother in this world and in the next." We do not know whether the Prophet had deliberately not assigned someone to Ali in order to honor him like this.

The brotherhood among the Emigrants and Helpers was unique. A local Muslim would provide his brother-in-faith from Makkah with food, shelter, and clothing. Some would go even further. In the case of Sa'ad bin Rabi'ah, he told his Emigrant brother Abdur Rahmaan to take half of everything he had. Abdur Rahmaan thankfully declined and instead asked to be shown the marketplace so he could buy and sell. Had it not been for this immense generosity, many Emigrants would have ended up being homeless. This brotherhood even joined a former slave with a freeman, like Bilaal bin Rabaah and Abdullaah bin Abdur Rahmaan. The bond of faith proved stronger than anything else.

The Prophet realized that taking financial and other help from the Helpers would compromise the dignity of the Emigrants. As such, he urged the Emigrants to help their local brothers-in-faith with their labor, working in their farms and assisting with other chores. The Prophet also discouraged the Helpers from giving away too much of their wealth. There had to be a delicate balance, and the Prophet was able to maintain it with excellence. The Emigrants deeply appreciated the sacrifices of the Helpers, and when, after the conquest of Khayber and Hunayn, wealth came to them, some of them returned the lands of their local brothers.

People of the Shed

The Prophet had established another group for a special kind of people. They came to be known as *As-haab As-Suffah*. Roughly translated, *Suffah* means a shed or a raised platform, and so they came to be known as People of the Shed. The Shed was a covered area in the Prophet's mosque that had some benches or raised platforms where the poor and the students of knowledge used to sit. This was the only area in the mosque that had a roof to protect them from the rain and sun, leaving the rest of the mosque exposed to the elements.

This was effectively the first Islamic seminary, a religious boarding school where the main teacher was Muhammad, the Messenger of Allaah.

How excellent and fortunate were those students who learned directly from the one to whom the revelation came! And how enviable is the status of those who were chosen to be this teacher's assistants!

The Companions who stayed at the *Suffah* did not have a house, or a tribe, or relatives, or anything else to support them. In material terms, they were the poorest of the poor, but in knowledge they were elite among the Prophet's Companions.

It is said that Allaah revealed the following verse about them:

> *Charity is for the poor, who in Allaah's cause are restricted (from travel), and cannot move about in the land (for trade or work). The one who does not know them, thinks that they are rich because of their modesty. You may know them by their mark, they do not beg of people at all.*[177] (Baqarah 2:273)

To support *As-haab As-Suffah,* the Prophet announced that "whoever has food for two persons should take a third one from them. And whosoever has food for four persons, he should take one or two from them." The Prophet himself took ten men, and Abu Bakr took three. The ones who got married would then leave the *Suffah,* and others would join to take their place. The Prophet deeply cared about *As-haab As-Suffah,* and they preferred the poverty of the Shed to earning money in the marketplace because it gave them more facetime with the Prophet.

According to some reports, the number of students would reach as high as eighty-nine (see Appendix), but it fluctuated for various reasons. The people of *Suffah* also included a few who had homes but preferred to stay there because of the opportunity to learn from the Prophet.

177 Baqarah 2:273.

One of them was Abu Hurayrah, whose real name was Abdur Rahmaan but whom the Prophet affectionately called "father of the kitten" because of his love for cats. He had come to Madinah in 6 AH (627/628 CE) and decided to spend every moment he could find with the Prophet, even though his mother had a house in the city. Because of this, Abu Hurayrah became one of the top students of the Prophet, narrating the highest number of Hadith (Prophetic traditions). Considering he spent only four years with the Prophet, this was an amazing feat. When someone expressed uneasiness about the number of Hadith Abu Hurayrah had narrated, he responded that he had conveyed so many of the traditions only because of Allaah's warning to those who conceal knowledge:

> *Verily, those who conceal the clear proofs, evidences and the guidance, which We have sent down, after We have made it clear for the People in the Book, they are the ones cursed by Allaah and cursed by the cursers.*[178]

At one point Abu Hurayrah explained how he was able to collect so many Hadith. "Do not find it strange that I have narrated too many Hadith! As our immigrant brothers were occupied with trade in the marketplace and our Ansaar brothers with agriculture in gardens and fields, I was memorizing the Prophet's blessed advice."

Sometimes when he was starving, Abu Hurayrah would ask a Sahaabi about a verse of the Qur'aan even though he knew the answer better than the Sahaabi did. He would keep walking with the Sahaabi until the latter reached his house, hoping that out of courtesy he would invite Abu Hurayrah inside and offer him some food.

Once, extreme pangs of hunger took Abu Hurayrah out of his house. He saw Abu Bakr passing by and asked him a question, which the latter answered and then moved on. Then Umar happened to come by, and the same thing happened. Neither realized what Abu Hurayrah was going through.

---

178 Baqarah 2:159.

Then came the Prophet, who immediately understood Abu Hurayrah's plight. He called him, "O Abu Hurayrah."

The latter responded, with utmost devotion, "At your service, O Messenger of Allaah."

The Prophet asked Abu Hurayrah to follow him to his house. There was no food in the Prophet's house except for a bowl of milk that someone had sent. The Prophet told Abu Hurayrah to call the rest of *As-haab As-Suffah*. Abu Hurayrah thought he might not get enough milk if everybody came, since it was a single bowl of milk. But this was a command from the Prophet, and Abu Hurayrah could not have disobeyed him.

Abu Hurayrah narrated the story himself. "I was upset because the Messenger of God had invited the *As-haab As-Suffah*. I was hoping to drink all of the milk and live by it for some time. I said to myself, 'I am only an envoy. I will share the milk among the *Suffah* Companions when they come.' In this case, I knew no milk would be left for me. However, I had no other choice but to follow the order from the Messenger of God. I went and called them. They came and sat after being permitted.

"The Prophet said, 'O Abu Hurayrah, take the jug and offer them milk.' I took the jug and started to give them the milk. Each of them, one by one, took the jug and drank until he was full and then passed it to the next person. After the last *Suffah* Companion drank, I gave the jug to the Messenger of God. He took it. There was only a little milk left inside. He raised his head and looked at me, smiling.

"'Abu Hurayrah!' he said.

"'Yes, Messenger of God,' I said.

"'Only you and I did not drink milk,' he said.

"'Yes, Messenger of God,' I said.

"'Sit down and drink,' he said. I sat down and drank. 'Drink some more,' the Prophet said. I did. He insisted that I should drink more. 'More, more!' he said.

"At last I said, 'I swear by God Who has sent you with the true religion that I am too full to drink any more!'

"'Then give me the jug,' he said. I did. He gave thanks to God. Then he said 'Bismi Allaah' and drank the rest."

A Fair Marketplace

On the periphery of Madinah, there was a large market that was dominated by the Jews. When the Prophet made rounds of the marketplace, he observed dishonest practices such as cheating and deception. The Prophet had an aversion to marketplaces in general, and he told his followers that markets were the most disliked place on earth to Allaah, while the mosques were the most beloved to Him. However, the Prophet was a realist, and he knew that people had to buy and sell in order to live. Therefore, he ordered the construction of a marketplace inside Madinah on the principles of Islam: honesty, integrity, and transparency.

He personally demarcated the boundaries of this marketplace and laid down certain laws. For example, the Prophet said that nobody who lived in Madinah could be a middleman between an outside buyer and a local merchant. It is well-known in our age that sometimes the middlemen make more profit than the seller. So the Prophet's edict required a direct connection between buyer and seller.

The Prophet also forbade the bartering of a small quantity of good-quality dates for a greater quantity of poor-quality dates. He said that is *Riba* (usury) and therefore prohibited. But he allowed selling the good-quality dates and then buying the poor-quality dates with money. When the Prophet found out that a merchant had good-quality dates on the top of the bag and rotten ones in the bottom, he told him, "He who cheats is not from us." One main purpose of these rulings was to connect business to religion and piety. A Muslim who cheated in his business dealings would go against his religion and earn the wrath of Allaah.

A Revelation against Cheaters

Abdullaah bin Abbaas reported that when the Prophet came to Madinah, the people of the city were notorious for cheating in measurements. So Allaah revealed Surah Al-Mutaffifeen (The Defrauders) in order to warn them.

> *Woe to Al-Mutaffifeen. Those who, when they receive by measure from men, demand full measure. And when they give by measure or weight to men, give less than due.*[179]

Allaah informed the Muslims that He had destroyed the people of the Prophet Shu'ayb because of their cheating in weights and measurements.

A New Prayer Direction

When the Prophet Muhammad was in Makkah, he faced Jerusalem in prayer because that was the direction in which Muslims were required to pray. Allaah had blessed Jerusalem and its environs.[180] After building the Ka'bah in Makkah with assistance from his older son, Ishmael, the Prophet Abraham had moved to Palestine. But the Ka'bah remained the First House of God on earth. The Prophet Muhammad loved and revered the Ka'bah,

179 Mutaffifeen 83:1–3.

180 Israa 17:1.

and when he prayed facing Jerusalem, he made sure the cube-shaped house was in the front.

After the Prophet's migration to Madinah, it was no longer possible to pray this way, as Makkah was to the south and Jerusalem to the north. Now when the Prophet prayed, he had to turn his back toward Makkah, a position that anguished him. He would at times look heavenward as if expecting Allaah to grant him his wish of praying toward Makkah. This happened for sixteen or seventeen months, until Allaah, the All-Aware, sent down a verse that brought much joy to the Prophet's heart:

> *Verily, We have seen the turning of your face towards the heaven. Surely, We shall turn you to a Qiblah (prayer direction) that shall please you, so turn your face in the direction of the Sacred Mosque (the Ka'bah). Certainly, the people who were given the Scripture (i.e., the Jews and Christians) know well that the (Ka'bah as the new prayer direction) is the truth from their Lord.*[181]

Imam Bukhari reported from the Companion Al-Baraa bin Aazib that "the first prayer which the Prophet offered facing the Ka'bah was the *Asr* (afternoon) prayer in the company of some people. Then one of those who had offered that prayer with him went out and passed by some people in a mosque who were in *ruku* (bowing position) during their prayers facing Jerusalem. He addressed them, saying, 'By Allaah, I bear witness that I have offered prayer with the Prophet facing Makkah (Ka'bah).' Hearing that, those people immediately changed their direction toward the House (Ka'bah) while they were in the bowing position."

It is also reported, in both Bukhari and Muslim, the two most authentic Hadith collections, that Abdullaah bin Umar said that "while the people were in Quba (Mosque) performing the *Fajr* (dawn prayer), a man came and said, 'A (part of the) Qur'aan was revealed tonight to Allaah's Messenger, and

181 Baqarah 2:144.

he was commanded to face the Ka'bah. Therefore, face the Ka'bah. They were facing Ash-Shaam (Jerusalem), so they turned toward the Ka'bah." There is another Hadith from Bukhari with similar wording except that the mosque is not identified and the prayer is *Asr* (late afternoon) prayer. It seems that this other mosque is what is known as "Masjid Al-Qiblatayn," or the mosque with two *Qiblahs* (prayer directions). This simply means that this mosque is one where the same prayer was performed while first facing Jerusalem and then facing Makkah.

A Question and a Controversy

The Companions of the Prophet were known to be extraordinarily concerned about their prayers and other acts of worship. They knew that worship was good only if Allaah accepted it. So, after the change in prayer direction, some began to ask questions: What was the status of prayer of those who prayed toward Jerusalem and died or were martyred before the direction was changed toward Makkah? Would Allaah accept their prayers?

The earnest concerns of these Companions met with a divine assurance in two verses in the Qur'aan:

> *The fools among the people will say: "What has turned them (Muslims) from their Qiblah to which they used to face in prayer?" Say (O Muhammad): To Allaah belong both east and the west. He guides whom He wills to the straight way. Thus We have made you Muslims a Wasat (justly balanced and the best) nation, that you be witnesses over mankind and the Messenger (Muhammad) be a witness over you. And We made the Qiblah which you used to face, only to test those who followed the Messenger (Muhammad) from those who would turn on their heels. Indeed it was very difficult except for those whom Allaah guided.*[182]

182 Baqarah 2:142–143.

The change in *Qiblah* was a major event, and it was both symbolic and tangible. It signified that the mantle of spiritual leadership was transferred from the progeny of one son of Prophet Abraham (Isaac) to the descendant of another son (Ishmael). The change also necessitated that all the prayer niches of all the mosques that existed at the time be redirected 180 degrees. In the mosque of the Prophet, the *As-haab As-Suffah* had to move to the north, and the people now prayed facing the south.

The Jews showed surprise at the change in the Muslim prayer direction, and they commented on it disapprovingly. Several verses were consequently revealed to address this issue. Some Jews also said that it was not pious of Muslims to turn away from Jerusalem in prayer. Another verse responded to this claim.

> *Righteousness is not that you turn your faces toward the east or the west, but [true] righteousness is (in) one who believes in Allaah, the Last Day, the Angels, the Book, and the Prophets and gives wealth, in spite of love for it, to relatives, orphans, the needy, the traveler, those who ask (for help), and for freeing slaves; (and who) establishes prayer and gives alms; (those who) fulfill their promise; and (those who) are patient in poverty and hardship and during battle. Those are the ones who have been true, and it is those who are the righteous.*[183]

Allaah also made it clear that He is everywhere, through His knowledge, and it did not matter which direction people faced in prayer. "And to Allaah belong the east and the west, so wherever you turn there is the Face of Allaah."[184]

The *Qiblah* change put both Jews and hypocrites through a test. The Qur'aan declared that the Jews knew from their scriptures that the *Qiblah* would be changed.

---

183 Baqarah 2:177.

184 Baqarah 2:115. The "Face" of Allaah is used figuratively. Allaah said in the Qur'aan: "There is nothing like unto Him." Shura 42:11.

Certainly, the people who were given the Scripture (i.e., the Jews and Christians) know well that (Ka'bah as the new prayer direction) is the truth from their Lord.[185]

As for the hypocrites, their hesitation exposed them. They were already known for procrastinating and making excuses when they should have been obeying the Messenger of Allaah. The new ruling about prayer direction served to expose their insincerity further.

The change in direction also indicated to those with insight that Muslims would not face Makkah in prayer unless Allaah would give them control over it. It was ironic that, although Makkah was the Muslims' *Qiblah*, at that moment it was an enemy territory that they could not enter to perform their worship.

Reflections: Some Muslims go to great lengths to determine the exact direction of the *Qiblah*, even if it means arguing with other Muslims. Verses 115 and 177 of Baqarah (above) remind us that we should be more concerned about observing the central tenets of Islam. Becoming divided over smaller issues is neither wise nor helpful. A few degrees' difference in the direction of the Qiblah would not invalidate anyone's prayer. It is the intention in the heart that God will look at even when we fall short outwardly.

American Muslims are keenly aware of the discord that arises every year over the sighting of the crescent of Ramadan and Eid Al-Fitr. The issue of local versus global moon sighting or determining the new moon through scientific calculation has been a bone of contention over the years, and people have written lengthy papers to assert the correctness of their position. The issue has become so polarizing that in some extreme cases members of the same family have prayed Eid on two different dates.

185 Baqarah 2:144.

Another issue that has caused much debate among Muslims of different ethnicities is *halaal* (lawful) versus *dhabeehah* (slaughtered) meat. Muslims have argued over whether they can consume beef, lamb, and chicken slaughtered by the People of the Book allowed in Islam, even questioning whether the Jews and Christians of today are the People of the Book that the Qur'aan has referred to. For a certain group of Muslims, if the source of the meat is a halaal animal that has been slaughtered by Jews or Christians such meat can be consumed, whereas for another group of Muslims the meat has to be dhabeehah, meaning the animal or chicken has been slaughtered by a Muslim according to Islamic guidelines. To the proponents of this argument, it does not matter that linguistically *dhabeehah* simply means something that has been slaughtered.

Yet another matter Muslims have been arguing over is whether to pray eight units of *taraweeh* prayers or twenty on Ramadan nights. Many Muslims firmly adhere to their belief in this matter, and they would like the mosque administration to do things their way. They forget that taraweeh is an optional prayer but maintaining peace and unity is obligatory.

Threats to the Prophet Continue

Despite the fact that the Prophet had left Makkah, the threats to his life continued in the new land. In fact, he was the chief target of the Quraysh. Even if the Quraysh could not lay their hands on him, they had the hypocrites and their allies in Madinah who bore a grudge in their hearts against the Prophet and Muslims.

Aayeshah, the Prophet's wife, reported that one night as he was preparing to go to sleep, he said, "Is there a pious person from among my Companions who should keep a watch for me during the night?"

She said, "We were in this state when we heard the clanging of arms. The Messenger of Allaah asked, 'Who is it?'

"The person said, 'This is Sa'ad bin Abi Waqqaas.'

"The Messenger of Allaah said to him: 'What brings you here?'

"He said: 'I fear for your safety, so I came to serve as your guard.' Allaah's Messenger invoked blessings upon him, and then he slept."

This state of vigilance continued until Allaah revealed: "Allaah will protect you from mankind."[186]

This verse meant that nobody could kill the Prophet, although physical harm might still come, as it did in the Battle of Uhud in 3 AH (624/625 CE). After the above verse came down, the Prophet declined to have personal security around him, on the grounds that Allaah would directly protect his life.

Permission to Fight Back

While the Muslims had endured insults and physical attacks in Makkah without any retaliation, after they migrated, God sent word to them that it was now all right if they fought back against their oppressors. The newly revealed verse told them:

> *Permission to fight back is granted to those who are fought against, because they have been wronged; and surely, Allaah is able to give them victory.*[187]

Abu Bakr said, "When I heard this verse, I knew that there would be fighting." Most scholars think this verse was revealed in Madinah, while some believe it came down after the Prophet had left Makkah.

---

186 Maa'idah 5:67.

187 Hajj 22:39.

After the permission to fight was granted, the Prophet cautiously started sending military expeditions to monitor and possibly capture the Qurayshi caravans. Later on he personally went with some expeditions that also involved fighting. In the Arabic language, these are called *sariyah* or *ghazwah. Sariyahs* are expeditions that the Prophet deputed but did not join, whereas *ghazwahs* are expeditions he personally led. Unlike in Makkah, life in Madinah involved frequent military campaigns meant to ward off threats and consolidate state power.

According to various opinions, the number of *sariyahs* was between thirty-six and one hundred, perhaps because some historians combined two expeditions or defined an expedition differently. Ibn Isshaaq accepted the opinion that the total number of *sariyahs* was forty-seven.

As for the number of *ghazwahs*, there are a number of opinions from scholars. According to Imam Bukhari, seventeen; Imam Muslim, nineteen; and Imam Haakim, twenty-one. Others have said there were between twenty-two and twenty-seven. Ibn Isshaaq has quoted twenty-seven. He said that out of these, fighting took place in only nine of them, namely Badr, Uhud, Banu Mustaliq, Khandaq, Banu Qurayzah, Khayber, Conquest of Makkah, Hunayn, and Taa'if.

In most of the early expeditions, the Prophet had sent a few Companions, primarily from his own family or from the Emigrants. He had not included the Helpers because some of those campaigns could involve offensive action, and the Second Pledge of Aqabah had not expressly mentioned that.

Testing the Water

In the early Madinah period, the Prophet sent or led a number of campaigns to intercept the Qurayshi caravans, which had to pass through the passage near Madinah in order to get to Syria. These caravans faced double jeopardy, for if they escaped interdiction on the way to Syria, they could be ambushed on their return. Some of the early campaigns included the following:

Sariyah of Al-Ees, where Hamzah bin Abdul Muttalib encountered Abu Jahl. Before a fight could break out, a man named Majdi bin Amr Al-Juhaani made peace. He had good relations with both parties.

Ghazwah Al-Buwaat, which took place in the Islamic month of Rabi Al-Awwal in 2 AH (623/624 CE). The Prophet had led a contingent of two hundred Companions to Buwaat to intercept a Qurayshi caravan with 2,500 camels laden with merchandise. With it were one hundred men, including Umayyah bin Khalaf. By the time the Prophet reached Buwaat, the caravan had left.

Ghazwah Safwaan, in Rabi Al-Awwal of 2 AH (623/624 CE). Karz bin Jaabir, a pagan Bedouin, raided the pastures of Madinah with a small group, looting some animals and killing a person or two. The Prophet quickly put together a contingent of seventy men and left in pursuit. He went as far as Safwaan, near Badr, but could not catch up with them.

Ghazwah Ushayrah. Although no fighting took place, this ghazwah played an important role in the Battle of Badr. The Prophet learned Abu Sufiyan had left Makkah with a trade caravan to Syria, and he wanted to intercept it. However, Abu Sufiyan got wind of the Prophet's plan and took a different route. Even though Abu Sufiyan escaped, the Prophet took advantage of his presence in the area and signed a nonaggression pact with Banu Mudlij and their allies Banu Dhumrah. Because of what happened on the way up, Abu Sufiyan was on high alert coming back down from Syria. He knew the Prophet was interested in his caravan.

Expedition to Nakhlah and PR Disaster

Toward the end of the month of Rajab, the Prophet prepared a scouting party of nine people. This was neither a battalion nor a regiment by any stretch of the imagination. Rather it was a surveillance team whose job was to report on the activities of the Quraysh in a certain area. The Prophet chose his cousin Abdullaah bin Jahsh as its leader. All of them were from the Emigrants. Abdullaah was given written sealed instructions and ordered not to read them until he had marched for two days. Perhaps the Prophet was so secretive because of spies and hypocrites in Madinah.

When the party had marched for two days, Abdullaah opened the Prophet's letter, which said, "When you read these instructions, march until you set up camp at Nakhlah, between Makkah and Taa'if. There, watch the movements of the caravan of Quraysh and collect news about them for us." The Quraysh could not have expected this surveillance, as Taa'if was south of Makkah and Madinah was to its north. The letter also said, "Do not compel any of your Companions to go with you."

When Abdullaah was done reading the Prophet's letter, he said, "I hear and obey." He then said to his Companions, "Allaah's Messenger has commanded me to march forth to Nakhlah to watch the movements of the caravan of the Quraysh and to inform him about their news. He has prohibited me from forcing any of you to go with me. So, those who seek martyrdom, they should march with me. Those who dislike the idea of martyrdom, let them turn back. Surely, I will implement the command of Allaah's Messenger."

Abdullaah's party consisted of Abu Hudhayfah bin Utbah, Ukkaashah bin Mihsan, Utbah bin Ghazwaan, Sa'ad bin Abi Waqqaas, Adi bin Amr bin Ar-Rabi'ah, Waaqid bin Abdullaah, Khaalid bin Bukayr, and Suhayl bin Baydaa. The group kept marching until it reached an area called Buhraan in Hijaz. Perhaps while taking a short break there, Sa'ad bin Abi Waqqas and Utbah bin Ghazwaan lost the camel that they were riding in turns. The two went searching for it while Abdullaah bin Jahsh and the rest of his Companions continued until they reached Nakhlah.

Not long after they reached Nakhlah, a Qurayshi caravan passed by, carrying raisins, food, and some trade items. Amr bin Hadrami, Uthmaan bin Abdullaah, and his brother Nawfal, as well as Al-Hakam bin Kaysaan, a freed slave of Hishaam bin Al-Mugheerah, were with the caravan. When they saw the Companions, they were frightened, but when they saw Ukkaashah bin Mihsan, their fears subsided, since his head was shaved. They said, "These people seek the Umrah (lesser pilgrimage), so there is no need to fear them."

The Companions conferred among themselves. This was the thirtieth day of Rajab, one of the four sacred months in which Allaah had prohibited fighting. They faced a dilemma: if they attacked the caravan, they would violate the prohibition and give the Quraysh a golden opportunity to smear them, but if they waited until the next day, when the month would be Sha'baan, the caravan would escape their grasp.

They said to each other, "By Allaah! If you let them pass, they will soon enter the sacred area and take refuge in it from you. If you kill them, you will kill them during the sacred month." It seems that perhaps they had forgotten that the Prophet had not instructed them to fight.

After some debate, they eventually decided to attack the caravan. Waaqid bin Abdullaah shot an arrow at Amr bin Al-Hadrami and killed him. Uthmaan bin Abdullaah and Al-Hakam bin Kaysaan gave themselves up, while Nawfal bin Abdullaah fled and outran them. The Companions captured the booty and returned to Madinah with their two prisoners. On the way Abdullaah bin Jahsh set aside one-fifth of the booty for the Messenger of Allaah and divided the rest among his Companions.

When the scouting party reached Madinah and the Prophet saw them, his face changed. The Prophet immediately understood the whole situation and admonished Abdullaah and his Companions, saying, "I did not command you to fight in the sacred month." The Prophet's concern was every bit justified. The Companions' actions had violated Allaah's injunctions, and they created a huge public-relations disaster. The Prophet refused to accept the booty and walked away.

When the Quraysh came to know of the attack, they railed against the Prophet, saying, "Muhammad and his Companions violated the sanctity of the sacred month and shed blood, confiscated property, and took prisoners during it."

The Messenger of Allaah was put on the defensive, and he was quite distressed. Abdullaah bin Jahsh and his Companions thought their mistake would cause their destruction in the Hereafter.

To comfort the Prophet and the Companions, Allaah sent down an amazing verse that on the one hand upheld His law about the sacred months and admonished the disbelievers on the other.

> *They ask you concerning fighting in the Sacred Months. Say, "Fighting therein is a great (transgression) but preventing (mankind) from following the way of Allaah, and to disbelieve in Him, and to prevent access to the Sacred Mosque (in Makkah), and to drive out its inhabitants are greater in transgression before Allaah. And forcing people to leave their faith is worse than killing.*[188]

Reflections: This verse is remarkable for its straightforward approach. It is criticizing Abdullaah bin Jahsh and his Companions for violating the sanctity of the sacred month but at the same time lambasting the pagans for their oppression of the believers. Had it not been for their persecution, the Muslims would not have left Makkah in the first place.

To paraphrase, it is as if Allaah is asking them, "Who are you to complain, when you have done worse things?" This verse is also applicable in our own time. We see that the powerful are oppressing and exploiting the weak, but when the oppressed fight back, they are accused of breaking the law and thrown in prison.

188 Baqarah 2:217.

The powerful nations invade and occupy weak nations, usurp their resources, and turn their people into second-class citizens. And when people of the weak nations resist the occupation, they are called militants, or worse, terrorists. When the powerful nations drop one-thousand-pound bombs on weak nations, they justify it in the name of defending freedom and democracy and ridding the world of evil. Bombing a poor nation into the Stone Age is considered the art of war, and the killing of the masses a mere collateral damage. But when a young man who could not take the destruction of his nation anymore attacks the aggressor with a Molotov cocktail, he is hunted down as a terrorist. When innocent people as young as eleven and as old as seventy-seven are picked up and thrown into the Gitmos of the world without ever being charged, their captors go unpunished because they are too powerful to be touched. When this happens, as it does all too often, justice becomes a casualty.

Coming of the Battle of Badr

On the way to Syria some days earlier, Abu Sufiyan had avoided interception by the Muslims. Upon reaching Bosra (also spelled Bozra or Bostra), the Syrian border town famous for its massive marketplace, Abu Sufiyan was able to sell his merchandise and buy local goods for customers in Makkah. Now it was time for him to return, and he was full of apprehension. It was one of the largest trade caravans he had ever led. It is reported that just about every household in Makkah had invested in this journey, hoping to make a good profit. The camels were laden with merchandise worth more than 50,000 gold dinars, a fortune at the time and even more so now if adjusted for inflation. One could say that some of that money belonged to the Muslims, who had not been allowed to take their wealth when they migrated to Madinah.

The Prophet had been sending teams of spies every few days to report on the Qurayshi caravans. On one of those occasions, he sent Talhah bin Ubaydullaah and Sa'eed bin Zayd. The two were able to locate the huge caravan, which consisted of a large number of camels that whipped up dust as they lumbered on, laden with the precious cargo. Talhah and Sa'eed followed the caravan for a while, and when it had gone some distance, they galloped back quickly to Madinah to report the news to the Prophet in the mosque.

The news was of utmost importance, and time was of the essence. The Prophet told the Companions that he had a critical mission to undertake and whoever had animals with them should go with him. When someone said he had his riding animal in another place and needed to get it, the Prophet said he would only take those who had the animals with them. In his characteristically cautious approach, the Prophet did not disclose the nature or destination of the mission. He did not want to reveal the plan in the mosque because of the potential presence of hypocrites who posed as Muslims but in their hearts were hostile to Islam. Once the Prophet was outside Madinah, he stopped and looked at those who had come with him. It was then that he told them where he was headed.

Reflections: Some of the Orientalists[189] have used this incident and others like it to accuse the Prophet Muhammad of highway robbery. When seen in a historical context, the Prophet's actions were nothing more than retaliatory. He was only going after the Qurayshi caravans and had every right to do so. It was the Quraysh who had driven him out of his birthplace, who had tortured Muslims, confiscated their homes and wealth and killed Sumayyah and her husband Yaasir in cold blood. There was no court system that could serve them justice, so the Prophet was using an avenue that was available to him to get back at the Quraysh.

189 According to Edward Said, late Columbia University professor, "Orientalism dates from the period of European Enlightenment and colonization of the Arab World. Orientalism provided a rationalization for European colonialism based on a self-serving history in which 'the West' constructed 'the East' as extremely different and inferior, and therefore in need of Western intervention or 'rescue.'" See *Orientalism* (Pantheon Books, 1978).

The Prophet had learned that only forty armed personnel were guarding this huge Qurayshi caravan, and with more than three hundred men at his command, the Prophet could easily capture massive wealth for his nascent Muslim community. However, Allaah had a different plan, and it was not a caravan but a war.

In Surah Anfaal, which was revealed about the Battle of Badr, Allaah says:

> *And (remember) when Allaah promised you (Muslims) that one of the two parties should be yours; you wished that the one not armed should be yours, but Allaah willed (war) to justify the truth by His Words and to cut off the roots of the disbelievers.*[190]

The Prophet's instantaneous action explains why the Companions were not heavily armed. There were some seven hundred Muslims in Madinah, but more than half did not participate because no general announcement was made about this campaign. The whole contingent had one hundred camels and only two horses for over three hundred people.

On the way down from Syria, Abu Sufiyan was in a state of paranoia. The incident at Ushayrah had been a close call. Not wanting to be accosted, or worse, captured, Abu Sufiyan was sending his own spies to find out if his caravan had been spied upon. Some Bedouins told him they had seen two men—meaning Talhah and Sa'eed—spying on his camp. So Abu Sufiyan said, "Show me where they camped."

When the Bedouins showed him where the Muslims had camped out, Abu Sufiyan, who was endowed with a keen sense of observation, minutely examined the area until he finally came across camel dung. He opened the dung and immediately realized the camels had eaten dates of Madinah. "These are the dates of Yathrib (Madinah)," he said, adding, "We are being

190 Anfaal 8:7.

monitored." Perhaps the dates of Madinah and their seeds had some distinguishing features.

Abu Sufiyan panicked. It was not only his own life that was at risk but also the safety of the rich Qurayshi caravan, in which every Makkan was invested. He quickly hired a seasoned guide and asked him to take the caravan by a less traveled route along the seashore. This strategy enabled him to bypass Madinah and thereby avoid being raided.

The next thing he did was send word to the Makkan chiefs to dispatch reinforcement. For this job he chose Dhumdhum bin Amr Al-Ghifaari, one of the fastest riders of Makkah. Dhumdhum was to convey Abu Sufiyan's SOS message to the Quraysh, saying that unless they sent help right away, their caravan would be confiscated. Moving at lightning speed, Dhumdhum made a week's journey in three days.

Aatikah's Dream Jolts Makkah

While Dhumdhum was galloping toward Makkah with the nerve-racking news, the Prophet's aunt, Aatikah, saw a dream that shook up the city. Aatikah bint Abdul Muttalib was the full sister of Abdullaah, the Prophet's father. Three days before Dhumdhum arrived in Makkah, Aatikah woke up from her sleep frightened.

She immediately called Abbaas bin Abdul Muttalib, her half brother, and said, "I saw a nightmare, and it is making me very scared. In my dream I saw that a crier is going to come to Makkah in three days, racing on his camel. And he first went to the mosque (Ka'bah) and cried out, 'O traitors, meet your death in three days from now!' Then the crier got on top of the Ka'bah and said the same thing, and then he went on top of Mount Abu Qubays and repeated his warning. Then the crier picked up a rock and threw it down. The rock came hurtling down, and when it landed at the foot of the mountain, it splintered, and its pellets hit every house of

Makkah." It was clear from the dream that something terrible was going to happen that would inflict great pain on the inhabitants of Makkah.

One may ask, What is the context of the word *traitor*, and who are the traitors of Aatikah's dream? A possible interpretation is that the traitors are the Quraysh who had turned against the monotheistic religion of their forefather, Abraham, and tortured those who believed in One True God.

Abbaas became visibly concerned about what his sister had told him. Aatikah was known to see true dreams, which are a blessing from Allaah. "This is a dangerous dream," he said to Aatikah, "and I'm worried that if you tell people, you will get in trouble, so keep this dream to yourself."

A short while later, Abbaas went against his own advice of secrecy and told his best friend, Waleed bin Utbah, about his sister's dream, all the while insisting that he not tell it to anyone. "Of course not," Waleed promised, but before long he told his father, Utbah. By the end of the day, the whole city was abuzz with talk of Aatikah's dream. As the saying goes, "If you want to keep a secret, do not tell it to anyone."

Abbaas did not know the secret was out. He went about his business that day and went to sleep without incident. The next day, the second day of the dream, he went to the Ka'bah in the late afternoon to make the ritual circumambulation, as was the local custom. There he saw Abu Jahl and his minions.

Abu Jahl, the man whom the Prophet had called "the Fir'awn (Pharaoh) of my *Ummah*," seemed distressed. He said, "O Abbaas! When you're done, come see me!" When Abbaas went to him, Abu Jahl sarcastically said, "O children of Abdul Muttalib, is it not enough that a male in your family has claimed to be a prophet, that now you have a prophetess also?" Abu Jahl kept lashing at him. "Is it true that a crier will come in three days? If that happens, we will see it, but if it doesn't happen, then, by Allaah, we will write a sign and place it by door of the Ka'bah, saying that the tribe of Abdul Muttalib is the most deceitful of the Arabs known to man!"

Abbaas was caught completely off guard, and in a moment of unpreparedness, he denied that Aatikah had seen any dream or that he had told anyone about it. The news of Abu Jahl's humiliating Abbaas and Banu Abdul Muttalib reached the women of Abbaas's clan, and that evening they came to Abbaas's house and sharply rebuked him.

"How could you accept that your men and now women should be humiliated?" they vented at Abbaas. "Have you no shame? Could you not have defended your women?" All of Makkah knew that before this incident Abu Jahl, a man from Banu Makhzum, had insulted the Prophet and made no secret of his dislike for Banu Haashim, whom he considered to be his rival. Abbaas regretted the way he had handled the matter and decided to get even with Abu Jahl.

The next morning, the third day of Aatikah's dream, Abbaas went out enraged, looking for Abu Jahl. Abbaas said, "When I came to the mosque, I saw Abu Jahl in the distance. As soon as he saw me, he turned pale and walked away."

Abbaas did not know that Abu Jahl had already heard the crier. Dhumdhum had arrived. To create high drama, he had cut the nose of his camel, torn his shirt, and disheveled himself. As yet another indication that something terrible had happened, he sat backward on his camel and cried out, "O Quraysh, your caravan! Muhammad and his Companions are lying in wait for your property, which is with Abu Sufiyan. I do not think that you will overtake it. Help! Help!" Abbaas said that the commotion made him forget about getting even with Abu Jahl.

The Quraysh began to prepare in an emergency mode. Dhumdhum had created so much hype that everybody, with a few exceptions, felt compelled to go. Among the tribes that decided not to go were the Banu Adiyy bin Ka'ab and Banu Zuhrah; the latter returned when they learned that Abu Sufiyan's caravan was safe. Among the noted individuals who either did not go or were reluctant to go were the following:

Abu Lahab did not want to go, perhaps because of his sister's dream, which was quite frightening in its detail. The other possible reason could be that he did not want to fight against his own nephew. Doing so would be in violation of the tribal custom and honor. It is said that Abu Lahab had asked Al-Aas bin Hishaam bin Al-Mugheerah, who owed him money, to go in his place and told him that if the latter did so, his debt would be forgiven. Al-Aas had agreed.

Umayyah bin Khalaf, the former owner of Bilaal, did not want to go to Badr, but Abu Jahal and Uqbah bin Abi Mu'yait went to him to bully him into going. They burned women's incense around him and said, "Perfume yourself, for surely you are a woman, and pencil your eyes." This enraged Umayyah. Pumped up, he bought one of the most expensive and fastest horses with the idea that if things went wrong, he would quickly flee.

Utbah bin Rabi'ah did not want to go either, but his reason for not wanting to go to war was in fact noble in its own way. "What kind of victory would it be when brother kills brother and father kills son?" he asked. Utbah was related to the Prophet. He is the same man who had sent some grapes to the Prophet and Zayd when they escaped from Taa'if and sat leaning against his orchard. It seemed he wanted to avoid a fratricidal war at all costs and did not mind even if his people blamed him for backing out. But eventually he did go.

Abu Jahl also incited Aamir bin Al-Hadrami to take revenge for the killing of one of his brothers, Amr bin Hadrami, who was killed in the *ghazwah* of Nakhlah by Abdullaah bin Jahsh. Utbah said he would pay the blood money for the killing of Amr, but Abu Jahl taunted him, asking what kind of a brother he was that he would accept a few pieces of gold for the killing of his brother. And so the cries of war were forcefully ignited.

One more thing was still making the Quraysh uneasy about leaving town: fear of an attack against their women and children by the Banu Bakr. Sometime earlier, a Qurayshi young man had killed the leader of the Banu Bakr, and the Quraysh, particularly Utbah, feared the former would exact revenge against their families while they were gone.

As they were pondering over this question, Shaytaan (Satan) took the form of Suraaqah bin Maalik and said, "O Quraysh, you know my nobility and place among my people. I will protect you. You have nothing to worry about." As an additional assurance, Suraaqah (meaning Satan) said he would go with them so that they could have peace of mind that there would be no foul play.

Utbah felt satisfied. And the Quraysh left with one thousand warriors, singing girls, wines, and tambourines. They had a hundred horses and were moving arrogantly, feeling confident of victory. Never before had they put together such a large force.

Allaah denounces their conceit in Surah Anfaal:

> *And be not like those who come out of their homes boastfully and to be seen of men, and hinder (men) from the path of Allaah; and Allaah is All-Encompassing of what they do. And (remember) when Shaytaan made their (evil) deeds seem fair to them and said, "No one of mankind can overcome you this day (Battle of Badr) and verily, I am close at hand to help you." But when the two forces came in sight of each other, he ran away and said, "Verily, I have nothing to do with you. Verily, I see what you see not. Verily, I fear Allaah for Allaah is severe in punishment."*[191]

191 Anfaal 8:47–48.

The Muslim Camp

The Prophet had not planned this expedition for war. In fact he thought that his forces would rather easily capture the Qurayshi caravan and go home. That is why some of the Companions did not join; they did not expect a war to break out. The Prophet had asked Uthmaan bin Affaan to stay home and take care of his wife Ruqayyah (the Prophet's daughter), who was seriously ill. She eventually died while the Prophet was away.

But Allaah wanted to test the Muslims and grant them victory if they persevered. In Surah Anfaal, which is full of references to the Battle of Badr, Allaah says:

> *As your Lord caused you to go out from your home with the truth; and verily, a party among the believers disliked it. Disputing with you concerning the truth after it was made manifest, as if they were being driven to death, while they were looking (at it). And (remember) when Allaah promised you one of the two parties, that it should be yours; you wished that the one not armed should be yours, but Allaah willed to justify the truth by His Words and to cut off the roots of the disbelievers, that He might cause the truth to triumph and bring falsehood to nothing, even though the criminals hate it.*[192]

When the Prophet realized that the planned raid on the caravan had of necessity turned into the threat of an imminent war, for which they were materially ill prepared, he addressed his Companions: "O people, advise me!"

This shows the Prophet's humility and wisdom. As the spiritual and worldly leader, he could have ordered them to prepare for war, and they would not have refused. But he chose to ask for their advice, and even so, very politely. He also knew that if they were part of the decision-making, they would own the decisions and plans that were made.

192 Anfaal 8:5–8.

Abu Bakr was the first person to get up. He promised full support to the Prophet in whatever he decided to do. The Prophet praised and thanked him.

But then he asked again: “O people, advise me!”

Umar got up this time, and he too promised full support; the Prophet praised and thanked him as well.

The Prophet repeated his request a third time: “O people, advise me!”

This time Miqdaad bin Amr got up and gave a passionate speech. “O Messenger of Allaah, go where Allaah tells you to go, for we are with you. We will not say, as the Children of Israel told Moses, ‘You and your Lord go fight, and we will stay home,’ but rather we will say, ‘You and your Lord go fight, and we will fight with you.’ By God, if you were to take us to Burk Al-Ghimaad (a far place), we would fight resolutely with you.” (Burk Al-Ghimaad is about five nights’ journey from Makkah. It is an expression that refers to going to great lengths to support someone.) The Prophet thanked and blessed Miqdaad. The first three speakers, Abu Bakr, Umar, and Miqdaad were all Emigrants from Makkah.

The Prophet repeated his request a fourth time: “O people, advise me!”

At that point Sa’ad bin Mu’aadh, a noble Companion from among the Helpers, got up. “It seems like you mean us, O Messenger of Allaah.” And when the Prophet agreed, Sa’ad spoke the words the Prophet wanted to hear. “We believe in you, we declare your truth, and we witness that what you have brought is the truth, and we have given you our word and agreement to hear and obey. So go where you wish; we are with you. And, by God, if you were to ask us to cross this sea and you plunged into it, we would plunge into it with you; not a man would stay behind. We do not dislike the idea of meeting your enemy tomorrow. We are experienced in war and trustworthy in combat. It may well be that God will let us show you something that will bring you joy, so take us along with God's blessing." The Prophet's face beamed with happiness at Sa'ad's profound words of support.

It was a sign of the Prophet's honesty that he did not expect the Helpers to participate in an external war. In the Second Pledge of Aqabah, the Helpers had sworn to defend the Prophet if attacked, but nothing was mentioned about their support if the Prophet were to go outside of Madinah and fight a war against someone. Therefore, in his exemplary sense of fairness, the Prophet wanted to stick to the letter of the agreement. Sa'ad, too, could have stayed to the letter of the pledge, but he emphasized the spirit of the agreement rather than the letter.

Having received Sa'ad's unconditional support, the Prophet said to his 310 or 313 Companions, "Forward in good heart, for Allaah has promised me one of the two parties, and, by Allaah, it is as though I now see the enemy lying prostrate."

They decided to meet the enemy at Badr.

Where Is Badr?

According to historians, Badr is a place about 160 miles southwest of Madinah and 250 miles north of Makkah. It was named after a water well that in turn was named after Badr bin Yakhlud, the person who had dug it. In fact there were several wells in Badr. As time went by, this area also became known as the Plains of Badr. It would take about ninety minutes by car to get to Badr from Madinah. One important reason that Badr may have been chosen was the availability of water.

War Is Deception

There is a saying in the Arabic language, *Al-harbu khidaa*; war is deception. In war Islam allows a strategy that can be interpreted differently, depending on a person's understanding or expectation. However, it must be noted that

Islam does not allow treachery under any circumstances. As the Prophet was heading toward Badr, he met an old man and asked him what he knew about Muhammad (meaning himself) and the Quraysh.

The man said, "First you tell me who you are."

The Prophet said, "If you tell us, we will tell you."

So the man said, "I have heard that Muhammad and his Companions left Madinah on such and such date, and so they should now be in such and such place (which was the area where the Prophet actually was). And I have heard that the Quraysh left on such and such date, and so they should be in such and such place." Both of his estimates were correct. Then the man asked the Prophet, "Of whom are you?"

The Prophet said, "We are from *Maa*," meaning water.

The old man was confused. "What does that mean? Is it from the water of Iraq?" the man kept muttering to himself while the Prophet and his Companions moved on.

In the meantime, the Companions by chance caught two of the Qurayshi servants and brought them to the Prophet, who quizzed them about the number in the Qurayshi army, but the servants did not know. So the Prophet asked them, "How many camels did they slaughter every day?" They said about nine or ten. The Prophet estimated that the Quraysh were between nine hundred and one thousand people. Then he asked them about the nobles of the Quraysh who had come, and they mentioned Utbah, Shaybah, Abul Bukhtari, Hakim, Nawfal, Al-Haarith, Abu Jahl, Umayyah, Suhayl, and others. The Prophet said, "Makkah has thrown to you the pieces of its liver, meaning its best."

The Prophet decided to set up camp at the first well of Badr, but Hubaab bin Mundhir asked, "O Messenger of Allaah, is this a place that

Allaah has ordered you to occupy so that we can neither advance nor withdraw from it, or is it a matter of opinion and military tactics?" When the Prophet replied that it was the latter, Hubaab advised that they should go to the wells closest to the enemy, fill up the wells that lay beyond that point, and build a cistern or reservoir so the Muslims would have plenty of water while the opponents had none. Abdullaah bin Abbaas reported that Gabriel had come to the Prophet and told him to accept Hubaab's advice, which the Prophet did. The Companions considered it to be good manners to make sure that they were not advising against Allaah's orders before they offered counteradvice to the Prophet.

Sa'ad bin Mu'aadh, one of the most brilliant and sincere Companions, said, "O Messenger of Allaah, let us make an observation booth for you to stand on and have your riding animal stand nearby; then we will meet the enemy. And if Allaah gives us victory, then that is what we desire, but if it is otherwise, you can ride your animal and join your people back in Madinah, who will protect you and give you good counsel and fight alongside you." The Prophet gratefully accepted his advice and sought Allaah's blessing for Sa'ad. Soon a stand was built for the Prophet.

Sa'ad was the leader of the Aws. When he accepted Islam at the invitation of Mus'ab bin Umayr, his entire tribe had joined him in the new faith. The Prophet loved him dearly. When he died of injuries sustained in the Battle of the Trench, the Prophet said, "The throne of the Most Merciful shook at the death of Sa'ad bin Mu'aadh." Some months after Sa'ad's death, when the Prophet put on a luxurious dress sent in as a gift by the king of Bahrain, he suddenly remembered Sa'ad and said, "The handkerchief of Sa'ad in Jannah is better than this."

Back in the Qurayshi Camp

When Abu Sufiyan finally met the Qurayshi troops, he tried to convince the Quraysh that, now that the caravan was safe, there was no need for war. But Abu Jahl said they would not go back until "we have gone to Badr, spent three nights there, have drunk some wine, our singing girls have sung for us, and Arabs are impressed by us." However, Banu Zuhrah accepted Abu Sufiyan's argument, and their leader, Al-Akhnas bin Shariq, ordered them to return.

Another important Qurayshi leader, Utbah bin Rabi'ah, paced back and forth among his troops and kept trying to avert the war. The Prophet, who had either overheard Utbah or been informed by Gabriel, said, "If there was any good in the Quraysh, it was represented by the man on the red camel. If they listen to this man, they will be fine."

But Abu Jahl, the artful manipulator, managed to rile Utbah by saying that when the latter saw Muhammad and his Companions, his lung became swollen with fear. Abu Jahl also suggested that Utbah was reluctant to go to war because of his son, Abu Hudhayfah, who was on the Muslims' side. That truly enraged Utbah, and he vowed to show his valor in the war. He and his brother and another son were the first ones to die in the battle. Alas, Utbah succumbed to the pre-Islamic pride and went against his own advice.

Among the people who came with the Quraysh were Banu Haashim, the clan of the Messenger of Allaah. They included Abbaas, his uncle, and Aqeel, his cousin and Ali's brother. But they came only grudgingly, in order to avoid Abu Jahl's taunts. They had no desire to fight, and the Prophet knew that.

Abu Jahl made sure that he did not neglect anything that would make him triumphant, including praying to Allaah for victory. So he prayed, "O Allaah! Whichever of the two camps (pagans or Muslims) severed the relation of the womb and brought us what is new, then destroy it this day." In another narration, he said, "Whichever of the two is on the truth, give it victory." It is ironic that Abu Jahl was supplicating to Allaah for the victory of the right party, not realizing that he was essentially asking for his own defeat. This shows that the pagans were sincere in their belief, even if misguided.

Allaah mentions Abu Jahl's supplication in Surah Anfaal:

O disbelievers, if you ask for a judgement, the judgement has now come unto you; and if you cease, it will be better for you, and if you return (to the attack), so shall We return, and your forces will be of no avail to you, however numerous they be; and verily, Allaah is with the believers.[193]

Allaah Answers the Prophet's Prayer

When the Quraysh came down at Badr at daybreak and the Prophet saw how arrogantly they were coming, he said, "O Allaah, these Quraysh have come with all their pride and arrogance; they defy You and call Your Messenger a liar. O Allaah, deliver Your help that You promised me."

The Prophet was very concerned about the situation. Having done his planning to the finest details, he had now turned to Allaah, the One without Whose permission no plan can proceed and no effort can succeed. He raised his hands in prayer and kept raising them. "O Allaah! I invoke You for Your covenant and promised victory. O Allaah! If You let this group of Muslims be defeated (today), You will not be worshipped." As he kept raising his hands higher, his shawl fell off his shoulders.

Abu Bakr took hold of his hands and said, "Enough, O Messenger of Allaah."

Allaah refers to the Prophet's prayer in Surah Anfaal: "Remember when you sought help of your Lord and He answered you (saying): 'I will help you with a thousand of the angels who will come rows upon rows.'"[194]

When the Prophet was done supplicating, a brief slumber overtook him and the Companions. Then suddenly he opened his eyes and read a verse

193 Anfaal 8:19.

194 Anfaal 8:9.

of the Qur'aan: "Their multitude will be put to flight, and they will show their backs."[195]

Then the Prophet turned to Abu Bakr and cried out, "O Abu Bakr! Glad tidings for you. Allaah's victory has approached. By Allaah, I can see Jibreel on his horse in the thick of a sandstorm." Ibn Abbaas said that on that day Gabriel (Jibreel) was leading five hundred angels while Michael (Mikaa'il) was leading another five hundred.

Scenes before the Battle

While the Prophet was arranging the battle rows, he accidentally poked Sawaad bin Ghaaziyah in the stomach with the tip of his spear. Sawaad said, "You have been sent with truth and justice, and you have hurt me. I want to retaliate for what you have done to me."

The Prophet lifted his shirt, exposing his stomach so Sawaad could take his revenge. Instead Sawaad kissed the Prophet's stomach. When the latter asked Sawaad why he had done that, Sawaad replied, "O Messenger of Allaah, we are about to plunge in war, and I do not know if I will come back alive, so I wanted the last thing before the battle to be for my skin to have touched yours."

When inspecting the troops, the Prophet noticed there were two young men who were too young to participate. Baraa bin Aazib and Abdullaah bin Umar were younger than fourteen. So they were sent back. Many of the Prophet's supporters were youths. They found Islam to be a revolutionary idea and looked to the Prophet as a tireless activist who had shaken up the foundations of their unjust and barbaric society.

The final count was approximately 313 men. Around 83 of them were from the Emigrants, and the rest were from the Helpers (62 Aws and 168

195 Qamar 54:45.

Khazraj). The Khazraj soldiers were double the Aws in number because their tribe was bigger and more of their members had embraced Islam. The Khazraj were also generally the poorer tribe, and the poor were quicker in accepting the new faith. For one thing, the poor and underprivileged looked at Islam as egalitarian.

In the entire army there were only two horses, which belonged to Zubayr bin Al-Awwaam and Miqdaad bin Al-Aswad, and around one hundred camels, which meant that three soldiers had to share one camel in the 160-mile journey, riding in turns.

Like the rest of the people, the Prophet was assigned a camel that he had to share with Ali bin Abi Taalib, who owned the camel, and Abu Lubaabah bin Abd Al-Mundhir. This turned out to be highly problematic for Ali and Abu Lubaabah. How could they even imagine riding a camel while the Prophet was walking? The Prophet was their ultimate spiritual and political leader as well as being older in age. They loved him more than themselves. Besides, where in the world has a general walked while a private ridden? So they went to the Prophet and insisted that he ride and they walk the entire journey.

The Prophet could have told them politely that in his opinion everyone should share the ride fairly. However, he chose something immensely beautiful. He said to Ali and Abu Lubaabah, "The two of you are not any younger or stronger than I am, and I am not in any less need of the reward than the two of you."[196]

The Prophet's ingenious answer made them speechless. As for the age, no doubt the Prophet was almost fifty-five, and Ali was twenty-five. True to his resolve, the Prophet walked and suffered the hardships of the long journey like the rest of the soldiers. The Prophet's conduct inspired his

196 The Prophet was telling Ali and Abu Lubaabah that he needed to earn as much reward as them.

Companions to emulate him. It is no wonder, then, that when Umar went to Jerusalem to take control of the city, he was walking while his servant was riding the animal, making people think that the servant was Umar and Umar the servant.

Before the start of the battle, the Quraysh had captured Hudhayfah and his father, Yamaan. These two Companions lived in Madinah but were neither Qurayshi nor from the Ansaar (Helpers). Hudhayfah's father had moved from Yemen. Because of their foreign lineage, the Quraysh did not have a direct hostility with them and, therefore, did not want to kill them. After some deliberation, the Quraysh decided they would set them free on the promise that they would not fight alongside the Muslims against the Quraysh. Hudhayfah and his father promised. When they reached the Prophet, they narrated the entire incident. The Prophet, who was outnumbered three to one against the Quraysh and could have used them in the battle, said that they should keep their promise. To honor their promise, Hudhayfah and his father did not join any battle that was against the Quraysh.

The Muslims were nervous on account of the larger and more heavily armed Qurayshi army, so Allaah caused them to doze off and sent down a light rain. It was a strange sight that a group of frightened people were napping just before a major battle. Sleep and fright are opposites.

Allaah reminds the believers of His wisdom and grace in Surah Anfaal:

(Remember) when He covered you with a slumber as a security from Him, and He caused water (rain) to descend on you from the sky, to clean you thereby, and to remove from you the Rijz (whispering, evil-suggestions) of Shaytaan (Satan), and to strengthen your hearts, and make your feet firm thereby.[197]

---

197 Anfaal 8:11.

The Muslim Formation

The Prophet gave the main flag to Mus'ab bin Umayr. Mus'ab was an Emigrant but was most beloved to the Helpers, many of whom had embraced Islam at his hands. On the right flank was Ali, representing the Emigrants, and on the left flank was Sa'ad bin Mu'aadh, representing the Helpers. The infantry was in the front, behind them the archers, and behind them the javelin throwers. The soldiers were arranged in rows so that not everyone was exposed to danger. Even today nations use this formation in battle. This arrangement also seems to be Allaah's choice, since the Qur'aan says that on the occasion of this battle, angels came down rows upon rows to help Muslims.[198]

First the Duels

In those days, armies would fight duels, called *Mubaarazah*, before an all-out war broke out. One of the first acts of war at Badr was an attempt by Al-Aswad bin Abd Al-As'ad to get water from the Muslim reservoir, but Hamzah bin Abdul Muttalib intercepted and killed him. Utbah bin Rabi'ah came forward next. He had already been incensed by Abu Jahl's taunting that he was a coward. So Utbah took his brother Shaybah and son Waleed and challenged the Muslims to send their equal.

A number of young Companions from Madinah, including Abdullaah bin Rawaahah, stepped forward from the Muslim side. Utbah asked them who they were, and when they identified themselves, he said he had not come to fight them. "Send us our equal from our own people," Utbah said.

The Prophet motioned Ali, Hamzah, and Ubaydah bin Haarith (the Prophet's distant uncle) to come forward. These were the Prophet's blood relatives, and in putting them in harm's way, he was setting an example for others to follow. It was quite common for leaders of the past and present to protect themselves and their families in war and let the poor fight and be killed. So by

198 Anfaal 8:9.

putting his own relatives in battle, the Prophet set an example of self-sacrifice. In the ensuing duel, Hamzah killed Shaybah and Ali killed Waleed. Ubaydah struck Utbah with his sword but was also struck back in the leg, which was almost severed. Hamzah and Ali rushed to his aid and finished off Utbah.

Before the start of the main battle, the Prophet picked up a fistful of pebbles and threw them at the enemy, saying, "May the faces be disfigured." They were small pebbles, but God's Hand was behind them, and they hit the Quraysh hard. In Surah Anfaal, Allaah called the Prophet's throwing of pebbles His own act: "And you did not throw what you threw but it was Allaah Who threw."[199]

Satan versus the Angels

When the main battle began, Satan, who had appeared to the Quraysh in Makkah in the guise of Suraaqah bin Maalik and promised to join them in the battle against the Muslims, saw angels coming down from heaven. They were not just any angels. Satan saw Gabriel and Michael, the mightiest angels, whom he could not have dared to take on. So he became afraid and began to slip away, saying, "I see what you do not see."

Allaah mentions in verse 48 of Surah Anfaal what Satan had said:

> *No one of mankind can overcome you this day and verily, I am your neighbor (meaning helper). But when the two forces came in sight of each other, he ran away and said, "Verily, I have nothing to do with you. Verily, I see what you see not. Verily, I fear Allaah for Allaah is severe in punishment."*[200]

A Qurayshi man saw Suraaqah fleeing and challenged him to stay and fight as he had promised. The man did not know it was Satan in Suraaqah's guise.

199 Anfaal 8:17.

200 Anfaal 8:48.

When he physically tried to stop Suraaqah, Satan took his original form and pushed the man so hard that he flew in the air.

Allaah commanded the angels to "cast terror into the hearts of the disbelievers" and "strike them over the necks, and smite over all their fingers and toes."[201]

And that is what happened. There were reports of enemies falling down even though none of the Companions were around. They were struck by the angels, who were pouncing on the disbelievers in a sandstorm. Ar-Rabi'ah bin Anas said, "In the aftermath of Badr, the people used to distinguish whomever the angels had killed from those whom they had killed by the wounds over their necks, fingers, and toes, because those parts had a mark as if they were branded by fire."

The Muslims won this battle easily even though they were outnumbered and outgunned. They had faced an enemy that was three times larger, yet the Muslims killed seventy disbelievers and took seventy prisoners. Sixteen Muslims received martyrdom that day.

After the battle Gabriel came to the Prophet and asked him about the status of those who fought in Badr. The Prophet said, "They were the best of Muslims." Gabriel said, "The same was the case of angels who participated in the Battle of Badr; they were the best of angels." From this it is evident that the angels of Badr had a special rank. Similarly, the Companions who fought in Badr had a special status with Allaah, Who praised them in the Qur'aan, and other Companions respected them.

After the battle was over, the Muslim martyrs were buried in individual graves, in a marked contrast to the Battle of Uhud, where two were buried in the same grave.

201 Anfaal 8:12.

The Death of Abu Jahl

Allaah had decided that the first battle would put an end to Abu Jahl. Some of the Helpers (Ansaar) had heard about Abu Jahl's extreme hostility for Islam and the Prophet. An Ansaari Companion named Mu'aadh bin Amr bin Al-Jamuh was looking for Abu Jahl, having heard of his infamy, and when he found him, he fell upon him, cutting off his foot and half his shank. However, Abu Jahl's son, Ikrimah, struck back, severing Mu'aadh's arm, which dangled from a tendon. Mu'aadh later had to break himself free of the dangling arm because it was obstructing his fighting.

Another Companion, named Mu'awwidh bin Afraah, saw Abu Jahl lying helpless, so he struck him and left him gasping for his last breath. Then Abdullaah bin Mas'ud came looking for Abu Jahl among the slain. Abdullaah found Abu Jahl still alive and put his foot on Abu Jahl's neck, saying to him, "Has God put you to shame, O enemy of God?"

Abu Jahl insulted him even in that state, saying, "You have climbed high, you little shepherd." Then Abdullaah cut off Abu Jahl's head.

The Death of Umayyah bin Khalaf

Umayyah bin Khalaf had survived the battle but was feeling very insecure, so when he saw Abdur Rahmaan bin Awf, his friend and fellow trader from the pre-Islamic days, he called out, "Won't you take me as a prisoner, for I am more valuable than these coats of mail that you have?" Abdur Rahmaan was carrying the body armor he had collected from the battlefield, so he took hold of Umayyah and his son Ali, intending to give them protection. The Madinah Charter had allowed any Muslim the power to give protection to anyone he wished.

As Abdur Rahmaan was walking with them, Bilaal, Umayyah's former slave and victim, saw Umayyah and grew furious. "May I not live if Umayyah lives," Bilaal shouted. He must have had flashbacks of the torture he had received at Umayyah's hands. The story of Bilaal's extraordinary torture and his clinging to faith under it was well-known in Madinah. So when other Companions heard Bilaal's cries, they came to his aid and surrounded the two.

Abdur Rahmaan told the Companions to leave the two alone because he had given them protection, but the rage against Umayyah was so great that they ignored Abdur Rahmaan. They started to poke the two with the spear that had slightly injured Abdur Rahmaan. In the meantime, someone swung his sword and cut off the foot of Umayyah's son. Realizing the gravity of the situation, Abdur Rahmaan told Umayyah to make an escape. People eventually succeeded in killing Umayyah and his son. Abdur Rahmaan used to say, "May Allaah have mercy on Bilaal. I lost my coats of mail, and he deprived me of my prisoners."

Perhaps as a sign of punishment from Allaah, Umayyah's body began to deteriorate so quickly that they could not bury him. Instead they decided to leave it there and throw sand and small rocks from a distance to cover it. Such was the end of a person who used to have Bilaal dragged through the streets of Makkah in the scorching sun with a rock on his chest in order to make him renounce his faith.

Talking to the Qurayshi Dead

The Prophet ordered the bodies of some of the Qurayshi leaders to be thrown into the empty wells of Badr instead of letting them rot in the sun and become food for the vultures. That indicates that combatants must show some basic respect to the dead of their enemies. This is in stark contrast to what the Quraysh did to the bodies of the Muslim dead in Uhud a year later. They mutilated the dead Muslims, including the body of Hamzah.

The Prophet stayed in Badr for three days, as was his custom. When he was leaving, he passed by the well where the bodies of Qurayshi leaders had been thrown, and addressed them: "Has your lord fulfilled the promise he made to you? My Lord has fulfilled the promise He made to me."

When Umar saw this, he said, "Ya Rasul Allaah (O Messenger of Allaah), are you talking to the dead who cannot hear you?" In another narration, he said, "Are you talking to bodies that have no soul in them?"

The Prophet replied, "O Umar, by the One in Whose hands my life is, they can hear me better than you can."

Reflections: Can the Dead Hear the Living? There is a difference of opinion among the Companions and scholars about whether the dead can hear. Those who say, yes, the dead can hear, use this incident. Among them is Abdullaah bin Umar. There are other examples from the Sunnah to support this view. For example:

1) The Prophet said, "If someone gives me salaam, Allaah asks an angel to convey it to me, and I respond to the salaam."
2) When the Prophet visited a cemetery, he would give greetings of salaam to those buried there.
3) It was said that the dead are punished when their relatives wail upon their graves.
4) Amr bin Al-Aas, a Companion, instructed his relatives to stand by his grave, saying, "Your presence will comfort me and calm me down so I may prepare for Munkar and Nakir."[202]

However, there are those who say that the dead cannot hear. Chief among them is Aayeshah, the Prophet's wife. She provided her evidence from the Qur'aan, citing among others the following verses:

202 Munkar and Nakir are two angels who visit the dead in the graves after they have been temporarily resurrected to answer some questions.

> *So verily, you cannot make the dead to hear, nor can you make the deaf to hear the call, when they show their backs and turn away. And you cannot guide the blind from their straying; you can make to hear only those who believe in Our Signs, and have submitted (to Allaah).*[203]

> *The living and the dead are not equal. Allaah can make hear anyone He wishes. And you cannot make those who are in the grave hear.*[204]

> *Verily, you cannot make the dead hear nor can you make the deaf hear the call, when they flee, turning their backs.*[205]

Qataadah, a student of Ibn Abbaas, said that what happened in Badr was something special but not the norm. He said that Allaah brought the Qurayshi leaders back to life so they could hear the Prophet and feel humiliated and ashamed for their disbelief.

Both Views Explained

Those who say that the dead can hear someone near their grave explain that the above verses meant that, even though the physical body has died, the soul still lives on. They say that the Qur'aan is using a similitude, a metaphor, to mean people whose hearts are hardened cannot hear the truth, just as a deaf person cannot hear what is being said.

On the other hand, in answer to those who say that the dead hear what goes on in their surroundings, one can argue that the Prophet did not correct Umar when he interjected and said, "Are you talking to the dead...?" Instead the Prophet by his response hinted to Umar that this

203 Ruum 30:52–53.

204 Faatir 35:22.

205 Naml 27:80.

was an exceptional situation and Allaah had caused the dead of the polytheists to hear the Prophet in order to cause them humiliation.

As for saying salaam to the people of the graveyard, some argue that it is not meant to be the salaam of *tahiyyah* (greetings) but rather the salaam of *du'a* (supplication), to which no response is expected.

Also, the dead hearing the footsteps of the living as they are departing the cemetery is not the same as the dead hearing the conversations of the living.

As for Amr bin Al-Aas's instructions to his family, this was his own juristic opinion.

It seems that the stronger opinion is that the dead cannot hear the living, except when Allaah allows them to in special circumstances, like the one after the Battle of Badr. And Allaah knows best.

The Aftermath of Badr

The Prophet had ordered the Companions not to harm his uncle Abbaas bin Abdul Muttalib, Abul Bukhtari, and some of the other people from the Banu Haashim clan.

The question is why the Prophet had issued such an order. The answer lies in the roles these people had played in helping the Muslims and in the circumstances that had led to their capture. Abbaas, the Prophet's uncle, had been a Muslim sympathizer and later a secret Muslim. He would keep an eye on the activities of the Quraysh and inform the Prophet if they planned to threaten the Muslims of Madinah. Like others of his clan, he had grudgingly come to Badr only to avoid being harassed by Abu Jahl and his minions. They were reluctant participants. Abul Bukhtari had helped the Muslims during the boycott and was one of the main people who had maneuvered to end that boycott.

Abbaas was a big man, but he was taken prisoner by a petite Ansaari Companion named Abul Yasaar Ka'ab bin Amr. When he was brought to the Prophet, Abbaas said, "Ya Rasul Allaah, this man did not capture me."

The Companion said, "No, I captured you."

Abbaas said, "I was captured by a horse rider whom I do not see anymore."

The Prophet interjected at that point and said to the Ansaari Companion, "You were helped by a noble angel."

Abu Hudhayfah Vows to Kill Abbaas

Abu Hudhayfah was a good Muslim, but he was deeply shaken by the death of his father, Utbah bin Rabi'ah; his uncle Shaybah; and his brother Waleed in the duel. His human emotions overpowered him, and he vowed to kill Abbaas, the Prophet's uncle, in revenge.

The Prophet noticed Abu Hudhayfah's sorrow and consoled him. Abu Hudhayfah said, "I am sad not because my father was killed, for he got what he deserved, but because I had hoped that my father's wisdom would lead him to Islam."

Abu Hudhayfah knew that the Prophet had ordered that Abbaas not be killed, but perhaps he reasoned that if his uncle had been killed for being on the side of the anti-Muslim army, so should Abbaas, as the latter also came with the pagan forces. He failed to realize that Abbaas had never fought against the Muslims and had never harassed or tortured them in Makkah. In fact Abbaas had provided tacit support to the Muslims and also suffered because of his kinship with the Prophet. Abbaas had played an important role in the Second Pledge of Aqabah. And finally, he had come with the Quraysh only under pressure.

When the Prophet heard about Abu Hudhayfah's vow, he asked Umar rhetorically, "Should the uncle of the Messenger of Allaah be put to the sword?" Umar understood what the Prophet meant, and he went to Abu Hudhayfah and sternly warned him against carrying out his threat.

Abu Hudhayfah was remorseful for his vow, and he once said, "I never felt safe after that unless martyrdom atoned for those words." He remained a good Muslim, and Allaah answered his wish. He died a martyr in the Battle of Yamamah against Musaylimah the Liar.

The Prisoners of War

A large number of prisoners were captured at Badr. As the Qurayshi POWs were being paraded before him, the Prophet suddenly remembered Mut'im bin Adiyy. Mut'im, a polytheist, had helped the Muslims with food supplies during the boycott and more importantly had protected the Prophet after the death of Abu Taalib. He had died before the Battle of Badr.

Remembering Mut'im's favors, the Prophet said, "Had Mut'im bin Adiyy been alive and spoken to me about these filthy prisoners, I would have let them go for his sake." Clearly, the Prophet wanted to return the favor and show his followers that thanking people for their kindness, no matter their religion, is a tenet of Islam. It is also to be noted that Mut'im's son, Jubayr, became a Muslim some months later.

The Prophet began to ponder over what to do with the prisoners. He was concerned on their behalf, but as he did in all important matters, he wanted to seek the opinion of his Companions. "O people! Allaah has made you prevail over them, and only yesterday, they were your brothers." The way the Prophet sought his Companions' advice implied that he expected leniency from them.

Umar bin Al-Khattaab stood up first and said, "O Allaah's Messenger! Cut off their necks!" But the Prophet turned away from him. The Messenger of Allaah repeated his statement, and Umar said the same thing, "Cut off their necks," adding, "Let me have my relatives from the Bani Adiyy, and hand over Aqeel to Ali, his brother, to execute."

Then Abu Bakr As-Siddiq stood up and said, "O Allaah's Messenger! I think you should pardon them and set them free in return for ransom." It is said, upon hearing Abu Bakr's advice, the grief on the face of Allaah's Messenger vanished. It also became quite clear that the Prophet also preferred to pardon them.

The Prophet freed some prisoners for ransom, as the poor community of the believers was much in need of food and other necessities. Some others were told they could go free if they taught one illiterate person among the Muslims how to read and write. One poor prisoner came to the Prophet and said he had no money to pay in ransom. The Prophet set him free on the condition that he would not fight against the Muslims again.

Abbaas tried to free himself without paying a ransom, claiming he did not have any money. The Prophet told him that he knew Abbaas had money and that he had instructed his wife, Umm Al-Fadl, what to do with the money if he were to die. Abbaas was surprised to learn that the Prophet knew about this private conversation. It was then that he sincerely and openly attested to his faith in Islam and the Prophet Muhammad.

In response to the very different advice of his two closest Companions—Abu Bakr and Umar—the Prophet said that Allaah had created some hearts soft and others strict. He compared Abu Bakr to Prophets Abraham (Ibraahim) and Jesus (Eesa), and Umar to Prophets Noah (Nuh) and Moses (Musa). The Prophet's comparison of Abu Bakr and Umar respectively to Prophets Ibraahim, Isa, Nuh, and Musa is supported by Allaah's Book.

Prophet Ibraahim: "And (remember) when Ibraahim said: 'O my Lord! Make this city (Makkah) one of peace and security, and keep me and my progeny away from worshipping idols. O my Lord! They have indeed led astray many among mankind. But whoso follows me, he verily, is of me. And whoso disobeys me, still You are indeed Oft-Forgiving, Most Merciful."[206]

Prophet Eesa: "If You punish them, they are Your servants, and if You forgive them, verily You, only You are the Almighty, the All-Wise."[207]

Prophet Nuh: "My Lord! Leave not one of the disbelievers on the earth!"[208]

Prophet Musa: "Our Lord! Destroy their wealth, and harden their hearts, so that they will not believe until they see the painful torment."[209]

Allaah Disapproves of the Prophet's Decision

The next day or so when Umar visited the Prophet, he found him and Abu Bakr crying. Umar said, "O Messenger of Allaah, please tell me why you are crying so I may join you." The Prophet informed him that Allaah had revealed a verse that disapproved of his letting go of prisoners for ransom. Although Allaah revealed another verse to forgive him, the Prophet thought the divine punishment would have almost afflicted him. The revelation said:

> *It is not (fitting) for a Prophet that he should have prisoners of war until he has fought (his enemies thoroughly or established himself) in the land. You desire the goods of this world, but Allaah desires (for you) the Hereafter. And Allaah is All-Mighty, All-Wise. Were it not for a previous ordainment from Allaah, a severe torment would have touched you for what you took. So enjoy what you have gotten of war booty, lawful*

206 Ibraahim 14:35–36.

207 Maa'idah 5:118.

208 Nuh 71:26.

209 Ta Ha 20:131.

and good, and have consciousness of Allaah. Certainly, Allaah is Oft-Forgiving, Most Merciful.[210]

Scholars have debated the wisdom behind Allaah's disapproval of taking ransom for freedom after the Battle of Badr. Some say it was because the Muslims were still weak and some of these prisoners could have come back to fight again. For sure, some did. Also, forgiveness is more effective when it is done from a position of strength. Some people take forgiveness as a sign of weakness, especially if it is done when one is weak.

Quraysh Grieve for Badr Rout

The first person to return to Makkah with the news of Qurayshi catastrophe at Badr was Haysuman bin Abdullaah Al-Khuzaa'i. In a grave and rapid voice, he announced the names of the Qurayshi top brass who had been killed. He said, "Abu Jahl is killed, Utbah is killed, Shaybah is killed, Waleed is killed, Umayyah is killed, and Uqbah is killed."

Safwaan, the son of Umayyah, who was sitting in the Hijr (near Ka'bah) and watching, thought Haysuman had lost his mind, so he asked him, "What happened to Safwaan bin Umayyah (meaning himself)?"

Haysuman said, "He is sitting in the Hijr." Safwaan was wrenched by grief, and the news sent shockwaves through Makkah. The pagans could not have imagined that their most senior leadership would be decimated so easily.

Abu Lahab's End

Abu Lahab, the Prophet's uncle, was equally shocked. He had not joined the Battle of Badr for his own reasons and instead had sent a proxy. Anxious to verify what Haysuman had said, he asked Mugheerah bin Haarith, "O son of my brother, tell me what happened in Badr."

210 Anfaal 8:67–69.

Mugheerah swore that the Quraysh had fought hard but the Muslims had killed them and captured them as they pleased. Then Mugheerah said something amazing. "There was another force that was fighting on behalf of the Muslims. They were not human beings; they were on the fastest horses. We could not have fought them."

Abu Raafiyah, one of the slaves of Abbaas who was standing by, shouted, "They were the angels." Abu Lahab became furious and slapped Abu Raafiyah across the face, threw him to the ground, and kept punching him.

Umm Al-Fadl, the wife of Al-Abbaas, could not bear this. She picked up a big piece of wood and hit Abu Lahab forcefully on the head, which created a gash in his head. As Abu Lahab's head began to bleed profusely, Umm Al-Fadl yelled at him, "Is this your manhood, that in the absence of the master you are killing his slave?"

Abu Lahab's wound festered. He contracted a disease that caused blisters on his body, and he smelled terrible. Even his family would not come near him. He would scream in his lonesome confinement. When he died a miserable death, no one from the family wanted to touch his body. So they got some slaves to throw clothes on his corpse in order to lift it and dump it behind a wall. They had to throw rocks at his body from afar to cover it.

In Madinah, Good News Tinged with Sadness

The first person to return to Madinah after the Battle of Badr was Zayd bin Haarithah. Upon arrival he started shouting, "Allaahu Akbar (God is greater)." People had been worried, as no news had reached them in the last three days, leaving them very concerned. Zayd's ecstatic outburst made them jump to their feet, and they surrounded him in expectation of the positive news. Zayd said what Haysuman had said to the Makkans: "Abu Jahl is killed, Utbah is killed, Shaybah is killed, Waleed is killed, Umayyah is killed, and Uqbah is killed." It seemed unbelievable for a moment that all of these Qurayshi leaders, much dreaded for their animosity and ruthlessness, were suddenly gone.

As Zayd broke the news, he heard from the Baqiyatul Gharqad (Jannatul Baqi') cemetery[211] the sound of a different kind of Allaahu Akbar. The Muslims were offering the funeral prayer for Ruqayyah, the Prophet's daughter, who had died of her illness. It was due to Ruqayyah's condition that the Prophet had instructed Uthmaan bin Affaan, his son-in-law, to stay in Madinah. Ruqayyah was the second-oldest daughter of the Prophet, after Zaynab.

Prisoners Treated Like VIPs

The Prophet had instructed the Companions to treat the prisoners of war well. He himself brought Suhayl bin Amr to his own house. The Companions, as usual, took the Prophet's orders to heart. They would give their prisoner bread and meat while themselves eating dates, to the extent that some of the prisoners were embarrassed and returned the meat. It is amazing that this was happening long before the 1949 Geneva Convention on the treatment of prisoners of war! There were no laws governing the treatment of POWs back then, and according to the prevailing customs, the prisoners were at the mercy of the victors, who could treat them however they wished.

One of the prisoners was Abul Aas bin Rabi'ah, who was married to Zaynab, the Prophet's eldest daughter. Abul Aas was the son of Haalah, the older sister of Khadijah. The two were married in pre-Islamic days. Abul Aas was not a Muslim at the Battle of Badr, but he loved Zaynab dearly and did not divorce her under pressure from Abu Lahab. They continued to remain married even after Zaynab had accepted Islam while Abul Aas had not. Surah Mumtahanah (chapter 60), which disallowed marrying a non-Muslim, had not been revealed yet.

---

211 The proper name of the cemetery near the Prophet's mosque is Baqiyatul Gharqad, but Muslims today commonly refer to it as Jannatul Baqi'.

While Abul Aas was held captive, Zaynab sent some jewelry as ransom for her husband. Among the jewelry was a necklace that belonged to Khadijah, her mother. When the Prophet saw it, his eyes teared up as it reminded him of his beloved wife Khadijah. He turned toward the Companions and said, "If it is okay with you, release the husband of my daughter and return her the necklace." They promptly complied. Abul Aas was let go on the condition that when he reached Makkah, he would send Zaynab back.

The Question of War Booty

When the Muslims won the Battle of Badr, the Companions began to capture whatever war booty they could from the battlefield. Soon they found themselves disagreeing over who should keep what. Those who had killed an opponent said the property of that person was theirs was according to the custom of those days. Others argued that if they had not chased the enemies or kept them at bay with their arrows, those properties could not have been captured. Yet others said they had a share in the war booty because they were guarding the Prophet, which prevented them from fighting or collecting the booty. In the meantime, Sa'ad bin Waqqaas came and asked the Prophet for permission to keep a beautiful sword that he had captured from someone he had killed. Because of these small disagreements, an otherwise celebratory mood was about to turn sour. It was then that Allaah sent down some verses to rectify the situation.

The first verse of Surah Anfaal (chapter 8) says, "They ask you about Al-Anfaal (the spoils of war). Say: 'The spoils of war are for Allaah and the Messenger.' So have consciousness of Allaah and settle all differences among you, and obey Allaah and His Messenger, if you are believers."[212] (Anfaal 8:1)

Although the verses could be applied to everyone who was arguing about the spoils, Sa'ad bin Waqqaas held the opinion that the above verses

212 Anfaal 8:1.

were revealed about him in particular. Later Allaah revealed verse 41 of Surah Anfaal (chapter 8), legislating that one-fifth of the spoils of war belonged to Allaah and His messenger. The way it worked was that 20 percent of this fifth went to support the family of the Messenger of Allaah, and the rest of it was used to support the orphans, the poor, and the wayfarers. The Prophet gave a share of the Badr spoils to Uthmaan, who could not leave Madinah because of his wife's illness.

Lessons of Badr

After the victory, Allaah reminded the Muslims that no matter how hard they had fought on the Day of Badr, they had had no power to win the war, because "there is no victory except from Allaah."[213] He did this to keep their hearts humble.

Allaah also laid down a timeless rule that numbers alone do not guarantee victory. And Badr was a case in point. Some 313 Muslims defeated the Qurayshi army of 1,000 because the Muslims had faith in Allaah. On the contrary, when the Muslims thought their big numbers would bring them victory in the Battle of Hunayn, they met with defeat initially. The other lesson we can derive from Badr is that when we do our part and rely on Allaah alone, He helps us in ways we had not even imagined.

Planting the Seeds of the Next War

Badr inflicted a deep wound in the pagan psyche. Most of their senior leadership had been killed, and their morale plunged. In the aftermath of the war, Abu Sufiyan emerged as the undisputed elder statesman. The person who had successfully steered the rich Qurayshi caravan to safety had earned the admiration of his people.

---

213 Anfaal 8:10.

One day, Abdullaah bin Abi Rabi'ah, Ikrimah bin Abi Jahl, Safwaan bin Umayyah, and other men from Quraysh who had lost their fathers, sons, or brothers in Badr went to Abu Sufiyan bin Harb and other Qurayshis whose wealth the former had been able to save. They said, "O people of Quraysh! Muhammad has grieved you and killed the chiefs among you. Therefore, help us with this wealth so that we can fight him; it may be that we will avenge our losses."

Allaah denounced their continued hostility toward Islam and cautioned the Muslims through a verse that said that the fight was not over yet. There was also a reminder to the pagans that, if they continued to reject faith and died as disbelievers, their abode in the Hereafter would be the fire.

> *Verily, those who disbelieve spend their wealth to hinder (men) from the path of Allaah, and so will they continue to spend it; but in the end it will become an anguish for them. Then they will be overcome. And those who disbelieve will be gathered unto Hell.*[214] (Anfaal 8:36)

The Beginning of Hypocrisy

Before the Battle of Badr, some people had wondered if the fledgling Muslim community would be able to cope with the economic hardships and the Quraysh's hostility. One of them was Abdullaah bin Ubayy, whom the Aws and Khazraj had been about to appoint their king two years before the battle. But the arrival of the Prophet to Madinah had forever ruined that possibility. Abdullaah had, consequently, become a stealth opponent of the Prophet and tried to undermine him at every opportunity. This was the beginning of *Nifaaq* (hypocrisy), and Abdullaah bin Ubayy became its champion.

214 Anfaal 8:36.

When the Muslims dealt a crushing defeat to the Quraysh, Abdullaah was shocked and grieved. With a tinge of wistfulness and sarcasm, he remarked, "It seems like the matter has been settled." His comments clearly indicated that he had lost all hope that he would ever be crowned the undisputed leader of Aws and Khazraj. Abdullaah had seen with his own eyes how much respect and loyalty the Prophet received from the Companions and how Allaah had helped him against a numerically superior enemy. Even his own son, also named Abdullaah, was a die-hard supporter of the Messenger.

So from here on, Abdullaah bin Ubayy and his ilk had only two choices: to either sincerely throw their lot behind the Prophet or to feign Islam outwardly in order to undermine it from within. Unfortunately, they chose the latter. Such people were more dangerous than an open enemy, who showed the courage of his conviction and did not hide his enmity. The hypocrites were mingling with the Muslims, only to spy on and plot against them. That is why Allaah denounced them in the harshest terms. Allaah commanded the Prophet in the Qur'aan not to ever pray over a hypocrite who had died.

When some of the hypocrites built their own mosque (Masjid Dhiraar) in which to gather and plot against the Muslims, Allaah ordered the Prophet to never set foot in it. Moreover, Allaah warned the hypocrites that on the Day of Judgment they would be thrown into the lowest layer of hellfire, called *Ad-Dark Al-Asfal.* The lowest layer is also considered the most intense.

Reflections: What Is Hypocrisy?

The word *Nifaaq* (hypocrisy) comes from the root *Naafaqa,* which means a desert rat's hole with two openings. When it is faced with a threat from a predator, it enters by one hole, and while the predator is trying to look into the entrance, it escapes by the other hole.

Hypocrisy is to claim that one is a Muslim while concealing disbelief in the heart. In fact, in Makkah it was the opposite. Many Muslims had faith in the heart but could not declare it publicly because of the persecution. Not only that, but under torture some Companions said words of disbelief outwardly. One of them was Ammaar bin Yaasir.

Terrified of what he had said under torture, Ammaar informed the Prophet, who asked him, "What was the state of your heart when you said that?"

Ammaar answered, "It was firm on faith."

The Prophet said, "If they repeat their torture, you repeat what you said."

Allaah supported His Prophet's stand and exonerated those who expressed disbelief under persecution:

> *Whoever disbelieves in Allaah after his belief—except one who was forced while his heart is at peace with the faith—but whoever opens their breasts to disbelief, on them is the wrath from Allaah, and theirs will be a terrible torment.*[215]

Allaah revealed several verses in the Qur'aan to warn Muslims against the hypocrites. Here is one example:

> *And of mankind, there are some who say: "We believe in Allaah and the Last Day" while in fact they do not believe. They try to deceive Allaah and those who believe, while they only deceive themselves, and perceive (it) not!*[216]

---

215 Nahl 16:106.

216 Baqarah 2:8–9.

Then Allaah sent down an entire chapter, Al-Munafiqoon (The Hypocrites), to denounce such people:

> *When the hypocrites come to you, they say: "We bear witness that you are indeed the Messenger of Allaah." Allaah knows that you are indeed His Messenger, and Allaah bears witness that the hypocrites are liars indeed.*[217]

The Prophet said, "The signs of a hypocrite are four: when he speaks, he lies; when he promises, he breaks his promise; when entrusted with something, he breaks the trust; and when he gets angry, he fumes."

May a Muslim Call Another Muslim a Hypocrite?

Hypocrisy is a condition of the heart, and no one can look into someone's heart. The Prophet said, "When a person says to his brother, 'O Kaafir (disbeliever),' then verily one of them has returned with it." This Hadith means that if the person who was called a disbeliever is in reality a believer, then the label of disbelief returns to the accuser.

Zaynab's Difficult Migration

True to his promise, when Abul Aas reached Makkah, he arranged for Zaynab's migration to Madinah. For some reason, he asked his brother Kinaanah to escort Zaynab, the Prophet's daughter. Kinaanah chose to do so in full view of the people. As he was leading Zaynab's camel, some angry people surrounded her and told Kinaanah there was no way they would allow her to leave. One of them struck the camel with a spear, which made it jump, throwing Zaynab off the camel's back. She was pregnant at the time, and the fall resulted in a miscarriage.

The news reached Abu Sufiyan. He ran to the scene and realized that Zaynab had been treated unfairly. Abu Sufiyan admonished Kinaanah for

217 Al-Munafiqoon 63:1.

making the trip in broad daylight and advised him to wait for a few days and try again in the cover of darkness. That is what Kinaanah did, and he escorted Zaynab to the outskirts of Makkah, where the Companions whom the Prophet had sent were waiting. It was one of the hardest moments for both Zaynab and Abul Aas, but Zaynab had to migrate to Madinah so she could freely practice Islam. Abul Aas was still hesitant about embracing the new faith.

Abul Aas Becomes Muslim

Abul Aas had another encounter with the Muslims, and it became a turning point for him. He had been to Syria for trade, and on the way back, he was intercepted by a Muslim expedition force that did not know who he was. While the Muslims captured his goods, he went straight to the house of Zaynab after nightfall to avoid detection and asked her for protection, which she readily gave him. He said to her that he wanted his merchandise back, as it belonged to others.

The next morning as the Prophet was about to finish leading the *fajr* (dawn) prayer, a voice rang out: "O you men, I have given protection to Abul Aas bin Rabi'ah." When the prayer was over, the Prophet turned around and asked if others had heard what he had heard. The Companions affirmed hearing a voice. The Prophet, who recognized it as Zaynab's voice, told them he had no knowledge of this matter, and he reminded them that all Muslims were entitled to give protection to whomever they liked. The Prophet went to his daughter's house and told her to take care of her guest but not to allow her husband to approach her, as he was not lawful to her. This incident happened after Surah Mumtahanah (chapter 60) had been revealed around the 6 AH (627/628 CE). The surah prohibited marriage between a Muslim and a polytheist.

Then the Prophet told the raiding party, "This man is related to us, as you know, and you have taken his property. If you return it to him, I will be happy, but if you keep it, then this is booty that Allaah has given to you and you have more right to it." It is amazing that despite the religious and political authority Allaah had given the Prophet, he was requesting his Companions to do this, not ordering them. The Companions said they would rather return everything they had taken from him.

Abul Aas went to Makah and returned the merchandise to its owners. But then he felt a stirring in his heart. Finally, Islam had entered it. He could no longer ignore the truth and the magnanimity of the religion of his wife and father-in-law. Abul Aas came out of his house and publicly recited the testimony of faith: "I testify that there is no God but Allaah and that Muhammad is His servant and Messenger." He told them he could have accepted Islam while he was in Madinah with the Prophet, but then people who had entrusted him with money would have thought he had done so only to rob them of their property. Then he joined his family. It is said that the Prophet joined Abul Aas with his daughter Zaynab in matrimony without a new *nikaah* (marriage contract).

Abu Sufiyan's Revenge

After the Battle of Badr, a few small skirmishes happened between the Muslims and the Quraysh, including Abu Sufiyan's ambush on an outlying district of Madinah with some logistical help from Banu Nadheer. Abu Sufiyan had vowed that he would not bathe or have sexual relations until he had avenged Badr.

In this raid Abu Sufiyan killed a few of the Ansaari Muslims and burned down some date-palm trees. When the Prophet learned of this, he went after Abu Sufiyan, but the latter was able to get away. This is known as the Raid of *Al Sawiq*. It is named so because Abu Sufiyan's raiding party had dropped sacks of *sawiq* (a kind of porridge or cereal) to lighten their load. The Muslims had captured a large amount of *sawiq*.

Just a short while later, the Prophet sent Zayd bin Haarithah to attack a Qurayshi merchant caravan led by Abu Sufiyan. While Abu Sufiyan got away, Zayd was able to capture a large quantity of silver and many camels. The Muslim attacks against the Qurayshi caravans increasingly threatened their livelihood, and they were forced to find a much longer route to Syria.

The Treatment of the Jews under Islam

Today, Muslim-Jewish relations are under great strain because of the occupation of Palestine and Israel's inhumane treatment of the Palestinians. However, historically, Jews flourished under Muslim rule. In fact, the coming of Islam saved the Jews from extinction. Had Islam not arrived on the scene, the Jews in the West would have steeply declined, and Judaism in the East would have become just another oriental cult.

The Jews found peace and freedom under Arab Muslim rule, so much so that many of them wrote in Arabic and adopted Muslim culture. The most outstanding Islamic rule was Muslim Spain, Al-Andalusia, where there was a true Jewish Golden Age. But it was not limited to Spain. Jews also thrived in other centers of Islam: in Baghdad, between the ninth and twelfth centuries; in Qayrawaan (in North Africa), between the ninth and eleventh centuries; and in Cairo, between the tenth and twelfth centuries. When the centers of Islam rose, so did the Jewish cultural and religious life. When Muslims went through their downfall, like in Spain, the Jewish progress also suffered a setback. In 1492, Muslims were expelled from southern Spain after eight hundred years of enlightened rule, and so were the Jews. Another Muslim empire, under the Ottomans, gave many of these Jews refuge.

According to Mark Cohen, a Jewish-American professor of Near Eastern studies at Princeton, during the Middle Ages, Jewish people under Muslim rule experienced tolerance and integration. Some historians refer to this time period as the Golden Age for the Jews, as more opportunities became available to them. In the context of day-to-day life, Abdel Fattah Ashour, a professor of medieval history at Cairo University, states that Jewish people found solace under Islamic rule during the Middle Ages. Author Merlin

Swartz referred to this time period as a new era for the Jews, stating that the attitude of tolerance led to Jewish integration into Arab-Islamic society.[218]

In his PBS documentary, *The Story of the Jews,* Simon Schama says, "With no accusation of Christ-killing to contend with, Jews under Islamic rule were spared the demonization they suffered in Christendom."[219]

Najib Saliba, professor of Middle East history at Worcester State College, MA, in his scholarly paper wrote: "I would like to emphasize that the treatment of the Christians and Jews by Muslim states, Arab or Ottoman, was far superior to the treatment Muslims and Jews received at the hands of Christian states, or Palestinians at the hands of the Jewish state of Israel."[220]

It was under Muslim rule, particularly in southern Spain, that some of the best-known Jewish personalities rose to prominence, such as the following:

Sa'adya Gaon, Rabbi Sa'adiah ben Yosef Gaon, who was born in Faiyum, Egypt, in 882 CE, was a prominent rabbi, Jewish philosopher, and exegete of the Geonic period. The first important rabbinic figure to write extensively in Arabic, he is considered the founder of Judeo-Arabic literature. He died in 942 CE.

Solomon bin Gabirol, who was born in Malaga, Spain, in 1021 CE, was also known as Solomon ben Judah and traditionally known by his Latinized name Avicebron. He was an Andalusian poet and Jewish philosopher with a Neoplatonic bent. He died in Valencia, Spain, in 1058 CE.

---

218 Mark Cohen, "The Neo-Lachrymose Conception of Jewish-Arab History," *Tikkun* 6, 3 (1991).

219 PBS, WNET (2014).

220 "Christians and Jews under Islam," annual symposium of the Antiochian Orthodox clergy in the Antiochian Village, Ligonier, PA, July 21–25, 2008.

Abraham Ben Meir Ibn Ezra was born at Tudela, Navarre, in Spain, in 1089 CE, and he died around 1167 CE, apparently in Calahorra. He was one of the most distinguished Jewish men of letters and writers of the Middle Ages.

Moshe ben Maimon Maimonides, or Musa bin Maymun, acronymed RaMBaM, and Latinized Moses Maimonides, was a preeminent medieval Spanish Sephardic Jewish philosopher, astronomer, and one of the most prolific writers of his time. Maimonides was educated at the University of Al-Qarawiyyin in Morocco. He was born March 30, 1138 CE, in Cordoba, Spain, and died December 13, 1204 CE, in Fustat, Egypt. His tomb is in Tiberias, Israel.

So in light of the historical information, we can clearly understand that the misfortune that befell the Jews in Madinah a few years later was not because they were Jews but because of what they did. No country can tolerate treason or treachery, and every society has stringent laws against treacherous behavior because it runs counter to core human values.

The Incident of the Banu Qaynuqa

Barely a year and some months after the migration of the Prophet to Madinah, it had become evident that the Jews were not happy with the Muslim victory at Badr. The Prophet was aware of the Jewish unease. He had hoped that the Jews would welcome him because they were the People of the Book and had knowledge of his coming in their scriptures. The Prophet had shown special respect for the Jews, making them partners in the Madinah Charter and fasting on the Day of Aashoora (10 Muharram), on which Jews fast to commemorate the fast of Prophet Moses.

After Badr, the Prophet went to the marketplace of Banu Qaynuqa, a Jewish tribe, and said, "O Jews, beware lest God bring upon you the vengeance that He brought upon the Quraysh. And become Muslims. You know that I am a Prophet who has been sent—you will find that in your scriptures and God's covenant with you."

The Prophet's warning was in line with what Prophets Moses and Jesus had told the Jews. God's messengers have a duty to convey His message, even if a people dislike it. The Jews of Banu Qaynuqa did not like what they heard, and they replied, "O Muhammad, you seem to think that we are your people. Do not deceive yourself because you encountered a people with no knowledge of war and got the better of them, for by God, if we fight you, you will find that we are real men!"

This was a veiled threat and totally uncalled for from an ally. The Prophet began to worry that Banu Qaynuqa's belligerent attitude was an indication that they would not live up to the treaty obligations for long.

Banu Qaynuqa had their *souq* (marketplace) in the outskirts of Madinah, called *Souq Al-Banu Qaynuqa*. They were primarily goldsmiths and blacksmiths; the latter profession gave them the skills to make weaponry. Naturally, they had a large cache of weapons stocked up in their fortress. The Jews generally lived in fortresses for protection. The Arabs were not familiar with the art of fort building.

The Banu Qaynuqa at times displayed ridicule for the Muslims when they came to their marketplace. They would jeer at them and even intimidate the Muslim women. One day, a Muslim woman came to their marketplace. After she had sold her merchandise, she decided to buy some gold from a Jewish merchant. The man suggested that she expose her body, which she refused to do. Then the merchant motioned someone to secretly tie the woman's garment to a pole. When she got up, her entire garment was pulled away, and she was left with nothing on. She began to scream for help. A Muslim man who was nearby killed the miscreant, and the Jewish mob killed the Muslim in return.

When the Prophet heard the news, he realized it was time to do something to address this situation and to prevent its recurrence. Allaah sent down these verses to warn the Banu Qaynuqa:

> *Say (O Muhammad) to those who disbelieve: "You will be defeated and gathered together to Hell, and worst indeed is that place of rest." There has already been a sign for you in the two armies that met. One was fighting in the cause of Allaah, and as for the other, in disbelief. They saw them with their own eyes twice their number. And Allaah supports with His aid whom He wills. Verily, in this is a lesson for those who understand.*[221] (Aal Imraan 3:12–13)

The vile action of Banu Qaynuqa, coming soon after their veiled threat to the Prophet, could not be taken lightly. So the Prophet laid siege to their fortress, appointing Abu Lubaabah bin Abd Al-Mundhir as his deputy. The Prophet himself wore the armor, known as *Zat al-Fudul*, and handed the white standard to his uncle Hamzah bin Abdul Muttalib.

Abdullaah bin Ubayy, the chief hypocrite and a leader of the Khazraj tribe, had ties with the Banu Qaynuqa. He came to the Prophet and said in a disrespectful manner, "O Muhammad, deal kindly with my clients," but the Prophet put him off.

He repeated the words, and the Prophet turned away from him, saying, "Let me go," whereupon Abdullaah thrust his hand into the pocket of the armor of the Prophet, which brought clear signs of anger on his face. He said to Abdullaah bin Ubayy, "Woe unto you. Let me go."

Abdullaah said, "No, by God, I will not let you go until you deal kindly with my clients. Four hundred men without mail and three hundred mailed protected me from all mine enemies; would you cut them down in one morning? By God, I am a man who fears that circumstances may change."

221 Aal Imraan 3:12–13.

The Apostle said, "You can have them."[222]

The siege had lasted for about fifteen days when the Banu Qaynuqa were compelled to surrender without fighting. About seven hundred of their fighting men were taken prisoner. This was toward the end of Shawwal or Dhul Qa'dah of 2 AH (623/624 CE).

While sparing their lives, the Prophet ordered the Banu Qaynuqa to leave the city within three days and allowed them to take all they could carry on their beasts of burden. They were allowed to collect their debts. Some even took the doors of their houses.

The Prophet assigned Ubaadah bin Saamit to oversee their departure until they were well away from the city. The Prophet told the Banu Qaynuqa they could always come to Madinah to carry out their business and stay therein for up to three days. After leaving Madinah, the Banu Qaynuqa stayed in Wadi Al-Qura for a month and finally settled along the Syrian border. The Prophet received significant booty from the Banu Qaynuqa, taking one-fifth for himself and the poor and distributing the rest among the Muslims.

The Assassination of Ka'ab bin Ashraf

Ka'ab bin Al-Ashraf was a Jewish leader in Madinah. His father was an Arab from the Taa'i tribe and his mother from the Jewish tribe of Banu Nadheer. He was considered Jewish because the Jews traced their lineage through their mothers. He was a wealthy man known for his handsomeness and poetry. He lived a life of luxury in his fort southeast of Madinah at the rear of the Banu Nadheer's habitations.

Ka'ab was shaken by the death of the big leaders of the Quraysh at Badr, and he openly lamented their loss in his poetry. In one of his lines, he said,

222 Ibn Isshaaq, *Sirat Rasul Allah*, 36.

"By Allaah, if Muhammad has indeed struck down those people, then it was better to be buried in the earth than to walk upon it!"

After Badr, he went to Makkah to incite the Quraysh against the Prophet. It is reported that he made a secret alliance with Abu Sufiyan, conspiring to kill the Prophet. Upon his return to Madinah, he lampooned the Prophet and wrote sensual, obscene poetry against Muslim women, sometimes identifying them by name.

When Ka'ab was in Makkah, Abu Sufiyan asked him which religion was better, his (meaning the Quraysh's) or Prophet Muhammad's. Ka'ab responded to Abu Sufyaan, "Yours is better."

Allaah revealed two verses exposing and denouncing Ka'ab:

> *Have you not seen those who were given a portion of the Scripture. They believe in Jibt (sorcerer and soothsayer) and Taaghoot (Satan) and say to those who disbelieve, "These people are better guided on the way," than the believers. They are those whom Allaah has cursed, and he whom Allaah curses, you will not find for him (any) helper."*[223]

The Prophet became quite irritated by Ka'ab's conspiracy and lewd poetry about Muslim women. Ka'ab had clearly crossed a red line. Being that he was part of the Banu Nadheer and they were allied with the Prophet through the Madinah Charter, Ka'ab's actions constituted treason and defamation.

The Prophet asked the Companions, "Who will rid me of Ka'ab Al-Ashraf? He has blasphemed Allaah and His Messenger." Muhammad bin Maslamah volunteered, and Abbaad bin Bishr, Al-Haarith bin Aws, Abu Abs bin Hibr, and Salkan bin Salaamah, Ka'ab's foster brother, promised to help.

223 Nisaa 4:51–52.

Ibn Maslamah said, "O Messenger of Allaah, do you wish that I should kill him?"

He said, "Yes."

Ibn Maslamah said, "Permit me to talk (to him as needed)." The Prophet permitted him to talk as he saw fit. Muhammad bin Maslamah chalked out a plan to meet with Ka'ab while his helpers stood by ready to make the move. He laid out an elaborate plan, and when the opportunity presented itself, he and his men pounced on Ka'ab and killed him.

When the Jews learned about the assassination of Ka'ab, they became scared and realized that the Prophet would not tolerate treaty violations or insults to Allaah and His Messenger. It is well-known that the Prophet forgave personal insults to him but dealt sternly with offense against the Prophethood.

Reflections: No doubt the killing of Ka'ab bin Ashraf was an assassination, but it must be understood in its context. First, Ka'ab was guilty of treason against the treaty to which he was a signatory, had committed defamation and character assassination of Muslim women, and had falsified his own scriptures by saying pagans were following the correct religion. Second, there were no courts of law in Arabia in those days that could deal with Ka'ab's case. Because he did not cease and desist from his hostile and defamatory behavior, Ka'ab was eventually dealt with according to the custom of that time. Finally, those who attack the Prophet on this issue should think with an open mind. How are the most *civilized* countries of the world dealing with people like Ka'ab fourteen centuries later? Do countries that employ political hit squads, fire missiles from drones on suspects, orchestrate disappearances of political opponents, and run underground prisons to torture people have any right to criticize the Prophet Muhammad?

Battle of Uhud

Having suffered heavy losses at Badr, the Quraysh were burning with the desire for revenge, and some among them were inciting others to wage another war against the Muslims. Besides revenge, there was one more reason to go to war against the Muslims: the declining Qurayshi income as a result of the Muslim interceptions of their caravan. Now they had to take a much longer route, and even then they did not feel safe from interception. To their chagrin some of the Arab tribes had become allies of the Muslims, thereby making their lives even more difficult. Trade was the economic lifeline of the Quraysh. Without it they could not survive.

The most enthusiastic about fighting were Ikrimah bin Abi Jahl, Safwaan bin Umayyah, Abu Sufiyan bin Harb, and Abdullaah bin Abi Rabi'ah. The Quraysh sent emissaries to all the tribes to unite against the Muslims. They managed to enlist the support of two well-known tribes, Kinaanah and Tihaamah, besides some desert Bedouins known as *Ahabish.* It was also decided that the 50,000-dinar profit from Abu Sufiyan's caravan that had escaped interception at Badr should be spent on equipping the army.

After coaxing and cajoling each other to war, the Quraysh gathered a massive fighting force of three thousand men. Never before in the history of the tribal warfare had such an army been raised. There were two hundred horses, three hundred camels, and seven hundred body armors. They had taken their women with them in order to cheer themselves up and to have someone to taunt them if they shied away from battle.

Abbaas, the Prophet's uncle, immediately sent a fast rider to Madinah to inform the Muslims of the Quraysh's move. The envoy found the Prophet in Quba and gave him the letter. The Prophet asked Abdullaah bin Ubayy, the hypocrite, who was near him, to read the letter. When he was done reading, the Prophet urged Ibn Ubayy to keep the matter confidential.

Madinah was put on high alert, and men kept weapons even during prayers just in case an emergency arose. A group of Ansaari volunteered to guard the Prophet; among them were Sa'ad bin Mu'aadh, Usayd bin Hudhayr, and Sa'ad bin Ubaadah. Lest they should be taken by surprise, armed groups of men began to patrol the entrances and roads leading to the city.

This was most likely Friday, the sixth of Shawwal, 3 AH (624/625 CE). The Prophet led Friday prayers and informed the people about the looming threat. An Ansaari Muslim from the Banu Najjaar, named Maalik bin Amr, had passed away. The Prophet led his funeral prayer, and after that he told the Companions he had seen a dream.

According to Al-Waaqidi in his *Kitaab Al-Maghazi* (*Book of Wars*), the Prophet said, "O people, surely I had a dream. I was wearing an impenetrable armor, and my sword, *Dhul Fiqaar*, broke at the tip; I saw cows slaughtered, and I led a ram behind me."

The people asked, "How do you interpret it?"

He replied, "The impenetrable armor is Madinah, so stay in Madinah. The break at the tip of my sword is injury to myself; as for the slaughtered cows, they are the dead among my Companions; the ram that I led is the troops we will kill, God willing."[224]

In Ibn Isshaaq's version, the Prophet said, "By God I have seen in a dream something that augurs well. I saw cows, and I saw a dent in the blade of my sword, and I saw that I had thrust my hand into a strong coat of mail. And I interpreted that to mean Madinah. If you think it well, (remain) in Madinah and leave them where they have encamped, for if they halt, they will have halted in a bad position, and if they try to enter the city, we can fight them therein."

224 Al-Waqidi, Muhammad bin Umar, Kitab Al-Maghazi, translated as The Life of Muhammad by Rizwi Faizer, Oxon, Canada, Routledge, 2013, 104.

This was a rare occasion in which Abdullaah bin Ubayy (the chief hypocrite) agreed with the Prophet, saying that the tribes of Yathrib (Madinah) had never lost a battle against outsiders when they fought from the city and never won when they fought from outside of it. However, some of the young and zealous Companions who had not attended the battle of Badr advised the Prophet to go out so that no one could say they were cowards.

The Messenger of Allaah went inside his house and put on double armor. While he was inside, Sa'ad bin Mu'aadh and Usayd bin Hudhayr, who had been quiet in the presence of the Prophet, began to chide the younger Companions for advancing their own opinion above the Prophet's. The young Companions felt sorry for their overzealousness, and when the Prophet came out, they said they would like to take back their advice. The Messenger of Allaah said, "It is not for a Prophet to wear his shield for war and then lay down his arms before Allaah decides in his favor."

When the Qurayshi troops reached Al-Abwaa, where the Prophet's mother was buried, some of them said, "We have our women with us, and we are fearful about them. So if one of them is taken, open the grave of Muhammad's mother and keep it as a ransom until your woman is released."

Abu Sufiyan sought the advice of the senior Qurayshi leaders, and they said, "Do not mention this thing, for if we do so, the Banu Bakr and Banu Khuza'ah will unearth our dead."

The Messenger of Allaah marched on Saturday, 7 Shawwal, with a thousand Companions. At the end of the night, just before daybreak, the Prophet moved, and when he got to *Ash-Shawt*, he observed the dawn prayer.

There he was close enough to the enemy that they could see one another. It was at this point that Abdullaah bin Ubayy went back to Madinah with three hundred men, a third of the army, saying he was unhappy the Prophet had not listened to his advice. Some of the Companions became angry with Ibn Ubayy and called him a traitor. Ibn Ubayy replied, "If we knew that you would fight today, we would accompany you. However, we do not think that you will fight today."

The Prophet asked the Companions if anyone could take them near the Quraysh by a road that bypassed the Qurayshi troops. Khaythamah Abu Sa'ad bin Khaythamah said he could, and he took them through the Harrah of Banu Haarithah until they came out in the territory of Mirba bin Qayzi, who was a bitter, old, blind man.

When he felt the approach of the Prophet and his Companions, he got up and threw dust in their direction, saying, "You may be the Prophet of God, but I won't let you through my garden. By God, Muhammad, if I could be sure that I should not hit someone else, I would throw it in your face."

The Companions rushed to kill him, but the Prophet forbade them, saying, "Do not kill him, for he is blind of sight and blind of heart."

The Messenger of Allaah marched until he reached the hillside in the area of Uhud, where they camped in the valley, with Mount Uhud behind them and Madinah in the front. In the middle was the Qurayshi army. The Messenger of Allaah told the Companions, "No one starts fighting until I issue the command to fight."

After the departure of Abdullaah bin Ubayy and his supporters, the Muslim army was reduced to just seven hundred men. The Prophet appointed Abdullaah bin Jubayr to lead fifty archers on Jabal Aynayn, which is now known as Jabal Ar-Rumaah (the Mount of the Archers). The Prophet said to them, "Keep the horsemen away from us, and be aware that we might be attacked from your direction. If victory was for or against us, remain in your positions. And even if you see us being picked up by birds, do not abandon your positions."

In a version in Al-Bukhari, the Prophet said: "If you see us snatched into pieces by birds, do not leave this position of yours till I send for you. And if you see that we have defeated the enemy and trodden on them, do not desert your position till I send for you."

The Prophet's advice was ingenious from a military standpoint, something the Muslims were going to truly fathom a little later. He divided the army into three battalions:

1. The Emigrants, under the command of Mus'ab bin Umayr Abdari
2. Aws, under the command of Usayd bin Hudhayr
3. Khazraj under the command Al-Hubaab bin Al-Mundhir

Interestingly, Mus'ab's non-Muslim clansmen were carrying the Qurayshi flag, as was their tradition.

Before the battle, the Prophet reviewed the army. He dismissed those whom he considered to be disabled or too young to stand the fight. Among them were Abdullaah bin Umar bin Al-Khattaab, Usaamah bin Zayd, Usayd bin Zaheer, Zayd bin Thaabit, Zayd bin Arqam, Araba bin Aws, Amr bin Hazm, Abu Sa'eed Al-Khudri, Zayd bin Haarithah Al-Ansaari (not the Prophet's adopted son), Sa'ad bin Habba, and Al-Baraa bin Aazib.

The Messenger of Allaah allowed both Rafi' bin Khadayj and Samurah bin Jundub to join the army even though they were too young. The former proved to be skillful at shooting arrows; the latter wrestled the former and beat him.

The Quraysh gave their main flag to the Banu Abd Ad-Daar clan and appointed Khaalid bin Al-Waleed to lead the right side of the horsemen and

Ikrimah bin Abi Jahl the left side. As the battle was about to begin, Abu Sufiyan came forward, and seeing the Ansaari fighters, he told them the Quraysh had nothing against them and that he only wanted to fight with the Makkan Muslims.

Abu Aamir, the father of Companion Hanzalah, also tried to discourage the Ansaari Muslims from fighting. He was a leader of the Aws and used to be called Abu Aamir the Raahib (the monk). He was respected among his people, but when the Prophet migrated to Madinah, Abu Aamir ran away to Makkah to avoid accepting Islam. The Prophet called him Abu Aamir the Faasiq (the Corrupt), and that is how the Muslims referred to him after that.

On the Day of Uhud, he told the Quraysh, "You will see how much my people love and respect me." So when the two armies were arrayed, Abu Aamir shouted, "O my people, I am Abu Aamir." When the Awsi Muslims saw him on the other side, they hurled some vile curses at him, and he turned to the Quraysh, saying some evil had befallen his people.

A Duel at Uhud

When the two armies faced each other, Talhah bin Abi Talhah, the flag bearer of the Quraysh, came to the front and challenged the Muslims to a duel.

Ali bin Abi Taalib accepted the challenge and struck Talhah a hard blow, which felled him to the ground, badly injured. Surprisingly, Ali walked away from Talhah without killing him. The Companions asked why he did not finish off Talhah. Ali replied that Talhah had begged him to spare his life in the name of family ties. He saw him lying helplessly with his lower garment lifted and private parts exposed.

"I felt pity for him," Ali said. Some other Muslims killed Talhah eventually. The flag was picked up by another man from Abd Ad-Daar, and one by one several of them were killed trying to keep the flag aloft.

The Prophet's Sword Given to Abu Dujaanah

On the Day of Uhud, the Prophet took out his sword and asked, "Who will take this sword with its right?" A number of Companions rushed to take it, among them Zubayr bin Al-Awwaam, Ali bin Abi Taalib, and Umar bin Al-Khattaab. But the Prophet did not give it to any of them, and he kept repeating his question. Then Abu Dujaanah Sammaak bin Kharshah came forward and asked, "O Messenger of Allaah, and what is its right?"

The Prophet replied, "That you strike the enemy with it until it bends."

Abu Dujaanah said, "O Messenger of Allaah, I will take it for that price," and he was given the sword.

Abu Dujaanah was a man of courage who used to swagger at war. He had a red band that he sometimes wore around his head. Whenever he was head-banded, everybody knew that he was determined to fight to the death. Therefore, as soon as Abu Dujaanah took the Prophet's sword, he tied a red band around his head and started strutting among the fighters with his chest puffed up. Watching him do that, the Messenger of Allaah remarked, "This is a sort of walking that Allaah detests except in such a situation."

Abu Dujaanah wreaked havoc among the Qurayshi troops. Nobody seemed to withstand his attack. Then Abu Dujaanah saw from a distance the person who was feverishly mobilizing the enemy troops. He rushed toward that person and raised his sword to strike, when suddenly he heard a woman's shrieks. Lo, it was Abu Sufiyan's wife, Hind. He pulled his sword back, telling himself, "This is the sword of the Messenger of Allaah, and it will not strike a woman."

Zubayr, a cousin of the Prophet, had been monitoring Abu Dujaanah since the man had received the sword over his own request. When Zubayr saw Abu Dujaanah's bravery and his respect for the Prophet's sword, he understood why he and not anyone else had been chosen for this honor.

After one-on-one fights, a general battle ensued, and the Muslims gallantly tore through the Qurayshi ranks, cutting down enemy after enemy. Hamzah was among the fiercest. Nobody could stand against him. He killed scores of enemy fighters in hand-to-hand combat. There was, however, a treacherous plan awaiting him, as martyrdom had been decreed for him.

The Story of Jubayr and His Slave Wahshi

Jubayr bin Mut'im's uncle, Tu'aymah bin Adiyy, had been killed at Badr, and Jubayr was seething with revenge. He told his Abyssinian slave Wahshi bin Harb, who was known as Abu Dasma, that if he killed Hamzah, the Prophet's uncle, he would be freed. So Wahshi, a renowned javelin thrower, followed Hamzah secretly in the battlefield of Uhud and watched with amazement how the latter was killing his opponents.

Wahshi's opportunity came when he saw Hamzah attacking Siba bin Abdul Uzzah. He trained his javelin at Hamzah and threw it with all his might. The spear hit Hamzah in the groin area and came out between his legs. Hamzah staggered and tried to move toward Wahshi, but then he collapsed. Wahshi pulled out his javelin after Hamzah's body became still and quickly informed the Quraysh that he had accomplished his mission.

Wahshi's Life after Uhud

The only reason Wahshi had killed Hamzah was to earn his freedom. He had no personal grudge against the uncle of the Prophet. Wahshi said, "After the Battle of Uhud, I continued to live in Makkah for quite a long time, until the Muslims conquered Makkah. I then ran away to Taa'if, but soon Islam reached that area as well. I heard that however grave the crime of a person, God would forgive him if he returned to Him. I, therefore, reached the Messenger of Allaah with the *Shahaadatayn* (testimonials of faith) on my lips.

"The Messenger saw me and said, 'Are you the same Wahshi, the Abyssinian?' I replied in the affirmative. Thereupon he asked, 'How did you kill Hamzah bin Abdul Muttalib?' I gave an account of the matter. The Prophet Muhammad was moved and said, 'I should not see your face until you are resurrected, because the heart-rending calamity fell upon my uncle at your hands.'"

Wahshi said, "So long as the Messenger of Allaah remained alive, I kept myself hidden from him. After his death the battle with Musaylimah (the false prophet) took place. I joined the army of Islam and used the same weapon against Musaylimah and succeeded in killing him with the help of one of the Helpers. If I killed the best of men (Hamzah bin Abdul Muttalib) with this weapon, the worst man, too, did not escape its terror."

Despite Hamzah's martyrdom, the Muslims dominated the battlefield. Aided by divine guidance, the Prophet had allowed only a narrow fighting area, thereby depriving the Quraysh of any benefit from their numerical advantage. More importantly, Allaah sent down forces that helped them against the Quraysh. This was the fulfillment of Allaah's promise, and the victory turned into defeat only because of the Muslims' disagreement and some archers' disobedience of the Prophet.

The Quraysh began to lose heart. When they saw their flag bearers falling one after another, they began to flee. The Prophet's Companions reported seeing the Qurayshi women running up the hills to safety, lifting their gowns in an attempt to move fast, showing their ankles.

The Tide Turns

When the Muslims saw that their enemies were fragmented and deserting the battlefield, they thought the battle had been won, and some of them started to collect the booty. When the archers saw this scene, a number of them also decided to seize the spoils of war. Their leader, Abdullaah bin Jubayr, reminded them of the command of the Messenger of Allaah that, win or lose, they were not to leave their places. Many of them went despite the chastisement, leaving the only vulnerable position of the Muslim army unguarded.

Khaalid bin Waleed, who was also retreating to safety, noticed this sudden opportunity. He quickly gathered some 150 people and launched a counterattack. The Muslims were not ready for an attack, and they ran for their lives, leaving the Prophet in the midst of the enemy. The tide of battle had turned against the Muslims. Abdullaah bin Jubayr and his remaining Companions valiantly fought but in the end were martyred.

Mus'ab bin Umayr

As is the case in battles, the Qurayshi forces paid special attention to the Muslim flag, which was being carried by Mus'ab bin Umayr. A man named Ibn Qamiyah Al-Laythi struck Mus'ab's right arm, with which he was holding the flag. When his right arm was severed, Mus'ab grabbed the flag with his other arm, and when that too was cut off, he grabbed the flag with the stumps of his arms until he was struck in the chest and fell down. It is said that Ali or some other Companion took the flag. There is also a narration that the Prophet called Mus'ab, and the man holding the flag said he was not Mus'ab but was an angel.

Mus'ab greatly resembled the Messenger of Allaah. So when Ibn Qamiyah returned to the Quraysh, he boasted, "I have killed Muhammad." This rumor had dual effects. One the one hand, the Quraysh began to celebrate and think they did not need to continue the fight, and on the other, some Muslims became distraught and saw no point in fighting. Some people believe that Satan had taken the shape of one of the Qurayshis and spread the rumor about the Prophet's death.

Anas bin An-Nadhr

It was then that Anas bin An-Nadhr, the uncle of Anas bin Maalik, passed by and saw some of the Companions sitting dejected. He asked what the matter was. They said, "The Prophet has been killed."

Anas said, "Then what would you do with life after him? Rise and die just as he died!" Anas then rushed to where the fighting was most intense.

Sa'ad bin Mu'aadh later told the Prophet that Anas had told him before being martyred, "Paradise! I smell its fragrance blowing from the other side of Uhud." Sa'ad said, "O Messenger of God, I could not fight as he fought."

Afterward they found Anas lying dead with more than eighty wounds, so disfigured that only his sister could recognize him by the marks on his fingers.

It is said that the following verse of Surah Ahzaab was revealed about Anas bin An-Nadhr:

> *Among the believers are men who have been true to their covenant with Allaah, of them some have fulfilled their obligations (i.e., have been martyred), and some are still waiting, but they have never changed (in their resolve) in the least.*[225]

In the chaos that followed, some Muslims killed other Muslims by mistake. Of those killed in such a manner was the elderly Companion Yamaan, father of the Prophet's confidant, Hudhayfah. In the din of the war, when he saw some Muslims attacking his father, Hudhayfah shouted, "My father, my father," trying to alert them but to no avail. His father was fatally wounded. Hudhayfah forgave the Muslims, and when the Prophet gave him blood money of one hundred camels from the state treasury, he gave them all away in charity. Because of his high esteem for Hudhayfah, the Prophet had confided to him the names of the hypocrites in Madinah, which gave

225 Ahzaab 33:23.

Hudhayfah the title, "the keeper of the Prophet's secret." After the Prophet's demise, whenever there was a funeral, people would look around to see if Hudhayfah was in attendance. His presence would signify that the deceased was not a hypocrite.

The Prophet's Courage

When the Prophet saw the Muslims fleeing the battlefield, he was in the midst of the enemy forces, yet he called his Companions out, unafraid that doing so would give away his location to the Quraysh and invite attack against him. Sure enough, a group of the Qurayshi fighters rushed toward him. The Prophet asked in a raised voice, "Who will sell his life for us?" Five of the Ansaar stood up to heed the Prophet's call. Four of them died defending him, and one was badly wounded. The Prophet himself shot so many arrows that his bow gave up.

Perhaps it was at that point that Utbah bin Abi Waqqaas threw rocks at the Messenger of Allaah, breaking his incisor and causing him to bleed. Utbah's rock also grazed his knees, and he fell in a ditch that Abu Aamir the Corrupt had dug. Ibn Qamiyah suddenly rushed on his horse and struck the Messenger of Allaah with his sword. Talhah swiftly moved to take the blow on his shield and lost some of his fingers in the attempt. However, he was able to blunt the impact of the sword on the Prophet. The sword's blow was hard, and despite Talhah's swift action, the Prophet's helmet was bent, and some of its rings pierced his cheeks. Abu Ubaydah bin Al-Jarraah broke his own teeth trying to pull the rings out from the cheeks of the Prophet. He also began to bleed. The Prophet said to Abu Ubaydah, "Whoever's blood has touched my blood, the fire (of Hell) cannot reach him."

Ironically, Utbah was the brother of Sa'ad bin Abi Waqqaas, a hero of Uhud on the Muslim side, about whom the Prophet said, "Shoot, may my mother and father be ransomed for you," a phrase he never used for anyone before or since. On the other hand, the Sahaabah used this phrase for the Prophet all the time to express their utmost love and respect for him. Both Sa'ad and Talhah shot numerous arrows that day while standing in front of the Messenger of Allaah, thereby guarding him with their own bodies.

Success or Failure Only with Allaah

When Utbah's rock and Ibn Qamiyah's sword struck the Prophet, in that moment of pain and disappointment he said, "How can a people achieve success after having done this to their Prophet, who is calling them to their Lord, the Exalted and Most Honored?" In another version, the Prophet said, "How can a people be successful when they have injured their Prophet?"

Then the Prophet invoked Allaah against some of the chiefs of Quraysh: "O Allaah! Curse Al-Haarith bin Hishaam. O Allaah! Curse Suhayl bin Amr. O Allaah! Curse Safwaan bin Umayyah."

The Prophet's supplication to Allaah against anyone can destroy them, but Allaah, Who is the most merciful and the knower of the unseen, intervened and gently chided His Prophet.

> *Not for you is the decision; whether He turns in mercy to (pardon) them or punishes them; verily, they are the wrongdoers.*[226]

While Allaah confirmed that the Qurayshi leaders whom the Prophet had prayed against were wrongdoers, He also reminded the believers that none but Allaah knows the final status of a person. Some years later, these Qurayshi leaders embraced Islam, and the Prophet himself pardoned them.

In several other places in the Qur'aan, Allaah has made clear that guidance, punishment, and forgiveness are not in the hands of anyone, including His messengers. The job of the messengers and prophets is only to convey

---

226 Aal Imraan 3:128.

the message. For example, He revealed the following verses: "Your duty is only to convey (the message) and on Us is the reckoning";[227] "Their guidance is not upon you, but Allaah guides whom He wills";[228] and "Verily, you guide not whom you like, but Allaah guides whom He wills."[229]

After Ibn Qamiyah had boasted that he had killed the Prophet, the first one to notice that the latter was alive was Ka'ab bin Maalik. Ka'ab recognized the Prophet beneath his face armor and shouted at the top of his voice, "O Muslims! Rejoice! This is the Messenger of Allaah!"

The Prophet gestured to Ka'ab to be quiet, but many Muslims had heard the good news and begun to gather around him. A group of Muslims escorted the Prophet to the higher ground. The foremost among them was Talhah, who himself was severely wounded. The Prophet needed to climb up, but his wounds and age prevented him from it. Talhah crouched below the ledge with great strain to his wounds and raised the Prophet on his back so he could climb up. The Prophet said of him that day, "He who wants to look at a martyr walking the face of the earth, let him look at Talhah, the son of Ubaydullaah."

Those accompanying the Prophet at this moment, besides Talhah, were Sa'ad bin Abi Waqqaas, Abu Bakr, Umar, Ali, Abu Ubaydah bin al-Jarraah, Abu Dujaanah, Sa'ad bin Mu'aadh, Zubayr bin Al-Awwaam, and Haarith bin Simmaah, among others. When the Prophet climbed up the hill, Ubayy bin Khalaf came rushing and shouted, "Where is Muhammad?"

The Sahaabah asked if they should take care of Ubayy, but the Prophet said, "Let him come." Then he took a lance from Al-Haarith and threw it at Ubayy, striking him in the neck.

---

227 Ra'd 13:40.

228 Baqarah 2:272.

229 Qasas 28:56.

Ubayy fell from his horse but managed to escape to the Quraysh, twisting and turning with pain and saying, "By God, Muhammad has killed me." The Quraysh chastised him for complaining so much, for all they saw was a scratch on his neck. Ubayy said, "Muhammad said to me in Makkah that he would kill me, and, by God, if he had only spat on me, he would have killed me."

How ironic it was that Ubayy believed in the promise of the Prophet Muhammad but disbelieved in his message. Ubayy remembered that years back in Makkah he used to threaten the Messenger of Allaah, saying, "Muhammad, I have got a horse called Awd, which I feed many measures of corn every day. I shall kill you while riding it."

The Prophet had responded to him, "No, I shall kill you, if God wills." In all his battles, the only person whom the Prophet killed with his own hands was Ubayy bin Khalaf.

The Quraysh had seen the direction in which the Prophet had gone. They were frantically shooting arrows at the Muslims, one of which struck an eye of Qataadah bin Nu'maan, who was shielding the Prophet with his body. Qataadah's eye was torn into pieces and ripped out of its socket. The Prophet picked up the eye and put it back. Qataadah reported that for the rest of his life the vision in that eye was better than in the other eye. This was a miracle that God gave the Prophet, and miracles are not bound by normal laws.

Hanzalah, Whom the Angels Bathed

Hanzalah was a sincere Companion of the Prophet. Ironically, he was the son of Abu Aamir Raahib, whom the Prophet had called *Faasiq* (the Corrupt). His father was called Faasiq instead of Raahib because of his treachery. Hanzalah's marriage was scheduled for Friday, the sixth of Shawwal. When he found out that the Battle of Uhud was about to begin the next day, Hanzalah came to the Prophet to ask if he should delay his marriage. The Prophet told him to proceed with the wedding.

When war broke out the next morning, Hanzalah jumped out of his bed, plunged into the fighting, and was martyred. After the battle the Sahaabah were surprised to see water dripping from his body. The Prophet informed them that Hanzalah had spent the night with his bride and was in the state of *janaabah* (sexual impurity) when he joined the fighting, so the angels had given him a bath. Thereafter he was known as "Hanzalah, the *Ghaseelul Malaaikah*," meaning the one whom the angels had bathed. His wife confirmed that Hanzalah had rushed to the battlefield without taking a bath. It is said that after Hanzalah's widow had passed the mandatory *iddah* (the waiting period), a number of Companions proposed to her because she was the wife of a special type of martyr.

Nusaybah bint Ka'ab

One of the unusual heroes of Uhud was Nusaybah bint Ka'ab, better known as Umm Umaarah. She was an early convert to Islam, a member of the Banu Najjaar tribe living in Madinah. Nusaybah was the sister of Abdullaah bin Ka'ab and the mother of Abdullaah and Habib bin Zayd Al-Ansaari.

She attended the Battle of Uhud like other women, to bring water to the soldiers, while her husband and two sons fought. But after the Muslim archers disobeyed the Prophet's orders and began deserting their positions, believing that victory was at hand, the tide of the battle turned, and it seemed that the Muslim defeat was imminent. When this occurred, Nusaybah entered the battle, carrying a sword and shield. She shielded the Prophet Muhammad from the enemy arrows and received several wounds while fighting. When a horse-mounted Qurayshi attacked her, she pulled on the horse's bridle and plunged her sword into its neck, toppling the horse onto its rider. Witnessing this, the Prophet called Abdullaah to help his mother.

Ibn Hajar al-Asqalaani, a famous Hadith scholar, said, "She (Nusaybah) witnessed the Pledge of Aqabah…She participated in the battles of Uhud,

Hudaybiyah, and Khayber and participated in *Umrah Al-Qadaa* (lesser pilgrimage). She also witnessed the victory of Makkah and participated in the battles of Hunayn and Yamamah, in which she lost one of her hands."

The Prophet said, "Whenever I turned left or right on the Day of Uhud, I could always see her (Umm Umaarah) fighting in my defense." So he supplicated, "O Allaah, make Umm Umaarah and her family my Companions in Jannah."

To Paradise without a Single Prayer

Among those Muslims who died in the Battle of Uhud was a man named Amr bin Thaabit bin Wuqaysh Al-Ash-hali, nicknamed Usayrim. On the day of the battle, he found himself alone in Madinah among women and children. The only men he found were the hypocrites or the very old. Feeling embarrassed, he went to the battlefront, and when the Muslims from Aws saw this fellow tribesman wielding a sword, they said, "What are you doing here? We do not want a non-Muslim's help."

Usayrim said, "I have become a Muslim." Then he joined the battle and was killed. Usayrim had embraced Islam after the dawn prayer on the day of Uhud and was martyred before the afternoon prayer. The Prophet confirmed his faith, saying, "He is from the people of Jannah."

Abu Hurayrah used to quiz his students: "Who was the Sahaabi who went to Paradise without praying a single prayer?"

Abu Sufiyan Looks for the Prophet's Body

Although the Quraysh had begun celebrating, they knew that a celebration without the body of the Prophet Muhammad for evidence could have no substance. Therefore, Abu Sufiyan began to earnestly look for evidence that the Prophet had been killed.

He mounted his horse and rode to the foot of Mount Uhud, where he had last seen the Prophet and his Companions standing, and shouted, "Exalt yourself, O Hubal! Make your religion prevail!"[230] Then he said, "Is Muhammad among you?" Neither the Prophet nor the Companions answered him. Then he asked, "Is Ibn Abi Quhaafah (Abu Bakr) among you?" They did not answer. He asked again, "Is Umar bin Al-Khattaab among you?" They did not answer him, for the Prophet had forbidden them from answering. Abu Sufiyan only asked about those three. That is because he and his people knew quite well that the call to Islam depended to a large degree on those men. This must not be seen as a slight against Uthmaan and Ali, who were also among the most prominent Muslims. Then Abu Sufiyan began to exult, saying, "As for those three, we have relieved you of them."

Umar could not restrain himself anymore, and he shouted, "O enemy of Allaah, those whom you have just mentioned, they are still alive. Allaah has preserved what you hate."

Abu Sufiyan answered, "The mutilation of your dead is something I did not order, but it did not displease me either." Then he shouted, "Hubal is sublime!"

The Prophet said to Umar, "Say Allaah is more sublime and exalted and mightier."

Abu Sufiyan said, "We have Al-Uzzah, and you have no Al-Uzzah."

The Prophet said, "Say Allaah is our Protector, and you have no protector."

Abu Sufiyan said, "War goes by turns, and this day was for that," referring to Badr.

230 Hubal was an important idol that the pagans worshipped.

Umar replied, "No, they are not the same. Our dead are in Paradise, while yours are in the fire."

Then Abu Sufiyan said, "O Umar, I beseech you by Allaah's name to tell me the truth: Have we killed Muhammad?"

Umar said, "No, and he is listening to you right now."

Abu Sufiyan said, "To me, you are more truthful than Ibn Qamiyah, and even more reliable."

Ibn Isshaaq said, "As Abu Sufiyan was leaving, he shouted, 'We will meet again at Badr next year.'"

The Messenger of Allaah said, "Say, 'Yes, that is an appointment that is binding on us.'"

Later on, the Messenger of Allaah dispatched Ali bin Abi Taalib to follow the returning Quraysh. He said to him, "Pursue them and see what they are going to do, and what they aim at. If they dismount horses and ride on camels' backs, this means that they are heading for Makkah, but if they ride horses and lead camels unmounted, they are leaving for Madinah. By the One in Whose Hand my soul is, if they attacked Madinah, I would march to them there, and I would fight them."

Ali followed them for a while and returned, saying, "I went out and traced them to see what they were up to. I saw them mount camels, leaving the horses unmounted. They were heading for Makkah."

Although the Quraysh rode their camels and headed back to Makkah, it was not without pondering over the idea of launching a second attack. It is reported that some of the Prophet's allies from the Khuza'ah tribe scared off the Quraysh by saying that the Muslims were furious and had gathered a large force to launch a counterattack against them. According to another report, it was Safwaan bin Umayyah who dissuaded the Quraysh from returning. The Prophet was relieved at the news. His greatest concern was the safety of the Muslim women and children in Madinah who were on their own. When the Quraysh left, some Muslim women came out of the city to provide water and other first aid to the wounded.

The Burial of the Martyrs

Now a very painful but necessary task lay ahead: the burial of some sixty-five to seventy martyrs. The Prophet had ordered that the bodies of the Muslims be collected and prepared for burial. When he saw what had been done to Hamzah's body, he sobbed, and at some point his sob became audible. He tried to stop Safiyyah, Hamzah's sister and his paternal aunt, from seeing his body, but she insisted, and the Prophet relented. Safiyyah came upon Hamzah's body and supplicated for him, exhibiting both grace and restraint.

Hind bint Utbah, whose father, uncle, brother, and son had been killed in Badr, had cut open Hamzah's stomach, removed his liver, chewed upon it, and spat it out. She had also cut his nose and ears and made a garland out of them. Abdullaah bin Jahsh, the Prophet's cousin, had been struck down not far from Hamzah, and his body also had been mutilated, like some other Muslims' bodies had been. Overcome with grief, the Prophet vowed that when Allaah gave him victory over the Quraysh, he would mutilate thirty of them.

Allaah, the All-Knowing and Merciful, sent down a verse that both consoled and guided the Prophet in this moment:

> *And if you punish them, then punish them with the like of that with which you were afflicted. But if you have patience with them, then it is better for those who are patient.*[231]

---

231 Nahl 16:126.

After this verse came down, the Prophet not only withdrew his oath but also forbade mutilation of the dead under any circumstances. He also said, "When one of you strikes a blow, let him avoid striking the face...for Allaah created Adam in His image."

The Prophet ordered that Hamzah and Abdullaah (uncle and nephew) should be buried together in the same grave. He also buried some other martyrs together, saying they were close friends in this world and that in the Hereafter people will be with those they love.

Then the Prophet met Hamnah bint Jahsh. She was told of the death of her uncle, Hamzah, and she said, "We belong to God, and to Him we return." Then she was told of the death of her brother, Abdullaah, and she said the same thing. Then she was told of the death of her husband, Mus'ab, upon which she shrieked and wailed.

The Prophet said, "A woman's husband holds a special place for her, as you can see from her self-control at the death of her uncle and brother and her shrieking over the death of her husband."

It is noteworthy that in Islam the mourning for the death of a relative is up to three days, except for the death of a husband, which is four months and ten days.

The Prophet came to the body of Mus'ab and exhibited great emotion. Mus'ab lived a princely life before Islam, but when faith entered his heart, he dedicated himself to serving God and His Messenger. Even other Companions drew inspiration from him. At Mus'ab's grave, the Prophet is said to have recited:

> *Among the believers are men who have been true to their covenant with Allaah, of them some have fulfilled their obligations (i.e., have*

> *been martyred), and some are still waiting, but they have never changed (in their resolve) in the least.*[232]

As mentioned earlier, some have said that the above verse was revealed about Anas bin An-Nadhr. However, its meaning could be applied to Mus'ab and all those who had vowed to defend Allaah's religion and His Messenger. This included the people who had participated in the two pledges of Aqabah.

The Prophet was informed that some of the Companions did not have enough clothes on them to shroud their bodies. It is said that Hamzah and Mus'ab only had a sheet wrapped around them, and when their heads were covered with it, their feet became exposed. The Prophet ordered that their feet be covered with a fragrant grass called *idhkhir*.

Among the Muslim dead were those who had no relatives present. The Prophet said words to console their souls and informed the Companions of Allaah's promise of an eternal bliss for them. Allaah sent down this verse about the martyrs of Uhud and martyrs in general:

> *Think not of those as dead who are killed in the way of Allaah. Nay, they are alive, with their Lord, and they have provision. They rejoice in what Allaah has bestowed upon them of His bounty and rejoice for the sake of those who have not yet joined them, but are left behind (not yet martyred) that on them no fear shall come, nor shall they grieve. They rejoice in a grace and a bounty from Allaah, and that Allaah will not waste the reward of the believers.*[233] (Aal Imraan 3:169–171)

The Prophet expounded on the above verses in a Hadith: "When your brothers were killed in Uhud, Allaah placed their souls inside green birds

232 Ahzaab 33:23.

233 Aal Imraan 3:169–171.

that tend to the rivers of Paradise and eat from its fruits. They then return to golden lamps hanging in the shade of the throne. When they tasted the delight of their food, drink, and dwelling, they said, 'We wish that our brothers knew what Allaah had given us so that they would not abandon Jihaad.' Allaah said, 'I will convey the news for you.'"

Two weeks before he died, the Prophet called one of his servants at night and went to the Baqiyatul Gharqad cemetery and prayed for the martyrs of Uhud, saying Allaah had ordered him to do so.

Lessons from the Battle of Uhud

From the Qur'aan and Hadith, it is evident that Allaah afflicts the believers to test their faith. It is easy to be a good Muslim when things are going well, but the real test is when one is patient and dignified in adversity. Uhud was a test for the Muslims, some of whom had just entered Islam. The Qur'aan says: "Allaah will not leave the believers in the state in which they are now until He separates the wicked from the good."[234]

The conduct of the Prophet also stood out very clearly on the day of Uhud. Allaah praised His Prophet's conduct and called it a special blessing from Allaah.

> *It was by God's grace that you (Prophet) dealt gently with your followers: for if you had been harsh and hard of heart, they would indeed have broken away from you. Pardon them, then, and pray that they be forgiven. Consult with them in matters of public concern; then, when you have decided upon a course of action, place your trust in God; God loves those who place their trust in Him.*[235]

234 Aal Imraan 3:179.

235 Aal Imraan 3:159.

Unlike the worldly leaders of the past and present, the Prophet did not scold the archers whose disobedience caused the death of some seventy Companions. There was no court martial. Taking a cue from their leader's conduct, the Companions also did not reproach each other.

Ibn Al-Qayyim Al-Jawziyah cited many of the rulings and noble lessons derived from the Battle of Uhud, among them the following:[236]

1. The believers learned that what happened to them was a direct consequence of disobeying the Messenger of God. As Allaah said:

   > *And Allaah had certainly fulfilled His promise to you when you were killing them, with His permission, until when you lost courage and fell to disputing about the Prophet's order and disobeyed after He had shown you that which you love. Among you are some who desire this world, and among you are some who desire the Hereafter. Then He turned you back from them in defeat that He might test you. And He has forgiven you.*[237]

2. Allaah's wisdom and method required that His messengers and their followers triumphed at times and were defeated at times, but the outcome was always in their favor. Because if they were continually victorious, nonbelievers would join them, and believers would be indistinguishable from others.
3. Sincere believers were distinguished from hypocrites, for when Allaah gave the Muslims victory over their enemies on the Day of Badr, some entered Islam whose motives were not as they appeared. So the wisdom of Allaah necessitated a test to differentiate between the believer and the hypocrite. In this battle, the hypocrites showed their true colors and spoke of what they had previously concealed.

236 Al-Jawziyah, Ibn Qayyim. *Zaad-ul-Ma'aad, Provisions for the Hereafter.* Translated by Jalal Abualrub. Orlando: Islamic Earning Media Publications, 2003.

237 Aal Imraan 3:152.

So the believers realized that they had an enemy from within and thus could be cautious of and prepared for that enemy.

4. Allaah tests His servants in both good times and bad, in victory and defeat. When they show firm obedience and servitude in what they like and what they dislike, then they are His true servants.
5. If Allaah had always given them victory in every circumstance and had always subdued their enemies, they would have become oppressive and arrogant. His servants are only kept righteous and balanced through the experience of both good times and bad, hardship and ease.
6. When Allaah afflicts them with setbacks, loss, and defeat, they become humble and submissive, making them deserving of His help.
7. For His believing servants Allaah has prepared in His Paradise positions that they cannot reach except through difficulties, trials, and above all His mercy. So He gives them the means to reach those positions.
8. When enjoying continuous health, wealth, and ascendancy, human souls acquire an oppressive and impatient nature. This is a disease that hinders one on the journey to Allaah and the Hereafter. So when Allaah intends to honor a soul, He gives it difficulties and hardships, which serve as treatment for that disease, just as a doctor makes a patient drink a bitter medicine or removes diseased parts from the patient. And if He left people to their own wishes, their inclinations would destroy them.
9. Martyrdom in the sight of Allaah is among the highest ranks earned by His allies. The martyrs are His privileged servants who are nearest to Him. In fact, after the rank of *Siddeeq* (the intimate and fervent supporter of a prophet) comes that of the *Shaheed* (martyr). The only way to attain this rank is through the circumstances leading to it (i.e., being overcome by an enemy).
10. Finally, when Allaah intends to destroy His enemies, he provides them with the causes of their destruction. The greatest of these causes after unbelief is their oppression, tyranny, and abuse of His

> sincere allies, their waging war against them and overpowering them. In this way, He purifies His servants of their sins and faults. And thereby He increases the causes of His enemies' destruction.[238]

Treachery at Al-Raji'

Al-Raji' is a place between Raabigh and Jeddah. Soon after the Battle of Uhud, in the third year of Hijrah (624/625 CE), the Banu Lihyaan had convinced the Adal and Qaara tribes to dispatch a delegation to the Prophet, asking him to send some of his learned Companions to invite their people to Islam and teach them the religion.

But behind this they had a very sinister plan. One of the Banu Lihyaan's men, Sufiyan bin Khaalid bin Nubayh Al-Hudhayli, had been killed by the Muslims, and they wanted to take revenge. So they said to Adal and Qaara, "We shall kill whoever killed our Companion, and we shall take the rest of them to the Quraysh in Makkah and exchange them for money, for the Quraysh desire nothing more than to have one of the Companions of Muhammad to mutilate and kill for those who were killed at Badr."

So the Adal and Qaara representatives went to the Prophet and said, "Indeed Islam is spreading among us, so send a group of your Companions to teach us the Qur'aan and Islam." It is said a number of people from these tribes had already accepted Islam. The Prophet chose six Companions for this job (seven according to Waaqidi). They were Marthad bin Abu Marthad Al-Ghanaawi, Khaalid bin Al-Bukayr Al-Laythi, Aasim bin Thaabit bin Abul-Aqlah, Khubayb bin Adiyy, Zayd bin al-Dathinna bin Mu'yawiyah, and Abdullaah bin Taariq. The Prophet put Marthad in command.

We should pause here for a moment to reflect on the men. The Prophet had once said that the scholars were the heirs of prophets because they

---

238 Al-Jawziyah, Ibn Qayyim. *Zaad-ul-Ma'aad, Provisions for the Hereafter*. Translated by Jalal Abualrub. Orlando: Islamic Earning Media Publications, 2003

inherited their knowledge. The six men the Prophet had sent were not just scholars; they had learned from the Prophet, who had certified them as teachers. In the context of the religious knowledge, one cannot think of a more stellar credential.

When the Companions reached Al-Raji', the Adal and Qaara betrayed them and called the men of the Hudhayl tribe against them. Suddenly the Muslims were surrounded by one hundred sword-wielding enemies who tried to convince them that they did not want to kill them but rather capture them for ransom. Marthad, Khaalid, and Aasim refused to accept the promise of the polytheists, and they fought. However, the odds were heavily against them, and they were killed.

The Hudhayl told them they would take the skull of Aasim bin Thaabit to Sulaafa bint Sa'ad bint Shuhayd, whose two sons, Musaafi and Julaas, had been killed by Aasim at Uhud. The mother had taken a vow to drink wine from the skull of her sons' killers. Sulaafa had also promised a huge reward to the one who would bring Aasim's head. Aasim had made a supplication that Allaah not allow any pagan to ever touch his body. Soon after Aasim was killed, a swarm of bees surrounded his body, and a sudden flood came into the valley and carried it away.[239]

As for Zayd, Khubayb, and Abdullaah, they were captured and bound. The Banu Lihyaan proceeded to Makkah to fetch the highest prize for their prisoners. Along the way, Abdullaah broke himself free and pulled out his sword, but they surrounded him and stoned him until he died.

In Makkah, Safwaan bin Umayyah bought Zayd in order to kill him in revenge for his father's death at Badr. He appointed his freed slave Nistas for this job. Zayd was brought to the Ka'bah, where Abu Sufiyan tried to show pity on Zayd and test his faith. He said, "By Allaah, I adjure you, don't you

239 Lings, *Muhammad: His Life Based on the Earliest Sources.*

wish that Muhammad were here in your place so that we might cut off his head, and that you were with your family?"

Zayd was unmoved by Ab Sufiyan's apparent words of sympathy and instead answered, "By Allaah, I do not wish that Muhammad now were in the place I occupy or that a thorn should hurt him, and that I were sitting with my family." Zayd was subsequently killed.

Abu Sufiyan used to say, "I have never seen a man so loved as Muhammad's Companions loved him."

Now it was Khubayb's turn to be killed. The Quraysh decided to kill him by crucifixion. He was imprisoned in the house of Ma'awiyah, a freed slave woman of Hujayr bin Abu Ihaab. She narrated that one day she saw Khubayb eating grapes that were as big as a man's head. She wondered where in the world such grapes grew.

When the time of execution came, Khubayb sought permission to pray two units of prayer. After the prayer he turned to his captors and said, "Were it not that you would think that I delayed out of fear of death, I would have prolonged my prayer." It is said that Khubayb was the first to start the custom of praying two units of prayer before an imminent death. Khubayb then raised his hands in supplication: "O Allaah, we have delivered the message of Your Messenger, so tell him tomorrow what has been done to us."

Usaamah reported from his father, Zayd bin Haarithah, that the Prophet was sitting among his Companions when he went into a trance like those in which Gabriel came to him with revelation. When the Prophet's condition returned to normal, he said, "And peace unto him and God's blessings. This is Jibreel, who brings me greetings from Khubayb."

Khubayb had also prayed, "O Allaah, count their number and kill them one by one; let none escape." His prayer was so passionate and full of faith that some of the pagans plugged their ears so as to keep from hearing his curse. Mu'aawiyah used to say that his father, Abu Sufiyan, threw him to the ground so that the curse would pass over him. For almost a month, Khubayb's prayer was the topic of discussion among the Quraysh. It is said that the Companion Sa'id bin Aamir used to have seizures, and Umar bin Khattaab asked him about it. Sa'id said he was present when Khubayb bin Adiyy was killed. He heard his curse, and whenever he remembered it, he would faint.

Greater Treachery at Bi'r Ma'unah

It is reported that Abu Bara Aamir bin Maalik, the leader of the Aamir tribe, came to Madinah to visit the Prophet. Abu Bara was a sincere person and a friend of the Messenger of Allaah and the Muslims. He brought two horses and two camels as presents to the Messenger of Allaah. However, the Prophet said to him, "I do not accept the presents of polytheists. If you want your present to be accepted, be a Muslim."

Abu Bara did not accept Islam but said to the Prophet, "O Muhammad! Your affair to which you invite is most excellent. If you were to send some of your Companions to the people of Najd and they invited them to your affair, I have good hopes that they would give you a favorable answer." The Prophet said he was afraid the people of Najd would kill his Companions. The Prophet's concern with Abu Bara's request, coming on the heels of the Al-Raji' massacre, was justified. However, Abu Bara assured him that the people of Najd would not harm those he gave protection to.

Although Abu Bara was not a Muslim, he was trustworthy, and in 4 AH (625/626 CE) the Prophet decided to send forty—or according to another opinion, seventy—of his best students for this task. Six of them were from the Emigrants, and the rest were from the Helpers. All of them were the People of Suffah and were called Al-Qurraa, meaning the reciters. They were among the elite group who had dedicated their lives to learning from the Prophet. Mundhir bin Amr was appointed as their leader, and the group carried a letter from the Prophet for the Banu Aamir.

After an arduous journey, the Muslims reached Bi'r Ma'unah, a well east of Madinah. The Companion Haraam bin Milhaan was chosen to deliver the letter of the Messenger of Allaah to Aamir bin Tufayl, who was a nephew of Abu Bara, the one who had given protection to the Prophet's emissaries. Aamir did not even bother to read the letter; he killed Haraam bin Milhaan.

Aamir bin Tufayl said he suspected that Haraam bin Milhaan did not come alone, so he asked his tribe, the Banu Aamir, to help him kill whoever else may have come with Haraam. The Banu Aamir refused because they knew Abu Bara had given protection to the Muslim delegation. Aamir bin Tufayl then asked the tribes of Sulaym, Usayyah, R'il, and Dakhwaan for help, and they agreed.

The Muslims waited for Haraam's return and were shocked to find themselves surrounded by a large number of sword-wielding pagans. They were clearly outnumbered, but their leader Mundhir bin Amr and his Companions decided to fight back. The odds were heavily stacked against them. They had come to teach, not to fight, so they had not brought body armor or weapons of war with them. They had what travelers typically carried with them: a basic sword to defend themselves against beasts and highway robbers.

Tragically, all of the Muslim teachers were killed except for their leader Mundhir bin Amr. Aamir bin Tufayl said to Mundhir, "If you wish, we will protect you."

Mundhir replied, "I will never submit or accept your protection unless you take me to the place where Haraam was killed and then free me from your protection." They took him to the place of Haraam's killing, where

Al-Mundhir fought with them and was killed. Ka'ab bin Zayd was severely wounded and left for dead. He was rescued from among the slain and lived until the Battle of the Trench, where he was martyred.

Two from the Muslim delegation, Al-Haarith bin Al-Simmaah and Amr bin Umayyah, were tasked with grazing the riding animals in the pasture. When they saw vultures circling above the campsite of their Companions, they were alarmed and began to fear the worst. Cautiously they came to the Muslim camp, hiding behind a mound of dirt. What they saw was shocking. Their Companions were dead, and the horsemen who had killed them were standing near their bodies. They discussed what they should do. Amr suggested going back to the Prophet and informing him. However, Al-Haarith decided to fight the pagans and was killed. Amr was taken prisoner, and when he told them that he was from the Mudar tribe, they let him go.

Amr hurriedly proceeded to Madinah, and while he was at Al-Qarqara, he met two men from the Banu Aamir who stopped to rest under the same shade as he. With the massacre of his Companions fresh on his mind, Amr decided to take revenge against these two from the Banu Aamir tribe. He waited for his opportunity and killed them while they slept.

When Amr reached the Prophet and told him what had happened to the Muslims, the latter said, "This is the result of Abu Bara's insistence." Amr then told the Prophet what he had done to the two from the Banu Aamir to avenge the death of the Muslims. The Prophet said, "Miserable is what you did. You killed two men who had a promise of protection from me." The Prophet then paid the blood money for the two men to their families.

When Amr was briefly detained by the pagans, Aamir bin Tufayl asked him to identify the Muslim dead. Amr found everyone except one. He said, "I am missing the freed slave of Abu Bakr named Aamir bin Fuhayrah."

Ibn Tufayl asked, "How was he with you?"

Amr said, "He was one of the most excellent of us and among the first Companions of the Prophet."

Ibn Tufayl said, "Did I not inform you about him? He was killed with a spear, and when the spear was pulled from him, the man was taken high in the sky until I could not see him anymore."

When the Prophet was informed of this, he said, "Indeed the angels have concealed his dead body. He has alighted in the uppermost heaven." This is the same Aamir bin Fuhayrah who used to bring the flock of sheep to erase the footprints when the Prophet and Abu Bakr were hiding in the Cave of Thawr at the time of migration. He was not a Muslim at the time.

Jabbaar bin Salaamah was the one who killed Aamir bin Fuhayrah. When Aamir was dying, he said, "By my Lord, I have succeeded." In another version, he said, "By the Lord of the Ka'bah, I have succeeded." Jabbaar said he kept wondering about the last words of Aamir until someone explained that Aamir meant he had attained Paradise. It was then that he accepted Islam.

The Prophet Invokes God's Help

The Messenger of God became extremely sad when those distinguished Companions were killed treacherously. Anas bin Maalik said, "I had never seen the Messenger of God feel as sad as when he was informed that his Companions had been martyred in Bi'r Ma'unah." It is reported that for forty days the Prophet invoked Allaah's wrath on the killers during the morning prayers.

Abu Bara was very regretful for what his nephew Aamir bin Tufayl had done, but he was sadder to know that the Messenger of God had said, "This is the result of Abu Bara's insistence." Aamir bin Tufayl died a miserable death. He was inflicted with a type of leprosy that spread all over his body.

He became delusional, and his people shunned him because they did not want to contract this disease.

The Banu Nadheer Violate the Madinah Charter

As mentioned earlier, when Amr bin Umayyah had wrongfully killed two men from the Banu Aamir, the Prophet immediately decided to pay blood money to their families. This was despite what the Banu Aamir had done to the Muslim teachers at Bi'r Ma'unah. Amr's two victims were under the Prophet's protection, and so he honored the obligation that came with it. But the blood money was a large sum of money—two hundred camels—and the Muslim community was still financially struggling. According to the Madinah Charter, the signatories were jointly responsible for some common matters. So the Prophet went to the Jewish tribe of Banu Nadheer to ask for their help in paying the blood money. The Banu Nadheer were also allies of the Banu Aamir.

On the way to see the Banu Nadheer, the Prophet and his Companions prayed in Quba, and when he arrived in the Jewish neighborhood, he asked them to contribute toward the blood money as the Madinah Charter required. They said, "O Abul Qaasim (father of Qaasim), we will do what you asked for." They asked him and his Companions to wait so that they could prepare food for them.

As the Prophet sat leaning against the wall of one of the houses, Huyayy bin Akhtab, the chief of the Banu Nadheer, consulted with some of his men and conspired to throw a big rock from the roof to kill the Prophet. Huyayy said to his men that this was their golden opportunity to eliminate the Prophet and crush Islam.

One of the Jewish notables, Sallaam bin Mishkaam, vehemently disagreed and said, "Obey me once, my people, for by God, if you do this, he (Prophet Muhammad) will surely be informed that we are acting treacherously against him. Surely this is the violation of the agreement between us and him. By God, if you do what you intend, this religion will surely stay among them until the Day of Judgment. He will destroy the Jews, and his religion will triumph." Huyayy rejected Sallaam's pleas, and as his designated man was getting ready to drop the rock on the Prophet, the angel Gabriel came and informed him of the plot. The Prophet quickly rose from his place and left without even saying anything to his Companions.

The Companions waited for a while and began to wonder where the Prophet had gone. Finally, Abu Bakr said that there was no point in waiting and that the Prophet must have left to take care of some important matter.

The Banu Nadheer also became nervous as to why the Prophet had left suddenly. Could he have known their plot? Al-Waaqidi reported in his book, *Kitab Al-Maghazi*, that one of the Jewish men, Kinaanah bin Suwayraa, told the Banu Nadheer, "Muhammad was informed about the treachery you planned against him. Do not deceive yourselves. By God, he is surely the Messenger of God, for he would not have stood up except he was informed about what you planned against him. Surely he is the last of the prophets. You desire him to be from the Banu Haroon, but God has placed him as He pleases. Surely our books and what we have studied of the Torah that was not changed state that his birth is in Makkah and the land of his emigration is Yathrib. His exact description does not disagree by a letter from what is in our book."[240] Ibn Suwayraa urged them to accept Islam, become the Prophet's close Companions, live in safety, and retain their wealth."

When the Sahaabah reached Madinah, the Prophet informed them about the Banu Nadheer's plot, and he sent Muhammad bin Maslamah to them with a stern message. Ibn Maslamah informed the Jews of what they had planned to do against the Prophet, even identifying the man they had appointed to do this dastardly job, Amr bin Jihaash. They were dumbstruck, as this was a top-secret plan.

240 Al-Waqidi, Muhammad bin Umar, Kitab Al-Maghazi, translated as The Life of Muhammad by Rizwi Faizer, Oxon, Canada, Routledge, 2013, 179

Ibn Maslamah told the Banu Nadheer that the Prophet had given them ten days to leave. They could take with them whatever they could, but none of them should be seen after ten days. The Banu Nadheer understood the severity of their action, which was both treachery and treason, and hence began to prepare for their departure.

Ibn Ubayy's False Promise

While the Jews were busy trying to pack, the hypocrite Abdullaah bin Ubayy sent word to them. "Do not leave your homes or your possessions. Remain in your fortress, for I have two thousand of my tribes and other Arabs who will enter with you in your fortress, and they will die to the last one of them before Muhammad reaches you. You will also be helped by the Banu Qurayzah and the Banu Ghatafaan." He also said if they were expelled, his people would also go into exile with them. Ibn Ubayy had made a similar promise to the Banu Qaynuqa, but this time most of the Jews did not pin much hope on his latest offer. When the Banu Qurayzah heard about what Ibn Ubayy had promised on their behalf, they acted honorably and flatly refused to help the Banu Nadheer against the Prophet, saying they had a treaty with him.

Despite internal opposition, Ibn Ubayy's offer of support made Huyayy change his mind, and he sent his response to the Prophet through his own son, Judayy. "We will not leave. You can do whatever you want." He was sure that he had enough food and water to outlast a prolonged siege for a year.

When the Prophet received Huyayy's message, he said, "Allaahu Akbar, the Jews have chosen war!" Then he ordered the Companions to arm themselves and march to the Banu Nadheer.

Judayy bin Akhtab's next stop was at Abdullaah bin Ubayy's house, where he saw Abdullaah's son, a sincere Muslim, putting on his armor and rushing out the door. When Judayy told him about his father's message (which he had just delivered to the Prophet) and asked for his support, Ibn Ubayy simply said he would contact his allies. The irony was not lost on Huyayy, the leader of Banu Nadheer. While his ally, Ibn Ubayy, was wavering on the promised support, his son, a Muslim, had already rushed to support the Prophet against Banu Nadheer.

The Prophet marched toward the Banu Nadheer and prayed *Asr* (the late-afternoon prayer) in their area while they watched from their fortress, ready for battle. As the Muslims came near their fortress, the Banu Nadheer started shooting arrows and throwing rocks at the Muslims. This barrage went on until dusk. The Prophet led the Muslims in *Maghrib* (sunset) and *Isha* (night) prayers, after which he left for Madinah with ten Companions, appointing Ali, or some say Abu Bakr, as the leader of the army.

The siege continued with small skirmishes, until one day the Prophet ordered the cutting down of some of the Banu Nadheer's best date-palm trees. They complained that a prophet would do such a thing. Allaah sent down a revelation in response, declaring this was done with His permission: "Whatever you have cut down of (their) palm trees or left standing on their trunks—it was by the permission of Allaah and so He would disgrace the defiantly disobedient."[241]

Seeing the writing on the wall and realizing that they were dealing with a Prophet whom Allaah would help, two men from the Banu Nadheer, Yaameen bin Umayr and Abu Sa'ad bin Wahb, accepted Islam. They and their families were promptly granted protection.

The cutting of the date-palm trees demoralized Huyayy, and he sent a message to the Prophet promising that he would leave. The Prophet responded that he and his people needed to leave at once, taking whatever

241 Hashr 59:5.

they could carry on the beasts of burden except for the weapons. Huyayy hesitated for a few days and then complied. The Banu Nadheer had been besieged for fifteen days. They were allowed to settle their dues and financial matters before leaving.

The Jews of the Banu Nadheer began to destroy their own homes so that the Muslims could not use them. They even took the doors of their houses. They packed their belongings on six hundred camels. Their women were exquisitely dressed and wore jewelry of gold, and their entourage was striking tambourines and playing pipes. The Companions were amazed to see the pomp of the departing Jews. They had never seen so much wealth.

Allaah referred to their exile and self-destruction in Surah Hashr:

> *It is He who expelled the disbelievers among the People of the Scripture from their homes at the first gathering. You did not think they would leave, and they thought that their fortresses would protect them against Allaah; but the decree of Allaah came upon them from where they had not expected, and He cast terror into their hearts so they destroyed their houses by their own hands and the hands of the believers. So take warning, O people of understanding.*[242] (Hashr 59:2)

The day the Banu Nadheer left was a sad day for the hypocrites, and they mourned quietly. Abdullaah bin Ubayy had failed to fulfill his promise, and Allaah directly quoted his false promise:

> *Have you not seen the hypocrites who say to their disbelieving brethren among the People of the Scripture, "If you are expelled, we indeed will go out with you, and we shall never obey anyone against you; and if you are attacked, we shall indeed help you." But Allaah is Witness that verily they are liars. Surely, if they (the Jews) are expelled, never will*

242 Hashr 59:2.

they (the hypocrites) go out with them; and if they are attacked, they will never help them. And even if they do help them, they (hypocrites) will turn their backs, and they will not be victorious.[243]

Aayeshah: Her Lineage and Traits

Earlier in the book, we discussed the Prophet's marriage to Aayeshah and her age at the time of marriage. While Aayeshah was married toward the end of the Makkan period, she did not begin to live with the Prophet until a year and a half after the migration to Madinah. Here we will mention some of the other details about Aayeshah.

Literally, her name means a living woman. Her lineage was Aayeshah bint Abi Bakr bin Abu Quhaafah Uthmaan bin Aarim bin Amr.[244] Her mother was Umm Rumaan Zaynab bint Aamir bin Uwaymir bin Abd Ash-Shams bin Attab Al-Kinaaniyah. Her siblings were:

- Abdullaah ibn Abi Bakr, whose mother was Qutaylah bint Abd Al-Uzzah
- Abdur Rahmaan ibn Abi Bakr, full brother
- Muhammad ibn Abi Bakr, whose mother was Asmaa bint Umays, widow of Jaa'far bin Abi Taalib
- Asmaa bint Abi Bakr, whose mother was Qutaylah bint Abd Al-Uzzah
- Umm Kulthoom bint Abi Bakr, whose mother was Habibah bint Kharijah (Before his death, Abu Bakr had informed Aayeshah that his wife Habibah was expecting, and he thought it would be a girl.)

Aayeshah was also called Umm Abdullaah because of Abdullaah bin Zubayr, whose mother was Aayeshah's half sister Asmaa. It is said that when Abdullaah was born, she carried him to the Prophet, who said to her, "His

243 Hashr 59:11–12.

244 Imam Mohibuddin Tabari, *The Mothers of the Believers* (Karachi: Darul Ishaat. 2010), 95.

name is Abdullaah, and you are Umm Abdullaah." The Prophet also called her *Muwaffaqah* (Blessed).[245]

She was extremely scholarly and inquisitive. Her contribution to the spread of the Prophet's message was extraordinary, and she advised and mentored the Muslim Ummah for forty-four years after the Prophet's death. She is also known for narrating 2,210 Hadith, not just on matters related to the Prophet's private life but also on those related to inheritance, pilgrimage, and eschatology, among others. She was highly regarded for her intellect and knowledge in various fields, including poetry and medicine, which received plenty of praise by early luminaries, such as the historian Al-Zuhri and her student Urwah bin Al-Zubayr. The Prophet spent his final days in her apartment, where he died and is buried.

The Broken Promise of Badr II

As mentioned earlier, Abu Sufiyan had thrown a challenge to the Prophet after Uhud, saying that he would meet the Muslims for round two at Badr, a challenge the Prophet had accepted. The meeting was set for the next year in the month of Dhul Qa'dah at Badr Al-Safraa. The place was known for its week-long marketplace. So when the appointed time came close, the Prophet started to prepare.

In the Qurayshi camp, Abu Sufiyan began to have second thoughts about going to Badr. He told his people, "We are going through a drought, our animals are lean and do not provide much milk, and there is no vegetation for them to graze on." Such a time, he argued, was not good for fighting.

In the meantime, Nu'aym bin Mas'ud, who was not yet a Muslim, arrived in Makkah. Abu Sufiyan asked about the Prophet's preparations. Nu'aym told him the Prophet had gathered a large fighting force, which

245 Ibid.

included men from the Aws sub tribes of Baliyy and Juhaynah. That made Abu Sufiyan more worried. He told Nu'aym that if he could somehow dissuade the Prophet from going to Badr, he would give the former twenty camels. That was a rather large reward, and Nu'aym agreed to travel back to Madinah. When he arrived in the city, for whatever reason Nu'aym did not go directly to the Prophet but instead began to tell the Sahaabah how big a fighting force Abu Sufiyan had gathered. Nu'aym said, "By God, I do not see any of you escaping."

The propaganda started to work. The hypocrites and their allies began to rejoice. When the rumor became widespread, Abu Bakr and Umar came to the Prophet and said, "O Messenger of Allaah, surely Allaah will demonstrate His religion." Unsure of the Prophet's decision, they reminded the latter that he had accepted Abu Sufiyan's challenge and advised that staying home would be seen as cowardice.

The Prophet replied, "By Him in Whose Hands my soul is, I shall surely set out even if no one were to set out with me." Here we see yet another example of the Prophet's extraordinary bravery and regard for his promise.

The Prophet addressed the people and informed them of the mission, and they marched to Badr Al-Safraa. Some 1,500 Muslims went there ready to fight but also ready to buy and sell.

To save face, Abu Sufiyan also left Makkah. He had 1,000 men, and when he reached Majanna, he told his people to return, saying it was a year of drought and not suitable for fighting. The Prophet stayed in Badr Al-Safraa for two weeks and then returned to Madinah with Muslim morale on the high. Faced with a public-relations defeat, Abu Sufiyan and Safwaan bin Umayyah began to look for another opportunity to fight the Muslims, a pursuit that culminated two years later in the Battle of the Trench, in which the Quraysh gathered the largest army the Arabs had known.

Not long after the trip to Al-Safraa, the Prophet led an expedition against the Ghatafaan tribe, who had been quite hostile to the Muslims. The latter gathered a large force, but the two sides did not fight. It was a war of nerves, and because of a lurking danger of the enemy attacking while the Muslims were praying, Allaah revealed verses concerning the Fear Prayer. This was a much-needed commandment, and it came as a relief to the Muslims:

> *When you (O Muhammad) are among them, and lead them in prayer, let one party of them stand up in prayer with you, taking their arms with them; when they finish their prostrations, let them take their positions in the rear and let the other party come up which have not yet prayed, and let them pray with you, taking all the precautions and bearing arms. Those who disbelieve wish, if you were negligent of your arms and your baggage, to attack you in a single rush, but there is no sin on you if you put away your arms because of the inconvenience of rain or because you are ill, but take every precaution for yourselves. Verily, Allaah has prepared a humiliating torment for the disbelievers.*[246] (Nisaa 4:102)

Unparalleled Love for the Companions

As the Prophet and his Companions were returning from an expedition, which was probably Dhaat Ar-Riqaa, Jaabir bin Abdullaah lagged behind because his camel was old and slow. Jaabir himself narrated this incident, and it shows the immense concern the Prophet had for his Companions. Imam Al-Bukhari collected it in his Saheeh, under Hadith 3:130.

Jaabir said, "I was with the Prophet in a *ghazwah* (military expedition) and my camel was slow and exhausted. The Prophet came up to me and said, 'O Jaabir.'

"I replied, 'Yes?'

246 Nisaa 4:102.

"He said, 'What is the matter with you?'

"I replied, 'My camel is slow and tired, so I am left behind.' So, he got down and poked the camel with his stick and then ordered me to ride. I rode the camel, and it became so fast that I had to hold it from going ahead of Allaah's Apostle.

"Then he asked me, 'Would you like to sell your camel?' I replied in the affirmative, and the Prophet purchased it for one *uqiyah* of gold."

The Prophet then asked him about his wife and whether she was a virgin, and Jaabir responded she had been married before. The Prophet said, "Would it not have been better if you had married a young virgin with whom you could play and have fun?"

Jaabir, who was perhaps twenty years of age at the time, said, "O Messenger of God, my father was killed at Uhud, leaving me my seven sisters to look after. I therefore married a woman who could take care of them and keep the family together."

The Prophet replied, "Then you have done the right thing, God willing. When we arrive at Siraar, we will have some camels slaughtered, and we will celebrate. Your wife will then hear that we have celebrated her marriage, and she will put out her cushions."[247]

Jaabir said, "But we have no cushions, Messenger of God."

The Prophet said, "But you will have. When you arrive at Madinah, you should arrange a good feast."

247 Putting up cushions was apparently an expression for a celebration of a happy occasion as well as for a woman's preparation for her husband's return from a journey.

When the Muslim army arrived at Siraar, which was only about five kilometers from Madinah, the Prophet had a number of camels slaughtered and cooked. The whole army shared in the celebration of the recent wedding of one of its soldiers. When the sun went down, the Prophet and his Companions moved into Madinah. The Prophet asked Jaabir to see him the next morning.

Jaabir told his wife about the Prophet's offer, and she advised him to do as the Prophet had instructed. The following morning, Jaabir took his camel and sat it down outside the Prophet's mosque. When the Prophet came out, he asked about the camel and was told that Jaabir had brought it. He asked for Jaabir to be called, and when he arrived, the Prophet said, "Take your camel, my nephew; it is yours." He then called Bilaal, who acted as treasurer, and told him to go with Jaabir and to give him an *uqiyah* of gold. Bilaal did as the Prophet bade him and gave Jaabir a fraction more. Jaabir said that the camel stayed with him a very long time.

This incident is one of many that show the degree of care and compassion the Prophet had for his Companions. When he realized that Jaabir was newly married, he was keen to make the whole community share in the celebration. Obviously the Prophet did not need to buy the camel, but realizing that Jaabir was poor and that he was supporting a large family, he bought it out of care and mercy. The act of buying the camel and giving it as a gift to its previous owner was a hallmark of the Prophet's character. This way the one who received help kept his dignity.

Allaah mentioned the Prophet's concern for his people in the Qur'aan thus:

> *Now there has come to you a Messenger from among yourselves; grievous to him is your suffering; anxious is he over you, gentle to the believers, compassionate.*[248]

248 Tawbah 9:128.

The Battle of the Trench

In 5 AH (626/627 CE), some of the Jews of the Banu Nadheer, including Sallaam bin Abul Huqayq and Huyayy bin Akhtab, went to the Quraysh and incited them to attack the Prophet Muhammad. The Banu Nadheer, who had been expelled earlier from Madinah because of their treachery, thought they could not take on the Muslims without the support of the Quraysh. There is a difference of opinion about the year. One opinion holds that the Battle of the Trench (also known as Khandaq or Ahzaab) happened in 4 AH (625/626 CE). This is based on Abdullaah bin Umar's statement that in the Battle of Uhud in 3 AH (624/625 CE), he was fourteen, and the Prophet had not selected him for fighting; however, in the Battle of Ahzaab, he was fifteen, and he was selected. However, Ibn Isshaaq reported that the Battle of the Trench took place in 5 AH.[249]

When visited by the leadership of the Banu Nadheer, the Quraysh asked them, "O Jews, you are the first people of scripture, and you know the nature of our dispute with Muhammad. Is our religion better or his?" The Jews replied that certainly the religion of the Quraysh was better.

So Allaah revealed: "Have you not seen those who were given a portion of the Scripture. They believe in sorcery and Satan and say to those who disbelieve, 'These people are better guided on the way' than the believers."[250]

The Quraysh were elated to hear what the Jews said about their pagan faith. They felt emboldened and promised to amass a huge force against the Prophet. The Jews quickly reached out to the tribes of Ghatafaan and Banu Sulaym. To the Ghatafaan they promised half of the dates of Khayber. These tribes were also joined by the Banu As'ad, Banu Murrah, and Banu Fuzara. However, the Banu Murrah pulled out when their leader Haarith

---

249 Ibn Isshaaq, Muhammad. *Sirat Rasul Allah*. Translated by A. Guillaume as *The Life of Muhammad*. 27th Ed. Karachi: Oxford University Press, 2014, 450.

250 Nisaa 4:51. It appears that this incident happened twice, and the above verse is applicable to both instances. The first incident involves Ka'ab bin Ashraf, who visited the Quraysh and made similar remarks.

bin Awf told them, "Disperse in your land and do not attack Muhammad. Indeed I think that Muhammad will be victorious." The Quraysh also reached out to their allies, so even without the Banu Murrah, the combined Jewish and Qurayshi forces were ten thousand strong. Abu Sufiyan was chosen to be the overall commander.

Allaah testifies that the Muslims were not scared of the Quraysh's big numbers.

> *And when the believers saw "Al-Ahzaab" (the Confederates), they said: "This is what Allaah and His Messenger had promised us, and Allaah and His Messenger had spoken the truth, and it only added to their Faith and to their submission (to Allaah)."*[251]

When the Prophet found that the Quraysh had put together a massive force in conjunction with a disparate group of other Arab tribes and the Banu Nadheer, he consulted with the Companions. He asked them whether the Muslims should go out to fight or meet the enemy from within the borders of Madinah. The threat was unlike any other in the past. Salmaan al-Farisi, a Persian Companion, advised the Prophet to dig a trench around Madinah to keep the enemy away. He had seen this strategy of war used successfully in his native country. The Prophet not only agreed but also helped with the digging of the trench. It is said that the trench was several miles long and covered the entire area of Madinah that was vulnerable to Qurayshi attack. On two sides Madinah was protected by lava rocks, and on one side by groves of date-palm trees. Only one side was exposed, and that was where the Prophet decided to dig the trench.

The Prophet joined his Companions in digging the trench and carrying away rocks and dirt, so much so that Baraa bin Aazib reported that the Prophet's body was covered in dust.[252] It was a very difficult time for a num-

251 Ahzaab 33:22.

252 Bukhari, Hadith #4016.

ber of reasons: the weather was cold and windy, the Muslims did not have much food, and the trench had to be dug mostly with bare hands. There were only a handful of pickaxes and shovels. On top of that, the thought of a huge army approaching was quite unnerving. As an ingenious commander, the Prophet realized something had to be done to divert the minds of his Companions away from these thoughts. So he began to chant poetry that Abdullaah bin Rawaahah had composed.[253] "O Allaah, there is no life except the life of the Hereafter. Forgive the Emigrants and the Helpers." In another version it says, "O Allaah, there is no good except the good of the Hereafter. Forgive the Emigrants and the Helpers."

The Muslims responded, "We have promised Muhammad (peace be upon him) that we will make Jihaad in the way of God as long as we live."

Bukhari reported in his Hadith collection that Ammaar bin Yaasir came to the Prophet and said, "They are killing me." He was complaining because he had been given two stones to carry while many others were carrying only one.

The Prophet responded, "Woe unto you, O Son of Sumayyah. No, rather you will be killed by a rebellious group." The Prophet also said that Ammaar's last drink would be milk. Then he affectionately removed the dust from Ammaar's head and clothes. This incident had historical significance. Years after the death of the Prophet, Ammaar was killed in the Battle of Siffeen (37 AH/657 CE) on the side of Ali. This Hadith is used to prove that in the dispute between Mu'aawiyah and Ali, Ali's position was correct.

During the digging of the trench, the Companions came upon a massive rock that they could not cut through. Since the path of the trench was demarcated by the Prophet himself, they did not want to go around the rock. So the Companions went to the Prophet and reported their problem. The Prophet got hold of a pickaxe and struck the rock, saying, "Bismi Allaah"

---

253 As-Sallaabee, *The Noble Life of the Prophet*, 3:1362.

(in the name of Allaah). In one of those small miracles that the Prophet was given aplenty, one-third of the rock crumbled, and a spark appeared from the tip of the pickaxe. The Prophet said, *Allaahu Akbar* (God is greater). He struck a second and third time, each time reciting *Allaahu Akbar* until the entire rock had broken into pieces.

Salmaan Al-Farisi saw the sparks and the Prophet's excitement and asked what was happening. The Prophet said that with the first strike he was given the keys of victory over Shaam (Syria, Jordan, Lebanon, and Palestine), with the second over Persia, and with the third over Yemen. Amazingly, all three lands were conquered not long after the Prophet passed away, and Shaam was the first.

While the massive Qurayshi army was at the doors of Madinah, Huyayy bin Akhtab, the exiled leader of the Banu Nadheer whom some Jews had described as the man of ill omen, called Abu Jahl of the Jews, came to the chief of the Banu Qurayzah, Ka'ab bin As'ad. Huyayy began to pester Ka'ab to join the war against the Prophet. To his credit, Ka'ab scolded him and said that the Banu Qurayzah had a treaty with the Prophet he could not violate.

Huyayy kept trying to convince Ka'ab that the victory would belong to the Quraysh and their allies because they were so large in number. Ka'ab eventually fell for this story and brought his own doom along with that of his people. He tore up the agreement with the Prophet. Some of the fair-minded Jews chastised Ka'ab and warned him that turning against the Prophet in times of war would be high treason, and while the Quraysh and Ghatafaan would return to their homes, the Banu Qurayzah would be left alone to deal with the Prophet once the war was over. They clearly saw the destruction of the Jews in the treacherous behavior of Ka'ab.

While the Prophet was sitting with some of his Companions, Umar arrived and said, "O Messenger of God, it has reached me that the Banu Qurayzah have destroyed the agreement and are preparing for war." The

Prophet sent Zubayr bin Al-Awwaam and later Sa'ad bin Mu'aadh, Usayd bin Hudhayr, and Sa'ad bin Ubaadah to verify the information. The latter three were from the Ansaar, and they occupied leadership positions in their community. Since the news was extremely worrisome, the Prophet wanted it affirmed by more than one source.

When the Muslim delegation reached the Banu Qurayzah, the latter began to disparage the Prophet, which led Sa'ad bin Mu'aadh to revile them. The Banu Qurayzah reviled Ibn Mu'aadh in return. Sa'ad bin Ubaadah asked Ibn Mu'aadh to ignore Banu Qurayzah's insults of the Prophet, saying, "The dispute between us is too serious for recrimination."[254] The Prophet had instructed this team to proclaim loudly if the news was incorrect or to otherwise indicate to him with some secret gestures if the news was correct. When they returned to the Prophet, Sa'ad bin Ubaadah said, "Adal and Qaara," suggesting that just as the two tribes had betrayed their trust, so had the Banu Qurayzah.

The Prophet proclaimed, "Allaahu Akbar, rejoice, O Muslims, in God's victory and His help."

The Bravery of the Prophet's Aunt

While the Prophet's reliance on Allaah manifested in all its profundity, the Muslims' anxiety intensified, as this was unlike anything they had ever faced. The external enemies were in the front while the fifth column was in the back, and it was the latter they were most concerned about. They realized that there was no way for them to engage the enemy in the front without making their women and children vulnerable to the Banu Qurayzah's attack from the rear.

The Muslim women and children were housed in various fortresses of the Ansaar. Safiyyah bint Abdul Muttalib, the Prophet's aunt, was in

254 Ibn Isshaaq, *Sirat Rasul Allah*, 453.

one such fortress. With the women and children in that fortress was the Companion Hassaan bin Thaabit, the poet. Hassaan was well accomplished in the art of poetry, and the Prophet had asked him on many occasions to defend the Muslims through poetry. But fighting was not Hassaan's cup of tea.

One night Safiyyah heard some noise outside the fortress, and she saw a man circling the building. Eventually the man began to scale the wall of the fortress. Safiyyah implored Hassaan to go and take care of this threat. Hassaan said to her, "O aunt of the Messenger of Allaah, please do not humiliate me. You know that this is not something I can do." Safiyyah then put on a man's cloak, covered her face in the manner of a man, and slid down a rope until she was able to strike the intruder with a club on his head. The man fell down and died. Safiyyah asked Hassaan to take the dead man's weapon, and again he excused himself, saying he had no need for the weapon.

Abu Bakr used to say, "We feared more for our children in Madinah from the Banu Qurayzah than from the Quraysh and Ghatafaan. I used to go to the hills of Sal and look at the houses of Madinah. When I saw them calm, I would praise God." In fact, the Banu Qurayzah did one night plot to attack the main part of Madinah, and they asked the Quraysh and the Ghatafaan each to provide them with one thousand men. When the Prophet found out, he sent five hundred men to repulse any attack against Madinah's population. All night the Muslim contingent patrolled the city, reciting *Allaahu Akbar* to foil any attack. About their situation Allaah revealed:

> *When they came upon you from above you and from below you, and when the eyes grew wild and the hearts reached to the throats, and you were harboring doubts about Allaah."*[255]

255 Ahzaab 33:10.

Just before the battle, it was a bitterly cold night. People were struggling to stay warm, but it was not possible in the open. Abu Sufiyan and his cavalry were circling the trench. The Prophet had asked Abbaad bin Bishr to push them away. Abbaad and his Companions managed to repulse them with stones and arrows. Khaalid bin Waleed and Amr bin Al-Aas also tried to cross over the narrowest part of the trench but were kept away by the arrows the Muslims shot at them.

Umm Salamah, the wife of the Prophet, said, "May Allaah bless Abbaad bin Bishr, for surely he was the most committed to the tent of the Messenger of Allaah, keeping watch over him always."

Some of the Muslim women and children, including the Prophet's wife Aayeshah, were housed in the fortress of the Banu Haarithah. Sa'ad bin Mu'aadh came by to say good-bye to his mother while wearing a body armor that was too small for him, leaving his forearm exposed. Sa'ad was a big man, but in her motherly affection, his mother said to him, "Catch up with the Messenger of God, my little son, for by God, you are late."

Aayeshah remarked, "By God, O Umm Sa'ad, I wish that the armor of Sa'ad covered up to his fingers." Later on Sa'ad was struck in his arm by an arrow in the same place Aayeshah had feared. His veins were ruptured, and some days later he died from excessive bleeding and other complications.

After several attempts, Ikrimah bin Abi Jahl, Nawfal bin Abdullaah, Amr bin Abd, and a few others managed to breach the trench. Amr began to call for a duel. Amr was known for his fighting skills. He had been wounded in Badr but had not been part of Uhud, and he badly wanted to make up for his absence. He called again, and no one came forward to take his challenge. Amr became upset and said tauntingly that his voice had become hoarse from asking a Muslim fighter to come forward. Was there no one among the Muslims who would take his challenge?

In the Muslim camp, Ali asked the Prophet three times to let him fight Amr, and finally the Prophet gave him permission. The Prophet gave Ali his sword, and with his own hands, he tied the turban on Ali's head, praying, "O Allaah, help Ali against him."

Amr was riding a horse, while Ali was on foot. When Amr saw Ali, he said, "Your father was my friend. You are a young lad. Rather I would like an older Quraysh, like Abu Bakr and Umar."

Ali ignored Amr and told him, "I desire to kill you." That both saddened and angered Amr. It is said that when Ali saw that Amr had taken his challenge, he told Amr that the fight would not be fair while the former was on horse and he on foot. That made Amr furious, and he quickly alighted and struck at Ali like a lion. Amr's blow pierced Ali's shield and became stuck in it. Ali quickly struck Amr with the other hand. It was a fatal blow, and Amr fell down. The dust rose where he had fallen, and people couldn't see anything until suddenly the cries of *Allaahu Akbar* rang out, and the Companions realized that Ali had killed Amr.

The death of Amr caused some of the Qurayshis to flee. Seeing that, Zubayr bin Al-Awwaam and Umar bin Al-Khattaab chased them as they tried to cross back to the other side of the trench. After some small fighting, the Quraysh retreated to their side, but one person, Nawfal bin Abdullaah bin Al-Mugheerah, fell in the ditch and was killed by the Muslims. Two others sustained wounds of which they died upon return to Makkah.

As night fell, the Quraysh withdrew to Al-Aqeeq frustrated and tired. They had not been able to achieve anything significant despite their overwhelming numerical superiority.

On the Muslim side, the Prophet had not prayed *Zhuhr*, *Asr*, or *Maghrib* prayers because he had been occupied with the preeminent danger throughout the day. So he asked Bilaal to call the *Adhaan* and led them into prayer.

A Brilliant Strategy of War

Nu'aym bin Mas'ud had just discovered Islam in his heart. He used to be close to the Banu Qurayzah, but when he resolved to embrace the faith, he immediately came to the Prophet and pronounced the testimony. Even his own people did not know that Nu'aym had accepted Islam. The Prophet told Nu'aym, "You are only one man among us, so go and create distrust among the enemy to draw them off us, if you can, for war is deception." This is the only time deception is allowed, and it makes sense since one never tells his enemies he will trust them with his plans.

Nu'aym asked the Prophet if he was allowed to use any strategy he deemed fit to carry out this mission, and when told he was, Nu'aym went to the Banu Qurayzah. He reminded the Banu Qurayzah of his ties with them, and when he was assured that they considered him above suspicion, Nu'aym said, "The Quraysh and the Ghatafaan are not like you; the land and property are yours, and your wives and children live in it. Whereas the Quraysh and the Ghatafaan have come from another land, and their families are elsewhere. If they see an opportunity, they will make the most of it, but if things go wrong, they will return to their land, leaving you to deal with Muhammad. So do not fight against Muhammad in violation of the treaty with him unless you have kept some of the leaders of the Quraysh as ransom to guard against their fleeing."

The Jews liked the idea, and it made sense to them. They readily agreed. Nu'aym's next stop was the encampment of the Quraysh. He went to Abu Sufiyan and assured him of his affection for them. When Abu Sufiyan said he did not suspect him of any wrongdoing, Nu'aym said, "Mark my words: the Jews have regretted their action in opposing Muhammad and have asked him, 'Would you like to get hold of some of the chiefs of the Quraysh and Ghatafaan so you can cut their heads off? Then we can join you in exterminating the rest of them.'" Nu'aym added that the Prophet had accepted the offer of the Banu Qurayzah.

Finally, Nu'aym went to the Ghatafaan and repeated what he had told Abu Sufiyan. Soon, the Banu Qurayzah sent an emissary to the Quraysh and demanded that they send some of their leaders as ransom against the Quraysh's running away from the battlefield. The Quraysh flatly rejected this demand, and both the Quraysh and the Banu Qurayzah became convinced that what Nu'aym had told them was true.

In the meantime, Allaah sent harsh and bitterly cold winds that upset the cooking pots and uprooted the tents of the Quraysh and Ghatafaan. The Qurayshi leaders began to complain about their dire state. Their camels and horses were dying, and the fact that they were away from their land worked against them. The Jewish demands rubbed salt in their wounds.

So Abu Sufiyan got up and told his people that he had had enough and was leaving. Evidently the war had not gone their way, and the stalemate was to the disadvantage of the Quraysh. Abu Sufiyan's decision was convincing, as others were equally tired and frustrated because of their plight. When the Quraysh began to pack and leave, the Ghatafaan also decided to return to their land, thus bringing to an end an existential threat the like of which the Muslims had not seen before.

Allaah sent down a verse to inform the Muslims that they had been helped by wind and angels, whom they did not see: "O you who believe! Remember Allaah's favor to you, when there came against you hosts, and We sent against them a wind and forces that you saw not. And Allaah is ever All-Seer of what you do."[256]

The Prophet looked at the empty campsites of the enemy and said, "The Quraysh will never be able to attack you after this; now you will take the offensive."

---

256 Ahzaab 33:9.

Dealing with High Treason

When the Quraysh, Ghatafaan, and their allies had left, the Prophet and his Companions also left for Madinah and took off their weapons. Around the afternoon prayer, Gabriel came to the Prophet and informed him that the angels had not laid down their weapons and that he should not, either. "God commands you, O Muhammad, to go to the Banu Qurayzah," Gabriel said. "I am about to go to them to shake their stronghold."

The Prophet ordered the people to march to the Banu Qurayzah and said none of them should pray Asr until they had reached their neighborhood. He sent Ali with the advance banner. When Ali reached the quarters of the Banu Qurayzah, they hurled insults at the Messenger of God. Ali tried to keep the Apostle at a distance so he would not hear the Banu Qurayzah's ill speech, but the Prophet indicated to Ali that he understood what was going on. The Prophet asked the Companions if anyone had passed by them, and when they said they saw Companion Dihya Al-Kalbi pass by, the Prophet said, "That was Gabriel."

Among the Jews were those who believed that Prophet Muhammad was indeed a prophet who was mentioned in their book, the Torah, and they disliked their leaders' decision to turn against the Prophet. Even the leaders knew the truth about the Prophet Muhammad, but arrogance, jealousy, and false pride kept them from accepting what they believed to be true. Now they feared the consequences.

Because the Banu Qurayzah fortress was strong and they were keeping Muslims at bay with their arrows, the Prophet commanded the Muslims to shoot arrows of their own and basically lay siege to the Banu Qurayzah until food and water shortage forced the besieged to surrender.

The siege continued for twenty-five days, and when the Banu Qurayzah's morale sank, their leader Ka'ab bin Asad addressed his people: "O Jews, you can see what has happened to you. I offer you three alternatives: One, we will follow this man and accept him as true, for by God, it has become plain to you that he is a prophet who has been sent and that it is he whom you find mentioned in your scripture. Then your lives, your property, your women, and your children will be saved."

They said, "We will never abandon the laws of the Torah and never change it for another."

Ka'ab said, "Then if you won't accept this suggestion, the second option is to let us kill our wives and children and send men with their swords drawn to Muhammad and his Companions, leaving no encumbrances behind us, until God decides between us and Muhammad."

They said, "Should we kill these poor creatures? What will be the good of this life when they are dead?"

Their leader then suggested a third option, saying, "Then tonight is the eve of the Sabbath, and it may be that Muhammad and his Companions will feel secure from us. So come down upon them and take them by surprise." The people rejected this plan as well.

The Abu Lubaabah Incident

The Banu Qurayzah then sent a message to the Prophet, saying that they wanted to consult with Companion Abu Lubaabah bin Abd Al-Mundhir, a request that the Prophet granted. The women and children went up to him weeping, which made Abu Lubaabah feel sorry for them. They said, "O Abu Lubaabah, do you think we should submit to Muhammad's judgment?" Abu Lubaabah said yes, and he moved his hand across his throat, indicating that slaughter awaited them.

Abu Lubaabah said that no sooner had he done this than he realized what a blunder he had committed. He had betrayed the trust of the Prophet, as the latter had not told him what he was going to decide. He was sent to the Banu Qurayzah only to talk to them. Abu Lubaabah rushed to the mosque in Madinah and tied himself to one of the pillars, saying, "I will not leave this place until God forgives me for what I have done."

The Prophet had waited for Abu Lubaabah a long time, and when he heard what had happened, he said, "If he had come to me, I would have sought Allaah's forgiveness for him, but in view of how he has behaved, I will not let him go from his place until God forgives him." It is said that six nights passed in this condition. Abu Lubaabah's wife would untie him for prayers and needs and then tie him back. Finally, Allaah revealed his forgiveness:

> *And (there are) others who have acknowledged their sins, they have mixed a deed that was righteous with another that was evil. Perhaps Allaah will turn unto them in forgiveness. Surely, Allaah is Oft-Forgiving, Most Merciful."*[257]

The Prophet laughed with happiness at Abu Lubaabah's forgiveness, and when Umm Salamah, the Prophet's wife, who was with him at the time, asked if she could announce the good news, he granted his permission. People rushed to free Abu Lubaabah, but he refused, saying he would not move until the Prophet himself freed him. So the Prophet untied him.

In a Hadith that Bukhari recorded from Samurah bin Jundub, the Messenger of Allaah expounded on the above verse. He said:

> *Last Night, two angels came to me in a vision and took me to a city, built with bricks made of gold and silver. We met some men part of whose bodies were as handsome as you ever saw and part as ugly as you ever saw. The two angels ordered these men to go to a river and submerge themselves in it; they did that and came back to us, and the*

257 Tawbah 9:102.

> *ugliness went away from them, thus becoming the most beautiful form. The two said to me, "This is the Garden of Eden, and your residence is in it." The two said, "As for the men who had part of their body handsome and part ugly, they have mixed a deed that was righteous with another that was evil."*

When Abu could not help them, the Banu Qurayzah surrendered to the Prophet. He ordered them bound and imprisoned. Fearing what might happen to the Banu Qurayzah, some of the people of Aws spoke to the Prophet, saying that the Banu Qurayzah were their allies, and they should be given to them or at least be dealt with leniently, just as the Banu Qaynuqa were at the behest of the Khazrajite Abdullaah bin Ubayy.

The Prophet remained silent, and the Aws continued pressing him until he said, "Would you be satisfied if I appointed a person from among you to judge?"

They said, "Yes, of course."

The Prophet then said, "That man will be Sa'ad bin Mu'aadh." Some other reports say that the Banu Qurayzah themselves had sought the mediation of Sa'ad, as they had trade ties with him in the pre-Islamic days.

The Aws began to press Sa'ad for a favorable judgment, but he kept silent. Then he broke his silence and spoke in the third person. "The time has come for Sa'ad to worry about the blame of God alone and disregard what people might say." The people put him on a mount and supported him from the sides. Sa'ad was still nursing his wounded arm. While he had been bleeding profusely, he prayed for martyrdom and at the same time for life until he had dealt with the Banu Qurayzah.

Sa'ad looked at his people and asked if they would accept his decision, and they said yes. Then he looked in the direction of the Messenger of

God, not making eye contact out of respect,[258] and asked if he would be satisfied with his judgment. The Prophet replied in the affirmative. As Sa'ad approached the Banu Qurayzah, passing through the lines of Muslims, the Prophet said, "Stand up for your master." Although he may have meant this statement only for the Aws to which Sa'ad belonged, everyone stood up and greeted him.

It is said that Sa'ad asked what the Torah said about treason and found out that a chance of peace was to be offered, and if the other party chose war, their men were to be put to death.

> *When you draw near to a city to fight against it, offer terms of peace to it. And if it responds to you peaceably and it opens to you, then all the people who are found in it shall do forced labor for you and shall serve you. But if it makes no peace with you, but makes war against you, then you shall besiege it. And when the Lord your God gives it into your hand, you shall put all its males to the sword, but the women and the little ones, the livestock, and everything else in the city, all its spoil, you shall take as plunder for yourselves. And you shall enjoy the spoil of your enemies, which the Lord your God has given you.*[259]

Sa'ad announced his judgment that the fighting men of Banu Qurayzah be killed, their property divided as spoils of war, and their women and children taken as captives. The Prophet confirmed his judgment, saying to Sa'ad: "You have given the judgment of Allaah above the seven heavens."[260]

Some of the Jews accepted Islam, and their lives, families, and properties were spared. The Prophet pardoned two other people, Zabir bin

258 The Companions did not look the Prophet in the eye when talking to him, except for a brief moment, because of their awe of him. Historically, people talked to kings with their eyes cast down.

259 Deuteronomy 20:10, English Standard Version.

260 Bukhari, vol. 5, book 59, Hadith #447.

Bata and Amr bin Sa'ad (or Su'da), the former because he had given refuge to Companion Thaabit bin Qays Ansaari in the Battle of Bu'aath in the pre-Islamic days, and the latter for exhorting the Banu Qurayzah not to be treacherous. The female captives from the Banu Qurayzah were given to the Sahaabah. The Prophet himself chose Rayhaanah bint Amr bin Khanaqah. He freed her and married her. Some reports say that she did not want to be married, wishing to remain as a maidservant, and that the Prophet honored her wish.

Reflections: Some non-Muslims have criticized the Prophet for the tragic end of the Banu Qurayzah. But an objective study of the events will clearly prove that the Prophet cannot be blamed for what happened to them. The Prophet had a mutual defense treaty with the Banu Qurayzah, which they broke during the time of war, thereby committing high treason. The Prophet tried to talk to them, but when he came to their neighborhood, they hurled insults at him. They said they wanted justice and did not expect the Prophet Muhammad could deliver it to them. In a profound statement, Abul Aala Maududi, commenting on Banu Qurayzah's attitude in *Tafheemul Qur'an*, said, "What these people needed was not justice, because justice demanded they should have been killed. They needed mercy, which they could get only from the Messenger of Allaah, but they rejected him."

The case of the Banu Qurayzah was different from the Banu Nadheer. While the latter had only conspired to kill the Prophet, the Banu Qurayzah plotted to eliminate the entire Muslim community.

What happened to the Banu Qurayzah at the end of the Battle of Khandaq was not because of who they were but because of what they had done. When the Muslims searched their fortress after their defeat, they found a large cache of weapons, which the Banu Qurayzah most certainly would have used against the Muslims if they'd had a chance. No nation allows treason, especially high treason, to go unpunished.

Sa'ad bin Mu'aadh Dies

After Sa'ad had rendered his judgment, his wound began to bleed again. The Prophet had cauterized it twice, but Sa'ad's time had come. The Prophet came by his bed, put Sa'ad's head in his lap, and said, "O Allaah, Sa'ad fought for you. He believed in Your Messenger and fulfilled his duties. Take his soul in the best way that You take the souls of Your creation."

Sa'ad opened his eyes and said, "Peace be upon you, O Messenger of Allaah. I testify that you delivered your message." Then the Prophet left for his house. Sa'ad died a little while later.

When Sa'ad died, Gabriel came to the Prophet and asked, "O Muhammad, who is this good man who has died among you? The doors of heaven are opened for him. The throne of the Merciful shook over his death."[261] The Prophet rushed back to Sa'ad's house so fast that the Companions complained because he had left all of them behind. The Prophet responded that he did not want to be preceded by the angels in washing Sa'ad's body, as had been the case with the body of Hanzalah in Uhud.

The Prophet joined others in carrying Sa'ad's coffin. People noted that Sa'ad's bier was unusually light. Sa'ad was a tall, heavyset man, and the hypocrites had insinuated that his bier was light because of the judgment he had passed against the Banu Qurayzah. The Prophet hushed them up, saying, "Angels are carrying his body." The Prophet buried Sa'ad and said *Allaahu Akbar* three times. The Companions repeated after him until the Baqiyatul Gharqad cemetery was shaking with the sound of *Allaahu Akbar.*

Suddenly, the people saw the face of the Messenger of Allaah changed with worry, and when asked, he said, "The grave was narrow for your Companion, and he was squeezed in it. If one is saved the squeezing, it would surely be Sa'ad. May God relieve him of it." According to this Hadith, it is part of the trial of the grave that it squeezes its inhabitant upon burial.

261 Ibn Isshaaq, *Sirat Rasul Allah*, 468.

The Prophet's Marriages between Uhud and Trench

The Prophet took three women into marriage between the Battle of Uhud and the Battle of Khandaq. All of them were widows of martyrs.

The first woman was Hafsah bint Umar, the daughter of Umar bin Al-Khattaab, the second rightly guided caliph of Islam.[262] This happened in 3 AH (624/625 CE). When Hafsah's husband, Khunays bin Hudhayfah, was martyred in the Battle of Badr and she had passed her *iddah* (the waiting period of four months and ten days), her father began to look for a possible suitor for her.

Umar first approached Uthmaan, whose wife, Ruqayyah, one of the Prophet's daughters, had just died. Uthmaan politely declined. Then Umar went to Abu Bakr, and he too declined. That made Umar upset, and he went to the Prophet to complain. The Prophet replied, "Allaah will marry Uthmaan to better than your daughter and will marry your daughter to better than Uthmaan." How true were these words, for indeed Uthman married another daughter of the Prophet, and the Prophet himself married Umar's daughter. Abu Bakr is reported to have said that the only reason he had declined Umar's offer of his daughter's hand was that he had heard that the Messenger of Allaah was interested in Hafsah.

The second woman was Zaynab bint Khuzayma, who was also the widow of a Badr martyr. When her husband, Ubaydah bin Al-Haarith, died in Badr, the Prophet married her to honor her husband and provide her support. The marriage took place in 4 AH (625/626 CE). She was nicknamed *Umm Al-Masaakeen* (the mother of the poor) because of her extraordinary kindness and charity toward the poor. Close to Aayeshah's age, the two younger wives Hafsah and Zaynab were welcomed into the household.

262 Sunni Muslims consider the first four caliphs—Abu Bakr, Umar, Uthmaan, and Ali—to be rightly guided in their life and governance, meaning they governed strictly according to the Book of Allaah and the Sunnah of His Prophet.

Sawdah, who was much older, extended her motherly benevolence to the younger women. Aayeshah and Hafsah had a lasting relationship. As for Zaynab bint Khuzaymah, however, she became ill and died eight months after her marriage.

The third woman was Hind bint Abi Umayyah, but she was called Umm Salamah after her son from an earlier marriage. Both she and her husband, Abdullaah bin Abdul As'ad, better known as Abu Salamah, had migrated to Abyssinia. When they came back from Abyssinia and tried to migrate to Madinah, they faced difficulty. The Quraysh grudgingly allowed Abu Salamah to migrate but refused to let Umm Salamah and their child go. Then her child was also separated from her and his arm broken in the skirmish over custody between the Quraysh and Abu Salamah's tribe. It was a while later that her child was returned to Umm Salamah and she was allowed to join her husband in Madinah.

When Abu Salamah died from the wounds he had suffered in the battle of Uhud, Umm Salamah became distraught. They were an exceptionally loving couple, and when the Prophet went to offer her condolences, he advised her to be patient. He said that Allaah may grant her someone better than Abu Salamah. She responded, "Who could be better than Abu Salamah?" The Prophet kept silent, and after she had passed her waiting period, he proposed.

In a testament to her wisdom and maturity, Umm Salamah did not immediately accept the Prophet's offer. She put forward three concerns, and the Prophet allayed them in the most beautiful manner. She said, "O Messenger of Allaah, I have young children from a previous marriage. You have other wives, and I suffer from jealousy. And I am older."

The Prophet replied, "As for your children, they are my children; as for jealousy, I will pray that Allaah will remove it from your heart; and as for older age, I am afflicted with the same condition."

Umm Salamah was a wise advisor to the Prophet, and this wisdom shone through after the Treaty of Hudaybiyah.

The Chief of the Banu Hanifah Embraces Islam

The Banu Hanifah tribe was a Christian offshoot of the Banu Bakr, who lived in the Yamamah area, now the Saudi capital Riyadh. They were a stubborn and opportunistic tribe. Back in the Makkah days, the Banu Hanifah was one of the tribes the Prophet had asked for protection, but they had treated him very rudely. It is the same tribe that produced Musaylimah Al-Khadhdhaab, the false prophet. The Saudi royal family traces its roots to the Banu Hanifah, going back five hundred years.

In 6 AH (627/628 CE), the Prophet sent Muhammad bin Maslamah on an expedition against the hostile tribe of Banu Bakr. The Muslims attacked the Banu Bakr and captured plenty of spoils. Around the same time, a group of Muslims who were patrolling the districts of Madinah and outlying areas came upon Thumaamah bin Uthal Al-Hanafi. Without knowing who he was, they captured him. When they got back to Madinah, they tied their prisoner to a column in the mosque of the Prophet.

When the Prophet was about to enter the mosque, he saw Thumaamah and asked his Companions, "Do you know whom you have taken?"

They said, "No, Messenger of God."

The Prophet said, "This is Thumaamah bin Uthal Al-Hanafi; you have done well in capturing him." Thumaamah was the leader of his tribe and an influential figure.

The Prophet then returned home to his family and said, "Get what food you can and send it to Thumaamah bin Uthal." He then ordered his camel to be milked for him. All this was done before he met Thumaamah or spoke to him. The Prophet then approached Thumaamah, hoping to encourage him to become a Muslim. "What do you have to say for yourself?" the Prophet asked Thumaamah.

He replied, "If you want to kill in reprisal, you can have someone of noble blood to kill. If, out of your bounty, you want to forgive, I shall be grateful. If you want money in compensation, I shall give you whatever amount you ask for." Hearing Thumaamah's response, the Prophet left him alone but continued to personally send him food and drink and milk from his camel.

Two days later, the Prophet went back to him and asked, "What do you have to say for yourself?" Thumaamah repeated what he had said earlier. The Prophet again left him, and when he returned the following day, he asked the same question to Thumaamah: "What do you have to say for yourself?" Once again, Thumaamah repeated what he had said twice before. The Prophet turned to his Companions and said, "Set him free."

For three days Thumaamah had seen the Prophet leading the Muslims in prayer and imparting religious knowledge. These sights, as well as the hospitality he had received as a prisoner, began to stir his heart and make him reflect. When he was set free, Thumaamah left the mosque of the Prophet and rode until he came to a palm grove, where he watered his camel and washed himself well. Then he turned back and made his way to the Prophet's mosque. There, he stood before a congregation of Muslims and said, "I bear witness that there is no god but Allaah, and I bear witness that Muhammad is His servant and His Messenger." He then went to the Prophet and said, "O Muhammad, by God, there was never on this earth a face more detestable than yours. Now, yours is the dearest face of all to me. I have killed some of your men. I am at your mercy. What will you want done to me?"

The Prophet replied, "There is no blame on you, Thumaamah. Becoming a Muslim obliterates past actions and marks a new beginning."

Thumaamah was greatly relieved, and with a joyful face he vowed, "By God, I shall place my whole self, my sword, and whoever is with me at your service and at the service of your religion."

Thumaamah was quickly learning the new faith's etiquette. He realized that no Muslim addressed the Prophet by his name, so when he spoke moments later, he said, "O Messenger of Allaah, when your horsemen captured me, I was on my way to perform *Umrah*. What do you think I should do now?"

The Prophet replied, "Go ahead and perform your *Umrah,* but perform it according to the laws of God and His Messenger." The Prophet then taught him how to perform *Umrah*.

Thumaamah left to fulfill his intention. When he reached the valley of Makkah, he began shouting in a loud, resonant voice, "Labbayk Allaahumma Labbayk. Labbayka laa shareeka laka labbayk. Innal hamda wa-n Ni'mata laka wal Mulk Laa Shareeka Lak." (Here I am at Your command, O Lord, Here I am. Here I am. No partner have You. Here I am. Praise, bounty, and dominion belong to You. No partner have You.) He was thus the first Muslim on the face of the earth to enter Makkah reciting the *talbiyah* (chants).

The Quraysh heard the sound of the *talbiyah* and felt both anger and alarm. With drawn swords, they set out toward the voice to punish the one who had thus assaulted their preserve. As they came closer to him, Thumaamah raised his voice even higher while reciting the *talbiyah* and looked upon them with pride and defiance.

One of the Qurayshi young men was particularly incensed. He was about to shoot Thumaamah with an arrow when the others grabbed his hand and shouted, "Woe unto you! Do you know who this is? He is Thumaamah bin Uthal, ruler of Yamamah. By God, if you should harm him, his people would cut off our supplies, with dire consequences for us." Swords were put back in their scabbards as the Quraysh went up to Thumaamah and said, "What's wrong with you, Thumaamah? Have you given in and abandoned your religion and the religion of your forefathers?"

Thumaamah replied, "I have not given in, but I have decided to follow the best religion. I follow the religion of Muhammad." Then he said, "I swear to you by the Lord of this house that after my return to Yamamah, no grain of wheat or any of its produce shall reach you until you follow Muhammad."

Under the watchful eyes of the Quraysh, Thumaamah performed the *Umrah* as the Prophet had instructed him. He dedicated his sacrifice to God alone. Thumaamah returned to his homeland and ordered his people to withhold supplies from the Quraysh. The boycott—the economic sanctions of the time—gradually began to hurt the Quraysh. Prices began to rise. Hunger began to bite, and there was even fear of death among the Quraysh.

In an amazing reversal of circumstances, the Quraysh, who had boycotted the Muslims in Shi'b Abi Taalib many years ago in Makkah, wrote to the Prophet, begging for help against Thumaamah's boycott. Their message said, "Our agreement with you (the treaty of Hudaybiyah) is that you should maintain the bonds of kinship, but you have gone against that. You have cut the bonds of kinship. You have killed and caused death through hunger. Thumaamah bin Uthal has cut our supplies and inflicted harm on us. Perhaps you would see fit to instruct him to resume sending us what we need."

The Prophet ignored their accusations and immediately sent an envoy to Thumaamah telling him to lift the boycott and resume supplies to the Quraysh. This Thumaamah did and brought relief to the Makkans.

The Battle of the Banu Al-Mustaliq

According to most accounts, the battle of the Banu Al-Mustaliq took place in the sixth year of AH (627/628 CE), although another opinion puts it in the fifth year and yet another in the fourth year. The Battle of Banu Al-Mustaliq (also known as the Battle of Al-Muraysi') is important because of several incidents that happened during and after. A number of verses were revealed concerning those incidents, and the Prophet's personal life was severely tested. For the first time, the laws of the Shari'ah were laid down about the hypocrites.

The Messenger of Allaah received news that Al-Haarith bin Abu Diraar, the leader of the Banu Al-Mustaliq tribe, was gathering forces to attack Madinah. This is the same tribe that fought on the side of the Quraysh in the Battle of Uhud. They also posed a general threat to the Muslims because the Banu Al-Mustaliq controlled a part of the road that led to Makkah.

The Prophet decided to quickly move against the Banu Al-Mustaliq in a surprise offensive. He prepared a fighting force of seven hundred people and proceeded to take care of this threat. The Muslim forces suddenly came upon the Banu Al-Mustaliq at a watering place of theirs called Al-Muraysi'. The Banu Al-Mustaliq could not withstand the surprise attack. Many were killed, and the rest fled, leaving behind their families and property as war booty. Among the captives was Juwayriyah bint Al-Haarith, the daughter of the tribe's leader.

Aayeshah narrated that"

When the Messenger of Allaah allocated the captive women of the Banu Al-Mustaliq, Juwayriyah bint Al-Haarith belonged to the share of Thaabit bin Qays bin Shammaas or one of his cousins. She signed a freedom agreement with Thaabit that she would be freed if she could pay the ransom. She came to the Prophet and said, "O Messenger of Allaah, I am Juwayriyah bint Al-Haarith, the chief of his people. I have

> *been afflicted with an adversity that you know.*[263] *I belong to the share of Thaabit bin Qays bin Shammaas, or a cousin of his, and I hold a freedom contract with him. Here I am seeking your help for the ransom." The Messenger of Allaah said, "Would you want what is better than this?" She said, "What is that, O Messenger of Allaah?" He replied, "I shall pay your ransom and marry you." She agreed. When the Muslims found out what had happened, they released all the captives and properties of the Banu Al-Mustaliq, saying they had become the in-laws of the Messenger of Allaah."*

Aayeshah said, "The marriage of the Messenger of Allaah to Juwayriyah was the cause of the setting free of one hundred families of the Banu Al-Mustaliq. I do not know of a woman who was greater in blessing for her people than she was." Following the incident, Al-Haarith bin Abu Diraar, Juwayriyah's father, came to Madinah with the ransom for his daughter. The Messenger of Allaah invited him to embrace Islam, and he accepted.

Because of the compassionate way the Prophet had treated Juwayriyah and the consideration the Muslims had shown to the captives of the Banu Al-Mustaliq, the whole tribe embraced Islam. At a time when the Prophet wished for even a small group to enter Islam, the conversion of an entire tribe was a supersized prize Allaah gave His messenger.

A "Rotten" Incident

On return from the Battle of the Banu Al-Mustaliq, a servant of Umar bin Al-Khattaab argued with an Ansaari over water, which was scarce at the time. Umar's servant struck the Ansaari man, causing him to bleed. The man asked other Ansaaris to come to his aid. Umar's servant ran to the Qurayshi tents and appealed for help. The matter came to a brawl between the Emigrants and the Helpers, even though their love for each other, especially the sacrifices

263 She had become a slave after having been not only a free woman but the first lady of her people.

of the Helpers for their Emigrant brethren, was legendary. Abdullaah bin Ubayy, the leader of the hypocrites, found a golden opportunity to instigate trouble. He told some of the fellow hypocrites that it was their fault because they had sheltered the Emigrants, who had now become rich and emboldened. "By God, our situation now with those rags of the Quraysh is, as the saying goes, 'Fatten your dog, and it will eat you.' By God, when we reach Madinah, the more honorable will drive out the weaker."

Zayd bin Arqam, who was a young boy at the time, heard all of Ibn Ubayy's slanderous rantings and reported them to the Prophet. When questioned, Ibn Ubayy swore by Allaah that he never made those derogatory remarks. The Prophet asked Zayd if he could have misheard or misunderstood Ibn Ubayy, but he insisted that he had heard it right. Some of the Helpers started to criticize Zayd for having reported such a thing, so much so that Zayd prayed to Allaah to reveal the truth about the matter. And Allaah did. An entire surah, called Munafiqoon (The Hypocrites) was revealed, exposing Ibn Ubayy and his ilk.

When the hypocrites come to you, they say: "We bear witness that you are indeed the Messenger of Allaah." Allaah knows that you are indeed His Messenger, and Allaah bears witness that the hypocrites are liars indeed.

They have made their oaths a screen. Thus they hinder (others) from the path of Allaah. Verily, evil is what they used to do. That is because they believed, and then disbelieved; therefore their hearts are sealed, so they understand not.

And when you look at them, their bodies please you; and when they speak, you listen to their words. They are as blocks of wood propped up. They think that every cry is against them. They are the enemies, so beware of them. May Allaah curse them! How are they denying the right path?

And when it is said to them: "Come, so that the Messenger of Allaah may ask forgiveness from Allaah for you," they twist their heads, and you would see them turning away their faces in pride. It is equal to them whether you ask forgiveness or not ask forgiveness for them, Allaah will never forgive them. Verily, Allaah guides not the people who are rebellious.

They are the ones who say: "Do not spend on those who are with Allaah's Messenger, until they desert him." And to Allaah belong the treasures of the heavens and the earth, but the hypocrites comprehend not.

They say: "If we return to Al-Madinah, indeed the more honorable will expel therefrom the weaker." But the honor belongs to Allaah, and to His Messenger, and to the believers, but the hypocrites know not.

O you who believe! Let not your properties or your children divert you from the remembrance of Allaah. And whosoever does that, then they are the losers. And spend of that with which We have provided you before death comes to one of you, and he says: "My Lord! If only You would give me respite for a little while, then I should give charity from my wealth, and be among the righteous."

And Allaah does not grant respite to anyone when his appointed time comes. And Allaah is All-Aware of what you do.[264]

Verse 8 of the surah directly referred to Abdullaah bin Ubayy's statement vindicating Zayd bin Arqam.

They say, "If we return to Madinah, the more honored will surely expel therefrom the more humble." And to Allaah belongs all honor, and to His Messenger, and to the believers, but the hypocrites do not know.[265]

264 Munafiqoon 63.

265 Ibid 63:8.

When the surah came down, the Prophet became happy. He took Zayd bin Arqam by his ear and said, "This is the boy whose ear was exonerated by Allaah."

When Umar heard what Ibn Ubayy had said, he asked the Prophet for permission to chop off the hypocrite's head, but the Apostle declined his request, saying "What if people say that Muhammad kills his Companions?"

The Prophet was upset about the near-brawl at the well, which had reopened the tribal prejudices after Islam had tamed it. He was visibly angry at the incident and said, "Is this what I was sent for? Leave it; it is rotten." But the Prophet was more worried about what Ibn Ubayy had said concerning the Emigrants. To distract people from harboring divisive thoughts, he ordered everyone to leave at once, even though they were tired and it was a hot day. When Sa'ad bin Ubaadah asked him why he had chosen such an unusual time to march, the Prophet said, "And did you not hear what your Companion said?" There was a clear wisdom in this order, for the Prophet did not want people, especially the hypocrites, to gossip about this matter.

Among the Muslims the one who was personally hurt and embarrassed by Ibn Ubayy's slander was his own son, also named Abdullaah, a sincere Muslim. What made things worse for the son was the rumor that some people had suggested to the Prophet that he should kill Abdullaah's father. Abdullaah never doubted the Prophet's sense of justice, but he wanted to confirm the news and also to suggest something to him.

"If you desire to kill my father, command me, for by God I could bring you his head before you get up from your seat," Abdullaah said, adding that if anyone else from the Muslims were to kill his father, his emotions would force him to kill that person, thus causing him to fall into a major sin. The contrast between father and son could not be sharper.

The Prophet assured Abdullaah that he did not want his father killed, and he also forbade him to do so. "Let us deal kindly with his Companionship when he is among us," the Prophet advised Abdullaah. The Prophet not only lived up to this advice, but when Ibn Ubayy died, he gave his own shirt as a shroud and led his funeral prayer.

The Story of Slander

This incident is known in Arabic as *ifk,* meaning a lie or falsehood. When used in the context of the Prophet's Seerah, the word refers to the slander of adultery against his wife Aayeshah. The books of Hadith have reported this incident in great detail from Aayeshah herself.

She said: "When the Messenger of Allaah wanted to go on a journey, he would cast lots among his wives, and the one whose lot was drawn would go with him. So he drew lots among us with regard to a campaign he was going out on, and mine was drawn, so I went out with the Messenger of Allaah. This was after the commandment of *hijaab* (head cover) had been revealed, so I traveled in my *howdah*[266] and stayed in it when we camped. We traveled until the Messenger of Allaah completed his campaign; then we returned.

"As we were approaching Madinah, we paused for a while; then they announced that the journey was to be resumed. When I heard this, I walked quickly away from the army to answer the call of nature; then I came back to my howdah. Then I put my hand to my chest and noticed that a necklace of mine that was made of onyx and carnelian had broken, so I went back and looked for it and was delayed because of that. In the meantime, the people who used to lift my howdah onto my camel came along and put it on the camel, thinking that I was inside. In those times women were more slender and not so heavy; they only ate mouthfuls of food. So the people did

266 A *howdah* is a seat, especially with a canopy and railing, for riding on the back of an elephant or camel.

not think anything of the howdah being so light when they lifted it up, as I was a young woman. They set off, and I found my necklace after the army had moved on.

"Then I came back to the place where we had stopped, and I saw no one to call or answer. So I went to the place where I had been, thinking that the people would miss me and come back for me. While I was sitting there, I fell asleep. Safwaan bin Al-Mu'attal As-Sulami Adh-Dhakwani had rested during the night behind the army. Then he set out just before daybreak and reached the place where I was in the morning, where he saw the outline of a person sleeping. He came to me and recognized me when he saw me, as he had seen me before hijaab was made obligatory for me.

"When he saw me and said, 'Truly, to Allaah we belong, and truly, to Him we shall return,' I woke up and covered my face with my *jilbaab* (outer garment). By Allaah, he did not speak a word to me, and I did not hear him say anything except, 'Truly, to Allaah we belong, and truly, to Him we shall return,' until he brought his camel and made it kneel so that I could ride upon it; then he set out leading the camel until we caught up with the army at *zhuhr* (afternoon) time.

"There are people who are doomed because of what happened to me, and the one who had the greater share therein was Abdullaah bin Ubayy bin Salul. When we came back to Madinah, I was ill for a month, and the people were talking about what the people of the slander were saying, and I knew nothing about it.[267]

"What upset me when I was ill was that I did not see the kindness I used to see on the part of the Messenger of Allaah. When I was ill, he would just come in and say, 'How is that lady?" That is what upset me.

---

267 Nobody had told Aayeshah that some people had accused her of committing adultery with Safwaan bin Al-Mu'attal.

"I did not feel that there was anything wrong until I went out with Umm Mistaah after I felt better, walking toward Al-Manaasi', which is where we used to go to relieve ourselves, and we would not go out for that purpose except at night. This was before we had lavatories close to our houses; our habit was similar to that of the early Arabs in that we went out into the deserts to relieve ourselves, because we considered it troublesome and harmful to have lavatories in our houses.

"So I went out with Umm Mistaah, who was the daughter of Abu Ruhm bin Al-Muttalib bin Abd Manaaf, and her mother was the daughter of Sakhr bin Aamir, the paternal aunt of Abu Bakr As-Siddiq. Her son was Mistaah bin Uthaathah bin Abbaad bin Al-Muttalib. When we finished what we had to do, Umm Mistaah and I came back toward my house. Umm Mistaah stumbled over her apron and said, 'May Mistaah be ruined!'

"I said to her, 'What a bad thing you have said! Are you abusing a man who was present at Badr?'

"She said, 'Good grief, have you not heard what he said?'

"I said, 'What did he say?' So she told me what the people of the slander were saying, which made me even more ill.

"When I returned home, the Messenger of Allaah came in to me and greeted me; then he said, 'How is that lady?'

"I said to him, 'Will you give me permission to go to my parents?' At that time I wanted to confirm the news by hearing it from them. The Messenger of Allaah gave me permission, so I went to my parents and asked my mother, 'O my mother, what are the people talking about?'

"My mother said, 'Calm down, for by Allaah, there is no beautiful woman who is loved by her husband and has co-wives but those co-wives would find fault with her.'

"I said, 'Subhaan Allaah! (Glory be to Allaah). Are the people really talking about that?' I wept throughout the whole night until morning. My tears never ceased, and I did not sleep at all; morning came while I was still weeping.

"Because the revelation had ceased, the Messenger of Allaah called Ali bin Abi Taalib and Usaamah bin Zayd and consulted with them about divorcing his wife.

"As for Usaamah bin Zayd, he told the Messenger of Allaah about what he knew of his wife's innocence and his fondness for her. He said, 'O Messenger of Allaah, she is your wife, and we do not know anything about her but good.'

"But Ali bin Abi Taalib said, 'O Messenger of Allaah, Allaah has not imposed restrictions on you, and there are plenty of other women besides her. If you ask her servant girl, she will tell you the truth.'

"So the Messenger of Allaah called Bareerah and said, 'O Bareerah, have you ever seen anything that might make you suspicious about Aayeshah?'

"Bareerah said to him, 'By the One Who sent you with the truth, I have never seen anything for which I could blame her, apart from the fact that she is a young girl who sometimes falls asleep and leaves her family's dough unprotected so that the domestic goats come and eat it.'

"The Messenger of Allaah then asked Zaynab bint Jahsh about my situation, and said, 'O Zaynab, what do you or have you seen?'

"She said, 'O Messenger of Allaah, may Allaah protect my hearing and my sight. By Allaah, I know nothing but good.' She is the one who used to compete with me among the wives of the Prophet, but Allaah protected her (from telling lies) because of her piety. But her sister Hamnah bint Jahsh kept on fighting on her behalf, so she was doomed along with those who were doomed.

"So then the Messenger of Allaah got up and asked who could sort out Abdullaah bin Ubayy bin Salul for him. While he was standing on the *minbar* (pulpit), the Messenger of Allaah said, 'O Muslims, who will help me against a man who has hurt me by slandering my family? By Allaah, I know nothing about my family but good, and the people are blaming a man of whom I know nothing except good, and he has never visited my family except with me.'

"Sa'ad bin Mu'aadh stood up and said, 'O Messenger of Allaah, by Allaah I will deal with him for you. If he is from the tribe of Al-Aws, then I will cut off his head, and if he is from our brothers of the tribe of Al-Khazraj, tell us what to do, and we will do it.'

"Then Sa'ad bin Ubaadah stood up. He was the leader of Al-Khazraj, and he was a righteous man, but he was overwhelmed with tribal sentiments. He said to Sa'ad bin Mu'aadh, 'By Allaah, you will not kill him, and you will never be able to kill him.'

"Then Usayd bin Hudhayr, who was the cousin of Sa'ad bin Mu'aadh, stood up and said to Sa'ad bin Ubaadah, 'You are lying! By Allaah, we will kill him, and you are a hypocrite arguing on behalf of the hypocrites!' Then the two groups, Al-Aws and Al-Khazraj, started to get angry and were about to come to blows, with the Messenger of Allaah standing there on the *minbar*, trying to calm them down, until they became quiet; then the Messenger of Allaah also fell silent.

"On that day I kept on weeping so much, my tears never ceased, and I did not sleep at all. My parents thought that my liver would burst from all that weeping. While they were sitting with me and I was weeping, a woman of the Ansaar asked for permission to see me. I let her in, and she sat and wept with me. While we were in that state, the Messenger of Allaah came in, greeted us, and sat down. He had not sat with me since the rumors had begun, and a month had passed by without any revelation coming to him concerning my case.

"The Messenger of Allaah recited the *tashahhud* (a glorification of God in prayer) when he sat down; then he said, 'O Aayeshah, I have been told such and such a thing about you, and if you are innocent, then Allaah will reveal your innocence, but if you have committed a sin, then seek Allaah's forgiveness and turn in repentance to Him, for when a servant confesses his sin and repents to Allaah, He accepts his repentance.' When the Messenger of Allaah finished what he had to say, my tears stopped completely, and I no longer felt even one drop.

"Then I said to my father, 'Answer the Messenger of Allaah on my behalf.'

"He said, 'I do not know what I should say to the Messenger of Allaah.'

"So I said to my mother, 'Answer the Messenger of Allaah on my behalf.'

"She said, 'I do not know what I should say to the Messenger of Allaah.'

"So even though I was just a young girl who had not memorized much of the Qur'aan, I said, 'By Allaah, I know that you have heard so much of this story that it has become planted in your minds and you believe it. So now if I tell you that I am innocent—and Allaah knows that I am innocent—you will not believe me; but if I admit something to you—and Allaah knows that I am innocent—you will believe me. By Allaah, I cannot find any example to give you except for what the Prophet Yusuf's father said: *So for me patience is most fitting. And it is Allaah Whose help can be sought against that (lie) which you describe.*'[268]

"Then I turned my face away and lay down on my bed. By Allaah, at that point I knew I was innocent and that Allaah would prove my innocence because I was innocent, but by Allaah, I did not think that Allaah would reveal Qur'aan that would be forever recited concerning my situation, because

---

268 Yusuf 12:18.

I thought of myself as too insignificant for Allaah to reveal anything concerning me. But I hoped that the Messenger of Allaah would see a dream in which Allaah would prove my innocence.

"By Allaah, the Messenger of Allaah did not move from where he was sitting and no one left the house before Allaah sent down revelation to His Prophet, and he was overtaken by the state that always overtook him when the revelation came upon him, until drops of sweat like pearls would run down him, even on a winter's day; this was because of the heaviness of the words that were being revealed to him. When that state passed—and the Messenger of Allaah was smiling—the first thing he said was, 'Be glad, O Aayeshah, Allaah has declared your innocence.'

"My mother said to me, 'Get up and go to him.'

"I said, 'By Allaah, I will not go to him, and I will not give praise to anyone except Allaah, may He be glorified, for He is the One Who has proven my innocence.'"

The verses that Allaah sent down are from Surah Nur (Light):

Verily, those who brought forth the slander are a group among you. Consider it not a bad thing for you. Nay, it is good for you. Unto every man among them will be paid that which he had earned of the sin, and as for him among them who had the greater share therein, his will be a great torment. Why then, did not the believers, men and women, when you heard it, think good of their own people and say: "This is an obvious lie?" Why did they not produce four witnesses against him? Since they have not produced witnesses, then with Allaah they are the liars![269]

269 Nur 24:11–13.

Because of this incident, Allaah also sent down laws to deal with slander; these laws included punishment in this life and warning for the Hereafter:

> *And those who accuse chaste women, and do not produce four witnesses, flog them with eighty stripes, and reject their testimony forever.*[270]

> *Verily, those who accuse chaste believing women, who never even think of anything touching their chastity and are good believers—are cursed in this life and in the Hereafter, and for them will be a great torment.*[271]

Abu Bakr used to financially support Mistaah, but after the slander he vowed he would not support him anymore. Allaah disapproved of Abu Bakr's vow and sent down the following verses:

> *And let not those among you who are blessed with graces and wealth swear not to give to their kinsmen. Do you not love that Allaah should forgive you and Allaah is Oft-Forgiving, Most Merciful.*[272]

So Abu Bakr immediately reversed himself, saying, "By Allaah, certainly I love that Allaah should forgive me. By Allaah, I shall never stop spending on him."

The greatest offenders were Abdullaah bin Ubayy, followed by Hamnah bint Jahsh, who spread the slander as a way of supporting her sister, Zaynab, and Hassaan bin Thaabit. Hamnah was the widow of Mus'ab bin Umayr, one of the closest Companions of the Messenger of Allaah and a martyr at Uhud. Both Hamnah and Hassaan were flogged. It is reported that Safwaan bin Mu'attal, the Companion who was falsely accused in the Story of *Ifk*, was impotent and had never touched a woman. He later died as a martyr.

270 Nur 24:4.

271 Nur 24:23.

272 Nur 24:22.

Surah Al-Ahzaab (33)

It is important to mention Surah Al-Ahzaab. There is hardly any surah in the Qur'aan that has as many legal and social rulings and as much guidance for the Prophet's family life as this. For instance, it refutes the cultural belief of the Quraysh about adopted sons. The chapter categorically rejects the notion that adopted children become one's own. In the Arab culture of the time, when someone adopted children, they treated them as their own offspring and gave them a share in inheritance. The adoptive parents also treated such children as *mahram*. A mahram is someone whom one cannot marry, like a daughter, son, sister, aunt, niece, uncle, and so forth.

The storm of criticism that arose over the Prophet's marriage to Zaynab, his cousin, is a case in point. Earlier Zaynab was married to the Prophet's adopted son, Zayd bin Haarithah. The Prophet had insisted on this marriage despite opposition from Zaynab's family, which was among the noblest families of the Quraysh. Zayd, on the other hand, was a freed slave. The marriage did not work out, resulting in a divorce. The Prophet kept advising Zayd not to divorce his wife. Allaah knew that the divorce would happen, and He ordered the Prophet to marry Zaynab once she had passed her waiting period. In Surah Ahzaab Allaah said:

> *And (remember) when you said to him on whom Allaah has bestowed grace and you have done a favor (Zayd): "Keep your wife to yourself, and have Consciousness of Allaah." But you did hide in yourself that which Allaah will make manifest, you did fear the people whereas Allaah had a better right that you should fear Him. So, when Zayd had completed his aim with her, We gave her to you in marriage, so that there may be no difficulty to the believers in respect of the wives of their adopted sons when the latter have no desire to keep them. And Allaah's command must be fulfilled.*[273]

273 Ahzaab 33:37.

The Prophet was initially hesitant, as the above verse said, concerned about the tempest it would create among the tradition-bound Arab pagans, but when Allaah pressed him, he proceeded with the marriage. As soon as the marriage had taken place, there arose a storm of propaganda against the Prophet. The polytheists, the hypocrites, and some others became united in their criticism of the Prophet's action. This was their chance to damage the moral excellence of the Messenger of Allaah. Finally, there was an opportunity to say, "Look, this man cannot be a Messenger of Allaah. How could a religious figure marry his own daughter-in-law, which even common people would abhor?" This was the second major attack on the personal honor of the Prophet, the first being the slander against his wife Aayeshah's character. The rumormongers concocted a story that the Prophet Muhammad had fallen in love with his daughter-in-law, and when the son came to know of this, he divorced his wife.

A Flawed Propaganda

There was no merit in the hypocrites' accusation. In fact it was a blatant lie. Zaynab was the Prophet's first cousin, daughter of his aunt Umaamah bint Abdul Muttalib, who was married to Jahsh bin Riyaab. The Prophet had known her from when she was a child until adulthood. If he had wished to marry her, Zaynab's parents would have been delighted. But to the contrary, he himself had arranged Zaynab's marriage with Zayd under his personal authority as the Prophet of Allaah, although her whole family had opposed it. But everyone had to submit to the Prophet's command.

Through a verse that is part of Surah Ahzaab, Allaah made it clear that believers cannot refuse an order of the Prophet:

> *It is not for a believer, man or woman, when Allaah and His Messenger have decreed a matter that they should have any option in their decision. And whoever disobeys Allaah and His Messenger, he has indeed strayed into a plain error.*[274]

274 Ahzaab 33:36.

Although this verse was revealed in response to another incident, its meaning is general. One should also note that Allaah has called the Prophet's decision His own.

The marriage to Zayd proved to be unsuccessful. When the differences could not be reconciled, the two were divorced. Allaah then ordered His Prophet to simply bring Zaynab into his household. There was no need for *nikaah*, as Allaah Himself had married Zaynab to the Prophet[275] Zaynab was always proud of this. She used to say that, of all the Prophet's wives, she was the only one whose marriage was conducted in Paradise.

By marrying Zaynab to the Prophet, Allaah dismantled the pagan custom of claiming relationship through adoption. This verse is clearly not the statement of a false Prophet making up verses trying to justify his desires. If the Prophet had ulterior motives, he could have gone about the matter in a much subtler way and gotten what he wanted. Instead, he was put on the spot to do something he felt uncomfortable with.

Aayeshah said, "If the Messenger of Allaah wanted to conceal anything that was revealed to him of the Book of Allaah, he would have concealed the verse that says: 'But you did hide in yourself that which Allaah will make manifest, you did fear the people whereas Allaah had a better right that you should fear Him.'"[276]

Sadly, some Muslim scholars have fallen into the mistake of reporting this matter as if the Prophet was suddenly overcome with the desire to marry Zaynab when he went to her house at a time when Zayd was not present and he saw her not properly dressed. This story is mentioned in Tafsir At-Tabari but without any chain of transmission. Ibn Kathir does not mention it at all in his commentary of the Qur'aan. In his monumental work on

275 Ahzaab 33:37.

276 Ahzaab 33:37. The Prophet initially kept to himself that Allaah had ordered him to marry Zaynab once Zayd had divorced her.

history, *Al-Bidaayah wa Al-Nihaayah* (*The Beginning and End*), Ibn Kathir discussed the marriage of Zaynab bint Jahsh and mentioned that there were some strange stories circulated by the early scholars, but many of them were dubious and should be abandoned.

A Dream that Changed the World

In 6 AH (627/628 CE), the Prophet saw in a dream that he had entered Makkah and was performing *Tawaaf* of the Ka'bah. The Qur'aan mentioned this dream in Surah Fath:

> *Indeed Allaah shall fulfill the true vision which He showed to His Messenger in very truth. Certainly, you shall enter Al-Masjid Al-Haraam, if Allaah wills, secure, having your heads shaved, and having your hair cut short, having no fear. He knew what you knew not, and He granted besides that a near victory.*[277]

One important element of this dream was the phrase *near victory*. Allaah said that He has already granted this victory, meaning it was decreed to happen. The Prophet Muhammad publicly proclaimed his intention to go for *Umrah* (lesser pilgrimage) and asked the tribes, including the non-Muslims, to accompany him on the journey. Some of the tribes declined his invitation, while others accepted it.

Giving himself enough time, the Prophet left on the first of the month of Dhul Qa'dah. His entourage included the Emigrants, the Helpers, and a number of other tribes. He led the procession riding on his she-camel, Al-Qaswa. Their total number was about 1,400 men. They took with them seventy camels and put on their *ihraam* (white unstitched garment), clearly showing to everyone that the purpose of their journey was Umrah and not a military expedition. No man in the whole group carried any arms except

277 Fath 48:27.

the undrawn sword usually worn by all travelers. Umm Salamah, the wife of the Prophet, accompanied him on this trip.

When the Quraysh learned that the Prophet was on his way to Makkah with 1,400 people, they became fearful, and their fear did not dissipate even when they learned that the Muslims were coming as pilgrims and had no weapons with them. The Quraysh quickly mobilized an army, including a cavalry force of two hundred, to stop the Prophet. They gave the command to Khaalid bin Waleed and Ikrimah bin Abu Jahl. This army advanced to Dhu Tuwa, a place the Prophet and his Companions would have to pass by, and took up position there.

Allaah sent Gabriel to inform the Prophet about Khaalid's move, which prompted the latter to ask if there was someone who could show them a road to Makkah that would avoid the Qurayshi blockade. When such a person was found, they proceeded via a route that was desolate and difficult. That road led them to the Valley of Al-Hudaybiyah, which was to the south of Makkah. This meant they went past Makkah and then headed north toward it.

When the Quraysh discovered the Prophet's maneuver, Khaalid and his team quickly returned to Makkah to defend it against what they thought to be a Muslim invasion from the south. For the first time, Khaalid realized that there was a force that was frustrating his plans against the Prophet Muhammad. He had not been able to lay his hands on the Prophet in Badr or Uhud or Khandaq despite his military genius. It must also be said that Allaah had some other plans for Khaalid.

By trying to prevent the Muslims from performing Umrah, the Quraysh were violating Allaah's commandment and their own tradition. But in their bigotry against the Muslims, they did not care. The Muslims were not afraid to defend against this blatant injustice, even by force, but if they did, the peaceful purpose of the whole affair would be lost, and the Quraysh would find great satisfaction in reviling the Muslims.

Upon arrival at the plains of Al-Hudaybiyah, Al-Qaswa, the she-camel of the Prophet, stopped and refused to move. Some of the Companions said the camel was being stubborn, but the Prophet told them, "He Who stopped the elephant has stopped her too," referring to the elephant in Abrahah's army that had come to destroy the Ka'bah the same year the Prophet was born.

Miracle and Compromise

A serious challenge at Hudaybiyah was lack of water. Few things are as scary as this in the desert. The Muslims and their animals faced a real threat. As usual, the Companions brought their problem before the Prophet. According to one narration, the Messenger of Allaah gave them an arrow from his quiver. They placed it in the well of Al-Hudaybiyah, and the water gushed out until they all satisfied their thirst and watered their animals.

The Prophet was in the mood of all possible compromise. He was headed to the sacred precincts where no fighting was allowed, where animals and plants were protected. Makkah was also his birthplace. He said, "By the One in Whose Hand my soul is, this day, if they ask me anything that will respect the ordinances of Allaah, I will grant it to them."

The Quraysh Send Delegates

The Quraysh were worried about the Muslim presence, but the core leadership did not want to directly engage with the Prophet. So they decided to send emissaries. The first person they sent was Budayl bin Waraqah Al-Khuzaa'i with some men of the Khuza'ah tribe. The Prophet told them that he had not come to fight but to perform Umrah. The delegation returned to the Quraysh, narrated what they had heard, and counseled them that the Muslims be permitted to fulfill their religious rites. The Quraysh remained unconvinced. They knew that a good number of the Khuza'ah had accepted Islam, and the tribe was friendly toward the Prophet and, therefore, perhaps viewed Budayl with suspicion. To some extent that was true. The Khuza'ah acted as the eyes and ears of the Muslims in Makkah.

In order to make sure that their first delegates had told them the truth, the Quraysh sent Al-Hulays bin Alqamah, the leader of their *Ahabish* allies, a group of strong Abyssinian bowmen. The Prophet knew that the *Ahabish* were a devout people, so when he saw them arriving, he ordered that the sacrificial cattle be paraded in front of them as material proof that the Muslims had peaceful intentions. Al-Hulays saw the seventy sacrificial animals and became convinced that the Quraysh were doing an injustice to Muslims by preventing them from Umrah. He returned without meeting the Prophet Muhammad and told the Quraysh to let the Muslims in.

Full of resentment, the Quraysh insulted Al-Hulays, saying he was an ignorant Bedouin. Al-Hulays was angered and told the Quraysh that he had not allied himself with them in order to stop the pilgrims from performing their religious duties. He even threatened that unless they allowed the Prophet Muhammad and his party into the sanctuary, he would remove himself and his tribe from Makkah.

The third person the Quraysh sent was Urwah bin Mas'ud Ath-Thaqafi. They assured him of their respect and pledged to abide by his advice. Urwah was an animated person, and he tried with his tongue and body language to convince the Prophet to return to Madinah, as the Quraysh had resolved that they would not allow the Muslims to perform Umrah that year. With his aggressive demeanor, Urwah tried to grab the beard of the Prophet to make a point, and Mugheerah bin Shu'bah pushed his hand away.

Urwah then looked at the Companions of the Prophet, which included Bilaal, Salmaan, and Suhayb, and derisively said, "O Muhammad, have you gathered together a motley group of people against your own to destroy them? Now the Quraysh have sworn a most solemn oath that so long as their eyelashes quiver on their eyelids, you shall not set foot again in Makkah by force. The scum surrounding you will flee from your side before the sun sets on another day."

The insulting words enraged Abu Bakr, a man steeped in gentleness, who shouted at Urwah with a derogatory word for the latter's idol, Al-Laat. "Be gone," Abu Bakr continued. "Do you think for a moment we could abandon Allaah's messenger?"

Urwah said to Abu Bakr, "Had it not been for a favor I owed you, I would have paid you back for this remark. But now we are even."

Urwah again tried to grab the beard of the Messenger of Allaah, and this time Mugheerah sternly warned him, "Take your hand away from the face of the Messenger before you lose it." Mugheerah was wearing a coat of mail, and Urwah could not recognize that it was his own nephew.

When he was told, he lashed at Mugheerah. "O wretched fellow, it was only yesterday that I washed your dirty parts!"

Urwah returned to Makkah, convinced that the Prophet Muhammad had not come to wage war but to perform a sacred ritual in fulfillment of a divine command. He said to the Qurayshi leaders, "O Men of Quraysh, I have visited Chosroe, Caesar, and the Negus in their respective courts. By God, I have never seen a king as beloved to his people as Muhammad is to his. His Companions revere him so much that they carefully lift every hair that falls off his body, and they save the water with which he performs his ablutions. When he speaks, their voices are hushed in his presence. They lower their eyes and do not look at his face in reverence for him. They will never allow any hand to fall on him. Judge then accordingly." The Quraysh still demurred.

The Quraysh Become Belligerent

When the Prophet saw no change in the Qurayshi position upon the return of their delegates, he sent an envoy of his own named Khiraash Al-Umayyah Al-Khuzaa'i to them. Khiraash entered Makkah riding on Tha'lab, one of the other camels of the Prophet, to signify the importance and authenticity of his mission. The Makkans slew the camel and were about to kill Khiraash when the Ahabish intervened and let him go free. This conduct of the Makkans only confirmed their belligerence.

The Muslims began to lose patience and considered fighting their way through. While they were still pondering what to do, some ruffians from Makkah went out under the cover of night to throw stones at the tents of the Muslims. About forty or fifty Muslim pilgrims encircled the attackers, captured them, and brought them to the Prophet for judgment. To the surprise of everyone, the Prophet forgave the attackers and allowed them to go free. The Quraysh were dumbfounded by Prophet Muhammad's generosity. While they had lost every argument they had against the Prophet, the Quraysh still stubbornly hung on to their position that Muslims will not be allowed to perform Umrah.

The Prophet then called Umar bin Al-Khattaab to go to the Quraysh to dissuade them from their stand. Umar pleaded with the Prophet not to send him. His reasoning was two-fold: one, none of his people, the Banu Adiyy bin Ka'ab clan, who would protect him against the Quraysh were left in Makkah, and two, they would not listen to him because of his well-known toughness against them. He suggested that the Prophet send Uthmaan bin Affaan, whose tribesmen were still in Makkah, and the Prophet agreed.

Uthmaan proceeded to Makkah, and on its outskirts he was met by Abaan bin Sa'id, who extended to him protection for the time it took to convey his message. Uthmaan approached the noblemen of Quraysh and handed over the Prophet's message. They suggested to him that he might make *Tawaaf* (ritual circling of the Ka'bah) if he wished, but Uthmaan declined, saying, "I shall never do so until the Prophet of God has done so himself." He continued to insist that the Muslims had come to Makkah simply in order to visit the holy shrine. The Quraysh told him that they had already sworn that the Muslims would not be allowed to enter Makkah this year. The negotiations lasted a long time, during which Uthmaan was forced to stay in Makkah. Soon the Muslims began to suspect that he had been treacherously killed.

The Covenant of Al-Ridwaan

The possibility of Uthmaan having been killed sent shockwaves among the Muslims. Besides being a sincere Muslim, Uthmaan was the Prophet's son-in-law. After Ruqayyah's death, the Prophet had married another of his daughters, Umm Kulthoom, to Uthmaan. He was also financially among the most generous in helping the cause of Islam. Any harm coming to Uthmaan would be downright personal to the Prophet.

There was no revelation from Allaah about the matter, so the Prophet called his Companions under a large tree in the middle of that valley, and there they took the oath to fight the Quraysh. Some say it was an oath to fight till death, while others say it only required that no one would run away. Their faith was certain, their conviction was strong, and their will was determined to avenge the blood of Uthmaan. This covenant was called the *Baiyatu Ar-Ridwaan* (Pledge of Al-Ridwaan), and Allaah praises it in the Qur'aan: "Surely, those who give Pledge to you (O Muhammad) they are giving Pledge to Allaah, the Hand of Allaah is over their hands."[278]

Two other verses not only praise the pledgers but also promise them abundant booty in the future:

> *Indeed, Allaah was pleased with the believers when they gave the pledge to you under the tree, He knew what was in their hearts, and He sent*

278 Fath 48:10.

down tranquility upon them, and He rewarded them with a near victory. And abundant spoils that they will capture. And Allaah is Ever All-Mighty, All-Wise.[279]

When the Muslims gave their pledge by putting their hand on the Prophet's, the latter used his other hand on behalf of Uthmaan to symbolize his presence. Thereupon, swords shook in their scabbards, and the Muslims realized that war was now inevitable. Everybody looked forward to the day of victory or martyrdom with a mind convinced and satisfied, and a heart reassured and at peace. The intervening moments were tense and full of nervous anticipation. While in this state, the news came that Uthmaan had not been murdered after all. Soon he returned safe and sound to the Muslim camp and told them about his ordeal.

The Quraysh's Response

Uthmaan informed the Prophet that the Quraysh had no doubt that the Muslims had come to Makkah for *Umrah*, but to save face and prestige, they had decided not to let the Muslims fulfill their religious rights that year. However, they were open to letting Muslims come the next year. One may find a similarity between the Quraysh's attitude and the situation of Prophet Joseph (Yusuf) when he was imprisoned even though he was blameless. The women of the ruling class of Egypt knew all too well that it was the wife of Aziz who had been trying to seduce Joseph, yet they decided to send him off to prison to satisfy their egos.

The Quraysh now wanted to enter into a treaty with the Muslims, and for this purpose they sent Suhayl bin Amr. When the Prophet saw Suhayl coming to negotiate on the Quraysh's behalf, he became optimistic. He also saw an omen in the name Suhayl, which comes from the root word that means easy, and said, "The people want to make peace, seeing that

279 Fath 48:18–19.

they have sent this man." Suhayl became a Muslim before the conquest of Makkah two years later and played a positive role during the confusion that engulfed the Muslims after the passing of the Prophet.

Suhayl repeated the Qurayshi position that there would be no Umrah that year, but the Muslims might come the next year if they so wished. He also suggested writing a treaty between the Muslims and the Quraysh. Sensing that the Quraysh had enslaved themselves to their egos, the Prophet called Ali bin Abi Taalib and said to him, "Write, 'In the name of Allaah, the Compassionate, the Merciful.'"

Suhayl objected, "Stop, I do not know either 'the Merciful' or 'the Compassionate.' Write, 'In Your name, O God.'"

The Prophet instructed Ali to write accordingly and continued. "Write, 'The following is the text of a pact between Muhammad, the Messenger of Allaah, and Suhayl bin Amr.'"

Suhayl interrupted again. "Had we accepted you as the Messenger of Allaah, there would not have been any problem between us. Rather write, 'This is a pact between Muhammad bin Abdullaah and Suhayl bin Amr.'

The Prophet asked Ali to erase the words "Messenger of Allaah," but Ali, shocked and deeply offended, declined. The Prophet asked him where the text was, and he personally removed it.

The Terms of the Treaty

- The Muslims shall return this time and come back next year, but they shall not stay in Makkah for more than three days.
- The Muslims shall not come back armed but can bring with them travelers' swords sheathed in scabbards and kept in bags.

- The two parties shall suspend war activities for ten years, during which they will live in full security, and neither will raise sword against the other.
- Muslims will return any man from the Quraysh who runs away to Madinah without his guardian's permission. But the Quraysh would be under no obligation to return a Muslim man who flees to Makkah.
- Whosoever wishes to join the Prophet Muhammad shall have the liberty to do so; and likewise whosoever wishes to join the Quraysh should be allowed to do so.

As the pact was being signed, Abu Jandal, Suhayl's own son who had become Muslim and who had freed himself from captivity, came to the Prophet and asked for asylum. Abu Jandal was crying and begging the Prophet to take him to Madinah. The treaty's clauses were fresh on everyone's mind. The Prophet still pleaded very hard with Suhayl to let his son go, but Suhayl refused and insisted that the provisions of the treaty needed to be applied to his son's case.

With a heavy heart, the Prophet accepted it and said, "O Abu Jandal, have patience and be strong, for Allaah will soon provide for you and your other persecuted Companions a way out of your suffering. We have entered into a treaty of peace with the Quraysh, and we have exchanged with them a solemn pledge that none will cheat the other." At that point Umar came closer to Abu Jandal and gestured toward his sword, suggesting that he seize it to defend himself. But it was the decree of Allaah that Abu Jandal was taken back to the Quraysh screaming and pleading. Abu Jandal's plight filled the Muslims' hearts with sadness and anger.

Muslims in Shock

The unequal, even humiliating, provisions of the treaty and Abu Jandal's heart-rending situation were too much for Umar to bear. As the Muslims were returning, Umar came to the Prophet and vented. "Are we not Muslims and they disbelievers?"

The Prophet simply said, "Yes."

Umar continued, "So why have we signed such a treaty?"

The Prophet said, "I am the Messenger of Allaah, and I will not disobey Him."

Umar pressed on. "Did you not tell us that we would go to the House and perform *Tawaaf* around it?"

The Prophet replied, "Yes, but did I tell you that you would go to it this year?"

Umar said, "No."

The Prophet continued, "Then you will go to it and perform *Tawaaf* around it." Umar then went to Abu Bakr to complain about the treaty and received the same answer from him.

The Prophet asked the Companions to shave their heads and sacrifice the animals that they had brought, but none of the shocked Muslims moved. When the Prophet repeated his command three times and no one obeyed, the Prophet went to his tent and expressed his sadness to his wife, Umm Salamah.

She, who was known for her wisdom, said, "O Messenger of Allaah, verily the Muslims will not disobey you; they are only zealous about their *deen* (religion) and their *emaan* (faith) in Allaah and your Message. Shave your head and slaughter your animals, and you will find that the Muslims will follow suit. Then march with them back to Madinah."

The Prophet came out, gave his sacrifice, and called the barber to shave his head. When the Muslims saw him in that state, they fell over each other while rushing to slaughter the animals and shave their heads.

Martin Lings writes in his Seerah book, *Muhammad: His Life Based on the Earliest Sources*:

> *The earth of the camp was strewn with the hair of the pilgrims. But suddenly there came a powerful gust of wind which lifted the hair from the ground and blew it towards Mecca, into the sacred territory; and everyone rejoiced, taking it as a sign that their pilgrimage had been accepted by God in virtue of their intentions, and they now understood why the Prophet had told them to perform their sacrifices.*[280]

A Clear Victory

In his shock and anger at the treaty, Umar had behaved improperly with the Prophet, and he was full of remorse in his heart. That was Umar; behind a stern outward demeanor, he was given to much self-reproach and crying. Imam Ahmad reported in his Musnad that Umar said, "We were with the Messenger of Allaah on a trip, and I asked him about a matter three times, but he did not answer me. So I said to myself, 'May your mother lose you, O son of Al-Khattaab! You were stubborn in repeating your question three times to the Messenger of Allaah; each time he did not respond to you.' So I mounted my camel, and went ahead for fear that a part of the Qur'aan might be revealed in my case. Suddenly, I heard a caller calling, 'O Umar!' So, I went to the Messenger while fearing that part of the Qur'aan was revealed about me."

The Prophet told Umar, "Last night, a surah was revealed to me that is dearer to me than this world and all that it contains: "Verily, We have given

280 Lings, *Muhammad: His Life Based on the Earliest Sources*, Rochester, Inner Traditions, 263

you (O Muhammad) a manifest victory. That Allaah may forgive you your sins of the past and the future."[281]

A number of important Companions held that the "manifest victory" mentioned in verse 1 was the Treaty of Hudaybiyah and not the Conquest of Makkah. After the surah came down, Umar felt corrected about his rush to judgment concerning the treaty, and for the rest of his life, he performed extra optional fasts and gave charity, seeking Allaah's forgiveness for his conduct on that day.

Time proved that the Hudaybiyah Treaty was indeed a great victory for the Muslims. History has shown that this pact was the product of profound political wisdom and farsightedness on the part of the Prophet, but above all it had Allaah's approval. The treaty brought about consequences of great advantage to Islam and indeed to Arabia as a whole. For the first time, the Quraysh had acknowledged that the Prophet Muhammad was an equal rather than a mere rebel, and they recognized the existence of a de facto Islamic government in Madinah. They accepted the right of the Muslims to perform the pilgrimage. It gave the Muslims the peace and security they needed on their southern flank to pay attention to matters of the relatively new nation.

Moreover, after this treaty Islam spread more widely and quickly than it had ever before. While those who accompanied the Prophet Muhammad for Umrah in their unsuccessful attempt were 1,400 strong, when he went a year later, he had 2,000 pilgrims with him. Just a year later, in 7 AH (628/629 CE), three of the most prominent men of Makkah, Amr bin Al-Aas, Khaalid bin Al-Waleed, and Uthmaan bin Talhah, embraced Islam, at which the Prophet joyously said, "The Quraysh have given us their own blood."

The greatest objection to the Hudaybiyah pact was to the provision that said any Qurayshi who ran away to the Muslims in Madinah without the permission of his guardian would have to be returned, but no such

281 Fath 48:1–2.

obligation was placed on the Quraysh in case a Muslim ran to them. The Prophet had explained to the Companions that a Muslim who returned to disbelief was not worthy of readmission to the Muslim community. On the contrary, in the case of a convert who wished to join the Muslims but was prevented from doing so, Allaah would soon make a way out for him.

The Story of Abu Baseer

Abu Baseer had accepted Islam in Makkah and was imprisoned like some other Muslims. However, he was able to break free and reach Madinah. His master, Azhar bin Awf, and Al-Akhnas bin Shariq sent two men with a letter to the Prophet, asking him to send back Abu Baseer. The Prophet called Abu Baseer and said to him, "We have agreed with the Quraysh to honor the Treaty of Hudaybiyah, which you well know. In our religion, we are not permitted to cheat. You should, therefore, return to your people. God will grant to you and the other persecuted Muslims a means of emancipation in His good time."

Therefore, Abu Baseer had to give himself up to the two Qurayshi escorts and accompany them back to Makkah. Once they arrived at Dhul Hulayfah, Abu Baseer and his guards stopped for a meal and some rest. He began to praise the sword of one of them, who was flattered and fell into Abu Baseer's trick. Then Abu Baseer asked the man if he could touch his sword, and as soon as he was allowed to lay his hand upon it, he struck the man with it and killed him. The other Qurayshi escort ran toward Madinah and reported to the Prophet what had happened.

Soon, Abu Baseer himself arrived, brandishing his sword. He said, "O Prophet of God, you have fulfilled your duty under the Treaty, and God has relieved you of your obligation; you have in fact surrendered me to my people as the treaty prescribed. But I was not willing to allow myself to be persecuted, enticed away, or forced to renounce my religion."

The Prophet did not hide his admiration, but he hinted that Abu Baseer could not stay in Madinah with the Muslims under the terms of the treaty.

Upon hearing those words, Abu Baseer left and set himself up in a place called Al-Ees on the coast of Jeddah near the Qurayshi trade route to Syria. When his story reached Makkah, the Muslims still stuck there felt elated, and about seventy of them ran away to Abu Baseer in Al-Ees. Abu Baseer and his Companions began to attack the Qurayshi caravans and confiscate their goods. Only then did it dawn on the Quraysh that it was a mistake to insist on the return of Muslim escapees. Therefore, they wrote to the Prophet, asking him, in violation of the Hudaybiyah Treaty, to accept their fugitives into Madinah, which the Prophet gladly did. It was an example of how God had turned an adverse situation into one of advantage to the Muslims.

The Case of Muslim Women Emigrants

A new situation arose with regards to Muslim escapees. This time it was the Muslim women of Quraysh who had escaped to Madinah. One of them was Umm Kulthoom, daughter of Uqbah bin Abi Mu'yait, the archenemy of the Messenger of God. Her two brothers, Umaarah and Al-Waleed, came to the Prophet to demand her return under the terms of Al-Hudaybiyah. The Prophet refused, arguing that the treaty did not apply to women. He said that if women called for assistance and shelter, their request could not be turned down. Furthermore, according to Islamic law, when a woman became Muslim, she could no longer remain married to her disbelieving husband. Allaah had already revealed verses to codify this law:

> *O you who believe! When believing women come to you as emigrants, examine them, Allaah knows best as to their Faith, then if you ascertain that they are true believers, send them not back to the disbelievers, they are not lawful (wives) for the disbelievers nor are the disbelievers lawful (husbands) for them.*[282]

282 Mumtahanah 60:10.

Triumphant Return to Makkah

A year after the Hudaybiyah pact, the Prophet, at the head of two thousand Muslims, proceeded to Makkah to perform the Umrah in accordance with the terms stipulated in the pact. As the Muslims reached Makkah, most of the Quraysh left their houses and took to the neighboring hills. According to the treaty, the Quraysh had no option but to permit the Muslims to visit Makkah and perform the pilgrimage, but they were loath to offer any welcome to the Muslims. The general view among the Quraysh was that if their young men and women came in contact with the Muslims, they were apt to be attracted by the new faith; therefore, any contact with the Muslims was to be avoided.

Expedition to Khayber

Upon returning from Hudaybiyah, the Prophet stayed in Madinah for about two months and then decided to march to Khayber, which had continued to pose a threat to the Muslims. It was the Jews of Khayber, particularly the Banu Nadheer's leader Huyayy bin Akhtab, who had instigated the Quraysh and financed the Battle of the Trench. Had it not been for the forceful persuasion of Huyayy, the Jewish tribe of Banu Qurayzah would not have betrayed the Prophet. Huyayy and his supporters were bitter at the outcome of the Battle of the Trench and would not mind fanning the flames of yet another war against the Muslim community of Madinah.

The land of Khayber, about ninety miles north of Madinah, had an excellent irrigation system that produced abundant harvests of dates and grain. The castles of Khayber had tunnels and passages that in wartime enabled the besieged to reach water sources outside the castles.

The Jews who farmed these lands were not only the best farmers of the country, but they were also leaders in industry and business, and they enjoyed a monopoly of the armaments industry. The best arsenals of Arabia were all in Khayber. Many of the Jews who had been banished from

Madinah had resettled in Khayber, and they were noted for their skills in metallurgy.

As the Messenger of God reached Khayber, he prayed, "O God, we ask you for the good of this town and the good of its people and the good of what is in it, and we take refuge in You from its evil and the evil of its people and the evil that is in it." Then he told the Companions, "Move forward in the name of Allaah."

It was the Prophet's habit to wait until the morning before raiding a people. If he heard the call to prayer, he held back; if not, he would proceed. At Khayber, when the dawn came, he did not hear any call to prayer, so he proceeded to confront the town, which was a collection of several well-fortified fortresses. When the workers saw the Prophet and his forces, they ran, crying out, "Muhammad is here with his forces."

The Prophet responded, "God is greater; Khayber is destroyed. When we arrive in a town, it is a bad omen for those who have been warned."

The Prophet ordered his army to halt in a valley called Al-Raji'. This put them strategically between the tribe of Ghatafaan and the Jewish tribes of Khayber, thereby making it difficult for the Ghatafaan to come to the aid of their allies. Despite the Prophet's advantageous position, the Ghatafaan still tried to join forces with the Jews. However, rumor spread that while the Ghatafaan were marching toward Khayber, the Muslims were raiding their towns and their women and property were at risk. The Ghatafaan quickly returned home.

In the ensuing skirmishes, the Muslims captured several Jewish fortresses early on. However, one fortress, Al-Qaamus of the Banu Abul Huqayq, turned out to be impenetrable. One after another, the Prophet sent Abu Bakr and Umar to capture the fort. Despite fighting hard and taking many casualties, they could not defeat the defenders of the fort. One day the

Prophet said, "Tomorrow I will give the flag to a man who loves Allaah and His Messenger. Allaah will conquer it by this means." So he called Ali, who was suffering from an eye disease. The Prophet rubbed some of his saliva in Ali's eyes, and he was miraculously cured. The Prophet gave the flag to him.

Ali carried the flag and fought valiantly. The most fearsome person that Ali encountered from this fortress was Marhab. He was a towering warrior who had killed many and had never been defeated. He challenged Ali to a duel, at which point the general fighting subsided. The Jews wanted to see the outcome of a fight in which Ali, not a tall man, was faced with Marhab, a giant. The scene was reminiscent of David's fight against Goliath.

Marhab struck Ali with a hard blow, but Ali took the blow on his shield, causing his shield to fall from his hand. Realizing the gravity of the situation, Ali took hold of the heavy door of the fort and used it as a shield instead. Ali outmaneuvered Marhab with his swiftness, and when Marhab's sword got stuck in Ali's shield, he struck at Marhab's neck, which he severed.

Marhab's death sent terror into the Jewish ranks, and they ran to take shelter inside Al-Qaamus. It is said that after the battle, seven Companions struggled to turn the door that Ali had been using as a shield with one hand. Al-Qaamus eventually fell. Seeing the writing on the wall, some of the lesser-known Jewish tribes gave up, and their lives were spared. When the people of Fadak, a nearby oasis, heard that Al-Qaamus and other forts had been defeated, they voluntarily surrendered and offered their garden as ransom. This garden became the personal property of the Prophet, since no one had fought for it.

When the dust of the battle had settled, the Muslims took many prisoners. Among them was Safiyyah, daughter of Huyayy bin Akhtab, the die-hard enemy of the Prophet and chief instigator against the Muslims. In general, the Prophet treated the men from the enemy side with compassion, sparing their lives and properties. He allowed them to cultivate their lands on the condition that they give half of the produce to the Muslims. He also informed them that it was up to him to allow them to continue this way in the future or remove them if circumstances warranted. He made the same arrangement with the people of Fadak.

Who Is Safiyyah bint Huyayy?

In his great wisdom, the Prophet put his own mantle on Safiyyah, indicating to the Muslims that he wanted to marry her. Safiyyah came from a noble Jewish family, and as a wife of the Prophet, she would receive the highest honor in the Muslim community. She was first married to Sallaam bin Mishkaam, who had divorced her. Her second husband, Kinaanah bin Al-Rabi'ah, had been killed after he lied about the wealth of the Banu Nadheer and tried to conceal it. Some say that the Prophet Muhammad gave Safiyyah the choice of returning to her people or becoming a Muslim and marrying him, and Safiyyah opted for the latter.

It is reported that while Safiyyah was married to Kinaanah, she had seen a dream in which the moon had fallen into her lap. When she had told this dream to her husband, he had interpreted the moon in the dream as referring to the Prophet Muhammad. Enraged, Kinaanah had slapped Safiyyah across her face, saying, "This simply means that you covet the king of the Hijaz." The marks of this beating were still on her face when the Prophet took her in.

Some modern scholars believe that the Prophet Muhammad married Safiyyah to reconcile with the Jewish community. This marriage may also have been an attempt to lessen Safiyyah's sorrow over losing her father and husband and to preserve her dignity. Safiyyah came to appreciate the love and honor the Prophet Muhammad gave her. She used to say, "I have never seen a more good-natured person than the Messenger of Allaah."

She was one of the best women in her worship, piety, devoutness, and charity. Upon entering the Prophet's household, Safiyyah became friends with Aayeshah and Hafsah. She offered gifts to Faatimah, the Prophet's daughter, and jewels to his other wives. When some of the wives of the Prophet taunted Safiyyah as a Jewess, she cried and complained to the Prophet, upon which he said, "Why did you not tell them, 'My father is Aaron, my uncle is Moses, and my husband is Muhammad?'" That really comforted Safiyyah.

When the Prophet was dying, out of profound love for him she said, "I wish it was I who was suffering instead of you." The Prophet attested to the sincerity of her words.

From Poverty to Abundance

After the Khayber campaign, the Muslims were in possession of abundant wealth. Aayeshah, the Prophet's wife, remarked that the first time they ate dates to their fill was after the Muslims' victory over Khayber. The Prophet distributed the spoils of war among 1,400 Muslims who had participated in the expedition. He also apportioned a share for Jaa'far bin Abi Taalib and the other emigrants who had arrived from Abyssinia just after the Khayber campaign. The Emigrants from Makkah who had received property from the Helpers of Madinah began to return that property now that they had their own.

The wealth from Khayber included the following:

- Large quantities of gold and silver
- The finest arsenals of Arabia, containing the newest weapons of the time, such as swords, spears, lances, maces, shields, armor, bows, and arrows
- Vast herds of horses, camels, and cattle, and flocks of sheep and goats
- Rich, arable lands with palm groves

The newfound wealth posed a challenge to the austere lifestyle of the Muslims. Even the Prophet's household was affected by it. Some of his wives began to ask for expensive gifts until their demands began to annoy him. To comfort the Prophet, Allaah sent down verses admonishing the wives of His Prophet and warning them that if the Prophet left them, Allaah would give him wives better than they. The Prophet gave them a choice of leaving him with generous gifts or staying with him in poverty. To the credit of the Prophet's wives, when they were offered a choice between a rich send-off (divorce) and a life of austerity with the messenger, they all preferred to live with him and forego the demands of material wealth.

The Poisoning at Khayber

The Prophet and his troops rested for a while at Khayber. Word came in that Zaynab bint Al-Haarith, the wife of a slain Jewish leader, had prepared a feast for the Prophet. Zaynab was doing it not to honor the Prophet but to avenge her people. She had found out that the Prophet loved lamb shoulder, so she roasted one after heavily poisoning it. The Prophet took a morsel, as did his Companion Bishr bin Al-Baraa. The Prophet immediately spat out the morsel without chewing it, saying the food had informed him it had been poisoned. Bishr had eaten the food, and not long after that, he died of poisoning.

The Prophet questioned the woman, and she admitted the crime, saying, "You know what you have done to my people. I did it so that if you were just a king, we would get rid of you; however, if you were a prophet, the food would inform you." While the Prophet pardoned her for the harm done to him, she was executed as a punishment for the death of Bishr. At the time of his death three years later, the Prophet said to Bishr's sister that he was feeling the pain from the effects of the poisoning at Khayber. Because of this, some Companions believed that the Prophet died as both an Apostle of God and a martyr. A Hadith in Sunan Abu Dawood says that anyone who is stung by a poisonous creature and dies from it is a martyr.[283]

283 Sunan of Abu Dawood, Hadith #2493.

One may ask, Why did the Prophet accept a meal invitation from a woman whose husband had been killed by the Muslims? An act of hospitality should not have been expected from such a woman. The answer may lie in the fact that the Prophet was trying to do everything to mollify the Jews of Khayber. He wanted to remind them that he had nothing personal against them and that what had happened to them was due to their treasonous actions and had not happened because they were Jews. It was also his habit not to turn down an invitation except for a valid reason, and he had advised his Companions of this.

Marriage to Umm Habibah

Before the expedition of Khayber, the Prophet had sent Amr bin Umayyah Al-Damri to Najaashi, the king of Abyssinia, asking him to send back the Muslim emigrants. He had also asked the king to conduct his marriage contract with Umm Habibah bint Abu Sufiyan. Her real name was Ramlah, and she was married to the Prophet's cousin Ubaydullaah bin Jahsh, from whom she had a daughter named Habibah. Upon migration to Abyssinia, Ubaydullaah had converted to Christianity. According to Allaah's laws, when Ubaydullaah left Islam, his marriage to Umm Habibah became void. As an act of mercy and appreciation for her sacrifices for Islam as well as for her lineage, the Prophet proposed to marry her, and she accepted.

As requested, Najaashi conducted Umm Habibah's *nikaah* (marriage contract) to the Prophet and gave her gifts on the Prophet's behalf. It is not known with certainty if Najaashi had become a Muslim at this time. Najaashi arranged for two boats and sent back sixteen men and scores of women and children to Madinah. They arrived as the Khayber campaign had just ended. This group had lived in Abyssinia for about fourteen years, and remarkably they continued to live there until seven years after the Prophet and the Muslims had migrated to Madinah. This phenomenon has led some historians to opine that Abyssinia was the Prophet's plan B if Madinah did not work out. It is worth nothing that the Muslims had lived in Abyssinia for fourteen years without trying to undermine the local government. The principles of Islam dictate living peacefully with and respecting the laws and traditions of those who give them refuge. These principles, regardless of what some detractors might say, are still in effect for all Muslims today.

The Unfulfilled Umrah

In the seventh year of Hijrah, a year after the Treaty of Hudaybiyah, the Messenger of God returned to Makkah to perform the Umrah that he and his Companions had been prevented from the year before. Besides those who were part of the previous year's group, there were also new pilgrims, bringing the total to two thousand. When the polytheists learned about the Muslims' imminent arrival, and as per the terms of the treaty, they vacated Makkah for three days and moved up to the mountains. The Muslims entered the city from the north and hardly saw any Makkans. The Messenger of God rode his she-camel, Al-Qaswa, with Companion Abdullaah bin Rawaahah holding her reins. The Prophet entered while reciting verses from Surah Al-Fath (chapter 48) and chanting, "At Thy command, O Lord! At Thy command, O Lord!"

When the Muslims had assembled in the precincts of the Ka'bah, the Prophet ordered Bilaal to get on top of the building and call the *Adhaan*, which he did. It was the first *Adhaan* in the House of Allaah, and two thousand believers responded to his call. Bilaal's stature in the eyes of the Messenger of God shocked the polytheists, who could not imagine that a former slave could rise to such a position of honor.

The Quraysh kept watch on the scene from the hills surrounding the valley of Makkah, and what they saw both awed and humbled them. They had never seen such discipline before—Muslims like Abu Bakr, Umar, Uthmaan, and Ali, to name a few, obediently heeding the call to prayer from a former slave—nor had they seen such a demonstration of equality and unity. The vast masses of the Muslims moved as one body, and the Quraysh could see with their own eyes that it was a body in which there were no distinctions between the rich and poor, high and low, black and white, and Arab and non-Arab.

The Quraysh also witnessed that the brotherhood, equality, and unity of men that Islam fostered were not theoretical concepts but were very real. It was a most impressive sight, and it could not have failed to touch the hearts of even the most hard-hearted idolaters. The deportment of the Muslims was exemplary. They were most anxious to obey the command of God and His Messenger. Instead of performing the naked circumambulation of the polytheists, the Muslims were dressed in modest attire, white two-piece clothes for men and loose, flowing garments along with head coverings for women. They were chanting words that the Prophet had taught them. And this demonstration by the Muslims was so unrehearsed, so spontaneous. To nothing in this world were the Arabs more allergic than to discipline, but they were transformed, within a few years, by the power of Islam.

Marriage to Maymunah bint Al-Haarith

While in Makkah, the Prophet married Maymunah bint Al-Haarith at the suggestion of his uncle Abbaas bin Abdul Muttalib. Her real name was Barra, but the Prophet called her *Maymunah,* meaning the blessed one, as his marriage to her also marked the first time in seven years when he could enter his hometown. She was the sister-in-law of the Prophet's uncle Abbaas. Maymunah and Abbaas's wife Umm Al-Fadl were full sisters. Her first marriage had ended in a divorce, and her second husband had died, making her both a widow and a divorcee. By marrying Maymunah, the Prophet demonstrated that it was not a stigma for a woman to be both divorced and widowed. With this marriage the Prophet established kinship ties with Banu Makhzum, the tribe to which Abu Jahl belonged.

After three days had passed in Makkah, the Quraysh sent Suhayl bin Abdul Uzzah to the Prophet to ask that he leave town. The Prophet asked the envoy if it would harm anything if the Quraysh allowed him to stay a bit longer, since he had just been married and was going to throw a feast for everyone. Suhayl refused, and so the Prophet left Makkah with the Companions.

Khaalid bin Waleed Accepts Islam

Soon after the Muslims had returned from Umrah, three of the luminaries of the Quraysh—Khaalid bin Waleed, Amr bin Al-Aas, and Uthmaan bin Talhah—entered Islam. They traveled to Madinah to pronounce their testimonies of faith before the Prophet, and thus they are considered among the last batch of Emigrants. The Prophet had declared that *Hijrah*—meaning migration for the sake of practicing one's religion—would be valid until before the Conquest of Makkah. Once Makkah became an Islamic territory, people could still move about but would not be called *Muhaajir* (Emigrants).

The story of Khaalid's conversion is quite heart-warming. Khaalid's brother Waleed had accepted Islam and was among those who had managed to free themselves from imprisonment in Makkah and join Abu Baseer's group in a place called Al-Ees. When the Quraysh started to feel the loss from this group's attacks against their caravan, they had written to the Prophet to take these people back into Madinah, which he gladly did. Sadly, when the Prophet's letter telling them to migrate to Madinah came, Abu Baseer was in the pangs of death, and he died while clasping the letter of the Messenger of Allaah. However, others headed to Madinah. When they reached the lava tract, Waleed's camel stumbled and threw him to the ground, badly injuring his finger. He had wrapped his finger in a bandage and said:

What are you but a finger shedding blood,
With no wound else upon the path of God.

But the wound became infected and proved fatal. However, before he died he managed to write a letter to his brother, Khaalid, urging him to enter Islam. The letter read:

> *In the name of God, the Merciful, the Beneficent*
>
> *I am infinitely amazed at the fact that you continue to turn away from Islam when you are as intelligent as I know you to be. No one can be so blind to the truth of Islam. God's Messenger asked me about you and said, "Where is Khaalid?" I said to him, "God will bring him to us." He said, "A man of his caliber cannot remain ignorant of Islam. If he would use his intelligence and his experience for the Muslims against the idolaters, he would benefit from it a great deal. We would certainly give him precedence over others." It is high time, brother, for you to make amends for the great benefits you have missed.*

When Khaalid read his brother's letter, he felt as if a curtain that had blurred his vision for a long time had been removed. He was pleased at the fact that the Prophet himself had inquired about him. He felt a strong desire to become a Muslim. That night he dreamt that he was in a narrow strip of land in a barren desert, and he was walking on and on until he came into an open, green, limitless field. It did not take him long to make up his mind that the right course for him was to become a Muslim. He decided to join the Prophet at Madinah.

Khaalid, however, felt that he needed to have a Companion to go with him. He approached Safwaan bin Umayyah, his friend. Safwaan's father and brother had been killed at the Battle of Badr, and his uncle had been killed at Uhud. Safwaan belonged to that generation of the Quraysh who viewed Islam with their deeply held prejudices and as something irreconcilable with their pagan traditions. He had resolved not to compromise with Prophet Muhammad.

Sawfaan was painfully surprised when Khaalid said to him, "Do you not see that Muhammad is gaining the upper hand against both the Arabs and the non-Arabs? It is certainly expedient for us to join him and share in whatever success he may achieve."

Safwaan completely rejected the suggestion, saying, "If all the Arabs followed Muhammad and I was the only one left, I would still not join him."

Realizing that Safwaan was determined to hold on to his grudges, Khaalid decided to seek out someone else. By chance, he met Ikrimah bin Abu Jahl, whose father had always been the most uncompromising enemy of Islam, until he was killed at Badr. Ikrimah's response was similar to that of Safwaan, except that he showed some empathy with Khaalid.

Khaalid then met Uthmaan bin Talhah, a close friend and the noble man who some years ago had escorted Umm Salamah to Madinah. The problem was that Uthmaan had lost six members of his family at the Battle of Uhud, his father, uncle, and four brothers. Khaalid hesitatingly asked Uthmaan, expecting a much harsher rejection than those of the other two. Surprisingly, Uthmaan not only responded sympathetically but agreed to join the Prophet in Madinah.

The two decided to depart in the dead of night separately and after a journey of a few hours meet at Ya'jaj. Per plan they continued their journey together until they arrived at Al-Haddah, where they met Amr bin Al-Aas. They were surprised to find themselves at an unusual place on a highway that led to Madinah. It was not long before they confided to each other what they were up to and decided to travel together. When they reached the outskirts of Madinah, they washed themselves up and changed their clothes.

Khaalid was the first one to meet the Prophet, and he later narrated his moving experience: "Allaah's Messenger was informed of our arrival, and he was pleased. I put on one of my best suits and went ahead to meet the

Prophet. On the way I was told that the Prophet was waiting for me. We then moved faster until we saw him at a distance, smiling. He wore his smile until I reached him and greeted him as God's Prophet and Messenger. He replied to my greeting with a face beaming with joy.

"I said, 'I declare that there is no deity but God, and that you are God's Messenger.'

"He said, 'Come forward.' When I drew nearer, he said to me, 'I praise God for guiding you to Islam. I have always been aware that you are endowed with great intelligence, and I have always hoped that your intelligence would lead you only to what is right and beneficial.'

"I said to him, 'Messenger of God, I am thinking of those battles at which I was fighting against the side of the truth. I request you to pray to God to forgive me.'

"He said, 'When you embrace Islam, all your past sins are forgiven.'

"I said, 'Messenger of God, is that a condition?'

"He said, 'My Lord, forgive Khaalid bin Al-Waleed for every effort he exerted to turn people away from Your path.' Uthmaan and Amr then pledged their allegiance to the Prophet. By God, ever since our arrival in the month of Safar in the eighth year of the Prophet's emigration, the Prophet consulted me about every serious matter that cropped up, ahead of all his other Companions."

The Conversion of Amr bin Al-Aas

Amr was no stranger to the Prophet. He was the statesman and smooth talker whom the Quraysh had sent to Najaashi (Negus) to bring back the first emigrants from Abyssinia. Despite his flowery prose and tact, Najaashi had refused to hand the emigrants back to Amr. His wit could not be a match for the verses of Surah Maryam that Jaa'far bin Abi Taalib had recited and that had driven Najaashi and his courtiers into tears. Amr, a gifted and pragmatic leader, had all this time been observing the rise of Islam and thinking of his place in a world that was changing around him. He had become ever more convinced that Islam would triumph over idolatry. Amr was happy with his position in his community—he was well respected as a leader, and people liked him for his wisdom and charisma. Among the things that prevented him from accepting Islam was the fear that he would lose his power and status.

But God has His plans. Amr tried to run away from Islam, only to find out that he was running into God's religion. Intimidated by the growing power of Islam, Amr decided to migrate to the Christian kingdom of Najaashi, the same place from which he had once tried to extradite the Muslim Emigrants and failed. He took a large number of expensive leather goods for the king. When he reached Najaashi's court, he saw Amr bin Umayyah, whom the Prophet had sent to the king with the request to conduct his marriage to Umm Habibah. Amr immediately thought of a plan. "Why don't I ask Najaashi to hand to me Muhammad's envoy so that I may kill him?" So he approached Najaashi and gave him the lavish gifts, which pleased the latter.

Amr then came to the point and told Najaashi, "O king, I wish you would hand over this man Amr bin Umayyah to me. He is envoy of a man who has killed our nobles." That enraged Najaashi, who slapped Amr bin Al-Aas in the face. His nose began to bleed profusely, and he collected the blood in his garment.

Najaashi said to Amr, "Do you want me to hand you the messenger of the Messenger of God, to whom the great Naamoos (Gabriel) came, the one who also came to Moses and Jesus, so that you may kill him!"

Thoroughly embarrassed, Amr asked Najaashi, "O King, do you testify (to Islam)?"

He said, "Yes, I am a witness to God (in confirming Islam)."

Amr said Islam began to enter his heart, and he asked Najaashi if he could take his allegiance of faith. Najaashi agreed, so in one of the profoundest ironies of fate, Amr accepted Islam in a land where he thought he would be protected from it. Najaashi ordered his physicians to treat Amr and gifted him new clothes. Amr realized that his pronouncement of faith to Najaashi was good enough, but he still wanted to recite it in front of the Prophet. With that thought, Amr quickly boarded a ship and headed to Madinah.

Amr said that, when he saw the Prophet, he was so awed by his personality that he could not bear to look him in the eye. Amr then extended his hand to the Prophet as if to pledge his allegiance but quickly pulled it back.

Surprised, the Prophet said, "O Amr, what is the matter?"

Amr said, "O Messenger of God, promise that my past sins will be forgiven."

The Prophet said, "Did you not know that Islam wipes out what sins came before it, and *Hajj* wipes out what came before it, and *Hijrah* (migration for religion) wipes out what came before it?"

That comforted Amr, and he recited the testimonials again as he had done in the presence of Najaashi: "I bear witness that there is no God besides Allaah, and I bear witness that Muhammad is the Messenger of Allaah."

Uthmaan bin Talhah Accepts Islam

It may be that when Uthmaan had escorted Umm Salamah and her young son to Madinah, Allaah had chosen to honor him in a way he could not have imagined. Uthmaan, like his two Companions, recited the testimonies of faith and entered Islam. Years had gone by since his noble act of escorting Umm Salamah to her husband in Madinah. After Umm Salamah's husband had died from wounds suffered in Uhud, the Prophet married her.

When the Prophet entered Makkah as victor in 8 AH (629/630 CE), he called for Uthmaan bin Talhah and gave the key to the House of God (Ka'bah) to him, even though Ali and Abbaas had sought it. In handing Uthmaan the key, the Prophet had said, "The key will be with you and your family until the end of time, and whoever takes it away from you will be unjust." For fourteen hundred years, the successive leaders of the Muslims who have ruled Makkah have honored the Prophet's command. To this day, the key of Ka'bah remains in the hands of Uthmaan's descendants.

The Battle of Mu'tah

In the eighth year of Hijrah (629/630 CE), the Prophet sent a three-thousand-man-strong force against the Romans and their Arab allies in Syria who had been harassing the Muslims there. This campaign turned out to be the most challenging and personally devastating to the Prophet. He had appointed Zayd bin Haarithah as the leader with the instruction that if Zayd were killed, Jaa'far bin Abi Taalib, who had just returned from Abyssinia, would lead, and if Jaa'far were killed, Abdullaah bin Rawaahah would take charge. The Prophet's words proved ominous.

When the Muslims reached the outskirts of Syria, they heard that Heraclius, the Roman emperor, had come to Balqaa with one hundred thousand Greek troops and had been joined by one hundred thousand men from Arab tribes of Lakhm, Judhaam, Al-Qayn, Bahraa, Bali, and others. The Muslims had not expected such a large force to have been arrayed against them. It would be nothing short of a miracle if three thousand men could defeat a massive, heavily armed army of two hundred thousand. They consulted among themselves, with many in favor of writing to the Prophet about the situation to know if he would send reinforcements.

However, Abdullaah bin Rawaahah encouraged the men to fight despite such low numbers, saying, "O men, what you dislike is that which you have come out in search of, martyrdom. We are not fighting the enemy with numbers or strength or multitude, but we are confronting them with this religion with which God has honored us. So come on! Both prospects are fine: victory or martyrdom."

Moved, the people said, "By God, Ibn Rawaahah is right."

So the Muslims marched on until they met the enemy in the village of Mashaarif. As a tactical move, the Muslims withdrew to Mu'tah, another village nearby. When the fighting began, Zayd bin Haarithah fought while holding the standard of the Messenger of Allaah in one hand. He himself took on many spears of the enemy forces until he succumbed to his injuries.

As instructed by the Prophet, Jaa'far bin Abi Taalib stepped in and seized the flag. He fought valiantly until he was hemmed in by soldiers from the other camp and martyred. Both of Jaa'far's arms were cut off, and his body was decapitated.

Abdullaah bin Rawaahah saw the situation and challenged the feeling of hesitation within him, chastising his soul for exhibiting even a moment's weakness, and then plunged himself into the thick of the battle, eventually attaining martyrdom.

The death of the three leaders one after another shocked the Muslims, and they began to wonder who might lead them next, until their eyes fell on Khaalid bin Waleed, who was fighting in the Muslim army for the first time since becoming a Muslim. Khaalid declined, saying he was humbled by the presence of those who had been Muslim a long time and who had sacrificed and fought for Islam. When Ansaari Companion Thaabit bin Arqam tried to give him the flag, Khaalid declined, saying, "You are more senior, and you participated in Badr." But Thaabit, aware of Khaalid's military genius, said he had taken the flag only in order to give it to him. Seeing he had no choice, Khaalid took the flag, trying to keep the enemy at bay to avoid fighting. Despite heavy odds, Khaalid was able to break up one contingent of enemy soldiers, but then he was surrounded. In a brilliant tactical move, Khaalid managed to safely retreat with his men.

In Madinah, the Angel Gabriel brought live pictures of the battlefield to the Prophet, who described the situation to the people gathered around him. The details were heart-rending. The leaders of the Muslim army were falling down, and the prospects of a victory seemed far-fetched. When Khaalid and the rest of the Muslims on the Mu'tah expedition came back, some people began to throw dust at them, calling them runaways and deserters. A number of the returnees felt so ashamed that they stopped coming out of their homes until the Prophet sent words of comfort to them.

The Prophet, whom Gabriel had fully apprised of the feat Khaalid had achieved, corrected the people, saying, "They are not runaways but rather those who will return (to fight) if Allaah wills."

Khaalid said, "On the Day of Mu'tah, nine swords were broken in my hand, and only a Yemenite sword had remained."

For Khaalid and others, the greatest sources of comfort besides the support of the Prophet were two verses in the Qur'aan that had been revealed after Badr. They exonerated the Muslim fighters who ran away from the battlefield as a strategy of war.

> *O you who believe! When you meet those who disbelieve, in a battlefield, never turn your backs to them. And whoever turns his back to them on such a day—unless it be a stratagem of war, or to retreat to a troop (of his own)—he indeed has drawn upon himself wrath from Allaah. And his abode is Hell, and worst indeed is that destination!*[284]

284 Anfaal 8:15–16.

The Prophet's Sorrow

All three leaders who died on the day of Mu'tah were dear to the Messenger of God, but two in particular were his beloved, Zayd, whom he had once adopted, and Jaa'far, who was his cousin. He had many memories of Jaa'far, an older brother of Ali, growing up in the household of Abu Taalib, where the Prophet himself grew up. Jaa'far also resembled the Prophet closely in physical features. Jaa'far had immigrated to Abyssinia to practice his religion freely, and after fourteen years he had come to Madinah when the Prophet had ordered him to do so.

The Prophet went to the house of Asmaa bint Umays, Jaa'far's widow, and asked for Jaa'far's sons to be brought to him. He embraced and kissed them, and then his eyes began to well up with tears. Seeing that, Asmaa said, "Why, O Messenger of God, has some news reached you about Jaa'far?"

The Prophet replied, "Yes, he was killed today." Asmaa stood and screamed, and the women of the family rushed toward her. The Prophet urged her not to say words of complaint and beat her chest.

The Prophet then encouraged Asmaa to rejoice because Jaa'far was flying around in Paradise with wings Allaah had given him in place of the two arms he had lost. Then he ordered his own daughter, Faatimah, to prepare food for Jaa'far's family, saying, "They are preoccupied today." The Companions reported seeing visible signs of grief on the Prophet's face for several days.

Zayd was the beloved of the Messenger of Allaah, and so was his son, Usaamah. When Umar became caliph (head of state), his son Abdullaah came to him complaining that Umar gave him less stipend from the treasury than he gave Usaamah. Umar said, "I do so because Usaamah was dearer to the Messenger of Allaah than you, and his father (Zayd) was dearer to him than your father (meaning himself)." Aayeshah once said that had

Zayd been alive after the passing of the Prophet, there was no way people would have chosen her father as caliph.

As for Abdullaah bin Rawaahah, besides being a sincere Companion, he was also an accomplished poet whom the Prophet sometimes asked to defend Islam through his poetry.

The End of the Hudaybiyah Pact

According to one of the Hudaybiyah treaty provisions, the Arab tribes had the option to ally themselves with the Quraysh or the Muslims. The Banu Bakr had chosen to join the Quraysh, while the Banu Khuza'ah had allied with the Prophet.

In disregard of the terms of the Treaty of Hudaybiyah, one night the Banu Bakr attacked the Banu Khuza'ah while they were at a watering well. And even when the Banu Khuza'ah sought refuge in the Ka'bah, many of them were killed there. In all, the Banu Bakr killed twenty-three people of the Khuza'ah. The Quraysh helped their allies with weapons, and one or two Qurayshi men took part in the attack under the cover of darkness.

The Khuza'ah immediately sent a deputation led by Amr bin Salim Al-Khuzaa'i to Madinah to inform the Prophet of what had happened and to ask for his help. Then Budayl bin Waraqah, another man from the Khuza'ah, came and provided more details of what the Banu Bakr had done and how the Quraysh had helped them. The Prophet told him, "May you be helped, O Amr bin Salim." Aayeshah reported that the Prophet was greatly angered by what he had heard. He asked for some water to perform ablution, and as he poured it over himself, she heard him say, "May I not be helped if I do not help the sons of Ka'ab."

The Quraysh soon realized what a terrible mistake they had made and sent Abu Sufiyan to the Prophet to manage the situation. Before Abu

Sufiyan had set foot in Madinah, the Prophet remarked, "I think you will see Abu Sufiyan coming to strengthen the agreement and ask for more time." On the way back to Makkah, Budayl, the Khuza'ah emissary, ran into Abu Sufiyan near a place called Usfaan. Abu Sufiyan asked Budayl if he had been to Madinah, which he denied. But Abu Sufiyan was not convinced. When Budayl was gone, Abu Sufiyan scoured the place where Budayl's camel had knelt and split open the camel dung. His eyes lit up. The contents of the dung showed the camel had eaten dates from Madinah. Abu Sufiyan feared he had come to plead his case with the Prophet a little too late and that Budayl had beaten him to it, which indeed was the case.

Upon arrival in Madinah, Abu Sufiyan was taken to the Prophet. Struggling to find the right words, he said, "O Muhammad, I was absent at the time of the truce of Hudaybiyah, so let us now strengthen the pact and prolong its duration."

Instead of addressing Abu Sufiyan's request, the Prophet asked him a loaded question: "Do you think your side has broken it?"

Abu Sufiyan was clearly put on the spot. He nervously answered, "God forbid!" The Prophet told Abu Sufiyan he would not extend the treaty or modify or replace it. That was hardly comforting to Abu Sufiyan, so he went to his daughter Ramlah (Umm Habibah), who was one of the wives of the Prophet.

Abu Sufiyan had not seen his daughter in the fifteen years since she had migrated to Abyssinia. He hoped that she would plead his case with the Prophet. But she said, "My father, you are the chief of the Quraysh. How is it that you have failed to enter Islam and continue to worship stones, which neither hear nor see?"

Abu Sufiyan became upset. "By God, since you left me you have gone to the bad."

Having not found any success with his daughter, Abu Sufiyan went to Abu Bakr and asked him to speak to the Prophet. Abu Bakr refused. Then he went to Umar asking for help. Umar said, "Should I intercede for you with the Prophet! If I had only an ant, I would fight you with it."

Next, Abu Sufiyan went to Ali, who was with his wife, Faatimah, the Prophet's daughter, and their little son Hasan. He reminded Ali of their ties of kinship and pleaded for him to intercede. He and Ali were great-grandsons of the two brothers Haashim and Abdush-Shams. Ali said, "When the Prophet is resolved to do something, it is futile to talk to him."

In a height of desperation, Abu Sufiyan pleaded with Faatimah to let her toddler boy act as a protector. Faatimah simply replied, "My son is too small to protect anyone, and none can give protection against the Messenger of Allaah."

Seeing Abu Sufiyan's sad plight, Ali suggested to him that, as chief of the Banu Kinaanah, he should himself give protection to the Quraysh even though there was no guarantee that the Prophet would honor his protection. Abu Sufiyan did just that. He got up and announced that he was giving protection to his people.

The Prophet said to him, "That is what you think, O Abu Sufiyan." With his words the Prophet made it clear to Abu Sufiyan that he was under no obligation to honor his protection. The Qurayshi chief returned to Makkah full of worries.

The Prophet gave the Quraysh three choices: they could pay the blood money for the dead of the Banu Bakr, terminate their alliance with the Banu Bakr, or accept that they had broken the Hudaybiyah pact.

The first option would have put an enormous financial burden on the Quraysh. Paying one hundred camels in ransom for each of the twenty-three victims of the Khuza'ah would have been too much for the Quraysh to bear. As for the second option, for political reasons they did not want to end their alliance with the Banu Bakr. Therefore, the Quraysh chose the last option and accepted that their actions had essentially abrogated the Treaty of Hudaybiyah.

Reflections: Western historians in general have portrayed the end of Hudaybiyah and the subsequent conquest of Makkah as a treacherous act on the part of the Prophet Muhammad, alleging that the Prophet signed a treaty with the Quraysh only to invade them a few years later. They conveniently ignore the fact that the Quraysh and the Banu Bakr had already broken the treaty and that the Muslims had every right to retaliate. Another important point to ponder is that the Prophet gave the Quraysh multiple choices, all of which were fair.

Preparing for the Conquest

The Prophet ordered the Muslims to prepare for a major military expedition, but he did not tell them where they were going. Some thought he wanted to go to Al-Shaam, Al-Thaqif, or Al-Hawaazin. To create more mystery, the Prophet sent Abu Qataadah bin Rabi'ah with eight people to Idam, which was not in the direction of Makkah. As a brilliant military strategist, the Prophet revealed the details at a time of his choosing. There were still hypocrites in Madinah who would be eager to defeat the Prophet's plans.

Within a short time, a massive ten-thousand-strong force was ready to go whenever or wherever the Prophet ordered. This was the highest number that the Muslims had ever readied. Not even for the Romans had such a force been raised. When the Prophet decided it was the right time to reveal the plan, he told the people that they were going to Makkah. He then prayed, "O Allaah, take the eyes and ears away from the Quraysh so that we may take them by surprise in their land."

Betrayal without Malice

The Prophet's secrecy would have been broken had it not been for divine intervention. A well-known Companion named Haatib bin Abu Baltaa'ah tried to secretly alert the Quraysh. Haatib had migrated from Makkah and fought against the Quraysh in Badr, earning him a distinguished place among the Companions. However, he still had family in Makkah, and by alerting the Quraysh, Haatib hoped to earn some leniency from them toward his kin. When he heard that the ten-thousand-strong army was marching on to Makkah, he asked a woman to carry his letter covertly to the Quraysh. In the meantime, Gabriel came down and informed the Prophet of what was happening unbeknownst to him. The Prophet immediately sent Ali and Zubayr bin Al-Awwaam to intercept the woman and get hold of the letter.

Ali and Zubayr overtook the woman in Al-Khulayqah and had her dismount from her camel. A search of her baggage did not turn up anything. The two Companions were certain that the Messenger of God could not be mistaken, so they threatened the woman that they would perform a body search if she did not hand over the letter. When she saw their resolve, she asked them to turn aside, and then she pulled the letter from her braid and gave it to Ali.

When Ali brought the letter to the Prophet, he called Haatib and asked for an explanation. Haatib assured the Prophet that he still believed in Allaah and His Messenger but said that he had family remaining in Makkah and he thought that perhaps with his gesture the Quraysh would be kind to them. Haatib's letter was addressed to Safwaan bin Umayyah, Suhayl bin Amr, and Ikrimah bin Abu Jahl, three of the most influential Qurayshis. The Prophet accepted Haatib's statement as truthful, but Umar bristled with anger and asked the Prophet's permission to cut off the latter's neck, accusing him of hypocrisy. The Prophet rebuffed Umar, saying, "He participated in Badr. How do you know that Allaah has not looked at the people of Badr and proclaimed, 'Do as you wish, for I have forgiven you.'"[285]

Then Allaah sent down verses 1–3 of Surah Mumtahanah:

O you who believe! Take not My enemies and your enemies as protecting friends, showing affection towards them, while they have disbelieved in what has come to you of the truth, and have driven out the Messenger and yourselves because you believe in Allaah, your Lord! If you have come forth to strive in My cause and to seek My good pleasure. You show friendship to them in secret, while I am All-Aware of what you conceal and what you reveal. And whosoever of you (Muslims) does that, then indeed he has gone (far) astray from the straight path. Should they gain the upper hand over you, they would behave to you as enemies, and stretch forth their hands and their tongues against you with evil, and they desire that you should disbelieve. Neither your relatives nor your children will benefit you on the Day of Resurrection. He will judge between you. And Allaah is the All-Seer of what you do.

Allaah has said that sometimes one may think of a thing as evil when it will turn out to be good. Haatib's incident seems to fall in that category. His actions were wrong, but they brought out two important points. One, the Prophet assigned a special status to the 310 Muslims who fought in the Battle of Badr, something that his Companions always remembered and respected. Badr was a defining moment, and no other war could compare to it. It was a struggle for the very existence of Islam. Allaah had called it "The Day of Distinction, the Day of Meeting of Two Groups," meaning the Muslims and the polytheists. Two, Allaah addressed Haatib as a believer despite a serious error on his part. There have been other occasions when the Muslims' mistakes were overlooked because what they had done was not born of malice. So while this incident exposed Haatib's fault, it also brought revelation that forever confirmed that he was a true Muslim.

285 Bukhari, vol. 5, book 59, Hadith #572.

The Campaign Begins

The Prophet left Madinah with the Muslim army on the tenth of Ramadan, 8 AH (629/630 CE). The army marched as one body, the Emigrants, the Helpers, and the tribes. Allaah had answered the Prophet's prayers that, despite such a large army rumbling toward Makkah, the Quraysh had no clue they were about to be attacked. The hypocrites and spies all had been unable to alert the Makkans of the imminent threat. As for Abu Sufiyan bin Harb, the most senior leader of the Quraysh, life had been on the edge since the Prophet had turned down his request for a treaty extension.

The Prophet's uncle, Abbaas, who by now was a Muslim still living in Makkah, had been secretly informed of what was coming. Abbaas worried that they would be doomed if the Prophet entered Makkah by force before its inhabitants had sought his forgiveness and protection. The Prophet and his army camped at Marr Al-Zahraan, and Abbaas joined him there. In a sign of both respect and protection, he was given the Prophet's white mule. Because war destroys lives and ruins habitats, Abbaas kept pondering over how to convey the news of the conquest to the Quraysh so that they might come and ask the Prophet to grant them protection.

While Abbaas was in this state, he heard some voices, including the voice of Abu Sufiyan. The latter had seen the numerous fires the Muslims had lit, but from a distance he could not tell who they were. Abbaas sprinted toward him and told him the Prophet had arrived with an army of ten thousand. He asked Abu Sufiyan to climb on the back of the mule and rushed him to the Prophet. These were tense moments. Whenever they passed by a Muslim group, the Muslims challenged them to identify themselves. When people saw Abbaas on the Prophet's mule, they said this was the Prophet's uncle, until the two passed by Umar's fire.

Umar looked at Abu Sufiyan behind Abbaas and shouted, "Enemy of God, Abu Sufiyan, praise be to Him Who has delivered you to us without effort." Abbaas rushed toward the Prophet before Umar could lay his hands on Abu Sufiyan. Umar ran in hot pursuit, and as Abu Sufiyan and Abbaas were standing before the Prophet, Umar asked permission to behead Abu Sufiyan. That infuriated Abbaas, who told Umar that had Abu Sufiyan been from the Banu Adiyy bin Ka'ab, he would not have been after the Qurayshi leader's head.

Taken aback, Umar said, "By God, your Islam was dearer to me than Al-Khattaab's Islam, had he accepted it." Umar's happiness for Abbaas's conversion demonstrated his love for the Prophet, since he knew how happy the Prophet was at Abbaas's conversion. Abbaas informed the Prophet that he had given protection to Abu Sufiyan. The Prophet asked his uncle to take Abu Sufiyan to his quarters and bring him back in the morning.

The next day, when Abbaas did as instructed, the Prophet asked Abu Sufiyan, "Isn't it time that you should recognize that there is no God other than Allaah?"

Abu Sufiyan answered, "You are dearer to me than my father and mother. How great are your clemency, honor, and kindness! By God, I have been thinking that had there been other gods, I would have been helped." He then accepted Islam and the unquestioned leadership of the Prophet. It was the same Abu Sufiyan who five years before had been looking for the body of the Prophet after the Battle of Uhud.

Reflections: This incident clearly shows that the Prophet was always eager to offer his opponents a chance to accept Islam because doing so would please God and result in forgiveness of their past sins and protection of their families and property. Subjugating the opponents was only a matter of last resort. The extremist behavior we see among some Muslims today runs counter to the Prophetic example. To be harsh and unforgiving toward non-Muslims is to forget that all of the Prophet's Companions were at one point non-Muslim. It was not the sword that forced them into submission to God, but rather the merciful character and lofty example of the Messenger of God.

One of the reasons the Companions revered the Prophet and cherished his company was his soft and forgiving nature. These traits of the Prophet were confirmed by Allaah Himself:

> *It is by God's grace that you were gentle with them, for if you had been harsh and hard-hearted, they would surely have deserted you; so bear with them and pray for forgiveness for them and consult them in matters.*[286]

The Prophet said, "If you hear something bad about your brother (or sister), find seventy excuses. If you cannot do it, then say: 'Perhaps he has an excuse I do not know.'"[287]

Muslims today are very quick to point out other Muslims' perceived faults—for example, not wearing the right *Hijaab* or not having a long enough beard or not following the right leaders without regarding their own faults. They claim to love the Prophet Muhammad but fail to emulate his example.

Jesus, another great Messenger of God, is reported to have said:

> *Judge not, that you be not judged. For with the judgment you pronounce you will be judged, and with the measure you use it will be measured to you. Why do you see the speck that is in your brother's eye, but do not notice the log that is in your own eye? Or how can you say to your brother, "Let me take the speck out of your eye," when there is the log in your own eye? You hypocrite, first take the log out of your own eye, and then you will see clearly to take the speck out of your brother's eye.*[288]

286 Aal Imraan 3:159.

287 Al-Bayhaqi, Hadith #7583.

288 Matthew 7:1–5.

Abbaas told the Prophet privately that Abu Sufiyan liked to be recognized for who he was and suggested he should be shown some favor and honor. The Prophet responded, "He who enters Abu Sufiyan's house will be safe, and he who locks his door will be safe, and he who enters the House of God will be safe." A verse in the Qur'aan had earlier reminded the people of Allaah's ancient decree that whoever entered the Sacred Mosque in Makkah would be safe.[289] This was an affirmation of the supplication of Abraham, the father of Arabs and Jews. Receiving a protected status for his house greatly pleased Abu Sufiyan. In this there is a lesson for Muslim leaders that they should be mindful of the personality of those they rule, because not everyone is alike.

Because of a tactical reason, the Prophet wanted Abu Sufiyan to see the Muslim army. So when Abu Sufiyan was ready to go back to Makkah, the Prophet asked Abbaas to stop Abu Sufiyan in the narrowest part of the valley so he would see the power and humility of the Muslim army. Regiment after regiment of Muslim forces passed by Abu Sufiyan, and he kept asking Abbaas who they were, and Abbaas informed him that they were the Muslims. The first to enter Makkah was Khaalid bin Waleed with the Banu Sulaym. He was leading a thousand people, and as he passed Abu Sufiyan, Khaalid recited the takbir, *Allaahu Akbar*, three times. Then came Zubayr bin Al-Awwaam with five hundred men; then the Banu Ghifaar with three hundred; then the Banu Aslam with four hundred, followed by the Banu Amr with five hundred.

But Abu Sufiyan was most anxious to see the battalion of the Prophet. Finally, the Prophet and his troops appeared. What Abu Sufiyan saw filled him with awe. It was a force of about five thousand soldiers, of which one thousand were wearing coats of mail, dust rising from the hooves of their horses. They could not be recognized because their faces were concealed by the armor they were wearing. The Prophet was riding his she-camel Al-Qaswa, and Abu Bakr and Usayd bin Hudhayr flanked him. Abu Sufiyan

289 Aal Imraan 3:96.

asked who were in the cavalry of the Prophet, and Abbaas told him they were the *Muhaajireen* (Emigrants) and the *Ansaar* (Helpers).

Despite the strength of the Muslim troops, the Prophet entered the city with his head down and his chin pressed against his chest in a gesture of extreme humility. He was glorifying Allaah and thanking Him for His favors. This was the city of peace, and he was determined to honor its sanctity. He had issued orders against bloodshed and destruction. Who except a Prophet of Allaah could have such an attitude toward a people who had persecuted him, driven him out, and fought against him? What other examples can we find in human history where a victor entered a vanquished city humbled and full of forgiveness?

Abu Sufiyan was so overwhelmed with this sight that he said to Abbaas, "No force can resist this army. O Abbaas! The kingdom of your nephew has flourished to a great extent."

Abbaas mildly rebuked him. "The source of the strength of my nephew is the Prophethood bestowed upon him by Allaah, and it has nothing to do with outward and material power."

Reflections: We see a parallel between the Prophet Muhammad's humble coming into Makkah riding a camel, and Jesus's entering Jerusalem while riding a donkey, full of humility. Some people asked who it was, and the crowd answered, "This is Jesus, the Prophet from Nazareth in Galilee."[290]

The Prophet had given his banner to Sa'ad bin Ubaadah. Seeing Abu Sufiyan, Ibn Ubaadah said, "O Abu Sufiyan, today is the day of fierce battle. Today, what is holy will be taken back. Today God will humiliate the Quraysh."

---

290 Matthew 21:1–11.

Abu Sufiyan was shaken, and when the Prophet passed by, he asked, "O Messenger of Allaah, did you command the killing of your people?" Perhaps this was the first time Abu Sufiyan had addressed him as the Messenger of Allaah.

What Abu Sufiyan heard from the Prophet would fill any heart with respect, faith, and emotion. The Prophet said, "Today is the day of graciousness! Today, God will make the Quraysh mighty." Then the Prophet ordered that his flag be taken away from Sa'ad bin Ubaadah and given to the latter's son, Qays, instead. When Sa'ad was told of the Prophet's order, he said he would not comply without proof, so the Prophet sent his turban with the envoy, and Sa'ad handed over the flag to his son.

The Prophet's words of compassion and honor filled Abu Sufiyan with joy. It was unlike any other day for him. Within a few hours, Abu Sufiyan had gone through feelings of fear, sadness, awe, and joy. He ran to his people and cried out, "O people, today whoever enters my house is saved, whoever locks his door is saved, and whoever discards his weapons is protected."

The people of Makkah who had not heard about the amnesty the Prophet had granted to Abu Sufiyan were stunned and fearful at the Muslims' arrival. What fate awaited the Makkans was a question on many people's minds.

Abu Bakr's Father Accepts Islam

Abu Bakr's father, Abu Quhaafah, was helped onto the hills of Abu Qubays by his youngest daughter, Qareebah. His hair had turned snow white, and he had been blind since before the *Hijrah*. He asked his daughter what she could see from the vantage point of the hill. She said, "I see a man moving in the midst of the crowd."

Abu Quhaafah said, "This is their commander," meaning the Prophet. Quraybah told him that the army had dispersed, and she was fearful on account of the large army she had seen. Her father comforted her by saying, "Little daughter, do not fear, for by God, your brother Ateeq (meaning Abu Bakr) is the closest Companion of Muhammad." He then instructed her to take him down to the house before the forces struck Makkah.

When the Prophet entered the Grand Mosque, Abu Bakr soon brought his father to him. Seeing the condition of his father, the Prophet said to Abu Bakr, "Why did you not leave the old man in his house so that I could have visited him?" Abu Bakr replied that it was his father who needed the Prophet, so it was only fitting that he should have come. The Prophet placed his hand on Abu Quhaafah's chest and asked him to pronounce the two testimonies of faith, which he did.

Khaalid's Skirmish in the Sacred Area

Khaalid was leading the right wing of the Muslim army. He was ordered to enter from the Al-Lit, a lower part of Makkah. He was accompanied by the tribes of Aslam, Sulaym, Ghifaar, Muzaynah, and Juhaynah, among others.

On the Qurayshi side, it was very hard for Safwaan bin Umayyah, Ikrimah bin Abi Jahl, and Suhayl bin Amr to let the Muslims take over Makkah without a fight. So they gathered a small force and decided to block Khaalid's advance. When they saw Khaalid and his men, they attacked with arrows and spears. They acted more out of desperation than any rational thinking, as by no means was Khaalid a soft target. He was a military genius whom the Prophet later called *Saifullaah* (Sword of Allaah). Khaalid and his forces routed them, killing some thirteen of the Quraysh and four of the Hudhayl, while scattering the rest, including their leaders. Two from Khaalid's camp were also killed—Kurz bin Jaabir and Khunays bin Khaalid bin Rabi'ah.

When the Prophet was informed, he asked Khaalid why he had fought, when he had been ordered not to fight in the city. Khaalid explained that he had fought only when he was attacked, and the Prophet accepted his answer, saying, "Allaah fulfills what is best."

Truth Vanquishes Falsehood

After things had calmed down, the Prophet performed the rituals of Umrah and asked for Uthmaan bin Talhah to bring the keys of the Ka'bah and open it for him. Inside, the Prophet found 360 idols. There could not have been a more depressing sight to find those idols in the ancient house that was built purely for the worship of One God, Allaah. For centuries people had worshipped Allaah alone in the house that Prophet Abraham and his son Ishmael had built. Then, in a great irony of history, Amr bin Luhayy Al-Khuzaa'i introduced idol worship in the Ka'bah, and gradually everyone, except for about eight people, began to worship them.

The Prophet pushed the idols with his stick while reciting, "Say, the truth has come and falsehood gone. Verily falsehood is bound to vanish."[291] Some reports say that the Prophet did not push the idols, only pointed his staff at them, and they fell down. He found some pictures depicting Prophet Jesus and his mother, Mary, and ordered that they be removed. There was also a portrait of Prophet Abraham, which Umar was ordered to erase.

The Prophet had the idols broken up and burned. Then he ordered whoever had an idol in his home to destroy it. The profundity of this moment could not be overemphasized. From the time that Amr bin Luhayy Al-Khuzaa'i had introduced Hubal in the Ka'bah, the House of God had remained in a state of desecration. And now, finally, the last Prophet of Allaah and the progeny of the Ka'bah's builders, Ibraahim and Ismaa'il, had cleansed this House and restored it to its original status. It was a glorious day, and the believers were beaming with joy. Since then the Ka'bah has been visited by billions of the faithful, and Allaah is glorified there every moment of the day and night.

Reflections: This is similar to what the Prophet Jesus did when he went inside the Temple in Jerusalem. "Jesus entered the temple courts

291 Israa 17:81.

and drove out all who were buying and selling there. He overturned the tables of the money changers and the benches of those selling doves. 'It is written,' he said to them, 'My house will be called a house of prayer, but you are making it a den of robbers.'"[292]

A large number of people had gathered outside the Grand Mosque, some nervous about what might happen to them. The Prophet addressed the people thus: "There is no God but Allaah. He has no associate. He has fulfilled the promise He made to his slave and helped him and defeated all the confederates. Bear in mind that every claim of privilege, whether of blood or property, is abolished except that of the custody of the Ka'bah and of supplying water to the pilgrims. Bear in mind that for anyone who is slain, the blood money is a hundred camels. O People of Quraysh, surely God has abolished from you all pride of the time of ignorance and all pride in your ancestry, because all men are descended from Aadam, and Aadam was made of clay.

"Allaah has made Makkah a sanctuary since the day He created the heavens and the earth, and it will remain a sanctuary by virtue of the sanctity Allaah has bestowed on it until the Day of Resurrection. It was not made lawful to anyone before me to fight in it. Nor will it be made lawful to anyone after me, and it was not made lawful for me except for a short period of time. Its animals (that can be hunted) should not be chased, nor should its trees be cut, nor its vegetation or grass uprooted, nor its lost items picked up except by one who makes a public announcement about it."

Then the Prophet turned to his own clan. "O Children of Haashim and Muttalib! I have been sent to you by Allaah as His Messenger, and the ties of love and kindness between you and me are unbreakable. You shouldn't, however, think that only a relationship with me will ensure your salvation on the Day of Judgment."

292 Matthew 21:12–13.

The Prophet then held up the key of the Ka'bah. Ali and Abbaas asked for it, but he called for Uthmaan bin Talhah. Giving the key back to Uthmaan, the Prophet said, "This key will be with you till the end of time, and if anyone were to take it away from you, that person will be the unjust." The Prophet's action symbolized what had been revealed to him: "Allaah commands you to return the things entrusted to you to the rightful owners."[293] Uthmaan's family had been the keeper of the key for many years, and the Prophet restored it to them with a command for all Muslims to follow. This was in keeping with his decision to retain two traditions from the days of ignorance: one was to restore the key to the Abd Ad-Dar, Uthmaan bin Talhah's tribe, and the other was to allow Abbaas (Banu Haashim) and his descendants to continue serving water to the pilgrims.

In handing the key to Uthmaan, the Prophet had displayed a magnanimity that only a Messenger of God could. Many years back, Uthmaan had refused to allow the Prophet to enter the Ka'bah. Instead of getting furious, the Prophet had calmly told him, "O Uthmaan, one day will come, I hope, when you will find me having this key and the power to give it to anybody I wish."

Uthmaan had said, "It means the Quraysh will have been eliminated then."

The Prophet had told him, "No, O Uthmaan! The Quraysh will attain real power and honor then."

How Should I Treat You?

After his sermon, the Messenger of God asked the people, "O Quraysh! What do you think I will do to you?" In another version, he asked, "How should I treat you?"

293 Nisaa 4:58.

The Quraysh said, "You are a noble brother and son of a noble brother. We only expect good from you."

The Prophet responded, "I will say to you what Yusuf (Joseph) said to his brothers: 'This day there is no blame on you: May Allaah forgive you, and He is the Most Merciful of those who show mercy.'"[294] He added, "You may leave; you are free."

One can only imagine the impact the Prophet's words had on the audience. As a defeated people, the Makkans were at the disposal of Rasul Allaah, but he spared them the humiliation and freed them. That is why they were called *Al-Tulaqaa*, the freed ones.

People began to come to him in groups to enter Islam. The old enmity had given way to a sense of gratitude. The Prophet was, after all, one of their own, and his victory was theirs. Those who came to declare their Islam included many women, among them Hind, the wife of Abu Sufiyan. She was clearly worried on account of what she had done to the body of Hamzah. Fearing that the Prophet might order her executed before she had embraced Islam, she came veiled and said, "O Messenger of Allaah, praise be to Him who has given victory to the religion that I choose for me." She then removed the veil from her face and announced she was Hind, the daughter of Utbah.

The Prophet said, "Welcome," as if nothing had happened.

Another woman who came to embrace Islam was Umm Hakim, the wife of Ikrimah. When she was done reciting the testimony, she pleaded with the Prophet to give her husband immunity, which he did even though Ikrimah was still at war with him and had fled Makkah after the botched attempt to stop Khaalid.

---

294 Yusuf 12:92.

The Prophet looked around in the crowd as if to find someone. "O Abbaas, where are your brother's two sons, Utbah and Mu'attib?" the Prophet asked. These were the sons of Abu Lahab to whom the Prophet had given his daughters Ruqayyah and Umm Kulthoom in marriage, although they had not been sent off to their husbands. He had done this before the Prophethood. When the Prophet started preaching, Abu Lahab had become infuriated and forced his sons to end their marriages. The men must have been embarrassed and afraid to face the Prophet, but Abbaas brought them, and they entered Islam. The Prophet's face lit up with joy, and he took them by hand and made a long supplication for them.

No Migration after the Conquest

Mujaashi bin Mas'ud As-Sulami said, "I came to the Prophet to offer him my pledge of migration. He said: 'The period of migration has expired and those who were to get the reward for this great act of devotion have got it. You may now give your pledge to serve the cause of Islam, to strive in the way of Allaah and to follow the path of virtue.'"[295]

As people kept streaming in, a person brought his father to the Prophet and said, "O Messenger of God! My father will pay allegiance to you and promise to migrate."

The Messenger replied, "There is no migration after the conquest of Makkah."

In another narration, Mujashi bin Mas'ud As-Sulami said, "I came to the Prophet to offer my pledge of migration. He said: 'Migration has ended; you may now give your pledge to serve the cause of Islam, in the Way of Allaah, and follow a path of virtue.'"

295 Muslim, Hadith #4595.

Up until this point, the Prophet had greatly emphasized the need to migrate to Madinah in order to escape persecution and practice Islam freely. Verses of the Qur'aan urged people to migrate. But now that Makkah was an Islamic territory, there was no need to migrate. However, it should be kept in mind that whenever a group of Muslims cannot practice their religion freely, they should migrate to a place where they can; this migration was not prohibited by the Prophet.

Those Not Covered Under Amnesty

The Prophet had ordered six men and four women killed because of the severity of their crimes and their lack of remorse. However, most of them were eventually forgiven. They were Abdullaah bin Abi Sarh; Abdullaah bin Hilal bin Khatal; Huwayrith bin Nuqaydh; Miqyas bin Subaaba; Saarah, a freed slave woman of Amr bin Haashim; Habbaar bin Al-Aswad; Ikrimah bin Abi Jahl; and Quraynah and Quraybah, two songstresses of Abu Khatal.

Abdullaah bin Abi Sarh was a Muslim who used to write down the revelation. Then Satan deceived him, and he started to make claims that sometimes when revelation came to him, he replaced a word that the Prophet had told him to write with one of his own and the Prophet did not know. Then he apostatized and ran to the Quraysh for protection. No Muslim believed in his claim of fabrication in the Qur'aan, as the Prophet was memorizing it himself and dictating it to several people. After the conquest of Makkah, Abdullaah asked his foster brother Uthmaan bin Affaan to protect him. Uthmaan hid him for some time. The Prophet showed reluctance to pardon Abdullaah, but when Uthmaan kept insisting, he relented.

Abdullaah bin Hilal bin Khatal had become a Muslim, but he had killed a Muslim slave and had apostatized. He had two singing girls, Quraynah and Quraybah, who used to sing satirical poems about the Prophet. The singing girls were also ordered to be killed. Abdullaah was killed by Sa'id bin Hurayth and Abu Barza Al-Aslami. One of the singing girls was killed, and the other was eventually pardoned.

Huwayrith bin Nuqaydh used to insult the Prophet in Makkah. He was killed by Ali bin Abi Taalib. The Prophet had made a distinction between someone's insulting him as a man and as a Prophet. He forgave insult to himself as a man but took revenge when God's Prophet or religion was mocked.

Miqyas bin Subaaba had killed an Ansaari Companion and joined the Quraysh as a polytheist. He was killed by Numayla bin Abdullaah.

Saarah was a freed slave woman of one of the Banu Abdul Muttalib and of Ikrimah bin Abi Jahl. Saarah had insulted the Prophet in Makkah. She was pardoned, and she lived until Umar's rule.

Even before the conquest of Makkah, the Prophet had a standing order that whenever Habbaar bin Al-Aswad was found, he should be burned in the fire. Then he changed his stance, saying, "Only the Lord of the Hellfire has the right to do so. Cut off his hands and legs if you have power over him; then kill him." His crime was very serious. He is the man who had caused Zaynab, the Prophet's daughter, to fall from the camel, resulting in the death of her unborn baby and severe injury to her. When Zaynab was migrating to Madinah from Makkah, escorted by her brother-in-law, Habbaar and some ruffians surrounded them and pierced the back of the camel with a spear, throwing Zaynab to the ground. Habbaar accepted Islam and was forgiven.

The offenses of Ikrimah bin Abi Jahl against the Prophet and the Muslims were well known. He was, like his father, among the harshest and most uncompromising opponents of Islam. He wanted neither to be captured and killed nor to accept Islam, so he fled to Yemen. As he boarded the ship, the captain announced, "O servant of God, you cannot travel in my ship unless you disavow partners to Him, for I fear that if you do not do so, we will perish." For the first time, Ikrimah truly realized the reach of Islam and the futility of his beliefs.

His wife, Umm Hakim, had already become a Muslim and asked the Prophet to pardon Ikrimah, a request that was granted. Umm Hakim rushed to the seashore in pursuit of Ikrimah and finally reached him in Yemen. She informed him that the Prophet had pardoned him and there was no point in him going into exile. Ikrimah relented, went to the Prophet, and recited the testimonies of faith.

The Prophet knew he was coming and said to his Companions, "Ikrimah, the son of Abu Jahl, is on his way to you, as a believer. Therefore revile not his father, for the reviling of the dead offends the living and does not reach the dead."[296] Ikrimah became a sincere Muslim and strove hard in the path of Islam, saying that he had to strive harder in order to compensate for his opposition to Islam and his delay in coming into it. He died as a martyr in the Battle of Yarmouk against the Byzantine Empire.

Safwaan bin Umayyah Flees

The word came that Safwaan, another archenemy of the Prophet, had fled toward the shore to cast himself into the sea. When he reached the seashore, he instead decided to go to Yemen. Safwaan was not among those the Prophet had ordered killed, but his hostility toward Islam was too great and his ego too big to allow him to accept Islam and live in Makkah. Umayr bin Wahb informed the Prophet about Safwaan's flight and asked for immunity. The Prophet granted it. Subsequently, Safwaan's wife, Faakhita bint Al-Waleed, also asked the Prophet to pardon her husband, and the request was again granted. She traveled all the way to Yemen and brought her husband back to Makkah, but Safwaan was still not ready to accept Islam, despite pardon. He asked for two months to make up his mind, and the Prophet granted him twice that.

296 Martin Lings, *Muhammad: His Life Based on the Earliest Sources*, Rochester, Inner Traditions, 316

When the Prophet decided to lead an expedition to Hawaazin, Safwaan went along as a polytheist to observe. As the Prophet was returning as a victor from Hunayn, he passed by a valley full of cattle and sheep and observed Safwaan looking at them covetously. The Prophet asked, "Abu Wahb (Safwaan), do you like this valley?"

He answered, "Yes."

The Prophet said, "It is yours with everything in it."

Safwaan was overwhelmed with this unparalleled generosity. He said, "No one can give away so much wealth and not care about it except a Prophet!" And it was at that point that he said, "I bear witness that there is no God but Allaah, and Muhammad is His Messenger."

The Case of Suhayl bin Amr

At the Prophet's triumphant return to Makkah, Suhayl had run into his house and locked the door. He had said if he were found, he would be surely killed because of the enormity of his crimes against Islam. He also remembered how rudely he had addressed the Prophet at Hudaybiyah and dictated the treaty, and how he had fought against him at Badr and Uhud. So he sent his son, Abdullaah, to the Prophet to ask for clemency. When Abdullaah asked the Prophet if he could pardon Suhayl, the Prophet replied, "Yes, he is protected, and he has the protection of Allaah, so let him appear." Then he instructed the Companions, "Whoever meets Suhayl bin Amr, do not stare at him. Let him leave, for by my life, Suhayl possesses a smile and nobility. And whoever is like Suhayl cannot ignore Islam. Surely he realized that what he was practicing could not profit him."

Abdullaah conveyed the Prophet's remarks to his father, and he exclaimed, "He was, by God, righteous, whether young or old!" Despite that, Suhayl hesitated in accepting Islam. He accompanied the Prophet in the next battle at Hunayn while still practicing polytheism. However, he could not ignore the powerful stirrings within him, and finally he embraced Islam.

Destruction of Al-Uzzah

Having rid Makkah of the man-made idols, the Prophet sent Khaalid bin Waleed to Nakhlah to destroy Al-Uzzah, one of the prominent deities, along with Al-Laat and Al-Manaat, that pagans worshipped in nearby towns. At the news of Khaalid's approach, the temple's priest hung his sword on the statue of the goddess and called upon her to defend herself and slay Khaalid, or he would become a monotheist. Khaalid demolished the temple and its idol and then returned to Makkah.

The Prophet asked him, "Did you see anything?"

Khaalid replied, "I saw nothing."

The Prophet said, "Then you have not destroyed her. Go back and destroy her."

So Khaalid returned, and what he saw frightened him. Out of the ruins of the temple, there came a black woman, entirely naked, with long and wildly flowing hair. Khaalid said afterward, "My spine was seized with shivering." But Khaalid was no wimp. He drew his sword and cut her down. When he went back to Makkah, Khaalid informed the Prophet and thanked Allaah that an evil practice had ended. His father used to sacrifice one hundred camels at Al-Uzzah's shrine and spend several days there to seek her blessings.

The Prophet Rebukes Khaalid

After the Conquest of Makkah, the Prophet sent groups of people to areas around the city to invite them to Islam. One group was led by Khaalid bin Waleed. The Prophet had clearly instructed them that they were callers to

Islam and not fighters. However, when Khaalid reached the Banu Jadhima, he ordered the people to lay down their arms, telling them that everybody else had accepted Islam. One of the Banu Jadhima men warned his people not to listen to Khaalid and said that if they did, Khaalid would tie them and kill them. In the ensuing confusion that followed, some of them laid down their arms, while a handful did not. Khaalid beheaded some of his prisoners, claiming that he was taking revenge for the killing of Abdur Rahmaan bin Awf's father.

When the Prophet was informed of Khaalid's actions, he raised his hands in prayer and said, "O Allaah, I am innocent of what Khaalid has done." Then he sent Ali to pay blood money to the victims' families and compensate them for property damage, leaving out not even a small thing. After paying all the claims, Ali still had some money left, which he gave away to the Banu Jadhima.

When it became clear that Khaalid had done this to avenge a personal grudge of the past, Abdur Rahmaan angrily said to Khaalid, "You have done a pagan act in Islam." To that the latter responded that he had done it only to avenge Abdur Rahmaan's father's murder at the hands of someone from the Banu Jadhima many years before. Abdur Rahmaan rebutted Khaalid and said he himself had killed his father's killer before Islam. In fact, Khaalid had avenged the murder of his uncle Faakih bin Al-Mugheerah, who had been killed in the same incident as Abdur Rahmaan's father.

When this additional detail reached the Prophet, he sternly reprimanded Khaalid, saying, "Gently, Khaalid, leave my Companions alone, for by God, if you had a mountain of gold and spent it for God's sake, you would not approach the merit of my Companions." The Prophet did not mean that he did not consider Khaalid his Companion, but he was simply emphasizing the merit of the early Muslims who emigrated and suffered enormously for Islam. Abdur Rahmaan was one of them. Khaalid later prayed for Allaah's forgiveness and apologized to Abdur Rahmaan until he was satisfied. This incident also shows that it takes time for a convert to renounce the remnants of his past.

The Battle of Hunayn

Although Makkah was now an Islamic territory and the Muslims could move about in it freely, two major tribes had not embraced Islam, and they harbored a grudge against the Muslims. One was the Hawaazin, who lived in the Valley of Hunayn midway between Makkah and Taa'if. God had considered Hawaazin so important that of the seven dialects in which He had sent down the Qur'aan, one was the Hawaazin's dialect (*Harf*). The Banu Sa'ad, the tribe of Halimah Saa'diyah, the Prophet's foster mother, was a subtribe of the Hawaazin. The other tribe was the Banu Thaqif of Taa'if, who considered themselves and their city respectively on par with the Quraysh and Makkah. Almost a decade earlier, the leadership of Taa'if had treated the Messenger of Allaah very harshly when he had visited them to call them unto Islam.

When the Hawaazin learned that Makkah had been conquered and its leadership all but converted to Islam, their reaction was not to join the Muslims but to fight them. They were deeply saddened to know about the destruction of Al-Uzzah, which had been the sister shrine to their own temple of Al-Laat. Just a month after the Conquest of Makkah, in the month of Shawwal, 8 AH (629/630 CE), the Hawaazin prepared a twenty-thousand-strong army that also included forces from the Banu Thaqif, Banu Jusham, Banu Sa'ad bin Bakr, Banu Awzaa, Banu Amr, and Banu Awf. Their commander in chief was a young man named Malik bin Awf An-Nasri. At age thirty, he not only was the leader of the Hawaazin, but other, smaller tribes had chosen him as their joint chief against the Muslims. Malik had established his credentials as a brave fighter and a man of princely demeanor.

Malik ordered his people to bring with them their women, children, and cattle to ensure they would not run away from the battlefield. An old wise man of the Banu Jusham, Durayd bin Al-Simmah, advised against it, but Malik ignored him. Durayd, who was blind, asked if the Banu Ka'ab, Banu Hilal, and Banu Kilaab were with the army. When told that they were not, he said, "If there was any nobility in this war, they would have preceded you, so do what they have done." Some people became inclined toward Durayd's opinion, as his experience in warfare and wisdom surpassed that of others among his people.

Malik hated to see the old man's opinion being respected so much. Concerned, he said, "O people of Hawaazin, by God, you either obey me, or I will fall onto my sword until it comes out from my back."

Malik sent out three spies to bring him information about the Muslim army. When they returned, they were disheveled as if somebody had manhandled them. They seemed to be terrified but somehow managed to say to Malik, "We saw white men on spotted horses who smote us, as you can see. We are fighting, not the people of this earth, but the people of heaven. Take our advice and withdraw, for if our men see what we have seen, they will suffer what we have suffered."

Malik was not convinced. "Shame on you!" he shouted. "You are the cowards." He ordered them to be imprisoned so that they could not demoralize the troops. Then he chose another man known for his bravery to bring the news of the Muslims, and he too returned the same way, shaken and in terror. But Malik refused to pay heed to anything, and after dark he gave orders to advance to the valley of Hunayn, through which he knew the Muslim army was bound to pass.

The Prophet came to know of Hawaazin's plans and prepared a force of 12,000 fighters—10,000 from the Muhaajireen and Ansaar, and 2,000 from the newly conquered Makkah, the *Al-Tulaqaa*, or the freed ones. Never before had the Muslim army been this large. This stood in stark contrast to all the previous battles, where the Muslim numbers were much smaller than those of their foes—for example, Badr with 310 versus 1,000 and Mu'tah with 3,000 versus 200,000. Even though the Hawaazin were still numerically superior, some Muslims thought since their own numbers were the highest ever, victory was assured. Al-Waaqidi in his *Kitab Al-Maghazi* attributed this opinion to Abu Bakr, who reportedly said, "O Messenger of God, we will not be defeated today because of our small numbers." There is also another opinion that the Prophet himself said this.

The Prophet left a man of Abdush Shams, Attaab bin Asid, in charge of Makkah and appointed Mu'aadh bin Jabal, a young but knowledgeable Companion from Al-Khazraj, to teach converts their new religion. Suhayl bin Amr and Safwaan bin Umayyah had not yet entered Islam but simply joined to defend their city against the Hawaazin. Before setting out, the Prophet had asked Safwaan to lend him a hundred coats of mail, which he was known to possess, and the weapons that paired with the body armor.

Safwaan asked, "Is it a question of 'Give or I will take'?"

The Prophet said, "It is a loan to be returned." Whereupon Safwaan even provided the camels for the transport of the war materiel.

The Hawaazin and their allies had positioned themselves in narrow passes and alleys. They were lying in ambush. From a strategic viewpoint, they had the upper hand. Because of the way the Muslim army had to enter the valley, the Hawaazin would face only a small number of them at any given time. The Hawaazin were renowned for their marksmanship with arrows, and they placed some of their best marksmen at high points close to those straight and narrow areas. They poured their arrows over the Muslims once they saw them, hoping that that would cause chaos among the Muslim army, and then the rest of his forces would launch a full-scale attack against them.

As the Muslim army moved with the first rays of light, hardly able to see the way, they were unaware that their enemies had taken positions and were ready to attack them as they approached. As soon as the front forces had reached the entrance to the valley, they were met with a barrage of arrows shot at them from all angles. They could hardly tell where the arrows came from, so they ran for cover. The unbelievers did not waste time; they attacked the Muslims as they retreated, bringing in large forces with cavalry and infantry units. Soon the Muslim army was in absolute chaos, with soldiers trying to flee.

In this moment of fear and chaos, the Prophet was calm and composed. He was riding his white mule called Ash-Shahba (some say Duldul) and moving toward the frontline where the enemy was. His uncle Abbaas was holding its right-hand rope, and his cousin Abu Sufiyan bin Al-Haarith bin Abdul Muttalib, who had recently embraced Islam, was holding the left-hand rope. The Prophet kept calling, "O servants of Allaah, come back to me; I am the Messenger of Allaah. I am the Prophet, not lying. I am the son of Abdul Muttalib." But the people were too overcome with fear to hear what the Prophet was saying.

Their running away from the battlefield led Abu Sufiyan bin Harb to remark, "Nothing will stop the deserters except the sea."

A brother of Safwaan Bin Umayyah, who was also, like him, a polytheist, quipped, "The sorcery is in vain today," equating Islam with magic.

Safwaan berated his brother. "Shut up. May your mouth be smashed. I would rather be ruled by a man of the Quraysh (meaning the Prophet) than by a man of the Hawaazin." Clearly, Safwaan's defense of the Muslims had to do with tribal pride rather than religion.

Allaah sent down verses describing the situation at Hunayn in both its early phase (disarray) and the later phase (victory).

Truly, Allaah has given you victory on many battlefields, and on the day of Hunayn (battle) when you rejoiced at your great number, but it availed you naught and the earth, vast as it is, was straitened for you, then you turned back in flight. Then Allaah sent down His tranquility on His Messenger, and on the believers, and sent down forces (angels) which you saw not, and punished the disbelievers. Such is the recompense of disbelievers. Then after that Allaah will accept the repentance of whom He wills. And Allaah is Oft-Forgiving, Most Merciful.[297]

Of the 12,000-strong Muslim army, only 180 Companions were left around the Prophet, including, among others, Abu Bakr, Umar, Abbaas, Ali, Fadl bin Abbaas, Abu Sufiyan bin Al-Haarith, Ayman the son of Umm Ayman, and Usaamah the son of Umm Ayman and Zayd bin Haarithah. The Prophet asked his uncle Abbaas, who had a strong voice, to call back the Muslims. Abbaas said, "O Companions of the Acacia tree (referring to the tree under which the Muslims gave the Pledge of Ridwan)." He also called, "O Companions of Surah Al-Baqarah."

Upon hearing Abbaas's voice, many started responding, "Here we are! Here we are!" The Muslims began to return in the direction of the Messenger of Allaah with such fervor that if some of their camels refused to obey, they disembarked and hurried on foot.

When a large crowd had gathered around the Messenger of Allaah, he commanded them to fight with sincerity. Then he took a handful of sand and threw it in the faces of the disbelievers, all the while praying, "O Allaah, fulfill Your promise to me." The sand entered the polytheists' eyes and mouths, and they began to retreat. A fistful of dust thrown at a large army would hardly do any damage, but this was a miracle of the Prophet, and he had Allaah's backing. This is what the Prophet had done at Badr. He had thrown dust in the direction of the Qurayshi army, saying, "May the faces be disfigured," and it had struck them like bullets. Allaah had called the Prophet's throwing of the dust at Badr His own action.

297 Tawbah 9:25–27.

In the second round, only a handful of Muslims were killed, one of whom was Ayman, Usaamah bin Zayd's elder brother. He was struck down at the side of the Prophet. The Muslims pursued the Hawaazin and their allies, killing and capturing many of them. As the tables began to turn, other Muslims came back, providing reinforcement to their ranks. A large number of the enemy fled, and among them was their leader Malik bin Awf, who sought protection with Banu Thaqif in Taa'if. The Hawaazin and their allies left six thousand prisoners of war; twenty-four thousand camels, sheep, and cattle; and a large quantity of gold, all of which became the property of the Muslims. It was by far the greatest war booty the Muslims had ever captured. The Prophet kept all of what was captured at Hunayn in a place called Al-Ji'raanah until he returned from dealing with the Banu Thaqif.

Victory was not achieved on the cheap, though. The Muslims had paid a very high price. Although the source books of biography have not listed all the casualties of the battle, they did mention that two tribes of Muslims—the Banu Sulaym and the Banu Rabaab—were almost totally destroyed because they were the front battalions in the first round. The Prophet held a funerary prayer for the martyrs of Hunayn and asked Allaah to admit them into Paradise.

Amazing Eyewitness Accounts

Ibn Kathir reported in his commentary on the Battle of Hunayn that a polytheist who had fought against the Muslims had said, "When we met the Messenger of Allaah and his Companions on the day of Hunayn, they did not remain in the battle more than the time it takes to milk a sheep! When we defeated them, we pursued them until we ended at the rider of the white mule (the Prophet Muhammad). At that time, men with white handsome faces intercepted us and said, 'Disgraced be the faces! Go back.' So we ran away, but they followed us. That was the end for us." Clearly, as the Qur'aan says, these were angels Allaah had sent whom the Muslims could not see.

One key lesson of Hunayn was that numbers did not grant victory. Had it been so, the Muslims would have been defeated at Badr, where they were outnumbered three to one. Also, when the Muslims thought their big numbers would help them win, Allaah did not send them help. However, when they put their trust in Allaah, angels came down to fight on alongside them.

The Battle for Taa'if

When the Hawaazin and their allies were routed from Hunayn, they ran to Taa'if for safety. The city was a stronghold of the Banu Thaqif. It was a walled city, and inside it were strong fortresses. Malik bin Awf sought refuge in one of those fortresses, as did many others who had run away from Hunayn. On the way to Taa'if, the Muslims passed by Malik's uninhabited fortress in Liyyah and, at the orders of the Prophet, destroyed it.

The Prophet called for the people to set up camp in the vicinity of the fortresses of the Banu Thaqif. The Companion Al-Hubaab bin Al-Mundhir rushed to the Prophet, saying, "O Messenger of God, if this decision was due to a command from Allaah, we submit, but if it is an opinion, then stay back from the fortress." Just as Al-Hubaab finished pleading, a volley of arrows from the enemy fortress fell upon the Muslims, killing some and injuring scores of others, including Abdullaah bin Abi Bakr. The Prophet asked Al-Hubaab to find a higher ground in the back of the fortress, and he found the place to which the encampment was moved. Today, the Taa'if Mosque stands where the Muslim camp was. Two of the Prophet's wives, Umm Salamah and Zaynab bint Jahsh, had accompanied him on this expedition. A tent was set up for each of them, and the Prophet prayed between the two tents.

The Muslims found the Banu Thaqif fortress one of the most difficult to storm or scale. The enemy archers and javelin throwers were on the watch, and the walls were too high to scale. One of the Companions, Tufayl bin Amr of the Daws tribe, to which the famous Hadith narrator Abu Hurayrah also belonged, went to his people and brought back a catapult. Some say it was Companion Salmaan Al-Faarisi who suggested this idea, and Yazid bin Zama'a or Khaalid bin Sa'id brought two catapults from Jurash. They used this tool of war, which was new to the Muslims, to throw heavy objects at the fortress to demolish it. But the Thaqif'ites responded with catapults of their own, throwing heated iron balls at the Muslims. It was a tough situation, so the Prophet decided to wait it out. Under the circumstances, waiting seemed to be the best course of action. Time was on the Muslims' side, and someday soon the Thaqif would run out of food and water.

Not long after that, the Prophet, due to either a revelation or his own strategy of war, ordered the Muslims to cut down the vineyards of the Banu Thaqif. Taa'if was famous for its grapes. The vineyards were lush green and produced abundant crops. The order was to cut the grape vines and burn them. When Umar informed the Prophet that the grapes were fully ready, the Prophet changed the order to cut down only those vines that had already been harvested.

Next, the Prophet announced that any slave who managed to come out of the fortress to the Muslim camp would be set free. About ten slaves responded, and the Prophet did as promised, assigning Muslims to host and protect them. The slaves converted to Islam of their own volition, and their Muslim hosts taught them how to read the Qur'aan and perform their acts of worship. Eventually, when the Banu Thaqif rank and file converted, their elders demanded the former slaves be sent back into slavery, but the Prophet refused, saying, "Those whom God set free cannot be touched." This angered the former slave owners, but they had no recourse against the Messenger of God.

As the siege continued, one day a leader of the Banu Thaqif, Abu Mihjaan bin Hubayb bin Amr bin Umayr Al-Thaqafi, shouted from his fortress, "O servants of Muhammad, by God you have not met anyone who is a better fighter than we are. You are staying in an evil prison; then you will turn away. Never will you be able to reach your desired goal. We are hard hearted. By God, we will never convert as long as you live. We have built an impenetrable fortress."

Umar could not hold himself back. He responded, "O Ibn Hubayb, we will cut your provisions until you leave this hole of yours. You are a fox in its den about to leave."

Abu Mihjaan said to Umar, "O Ibn Khattaab, if you cut the ropes of grapes, we will restore them through watering and new soil."

Umar said, "You will not be able to water or cultivate the soil, for we will never leave your door until you die." Abu Bakr asked Umar to refrain from that statement and informed him that God had not permitted His Prophet to take the fortress of Taa'if in this expedition. When Umar went to the Prophet to confirm what Abu Bakr had said, the Prophet said that that was true.

Umar then asked the Prophet if he should ask the people to prepare to return, and the Prophet said yes. When the people heard the announcement, some of them began to say they must not leave but rather wait for the Banu Thaqif to surrender or die. When the matter became heated, some of the people went to Abu Bakr, and he informed them that the Prophet had received a revelation. Then they went to Umar, hoping to get his support, but he flatly rejected the people's opinion, reminding them that he was sorely mistaken in Al-Hudaybiyah and did not want to commit the same mistake.

The Prophet said to Abu Bakr, "I dreamed that I was given a bowl filled with butter, and a rooster pecked at it and spilled what was in it."

Abu Bakr, who also knew how to interpret a dream, said, "I do not think that you will get what you desire on this day." The Messenger of God concurred with Abu Bakr's interpretation.

However, to teach some overzealous Muslims a practical lesson, the Prophet allowed them to go fight the next morning, and so they did. However, they achieved no victory, only fatigue and injury. So the Prophet said, "Indeed we will return home if God wills," and the people became happy. The Prophet laughed at their change of stance.

The Banu Thaqif felt rather arrogant about being undefeated, and they bragged about it. As the Muslims departed Al-Taa'if, some people asked the Prophet to invoke God's punishment against the Banu Thaqif. Instead, he prayed, "O God, guide the Thaqif and bring them to Islam." It is the same place where many years earlier the Prophet had been pelted with stones and bloodied. Even then, when he was asked by the angels for permission to topple the mountain on the Banu Thaqif, the Prophet had declined and said he hoped that their children would embrace Islam one day.

The Distribution of Spoils

From Taa'if, the Prophet came back to Al-Ji'raanah to take care of what the Muslims had captured at the Battle of Hunayn. However, the Prophet delayed distributing the war booty, hoping that the Hawaazin and their allies would come, accept Islam, and reclaim what they had lost. The Hawaazin eventually came but only after the Prophet had already distributed the wealth.

When the Prophet looked at the prisoners, he found most of them clad in raggedy clothes. Overwhelmed with compassion, he immediately sent some men to buy a new garment for each of the six thousand prisoners. As some people began to show unease about the war booty, the Prophet decided to distribute without delay from his own share, the fifth that Allaah had allocated to him and the poor. A verse in the recently revealed Surah Tawbah had already allowed him to spend from the mandatory alms, the *zakaat*, on people whose hearts needed to be reconciled for Islam, as well as on freeing slaves and helping the indebted, a total of eight categories of people.

> *The alms are for the poor and the needy, and for those who are employed collect them, and those whose hearts are to be reconciled, and to set free slaves and captives, and for the relief of debtors, and for Allaah's cause, and for the wayfarer—an obligation enjoined by Allaah, And Allaah is All-Knowing, All-Wise.*[298]

The most important among those whose hearts needed to be reconciled were the top leaders of the Quraysh. Some of them had accepted the new faith, but it had not been established in their hearts quite yet. There were also those who had come close to accepting Islam but needed a little push, which could be both psychological and material. The Prophet was acutely aware of their personalities. There were also those from the Al-Tulaqaa, the general category of people who had been pardoned at the Conquest of Makkah.

So the Prophet gave Abu Sufiyan a hundred camels, and when he asked for equal amounts for his two sons, Yazid and Mu'aawiyah, the Prophet obliged. A sum of three hundred camels was a massive amount of wealth. Safwaan bin Umayyah also received three hundred camels. Safwaan had earlier been given a valley with all its possessions when he had shown a yearning for it. It was at that point that he had said that only a Prophet could be so generous and not care how much he was giving away.

Hakeem bin Hizaam, a nephew of Khadijah, the Prophet's first wife, was given a hundred camels. When he asked for another hundred, the Prophet approved it but with this advice: "This property is a fair green pasture. Whoever takes it in generosity of soul shall be blessed therein, but whoever takes it for the pride of his soul shall not be blessed therein, and he shall be as one who eats and is not filled. The upper hand is better than the lower hand, and begin your giving with such of your family as are dependent upon you."

298 Tawbah 9:60.

Hakim said, "By Him who sent you with the truth, I will not receive anything from any man after you."[299] He took only the original one hundred camels.

The Prophet gave Al-Haarith bin Harith bin Kilda a hundred camels. He also gave some chiefs of the Quraysh and other clans a hundred camels; he gave others fifty or forty, depending on his best judgment. The word spread that "Muhammad grants generously and does not fear poverty."

The news brought a large group of Bedouins, who jostled for the booty and even took away a garment of the Prophet, which prompted him to say, "O people! Give me back my garment! For I swear by the One in Whose Hand is Muhammad's soul, that if I had as many camels as the trees of Tihaama, I would distribute them among you. You know quite well that I am neither mean nor coward nor liar." Then he plucked out some hair from his camel's hump and, holding it between his two fingers, said, "O people, I swear by Allaah that I get nothing but one-fifth of your booty, and this very fifth goes back to you."

When the Prophet was finished with leaders and new converts, he allocated shares to the rest. A footman's share was four camels and forty sheep, and a horseman would get twelve camels and a hundred and twenty sheep. Out of his wisdom, he did not give the Muhaajireen and Ansaar lavish portions despite their sacrifices.

The victory of Hunayn and the supremacy that the Muslims had gained in relation to the Banu Thaqif, coupled with the Prophet's peerless generosity, opened up new rounds of conversion. Suhayl bin Amr accepted Islam unconditionally, and he remained steadfast in the times of trial that immediately followed the Prophet's death three years later.

299 Lings, *Muhammad: His Life Based on the Earliest Sources*, Rochester, Inner Traditions, 322

Among others who entered Islam at Al-Ji'raanah were some of the leading men of Makhzum: two brothers of Abu Jahl; Khaalid's half brother Hishaam; and a second son of the Prophet's aunt Aatikah, Zuhayr, whose brother had recently been martyred at Taa'if. It was Zuhayr who, some ten years previously, in defiance of Abu Jahl, had been the first to speak in favor of ending the anti-Muslim boycott. The Prophet's aunt Aatikah had already entered Islam before either of her sons.[300]

The Prophet had sent word to Malik bin Awf that if he were to come and accept Islam, his property and family would be returned. When he had finished distributing the booty, a delegation of Hawaazin arrived. It was led by the Prophet's foster brother from the Banu Sa'ad. There were fourteen Muslims among them, and the remainder now entered Islam. They insisted that the Prophet consider the entire tribe of Hawaazin as his foster kinsmen and treat them with generosity. "We nursed you on our laps and suckled you at our breasts," they said. The Prophet informed them he had already distributed the war booty and asked which they considered dearer, the possessions or their wives and children. They said, "Give us back our sons and our wives."

The Prophet immediately let go of what he and his clan had, and as for others, he said he would ask the Muslims to do likewise. Then he instructed the people of Hawaazin, "When I have led them in the afternoon congregational prayers, say: 'We ask the Messenger of God to intercede for us with the Muslims, and we ask the Muslims to intercede for us with the Messenger of God.'" They did as they were told, and the Prophet turned to the congregation and explained that they were asking for their children and their wives to be returned to them. All Emigrants and Helpers immediately complied. There were a few from the new people who refused but eventually were won over.

While this was happening, an elderly woman pushed her captors, saying, "Move away. I am your Prophet's sister." The soldiers brought her to the

300 Lings, *Muhammad: His Life Based on the Earliest Sources.*

Prophet, who asked her to prove her claim. The woman said, "I still have marks where you bit me in the arm while I carried you over my waist." Then she raised her sleeve to show the mark. The Prophet grew overwhelmed with emotion as he realized she was his foster sister Shaymaa. He asked about her parents, Halimah and Al-Haarith bin Abdul Uzzah, and when she said they had passed away, tears flowed from his eyes. He spread his mantle and had Shaymaa sit on it. Then he gave her lavish gifts and the choice of living with him or returning to her tribe. She chose the latter. The Prophet gave his foster sister some more camels and some sheep and goats, and he bade her farewell.

Then, as the delegation was leaving, the Prophet asked them for news of their leader, Malik. They told him that he had joined Thaqif in Taa'if. "Send him word that if he comes to me as a Muslim, I will return his family to him and his possessions, and I will give him a hundred camels." He had deliberately lodged Malik's family with his aunt Aatikah in Makkah and had withheld his property from being distributed. Upon hearing of the generous promise of the Prophet, Malik did not hesitate to slip out of Taa'if on his mare under the cover of night. Upon arrival at the Prophet's camp, he proclaimed his conversion to Islam, picked up his family, his property, and the prize of one hundred camels, and then went home. The Prophet put him in command of the already large and increasing Muslim community of Hawaazin, with instructions to give Thaqif no respite.

The Ansaar Feel Left Out

The wisdom behind the Prophet's extremely lavish gifts to the leaders of the Quraysh was not completely clear to the Ansaar (Helpers). They could not be blamed for their hurt feelings, as after the Emigrants (*Muhaajireen*), they had made the most sacrifices. They could not understand why erstwhile enemies of Islam, who had just embraced the faith and who had yet to prove their commitment, could receive so much wealth while they and their Emigrant brothers would get nothing. They had received only a meager share of the spoils and no gifts.

Many of the Ansaar were poor, and they had given away part of what they had to those who had emigrated to Madinah. Allaah had already praised them for their sacrifices and selflessness in a verse about the spoils of war.

> *And there is also a share in this booty for the poor Muhajirin, who were expelled from their homes and their property, seeking bounties from Allaah and His good pleasure, and helping Allaah and His Messenger. Such are indeed the truthful. And those who, before them, had homes (in Madinah) and adopted the faith, love those who emigrate to them, and have no jealousy in their breasts for that which they have been given, and give them (emigrants) preference over themselves even though they were in need of that.*[301]

Some of the Ansaar began to talk about the apparent unfairness in the booty distribution. "The Prophet has joined his people," some of them said. There also was a feeling that the Prophet would now stay in Makkah, his birthplace. Soon their concerns spread among the people. When the matter intensified, Sa'ad bin Ubaadah, a leader of the Ansaar, went to the Prophet and informed him, "O Messenger of Allaah, this group of the Helpers is upset at the distribution of the booty. You have allotted shares to your own kinsmen and given lots of gifts to the Arab tribes. But this group has received nothing." The Prophet asked Sa'ad what he thought. He said, "O Messenger of Allaah, I am but one of them."

The Prophet came closer to a group of the Ansaar who had gathered there and said, "O Ansaar, I have been informed that you are upset with me on account of a recent incident. Did I not find you in error, and God guided you; poor, and God enriched you; enemies one to another, and God reconciled your hearts?"

---

301 Hashr 59:8–9.

They said, "Yes, indeed, God and His Messenger are most bountiful and most gracious."

The Prophet asked them, "Will you not say something in return?" The Ansaar felt perplexed; how could they respond to the Messenger of God? The Prophet solved their predicament. "If you had wished, you could have said to me, and in so doing you would have been truthful, 'You came to us opposed and rejected, and we accepted you; a fugitive, and we sheltered you; poor, and we comforted you."[302]

Then the Prophet added, "O Ansaar, do you feel anxious about the things of this world wherewith I have sought to incline these people toward the faith that is already established in your hearts? Are you not satisfied that the people go with sheep and camels while you take with you the Messenger of Allaah to your homes? By God, if the people went one way and the Ansaar another, I would go the way of the Ansaar. O Allaah, have Mercy upon the Ansaar, and on their sons, and on their sons' sons."

The Ansaar began to weep until their beards became wet with tears, and they said to the Prophet, "We are well content with the Messenger of God as our lot and our share."[303]

Before returning to Madinah, the Prophet and the Companions who were in ihraam—wrapped in the two white sheets worn by male pilgrims—went to Makkah and performed Umrah. He left Attaab bin Asid in charge of the city and Mu'aadh bin Jabal responsible for educating new Muslims, just as he had appointed them before going to Hunayn. The Prophet and the rest of the army reached Madinah around the beginning of Dhul Qa'dah, after almost three months.

---

302 Bukhari, chapter on Khumus, Hadith #375; Ibn Isshaaq, *Sirat Rasul Allah*.

303 The Prophet's supplication about the *sons* of Ansaar did not mean he was not praying for their *daughters*. Rather, it was customary in those days to say *sons*, but it also meant daughters and the whole family.

Urwah bin Mas'ud Accepts Islam

Urwah did not fight against the Muslims in either Hunayn or Taa'if. He was away building mangonels (modern cannons). When he returned to Taa'if, the Prophet and his army were already gone. He had encountered the Prophet at the time of Hudaybiyah and had seen the respect the Companions showed to the Prophet. It is Urwah who at that time had said to the Quraysh, "I have visited the kings of Persia, Rome, and Abyssinia, but I have not seen any leader more revered and respected by his people than Muhammad. If he orders them to do anything, they do it without delay. If he performs *Wudu* (ablution), they all seek the remainder of the water he used. They never look at him in the eyes, out of respect."

In a Hadith the Prophet Muhammad had said that Urwah bin Mas'ud resembled the Prophet Jesus most closely in appearance. Describing his experience during the Ascension (Mai'raaj), the Prophet had said, "I was shown the Prophets in front of me, and Musa (Moses) resembles the men of the tribe of Shanu'ah, and I saw Eesa (Jesus), son of Maryam (Mary), and the person who resembles him most is Urwah Ibn Mas'ud, and I saw Ibraahim, and the person who resembles him most is your Companion (referring to himself), and I saw Gabriel (Jibreel), and the person who resembles him most is Dihyah."[304]

Urwah must also have come to know of the grace the Prophet had shown to the Hawaazin and the Banu Sa'ad. Malik bin Awf, a dynamic Hawaazin leader, had accepted Islam. So when Urwah realized that he could no longer remain in a state of denial about Islam, he went to Madinah and embraced the faith before the Prophet. Given his leadership position and popularity among the Banu Thaqif, he was full of confidence that if he invited his people to adopt his new faith, they would. He asked the Prophet for permission to go back as a caller to Islam.

The Prophet said, "Surely they will kill you!"

---

304 Reported by Imams Muslim and At-Tirmidhi from Jaabir bin Abdullaah.

Urwah replied, "O Messenger of God, indeed I am more loved by them than the eldest of their children."

He asked for permission again, and the Prophet replied as before, but upon Urwah's insistence, he relented and said, "If you wish, leave."

Urwah reached Taa'if after five days of arduous journey and entered his house. People disliked that he did not first stop to visit Al-Laat, their idol. When they complained about his behavior, Urwah did not waste time in inviting them to Islam. That upset them, so they beat him up severely and left his house, contemplating what to do with him next. When dawn came, Urwah went to one of the rooms and issued the call for prayer. It is said one of the men from his allies, Wahb bin Jaabir or Aws bin Maalik, shot an arrow at Urwah and struck him, causing him to bleed profusely. When Urwah's own men confronted the shooter, he said, "Do not fight for me. Indeed I have God, and God favors me with it. God drove me to it. I testify that Muhammad is the Messenger of God. He informed me that you would kill me." Then he instructed his men to bury him alongside the Muslim martyrs of Taa'if.

When the news of Urwah's death reached the Prophet, he said, "Urwah is like the hero of (Surah) Ya-Seen, who invited his people to God, and they killed him."[305]

The Banu Thaqif Submit to Islam

After the men of Taa'if had killed Urwah, their fear of the Muslims increased. They were already living in fear because of the frequent raids of Malik bin Awf on their men and property. Now they had earned the ire of the people of Urwah bin Mas'ud. Additionally, while Islam was spreading, the Thaqif's own lives had become restricted. The leaders consulted and

305 Yaasin 36:20–27.

decided to send someone to Madinah to seek guarantees of protection from the Messenger of Allaah. Their man of choice was Abd Yaaleel bin Amr, but he balked at the idea. He feared that if he went to the Messenger and returned as a Muslim, he might face a situation similar to Urwah's. He said he would go only if others also went with him. So they gathered several other men, and this group headed for Madinah.

In Madinah, the group from Thaqif was received hospitably and invited to Islam. Urwah's own nephew, Mugheerah bin Shu'bah, who had long ago become Muslim, hosted them. The delegation learned the tenets of Islam and observed the pious lives of the Companions. As for accepting Islam, they said they would not until some of their conditions were met. This insistence upon conditions was unique to the Banu Thaqif, as all other tribes had entered into Islam unconditionally. Among the conditions was that the Prophet should write a document pledging protection to them, to which the Prophet agreed. Then they asked that the idol of Al-Laat not be destroyed for three years. When the Prophet refused, they reduced it to two years, then one year, and then one month. When the Prophet rejected even the one-month condition, they requested that they not be forced to destroy Al-Laat with their own hands, and to that the Prophet agreed. The Prophet sent Mugheerah and Abu Sufiyan bin Harb to destroy the idol.

Another condition was that the Prophet should exempt them from offering prayers. The Prophet said to them in reply, "There is no good in a religion that is devoid of prayers." So they agreed.

Then they asked that the Banu Thaqif be allowed to continue committing adultery, practicing usury, and drinking wine. This led to an interesting dialogue between them and the Messenger of Allaah.

Abd Yaaleel said, "As for adultery, we mostly remain bachelors or cannot get married, so we must indulge in it."

The Prophet responded, "That is unlawful for you. Allaah has commanded, 'And come not near unto adultery. Verily, it is an abomination and an evil way.'"[306]

Abd Yaaleel said, "What do you say about interest, since our entire property is nothing but interest?"

The Prophet replied, "You have a right to get back the original sum that you lent, for Allaah has ordered, 'O you who believe, fear Allaah and give up what remains due you in interest, if you are believers.'"[307]

Abd Yaaleel said, "As regards wine, it is the juice of our lands and a must for us."

The Prophet replied, "Allaah has forbidden it: 'O you who have believed, indeed, intoxicants, gambling, sacrificing on altars (to other than Allaah), and divining arrows are but defilement from the work of Satan, so avoid it that you may be successful.'"[308]

The Banu Thaqif delegation grudgingly agreed. As they were returning, they asked the Prophet to appoint someone who would teach them the rituals and dos and don'ts of the religion. The Prophet chose Uthmaan bin Abi Alaa. He was the youngest among them, but the Prophet had noticed his keen interest in Islam.

The Prophet's Invitation to Rulers

After the treaty of Hudaybiyah, the Prophet had sent envoys to rulers of Persia, Abyssinia, Bahrain, Egypt, and Rome. As God's Messenger for the entirety of mankind, he needed to invite all of humanity. Inviting the

306 Israa 17:32.

307 Baqarah 2:278.

308 Maa'idah 5:90.

leaders had special significance, for if they accepted Islam, their subjects would follow suit. None but Negus, the ruler of Abyssinia, accepted Islam.

His message to the King of Persia said:

In the Name of Allaah, the Most Beneficent, the Most Merciful

From Muhammad, the Messenger of Allaah, to Khusraw (Chosroe) Parvez, the king of Persia. Peace be upon him who follows true guidance, believes in Allaah and His Messenger, and testifies that there is no god but Allaah alone without associate, and that Muhammad is His slave and Messenger. I invite you to accept the religion of Allaah. I am the Messenger of Allaah sent to all people in order that I may infuse fear of Allaah in every living person, and that the charge may be proven against those who reject the truth. Accept Islam as your religion so that you may live in security; otherwise, you will be responsible for all the sins of the Magians (Zoroastrians).

Abdullaah bin Hudhaafah As-Sahmi was chosen to carry the letter to Khusraw. Abdullaah got his camel ready and bade farewell to his wife and son. He set out alone and traversed mountains and valleys until he reached the land of the Persians. He sought permission to enter into the king's presence, informing the guards of the letter he was carrying. Khusraw Parvez thereupon ordered his audience chamber to be made ready and summoned his prominent aides. When they had assembled, he gave permission for Abdullaah to enter.

Abdullaah entered and saw the Persian potentate dressed in delicate, flowing robes and wearing a great, neatly arranged turban. On Abdullaah were the plain, coarse clothes of the Bedouin. His head was held high, and his feet were firm. The honor of Islam burned fiercely in his breast, and the power of faith pulsated in his heart. As soon as Khusraw Parvez saw him approaching, he signaled to one of his men to take the letter from his hand.

"No," said Abdullaah. "The Prophet has commanded me to hand over this letter to you directly, and I shall not go against a command of the Messenger of God."

Khusraw said, "Let him come near me." Khusraw took the letter from Abdullaah and called an Arab translator to read its contents. He began reading. "In the name of Allaah, the Beneficent, the Merciful. From Muhammad, the Messenger of God, to Khusraw, the ruler of Persia. Peace on him who follows the guidance…"

Khusraw did not wait for the letter to be finished; he became filled with rage. He snatched the letter from the translator's hand, tore it into pieces, and shouted, "Does he dare to write to me like this, he who is my slave?" He was angry that the Prophet's letter had not mentioned him first. He then commanded Abdullaah to be expelled from his assembly.

Abdullaah was taken away, not knowing what would happen to him. But he did not want to wait to find out. He said, "By God, I don't care what happens to me, after the letter of the Prophet has been so badly treated." He managed to get to his camel and rode off.

When Khusraw's anger had subsided, he commanded that Abdullaah be brought before him. But Abdullaah was nowhere to be found. They searched for him all over but to no avail.

Back in Madinah, Abdullaah told the Prophet how Khusraw had torn his letter to pieces, and the Prophet's only reply was, "May God tear up his kingdom."

Meanwhile, Khusraw wrote to Bazaan, his deputy in Yemen, to send two strong men to "that man who has appeared in the Hijaaz" with orders to bring him to Persia. Bazaan dispatched two of his strongest men to the Prophet and gave them a letter for him, in which he was ordered to go with the two men to meet Khusraw without delay. Bazaan also asked the two men to get whatever information about the Prophet they could and to study his message closely.

The men set out, moving very quickly. At Taa'if they met some Quraysh traders and asked them about Muhammad.

"He is in Yathrib (Madinah)," they said, and they went on to Makkah feeling extremely happy. This was good news for them, and they went around telling the other Quraysh, "You will be pleased. Khusraw is out to get Muhammad, and you will be rid of his evil."

The two men meanwhile made straight for Madinah, where they met the Prophet, handed him the letter of Bazaan, and said to him, "The king of kings, Khusraw, has written to our ruler Bazaan to send his men to get you. We have come to take you with us. If you come willingly, Khusraw has said that it will be good for you, and he will spare you any punishment. If you refuse, you will know the power of his punishment. He has power to destroy you and your people."

The Prophet smiled and said to them, "Go back to your mounts today and return tomorrow."

On the following day, they came to the Prophet and said to him, "Are you prepared to go with us to meet Khusraw?"

The Prophet replied, "You shall not meet Khusraw after today. God has killed him, and his son Shirwaih has taken his place."

The two men stared in the face of the Prophet. They were completely dumbfounded. "Do you know what you are saying?" they asked. "Shall we write about this to Bazaan?"

The Prophet answered, "Yes, and say to him that my religion has informed me about what has happened to the Kingdom of Khusraw, and tell him that if he should become Muslim, I would appoint him ruler over what he now controls."

The two men returned to Yemen and told Bazaan what had happened. Bazaan said, "If what Muhammad has said is true, then he is a Prophet. If not, then we shall see what happens to him."

Not long afterward, a letter from Shirwaih came to Bazaan, in which he said, "I killed Khusraw because of his tyranny against our people. He regarded as lawful the killing of leaders, the capturing of their women, and the expropriating of their wealth. When this letter reaches you, take the allegiance of whoever is with you on my behalf." As soon as Bazaan had read Shirwaih's letter, he threw it aside and announced his entry into Islam. The Persians with him in Yemen also became Muslim.[309]

The Letter to Heraclius, and His Stance

In the name of God, the Beneficent, the Merciful

This letter is from Muhammad, the slave of God and His Messenger, to Heraclius, the ruler of the Byzantines. Peace be upon him who follows the right path. I am writing to call you to Islam. If you become a Muslim, you will be safe, and God will double your reward, but if you reject this invitation of Islam, you will bear the sin of having misguided your subjects. Thus do I urge you to heed the following: "O People of the Scriptures! Come to a word common to you and us that we worship none but Allaah and that we associate nothing in worship with Him, and that none of us shall take others as Lords beside Allaah." Then if they turn away, say: "Bear witness that we are Muslims."[310]

309 Abdul Wahid Hamid, *Companions of the Prophet*, Muslim Education and Literary Services, UK, vol. 1.

310 Aal Imraan 3:64.

Unlike Khusraw, Heraclius treated the letter of the Prophet with respect and was hospitable toward the emissary, Dihya Al-Kalbi. The Roman emperor of the time was nearly the same age as the Prophet, and from the early Christian scriptures he had learned that the time for a Prophet had come. Even before the Prophet had sent his letter, an interesting incident pointed to Heraclius's knowledge of his coming.

Abu Sufiyan bin Harb narrated to Abdullaah bin Abbaas that Heraclius had sent for him while he was on a trade journey in Shaam. This was a time when Muslims and the Quraysh were enjoying a period of mutual peace because of the Treaty of Hudaybiyah. So he, along with others, went to Heraclius at Jerusalem.

Heraclius called them into the court, where he had Roman governors around him. Then he called for a translator and asked the Qurayshi traders, "Who among you is the most closely related to this man who claims to be a prophet?"

Abu Sufiyan replied, "I am the nearest relative to him."[311]

Abu Sufiyan narrated the rest of his encounter with Heraclius thus:

Heraclius: "Bring him (Abu Sufiyan) close to me and let his Companions come forward and make them stand behind his back." He then told his translator, "Tell them that I will ask him about this man, so if he lies to me, deny what he says."

Abu Sufiyan: "By Allaah! Had I not been afraid of my Companions' exposing of my lies, I would have lied about him. The first question he asked me was, 'What is his family status among you?' I replied, 'He belongs to a noble family among us.'"

311 Abdu Manaaf was the fourth ancestor of the Prophet and Abu Sufiyan.

Heraclius: "Has anybody among you ever claimed the same (i.e., to be a prophet) before him?"

Abu Sufiyan: "No."

Heraclius: "Was anybody among his ancestors a king?"

Abu Sufiyan: "No."

Heraclius: "Do the nobles or the weak (and poor) follow him?"

Abu Sufiyan: "It is the weak who follow him."

Heraclius: "Are his followers increasing or decreasing?"

Abu Sufiyan: "They are increasing."

Heraclius: "Does anybody among those who embrace his religion become displeased with the religion and renounce it?"

Abu Sufiyan: "No."

Heraclius: "Have you ever accused him of telling lies before his claim?"

Abu Sufiyan: "No."

Heraclius: "Does he break his promises?"

Abu Sufiyan: "No. We are in a truce with him, but we do not know what he will do in it."

Heraclius: "Have you ever had a war with him?"

Abu Sufiyan: "Yes."

Heraclius: "What was the outcome of the battles?"

Abu Sufiyan: "Sometimes he was victorious, and sometimes we."

Heraclius: "What does he order you to do?"

Abu Sufiyan: "He tells us to worship Allaah alone and not to worship anything along with Him, and to renounce all that our ancestors had said. He orders us to pray, to speak the truth, to be chaste, and to keep up the ties with our relatives."

Heraclius (to his translator): "Tell him: 'I asked you about his family and your reply was that he belonged to a very noble family. In fact all the prophets come from noble families among their respective people.

"'I questioned you whether anybody else among you claimed such a thing, and your reply was in the negative. If the answer had been in the affirmative, I would have thought that this man was following the previous man's statement.

"'Then I asked you whether anyone of his ancestors was a king. Your reply was in the negative, and if it had been in the affirmative, I would have thought that this man wanted to take back his ancestral kingdom.

"'I further asked whether he was ever accused of telling lies before his claim of prophethood, and your reply was in the negative. So I wondered how a person who does not tell a lie about others could ever tell a lie about Allaah.

"'I then asked you whether the noble people followed him or the weak. You replied that it was the weak that followed him. And in fact all the prophets have been followed by this very class of people.

"'Then I asked you whether his followers were increasing or decreasing. You replied that they were increasing, and in fact such is the way of true faith, until it is complete in all respects.

"'I further asked you whether there was anybody who, after embracing his religion, became displeased with his religion and discarded his religion. Your reply was in the negative, and in fact this is the sign of the true faith.

"'I asked you whether he had ever betrayed. You replied in the negative, and likewise the Apostles never betray.

"'Then I asked you what he ordered you to do. You replied that he ordered you to worship Allaah and Allaah alone and not to worship anything along with Him and forbade you to worship idols and ordered you to pray, to speak the truth and to be chaste.

"'If what you have said is true, he will very soon occupy this place underneath my feet, and I knew (from the scriptures) that he was going to appear, but I did not expect that he would be from you (your people), and if I knew I could reach him, I would go out of my way to meet him, and if I were with him, I would certainly wash his feet.'"[312]

Abu Sufiyan: "Then I told my Companions: 'The matter of Ibn Abi Kabsha (the Prophet) has become so great that even the king of the Sons of Yellow (i.e., Romans) is afraid of him.' Then I became sure that he (the Prophet) would be the conqueror in the near future until I embraced Islam."[313]

---

312 Bukhari, vol. 1, Hadith #6. Abu Sufiyan appears to have narrated this story after he became a Muslim.

313 [102] Ibn Abi Kabsha was a derogatory term that the pagans used for the Prophet. Among ancient Arabs, a man named Ibn Abi Kabsha had traveled to parts of the world and found a people who believed in astrology and worshipped a star called Shiyara. Upon return he suggested to the Arabs that they leave the idols and worship Shiyara, but they rejected. So when the Prophet told the pagans to stop worshipping idols and to worship Allaah alone, they called him Ibn Abi Kabsha.

Did Heraclius Embrace Islam?

There are two opinions on whether Heraclius accepted Islam. One said Heraclius did become a Muslim, while the other said that, although he believed in the Prophet's message, he refused to embrace Islam because of the fear of losing his throne and, worse, being killed by the Romans. A Hadith of the Prophet said that Heraclius did not accept Islam, which supports the second opinion.

Shihaab Al-Zuhri said that the Roman governor of Jerusalem saw Heraclius in a sad mood one day when he was visiting the city. When asked, Heraclius said that from looking at the stars, he had determined that the king of those who practice circumcision would conquer the lands he was sitting on. He also consulted one of his friends in Rome who had knowledge of these matters. The friend confirmed that the king's conclusion was sound. One of the king's advisors thought that the reference to circumcised people meant the Jews, who were then living under the authority of the Romans. The advisor suggested killing all male Jews so that what the king suspected would not ever happen. However, the king came to know that the Prophet's envoy was also circumcised, and he was an Arab.

So when the Prophet's Companion Dihya brought his message to Heraclius, the latter called his notables to the palace and ordered the doors shut. Then he said, "O Romans! If success is your desire and if you seek right guidance and want your empire to remain, then pledge allegiance to this Prophet." The people were shocked, and they tried to run away but found the doors closed. Heraclius realized their hatred toward Islam, and when he lost hope of their embracing Islam, he ordered that they be brought back in his audience. When they returned, he said, "What I said just now was only to test your faith, and I have seen it."

Another version claims that after his people rejected his suggestion, Heraclius turned to Dihya and said, "What you should do now is visit Patriarch Dagatir. He is of the most senior of the Christian scholars. Call him on to Islam as well." Some say that the Prophet had already sent a letter to Patriarch Dagatir with Dihya.

Dagatir, who was a great scholar, reacted positively to the Prophet's message and said, "I swear by Allaah that your master is the prophet sent by Allaah. We knew his name and his attributes." Dagatir embraced Islam and retreated into his home to seclude himself from people. When the news of Dagatir's conversion broke, the Romans surrounded his house and denounced him. Dagatir, realizing that his end might be near, wrote a letter to the Prophet and said to Dihya, "Take this letter to our master. Convey my greetings to him and inform him that I bear witness that there is no deity save Allaah and that Muhammad is his Messenger. I have believed in him and acknowledged him, and I am his subject. But as you can see, these men are denying this. Relay exactly all of that which you see to our master."

When Dihya returned, he informed the Prophet about Dagatir and Heraclius. Regarding Heraclius the Prophet said, "He will remain on the throne for a while longer. As long as my letter remains with them, so will be his kingdom."

There are several factors that lend support to the second opinion, that Heraclius preferred retaining his kingdom to embracing Islam:

- Within two years of the Prophet's invitation, Heraclius fought the Muslims in the Battle of Mu'tah, during the eighth year of Hijrah (629/630 CE).
- It is possible that Heraclius professed Christianity outwardly but accepted Islam in his heart, but that notion is rejected on the basis of a Hadith collected by Imam Ahmed in his *Musnad*. In response to Heraclius's letter to the Prophet in which he said, "I am a Muslim," the Prophet said, "He has lied; he is still practicing his Christianity."
- The Prophet later led a large expedition to Tabuk against Heraclius. The last army he had ordered to be sent was also against the Romans,

an army that had halted because of the Prophet's illness and would become the first expedition of Caliph Abu Bakr.

The Letter to Maqawqis, the Ruler of Egypt

The Prophet's letter to Maqawqis was very similar to his letter to Heraclius. Maqawqis was said to be a representative of the Byzantine Empire, and like Heraclius, he believed that the time for a new messenger had come. He did not accept the Prophet's invitation to enter Islam, nor did he reject it. He chose to be evasive about the subject but treated the Prophet's letter and his emissary, Haatib bin Abi Baltaa'ah, with great respect. In his *History of the Prophets and Kings*, At-Tabari wrote that when it was time for the emissary to leave, Muqawqis sent him with lavish gifts for the Prophet, including Coptic Christian sisters Maariyah Al-Qibtiyah and Sereen, a female mule named Duldul, a donkey named Ya'foor, one thousand ounces of gold, and twenty fine garments.

The Prophet married Maariyah, who bore him a son, whom he named Ibraahim after his ancestor, Prophet Abraham. His other sons had died in infancy, and the birth of Ibraahim, when the Prophet was around sixty, brought much joy to him and the Muslim community. But this joy did not last very long. Barely eighteen months later, Ibraahim fell seriously ill and died. The Prophet could not do anything against the decree of Allaah.

When sorrow overwhelmed him, the Prophet said, "Indeed, O Ibraahim, we are bereaved by your departure. The eyes shed tears, and the heart is saddened, but we will not say anything except that which pleases our Lord." Then the Prophet put a marker on Ibraahim's grave, saying, "Tombstones do neither good nor ill, but they help appease the living. Anything that man does, God wishes him to do well."[314] Then the Prophet consoled Maariyah, telling her that Ibraahim would have his own nurse in Paradise.

314 Muhammad Ibn-i Sa'ad, Tabaqat, 1:131–144.

Ibraahim's death was followed by a solar eclipse, and some people began to say that the sun had eclipsed to express grief at his death. The Prophet quickly set them right, saying, "The sun and the moon are signs of Allaah. They are not eclipsed for the death or birth of any person. When you witness an eclipse, remember Allaah and turn to Him in prayer."[315]

Tabuk: A Difficult Expedition

The expedition of Tabuk in the Rajab of 9 AH (630/631 CE) was unlike any other the Prophet had undertaken, for a number of reasons. It was the farthest the Muslim army had ever been to fight, about one thousand kilometers from Madinah, near the border with the present-day Jordan. For the first time, the Prophet had disclosed the actual destination from the start. And it was an exceptionally hot summer. Traveling one thousand kilometers on camel and horseback was a grueling endeavor even for the most seasoned traveler. Another reason, although lesser in importance, was that the dates were ripe. It was harvest time in Madinah.

Why did the Prophet want to take on the Romans? There are different reports. The Prophet had received information that the Romans and their Arab allies in Syria were preparing to attack the Muslims. They controlled Southern Syria as well as Jordan in what was then known as *Bilaad Al-Shaam* (the Land of Al-Shaam—Syria, Jordan, Palestine, and Lebanon). The Byzantine Empire (Eastern Roman Empire) was one of the two superpowers of that era; the other was the Persian (Sasanid) Empire. Any threat from the Romans had to be taken very seriously. For expediency and tactical reasons, the Prophet decided to meet the Romans in their own territory rather than in his.

Al-Waaqidi wrote in his book, *Kitab Al-Maghazi*, that a number of sources told him that Nabatean traders who came to Madinah informed the Muslims that the Byzantines were planning to attack their city. Besides

315 Muslim, The Chapter of Prayer, Hadith #1967.

their own forces, the Romans had also gathered the Arab tribes of Lakhm, Judhaam, Ghassaan, and Aamilah to fight the Muslims. The Nabateans also reported that Heraclius had advanced a year's salary to the soldiers because he perceived this to be a long and drawn-out fight, and these forces had already advanced as far as Balqaa.

The Prophet asked for not only manpower but also any and all financial and material help people could provide. The Prophet's clarion call brought forth the spirit of sacrifice among his Companions, with Abu Bakr bringing all that he had at home and Umar half that. When the Prophet asked Abu Bakr if he had left anything for his family, he famously said, "Yes, Allaah and His Messenger." Umar said he had brought half.

Uthmaan, the Prophet's son-in-law, provided three hundred camels loaded with provision and arms, two hundred ounces of gold, and one thousand dinars, which prompted the Prophet to say, "After this day, nothing will harm Uthmaan no matter what he does."

Abdur Rahmaan bin Awf gave two hundred ounces of silver. Even women gave away their prized jewelry to fund the expedition. A massive force of thirty thousand fighting men was prepared.

There was also a special group of people who had nothing to offer except themselves, and Allaah praised them in the Qur'aan for their sincerity. They were seven poor men (later called "Seven Weepers") from the Banu Amr bin Awf or from the Banu Muqarrin who did not have mounts, so they came to the Messenger of Allaah to ask for help. The Prophet told them he did not have riding animals to give them, which caused them to return home, crying at their inability to join the campaign against the Romans.

Allaah revealed a verse to the Prophet to praise and console them: "Nor (is there blame) on those who came to you to be provided with mounts, when you said: 'I can find no mounts for you,' and they turned back, with their eyes overflowing with tears of grief that they could not find anything to spend."[316]

Besides those seven poor men, there were also people like Abdullaah bin Umm Maktoom, the blind Companion, as well as the elderly, who could not go. The Messenger of Allaah told his Companions, "Some people have remained behind you in Madinah; they never spent anything, crossed a valley, or afflicted hardship on an enemy, but they shared the reward with you."

The Prophet had instructed Ali to remain with his family. The hypocrites attacked Ali for staying in Madinah. Their words were so hurtful that Ali could no longer bear them, for he loved the Prophet more than his own life. He immediately put on his armor and rode out to catch up with him, which he did before reaching the first halt, with the intent of seeking his permission to join him. No sooner had he caught up with the Prophet than he told him of the gossip in Madinah.

The Prophet denounced the hypocrites, saying, "They lie. I asked you to remain for the sake of those I had left behind. So return, and represent me in my family and yours. O Ali, are you not content that you should be to me as Aaron was to Moses, except that after me there is no prophet?" Prophet Moses had left Aaron, his brother, with the Israelites when he had gone to Mount Sinai to receive the Ten Commandments.

There was also a group that Allaah condemned for their conniving. They came up with every excuse in their arsenal to stay back in Madinah. One of them tried to discourage the others by saying, "Do not go; it is too hot."

---

316 Tawbah 9:93.

So Allaah exposed him in the Qur'aan:

> *Those who stayed away rejoiced in their staying behind the Messenger of Allaah. They hated to strive and fight with their properties and their lives in the cause of Allaah, and they said: "March not forth in the heat." Say: "The fire of Hell is hotter," if only they could understand!*[317]

Ibn Ubayy, the leader of the hypocrites, pretended to leave Madinah for Tabuk but surreptitiously separated from the Prophet and returned with his supporters. He had done this once earlier, right before the Battle of Uhud.

The Story of Abu Dharr Al-Ghifaari

Whenever the Prophet was informed that someone dropped out from the Tabuk army, he would say, "Let him be, for if there is any good in him, Allaah will join him to you; if not, God has rid you of him." The word came out that Abu Dharr Al-Ghifaari had fallen behind. In reality, the camel of Abu Dharr was walking slowly, so he took off his gear from the mount and put it on his back. While he was walking in this state toward the army, some of the Companions spotted him; the Prophet said he hoped it was Abu Dharr, and for sure it was he. The Apostle said, "God have mercy on Abu Dharr. He walks alone and will die alone and be raised alone."

What the Prophet had said came true. Abu Dharr's real name was Jundub bin Junadah, and his Kunniyah (genitive name) was Abu Dharr. He accepted Islam in the Makkan period and came to Madinah after the Battle of Khandaq. He devoted himself to serving the Messenger of Allaah and led a very austere life. After the death of the Prophet, he left for the Syrian Desert and stayed there during the caliphates of Abu Bakr and Umar. He returned during Uthmaan's caliphate, but because of his criticism of the comfortable lifestyle of some people and their countercriticism of him, the caliph sent him to live in Rabadha outside of Madinah.

317 Tawbah 9:81.

When death approached Abu Dharr, only his wife and servant were around him. He instructed them that when he died they should shroud his body, leave it by the roadside, and ask the first caravan to help bury him. Companion Abdullaah bin Mas'ud and his group were the first ones to pass by. Abu Dharr's servant said, "This is Abu Dharr, the Prophet's Companion. Help us bury him."

Ibn Mas'ud began to cry profusely, saying, "The Prophet was right. You walked alone (in Tabuk), and you died alone, and you will be raised alone."

The Ruins of Thamood

During the march across the desert, the army took the route that would pass by the remnant of homes that once belonged to the people of Thamood. The fate of the people of Thamood was well known to the Muslims, as Allaah had mentioned their disobedience and the resulting punishment in the Qur'aan. The Prophet told the Companions not to use the water from the wells of Thamood but to pass through the area quickly, as the wrath of Allaah had descended upon it.

The Miraculous Spring at Tabuk

At a halt several miles outside Tabuk, the Prophet told his army, "Allaah willing, tomorrow you will reach the spring of Tabuk. You will not reach it until the sun is hot. Whosoever reaches it must not touch its water until I arrive." However, two of the first men to reach the spring had not heard the Prophet's order. They drank from it and used the water to make dough.

Later in the day, when the rest of the army reached the spring, the spring had become reduced to a trickle. The Prophet ordered that the dough be fed to the camels. Then he instructed that the remaining water should be scooped up in handfuls and poured into a waterskin. After sufficient water had been collected, the Prophet washed his hands and face with it, then poured it over the rock that covered the mouth of the spring, passing his hands over it while supplicating to Allaah. With a thunderous sound, the water gushed forth, and the entire army satisfied its needs.

Mu'aadh bin Jabal happened to be standing by the Prophet as the water gushed forth, and the Prophet turned to him, saying, "O Mu'aadh, perhaps you will live to see this place become an oasis with many gardens." And so it was that in the years to follow, the prophecy was fulfilled.

The War That Was Not

Finally, when the Muslim army arrived in Tabuk and camped out, there was no sign of the enemy. The Prophet stayed in Tabuk for twenty days and concluded that the rumors of the impending Roman attack were false. It turned out that Heraclius had actually stayed in Hims. It is possible that Heraclius did not want to fight a man who, according to some reports, he believed to be the Messenger of Allaah. It is one thing for him to have not embraced Islam because of political considerations, but quite another to fight in defiance of his belief, as the latter would have led to his ruin.

Some might ask, What was gained from this difficult expedition? The answer is, moral and psychological victory over both the Romans and the Arab tribes who were allied with them. Throughout history, psychological warfare has been used as an instrument of war. With the expedition, the Muslims sent a clear message that they had the courage and conviction to stand up to a superpower and bring war to their doorsteps. It showed that the Muslims were a power to be reckoned with.

As the Muslim army was heading back, the Prophet sent Khaalid bin Waleed with a cavalry of four hundred to Dumaat Al-Jandal, which lay to the northeast of Tabuk and was just five halts from Damascus. Dumaat Al-Jandal was an important location on the road between Iraq and Madinah as well as on the road to Syria. Khaalid's mission was to capture Ukaydir bin Abdul-Maalik, king of Kindah.

When Khaalid wondered how he would be able to find Ukaydir, the Prophet told him, "You will find him hunting cows, and you will take him." Lo, Khaalid found Ukaydir just as the Prophet had described, and captured him. A small battle ensued, in which Khaalid killed Ukaydir's brother Hassan. Khaalid convinced Ukyadir to surrender, give up some of his wealth, and go to the Prophet, who would decide what to do with him.

The Prophet signed a treaty with Ukaydir on the condition that he would pay *jizyah*, a form of tax on non-Muslims in return for protection and personal freedom. The kingdom of Kindah became Islamic territory. Because of the Roman influence, Kindah and the tribes allied with the Byzantines lived a pompous life. So when Ukaydir's brother Hassan was killed and his fine dress came into the hands of the Muslims, the Companions started to touch it admiringly. When the Prophet saw this, he said, "Does this amaze you? By Him who holds my soul in His Hand, the handkerchief of Sa'ad (bin Mu'aadh) in Paradise is better than this."

The Story of Ka'ab bin Maalik and Two Others

In contrast to the hypocrites, there were three sincere Muslims who could not join the Tabuk expedition because of their procrastination. They were Ka'ab bin Maalik, Muraarah bin Al-Rabi' and Hilaal bin Umayyah. Their Islam was beyond any doubt, but they fell into a huge trial due to their poor judgment. A fourth person was Abdullaah bin Khaythamah, but he eventually joined the Prophet in Tabuk after ten days and was not denounced for the delay.

Ka'ab himself told this story, and his son Abdullaah narrated it.[318]

318 Bukhari, vol. 5, book 59, Hadith #702.

"I did not remain behind Allaah's Apostle in any *ghazwah* that he fought except the ghazwah of Tabuk, and I failed to take part in the *ghazwah* of Badr, but Allaah did not admonish anyone who had not participated in it, for in fact, Allaah's Apostle had gone out in search of the caravan of the Quraysh till Allaah made them (i.e., the Muslims) and their enemy meet without any appointment. I witnessed the night of Al-Aqabah (pledge) with Allaah's Apostle when we pledged for Islam, and I would not exchange it for the Badr battle although the Badr battle is more popular among the people than it (i.e., Al-Aqabah pledge). As for my situation (at the time of the Tabuk expedition), I had never been stronger or wealthier than I was when I remained behind the Prophet in that *ghazwah.*

"By Allaah, never had I two she-camels before, but I had them at the time of this *ghazwah.* Whenever Allaah's Apostle wanted to make a *ghazwah,* he used to hide his intention by apparently referring to different *ghazwah* till it was the time of that *ghazwah* (of Tabuk), which Allaah's Apostle fought in severe heat, facing a long journey, desert, and the great number of enemy. So the Prophet announced to the Muslims clearly (their destination) so that they might prepare for their *ghazwah.* So he informed them clearly of the destination he was going to. Allaah's Apostle was accompanied by a large number of Muslims. Any man who intended to be absent would think that the matter would remain hidden unless Allaah revealed it through Divine Revelation.

"So Allaah's Apostle fought that *ghazwah* at the time when the fruits had ripened and the shade looked pleasant. Allaah's Apostle and his Companions prepared for the battle, and I started to go out in order to get myself ready along with them, but I returned without doing anything. I would say to myself, 'I can do that.' So I kept on delaying it every now and then till the people got ready and Allaah's Apostle and the Muslims along with him departed, and I had not prepared anything for my departure, and I said, 'I will prepare myself (for departure) one or two days after him, and then join them.' In the morning following their departure,

I went out to get myself ready but returned having done nothing. Then again in the next morning, I went out to get ready but returned without doing anything.

"Such was the case with me till they hurried away and I missed the battle. Even then I intended to depart to overtake them. I wish I had done so! But it was not in my luck. So, after the departure of Allaah's Apostle, whenever I went out and walked among the people (left in Madinah), it grieved me that I could see none around me but one accused of hypocrisy or one of those weak men whom Allaah had excused.

"Allaah's Apostle did not remember me till he reached Tabuk. So while he was sitting among the people in Tabuk, he said, 'What did Ka'ab do?' A man from the Banu Salamah said, 'O Allaah's Apostle! He has been stopped by his two *burdas* (i.e., garments), and he's looking at his own flanks with pride.' Then Mu'aadh bin Jabal said, 'What a bad thing you have said! By Allaah! O Allaah's Apostle! We know nothing about him but good.' Allaah's Apostle kept silent.

"When I heard that he (the Prophet) was on his way back to Madinah, I became immersed in my concern and began to think of false excuses, saying to myself, 'How can I avoid his anger tomorrow?' And I took the advice of wise members of my family in this matter. When it was said that Allaah's Apostle had come near, all the evil false excuses left my mind, and I knew well that I could never come out of this problem by forging a false statement. Then I decided firmly to speak the truth.

"So Allaah's Apostle arrived in the morning, and whenever he returned from a journey, he used to visit the mosque first and offer two units of prayer therein and then sit with the people. So when he had done all that, those who had failed to join the battle (of Tabuk) came and started offering (false) excuses and taking oaths before him. They were somewhere around eighty men. Allaah's Apostle accepted the excuses they had expressed, took their pledge of allegiance, asked for Allaah's forgiveness for them, and left the secrets of their hearts for Allaah to judge.

"Then I came to him, and when I greeted him, he smiled a smile of an angry person and then said, 'Come over.' So I came walking till I sat before him. He said to me, 'What stopped you from joining us. Had you not purchased an animal to carry you?' I answered, 'Yes, O Allaah's Apostle! But by Allaah, if I were sitting before any person from among the people of the world other than you, I would have avoided his anger with an excuse.'

"'By Allaah, I have been bestowed with the power of speaking fluently and eloquently, but by Allaah, I knew well that if today I told you a lie to seek your favor, Allaah would surely make you angry with me in the near future, but if I tell you the truth, though you will get angry because of it, I hope for Allaah's forgiveness. Really, by Allaah, there was no excuse for me. By Allaah, I had never been stronger or wealthier than I was when I remained behind you.'

"Then Allaah's Apostle said, 'As regards this man, he has surely told the truth. So get up till Allaah decides your case.' I got up, and many men of the Banu Salamah followed me and said to me, 'By Allaah, we never witnessed you doing any sin before this. Surely, you failed to offer excuses to Allaah's Apostle as the others who did not join him have offered. The prayer of Allaah's Apostle to Allaah to forgive you would have been sufficient for you.' By Allaah, they continued blaming me so much that I intended to return (to the Prophet) and accuse myself of having told a lie, but I said to them, 'Is there anybody else who has met the same fate as I have?' They replied, 'Yes, there are two men who have said the same thing as you have, and to both of them was given the same order as given to you.' I said, 'Who are they?' They replied, 'Muraarah bin Al-Rabi' and Hilaal bin Umayyah,' two pious men who had attended the *Ghazwah* of Badr, and in whom there was an example for me. So I did not change my mind when they mentioned them to me.

"Allaah's Apostle forbade all the Muslims to talk to us, the three aforesaid persons out of all those who had remained behind in that *ghazwah*. So we kept away from the people, and they changed their attitude toward us till the very land (where I lived) appeared strange to me as if I did not know it.

"We remained in that condition for fifty nights. As regards my two fellows, they remained in their houses and kept on weeping, but I was the youngest of them and the firmest of them, so I used to go out and witness the prayers along with the Muslims and roam about in the markets, but none would talk to me, and I would come to Allaah's Apostle and greet him while he was sitting in his gathering after the prayer, and I would wonder whether the Prophet did move his lips in return to my greetings or not. Then I would offer my prayer near to him and look at him stealthily. When I was busy with my prayer, he would turn his face toward me, but when I turned my face to him, he would turn his face away from me.

"When this harsh attitude of the people lasted long, I walked till I scaled the wall of the garden of Abu Qataadah, who was my cousin and dearest person to me, and I offered my greetings to him. By Allaah, he did not return my greetings. I said, 'O Abu Qataadah! I beseech you by Allaah! Do you know that I love Allaah and His Apostle?' He kept quiet. I asked him again, beseeching him by Allaah, but he remained silent. Then I asked him again in the Name of Allaah. He said, 'Allaah and His Apostle know it better.' Thereupon my eyes flowed with tears, and I turned and jumped over the wall.

"While I was walking in the marketplace of Madinah, suddenly I saw a Nabatean (i.e., a Christian farmer) from the Nabateans of Al-Shaam who came to sell his grains in Madinah, saying, 'Who will lead me to Ka'ab bin Maalik?' The people began to point (me) out for him till he came to me and handed me a letter from the king of Ghassaan, in which the following was written: 'To proceed, I have been informed that your friend (i.e., the Prophet) has treated you harshly. Anyhow, Allaah does not let you live at a place where you feel inferior and your right is lost. So join us, and we will console you.'

"When I read it, I said to myself, 'This is also a sort of a test.' Then I took the letter to the oven and made a fire therein by burning it.

"When forty out of the fifty nights had elapsed, behold! There came to me the messenger of Allaah's Apostle and said, 'Allaah's Apostle orders you to keep away from your wife.' I said, 'Should I divorce her?' He said, 'No, only keep away from her and do not cohabit with her.' The Prophet sent the same message to my two fellows. Then I said to my wife. 'Go to your parents and remain with them till Allaah gives His verdict in this matter.'

"The wife of Hilaal bin Umayyah came to the Apostle and said, 'O Allaah's Apostle! Hilaal bin Umayyah is a helpless old man who has no servant to attend to him. Do you dislike that I should serve him?' He said, 'No (you can serve him), but he should not come near you.' She said, 'By Allaah, he has no desire for anything. By Allaah, he has never ceased weeping till his case began till this day of his.'

"On that, some of my family members said to me, 'Will you also ask Allaah's Apostle to permit your wife (to serve you) as he has permitted the wife of Hilaal bin Umayyah to serve him?' I said, 'By Allaah, I will not ask the permission of Allaah's Apostle regarding her, for I do not know what Allaah's Apostle would say if I asked him to permit her (to serve me) while I am a young man.'

"Then I remained in that state for ten more nights after that, till the period of fifty nights was completed starting from the time when Allaah's Apostle prohibited the people from talking to us. When I had offered the Fajr prayer on the fiftieth morning on the roof of one of our houses, and while I was sitting in the condition that Allaah described (in the Qur'aan), my very soul seemed straitened to me, and even the earth seemed narrow to me for all its spaciousness; there I heard the voice of one who had ascended the mountain of Sala' calling with his loudest voice, 'O Ka'ab bin Maalik! Be happy.' I fell down in prostration before Allaah, realizing that relief had come. Allaah's Apostle had announced the acceptance of our repentance by Allaah when he had offered the Fajr prayer. The people then went out to congratulate us. Some bringers of good tidings went out to my two fellows, and a horseman came to me in haste, and a man of the Banu Aslam came running and ascended the mountain, and his voice was swifter than the horse. When he whose voice I had heard came to me conveying the glad tidings, I took off my garments and dressed him with them; and by Allaah, I owned no other garments than them on that day. Then I borrowed two garments and wore them and went to Allaah's Apostle.

"The people started receiving me in batches, congratulating me, saying, 'We congratulate you on Allaah's acceptance of your repentance.' When I entered the mosque, I saw Allaah's Apostle sitting with the people around him. Talhah bin Ubaydullaah swiftly came to me, shook hands with me, and congratulated me. By Allaah, none of the Muhaajireen (Emigrants) got up for me except him, and I will never forget this for Talhah.

"When I greeted Allaah's Apostle, his face was bright with joy. He said, 'Be happy with the best day that you have got ever since your mother delivered you.' I said to the Prophet, 'Is this forgiveness from you or from Allaah?' He said, 'No, it is from Allaah.' Whenever Allaah's Apostle became happy, his face would shine as if it were a piece of moon, and we all knew that characteristic of him.

"When I sat before him, I said, 'O Allaah's Apostle! Because of the acceptance of my repentance, I will give up all my wealth as alms for the sake of Allaah and His Apostle.' Allaah's Apostle said, 'Keep some of your wealth, as it will be better for you.' I said, 'So I will keep my share from Khayber with me,' and added, 'O Allaah's Apostle! Allaah has saved me for telling the truth; so it is a part of my repentance not to tell but the truth as long as I am alive.'

"By Allaah, I do not know anyone of the Muslims whom Allaah has helped for telling the truth more than me. Since I have mentioned that truth to Allaah's Apostle till today, I have never intended to tell a lie. I hope that Allaah will also save me (from telling lies) the rest of my life. So Allaah revealed to His Apostle:

> *"Indeed, Allaah has forgiven the Prophet, the Muhajirin and the Ansaar who followed him in the time of distress (Tabuk expedition), after the hearts of a party of them had nearly deviated (from the right path), but He accepted their repentance. Certainly, He is unto them full of kindness, Most Merciful. And (Allaah has forgiven) the three who stayed behind, until for them the earth, vast as it is, was straitened and their souls were straitened to them, and they perceived that there is no fleeing from Allaah, and no refuge but with Him. Then, He forgave them that they might beg for His pardon. Verily, Allaah is the One Who forgives and accepts repentance, the Most Merciful. O you who believe! Have consciousness of Allaah, and be with those who are true (in words and deeds).*[319]

"By Allaah, Allaah has never bestowed upon me, apart from His guiding me to Islam, a greater blessing than the fact that I did not tell a lie to Allaah's Apostle that would have caused me to perish as those who have told a lie perished, for Allaah described those who told lies with the worst description He ever attributed to anybody else."

A Celebrated Poem

When the Prophet returned from Tabuk, the people of Ansaar, particularly their children, welcomed him with a beautiful song to show their love, longing, and appreciation for him. The words of this poem, popularly known as *Tala'al Badru Alayna*, continue to captivate Muslims more than 1,400 years later:

319 Tawbah 9:117–119.

Tala'al-badru alaynaa
The full moon rose over us

Min thaniyyaatil-wadaa
From the Valley of Wadaa

wajabath-shukru alaynaa
And it is incumbent upon us to show gratitude

Maa da'aa lil-laahi daa
For as long as anyone in existence calls out to God

Ayyuhal mab'uthu feenaa
O our Messenger (Emissary) amongst us

Ji'ta bil amril muṭaa
Who comes with the exhortations (commandments) to be heeded

Ji'ta sharraftal madinah
You have brought nobility to this city

Marḥaban ya khayra daa
Welcome you who calls us to a good way

Islam the Irresistible

The Prophet had prevailed over Makkah and returned from the expedition of Tabuk with a psychological victory. Makkah, the place of the Muslim *Qiblah*, was finally in the hands of the Muslims. The Qurayshi nobles, who had long tried to crush Islam, had entered the faith one after another. They included sons and daughters of erstwhile enemies who had died in Badr and Uhud. The religion of Allaah was reaching beyond the Arabian Peninsula.

Abu Bakr Leads the First Hajj

The Messenger of Allaah was far busier now. His city, Al-Madinah,[320] was humming with activity. A number of watershed events had taken place that had put the city not just on the map of Arabia but on the world map. The Conquest of Makkah and the expeditions of Hunayn, Taa'if, and Tabuk (not to mention many other smaller expeditions) had on the one hand set off alarm bells in Persia and Rome and on the other hand brought the Arab tribes to Madinah to embrace Islam. People were coming into Islam either because they were convinced of its truth or because they could no longer oppose it. There was a steady stream of tribal representatives coming to Madinah, and many more were yet to come.

And then it was Hajj time once again. The Prophet himself was unable to go to Makkah because of urgent state matters. So he ordered Abu Bakr to lead the Hajj delegation in the ninth year of Hijrah (630/631 CE). This was the first time that the administration of Hajj was fully in the hands of the Muslims. Abu Bakr began preparations, as did three hundred other Muslims.

When Abu Bakr reached Dhul Hulayfah, he heard the sound of Al-Qaswa, the Prophet's she-camel, with whom he was familiar. He looked around, wondering if the Prophet himself had decided to come. Instead he saw Ali, who had ridden Al-Qaswa from Madinah. In the past, the Prophet had lent his personal things—a sword, a turban, or a riding animal—to tell people that he had sent the bearer in an official capacity. Abu Bakr asked, "Have you come as a commander or a messenger?"

Ali replied, "Indeed as a messenger." And he informed Abu Bakr that his mission was to recite a number of verses of Surah Tawbah (Repentance) that had come down concerning the polytheists after he

320 *Madinah* in Arabic means a city, but when used with article *Al*, it becomes Al-Madinah, the city, referring to the city of the Prophet.

had left Madinah. Some of the commandments that were revealed in this surah follow:

- The polytheists had four months to move about in the land, repent, or face retribution.
- Those polytheists who had a special treaty with the Prophet and had adhered to it would be accorded all its provisions until it expired.
- This year they would be allowed to perform Hajj, but they would not be allowed to circumambulate the Ka'bah naked or clap or whistle.
- After this year no polytheist would be allowed to perform Hajj.
- A polytheist who asked for protection and safe exit would be taken to a place of safety after Islam had been explained to them.

Reflections: A number of the verses of Surah Tawbah appear to be very harsh toward the idolaters. Some non-Muslims, especially those in the West, have used these verses in support of their argument that the Qur'aan commands Muslims to kill all nonbelievers wherever they can find them. What the non-Muslim commentators have concealed is the context in which Surah Tawbah was revealed. The verses were clearly aimed at the polytheists of that time who had killed, persecuted, and expelled Muslims and had continued to plot and conspire against them. These polytheists had persistently refused to allow the Muslims to live in peace and worship One God freely. These verses were not directed at the People of the Book (Jews and Christians) or any other people.

After twenty-two years of extreme hostility and threats against the Muslims, Allaah was telling the Muslims that they could retaliate even if that meant acting preemptively. Fairness demands that that permission should be seen through the lens of history. Today, some nations have made it part of their strategic doctrine to act preemptively against a perceived threat to their national security, and they have resolved that they will not allow other nations to achieve military and economic parity with them because doing so would endanger their supremacy. We have witnessed that, in the name of preemption, some nations have invaded other countries or fired drone missiles at people who were simply suspected of engaging in hostility against them. In many cases, the victims' identities were not known and their guilt not established. Some of those strikes end up killing completely innocent people, such as those who had gathered to celebrate a wedding or some other innocuous event.

In the case of the polytheists, the Qur'aan had issued them with a cease-and-desist order and warned of the consequences if they failed to comply. One of the verses instructed the Muslims to take the polytheists to a place of safety, if they requested. It was very generous compared to what the polytheists had done to the Muslim emigrants.

Accordingly, on the Day of Nahr (the tenth of Dhul-Hijjah), Abu Bakr sent Abu Hurayrah along with other announcers to Mina to tell people that no pagan would be allowed to perform Hajj after that year and that no naked person could perform the Tawaaf around the Ka'bah. Ali, in keeping with the orders of Allaah's Messenger, read out the recently revealed verses of Surah Tawbah (chapter 9) to the people.

The Year of Delegations

After the Conquest of Makkah, it had become clear to the tribes that there was no way they could ignore Islam. Some had seen the godly lifestyles of Muslims, which had begun to impress them, while others were awed by Islam's rising military power. They had seen that the Muslims were knocking at the borders of the Byzantine Empire and were not afraid to take on a superpower.

Delegations started to pour into Madinah to explore and enter Islam. The Prophet had ordered tents erected in the courtyard of the mosque for visitors to hear the Qur'aan, observe the prayers, and ask him any questions they might have.

According to one estimate, about seventy delegations and a number of individuals came to Madinah, most in 9 AH (630/631 CE) but some in previous years. Many simply joined the ranks of the believers, while a few brought unique perspectives that are worth mentioning. Some wanted the Prophet's forgiveness for offenses they had committed against Islam. In one case, the leader of a group—such as Farwah Bani Amr Al-Judhami, who was an Arab leader in the Byzantine army—sent an emissary to the Prophet to pledge allegiance. In the Battle of Mu'tah, he had seen the bravery and discipline of a small Muslim army that was pitted against a force almost seven times larger. Farwah came away from this experience thinking that it must be their religion that had made them fearless. He accepted Islam and sent an emissary to let the Prophet know of his conversion. When the Byzantines found out, they tried to force him to recant, and when unsuccessful, they crucified him. Farwah chose death over apostasy and is considered to be a martyr.

Among the individual visitors was Ka'ab bin Zuhayr, the renowned poet of Makkah who had long attacked Islam and the Prophet through his satirical poems. It was the Prophet's tradition to overlook insults to himself as a man, but he was stern in dealing with blasphemy against Allaah or with the lampooning of the institution of prophethood. Because of the nature of Ka'ab's offense, the Prophet had ordered that if found, he should be killed. Ka'ab's brother, Bujayr, was a Muslim, and he pressed Ka'ab to go to the Prophet, saying the Prophet forgave anyone who repented and embraced Islam. Ka'ab agreed.

Arriving in Madinah, Ka'ab stayed with a man from Juhaynah as a guest. After the dawn prayer, Ka'ab went to the Prophet and put his hand in his. The Messenger of Allaah had never seen Ka'ab before. Ka'ab said, "O Messenger of Allaah! Ka'ab bin Zuhayr has come to you as a repentant Muslim. Will he be secure and forgiven if I bring him?"

The Messenger of Allaah said, "Yes."

Ka'ab quickly said, "I am Ka'ab bin Zuhayr."

Hearing that, one of the Helpers rose to his feet and asked the Messenger's permission to cut Ka'ab's neck. The Prophet said, "Leave him alone! He has become a Muslim." Ka'ab became very happy and quickly came up with a poem in which he apologized for his wrongs and praised the Prophet and the Emigrants. The Prophet appreciated his poem but suggested that Ka'ab would do well to praise the Helpers also, which he did. Some say that the Prophet was so pleased with Ka'ab's poem that he gave him his cloak.

Among the delegations was one from the king of Himyaar (Yemen) to convey the ruler's allegiance to Islam. In the meantime, Ali had sent the good news from Yemen that the people there had accepted Islam. The Prophet had sent Khaalid bin Waleed to invite the Hamdaan, and he had been inviting them to Islam for six months, but they had refused. It was not until the Prophet sent Ali that the Hamdaan finally submitted. When the Prophet received Ali's message, he fell into prostration and supplicated, "Peace be upon Hamdaan. Peace be upon Hamdaan."

Some delegations were coming with their unique complaints and requests and asking the Prophet to pray to Allaah for them, knowing the Prophet's prayer would be accepted.

The delegation from Fazaarah professed Islam, but they complained about the drought in their region. The Messenger of Allaah ascended the pulpit, lifted his hands up, and implored Allaah to send down rain in a way that would benefit the Banu Fazaarah, not inundate them. The Prophet prayed, "O Allaah, let the rain fall down and water their country and animals, and spread Your mercy and bring back to life the dead land. O Allaah, send rain that is saving, comforting, useful, and not harmful. O Allaah, let it be the rain of mercy and not the rain of wrath."

The Christians of Najraan Come to the Prophet

In the year 9 AH (630/631 CE), the Prophet had sent an envoy to Abdul Haaris bin Alqamah, the grand bishop of Najraan and an official representative of the Roman Church in the Hijaaz. The message was similar to several he had sent to rulers, in which he had invited them to Islam and promised safety and prosperity if they did. Since he had received no response, the next year he sent Mugheerah bin Shu'bah to explain Islam's teaching. After discussing Islam with Mugheerah, the Christians of Najraan decided to send a delegation to the Messenger of Allaah to ask questions firsthand.

Muhammad bin Isshaaq bin Yasaar reported in his *Seerah* book that the Christians of Najraan, a place in or near Yemen, sent a sixty-three-man delegation. The large size of this delegation attested to the importance they ascribed to this matter. It included fourteen high-ranking priests. Three of these men were chiefs of this delegation: Al-Aaqib, their leader to whom they referred for advice and decision; As-Sayyid, their scholar and leader in journeys and social gatherings; and Abu Haarithah bin Alqamah, their patriarch, priest, and religious leader. Abu Haarithah was an Arab man from the family of Bakr bin Waa'il, but when he embraced Christianity, the Romans and their kings built churches to honor him.

The Prophet was very hospitable toward the Christian delegation from Najraan, a cluster of seventy-three villages on the outskirts of Yemen. The Qur'aan has mentioned it by its ancient name, Ukhdood. Today, Najraan is a city in the southwestern part of Saudi Arabia. They were well established in their land, with a strong military. A number of historians have mentioned that the Prophet allowed them to pray as they wished, and they did so facing the east.

The Prophet invited the Christian delegation to believe in the Oneness of God, and they replied that they already believed that God was One. The Prophet told them that some of their beliefs, like believing God has a son or is part of a Trinity, negated their belief in One God. They said that Jesus was the Son of God because he was created without a father. In response, the Prophet recited to them a verse from Surah Aal Imraan: "Verily, the likeness of Eesa before Allaah is the likeness of Adam. He created him from dust, then said to him: 'Be!' And he was."[321]

The Christian delegation argued that Jesus was God because he brought the dead to life and cured the leper and the blind. The Prophet told them that Jesus did all of that by Allaah's permission and not of his own power, but they remained unconvinced. The Prophet gave them another day to think. The next day, they still refused to accept Islam, so Allaah commanded the Prophet to challenge them to invoke Allaah's curse on the liar. The Prophet recited to them the verses that Gabriel had brought to him:

> *Then whoever disputes with you (O Muhammad) concerning him (Jesus) after the knowledge has come to you, say: "Come, let us call our sons and your sons, our women and your women, ourselves and yourselves, then pray and invoke Allaah's curse upon the liars."*[322]

When the day of the swearing (*mubaahalah*) came, the Prophet came with Ali, Faatimah, Hasan, and Hussain. The Christian delegation was nervous to see that the Prophet Muhammad had brought his only surviving daughter, her husband, and her two children. They said to each other that the Prophet had certainty about his position; otherwise, he would never invoke God's curse on his own family. The Christian delegation began to feel hesitant. They consulted with Al-Aaqib, who said to them, "By Allaah, O Christians! You know that Muhammad is a Messenger and that he brought you the final word regarding Jesus. You also know that no prophet conducted *mubaahalah* with any people when the old among them remained safe and the young people grew up. Indeed, it will be the end of you if you do it. If you have already decided that you will remain

321 Aal Imraan 3:59.

322 Aal Imraan 3:61.

in your religion and your creed regarding Jesus, then sign a treaty with Muhammad and go back to your land."

The delegation then came to the Prophet and said, "O Abul Qaasim! We have decided not to do *mubaahalah* with you and that you remain in your religion, while we remain in our religion. However, send with us a man from your Companions, a really trustworthy man whom you are pleased with, to judge between us concerning financial matters."

Many a Companion eagerly waited to see whom the Prophet would choose. He called Abu Ubaydah bin Al-Jarraah and told the Christian delegation, "This is the trustee of this Ummah." They accepted Islamic rule without a fight and agreed to pay *jizyah*.[323]

Subsequently, the Prophet had a detailed contract written between him and the people of Najraan, spelling out their rights and duties and the amount of *jizyah* they would need to pay.

Reflections: *Jizyah* has been the subject of intense debate among the non-Muslim scholars, some calling it humiliating and exploitative. If we look at the rationale behind *jizyah*, it seems more than fair. The non-Muslim subjects received all the state benefits, protection, and exemption from military service for a small payment, while Muslims pay a mandatory 2.5 percent and share the burden of defending the state with their own lives. There were many categories among non-Muslims who were exempted from paying the *jizyah*, such as women, children, elders, those with physical and mental disabilities, the ill, monks, hermits, slaves, those who could not pay, non-Muslim foreigners who only temporarily resided in Muslim lands, and non-Muslims who chose to join the military service. This is not practiced in Muslim lands today.

323 The information about the delegation of Najraan is compiled from Tafsir Ibn Kathir, Bukhari, and Muhammad ibn Isshaaq.

The Banu Hanifah and Portents of Trouble

The Banu Hanifah was a subtribe of the Banu Bakr and no stranger to the Prophet. It was one of the tribes whom the Prophet had asked for protection against the Quraysh in his Makkah days before migration. The Banu Hanifah had rejected his request with utmost rudeness. Then after Hudaybiyah, the Banu Bakr, the parent tribe, had joined the Quraysh and attacked the men of Khuza'ah who were allied with the Prophet inside the Sacred Mosque. That violation of the treaty had paved the way for the Conquest of Makkah. In the sixth year of Hijrah, the Muslims had by chance captured Thumaamah bin Uthal Al-Hanafi, the leader of the Banu Bakr, who had accepted Islam after his release from captivity. However, many of his tribesmen did not follow him in Islam.

When they went to Madinah in 9 AH (630/631 CE), the Banu Hanifah brought a delegation of seventeen people, including Musaylimah bin Habib, who caused major turmoil and bloodshed among the Muslims some years later. The delegation left Musaylimah with the riding animals while the rest went to see the Prophet. They embraced Islam at the Prophet's invitation and were given generous gifts. Before leaving, they remembered that Musaylimah was taking care of the animals and did not get a gift, so they said to the Prophet, "We left one of our comrades in the camp to look after our mounts."

The Prophet said, "He is not the least among you, that he should stay behind to guard the property of his comrades." When Musaylimah heard that, he misused the Prophet's words to claim that the latter praised him and recognized his high status.

Musaylimah, whom the Prophet called the arch-liar, later embraced Islam, only to turn apostate and claim prophethood. It is reported that Musaylimah was a magician and that through magic he deceived many into thinking that he had miraculous powers. Some started to follow him and his concocted religion, which had some elements of Islam mixed with Musaylimah's own fabrications.

Musaylimah claimed co-prophethood and sent a message to the Prophet Muhammad that said, "From Musaylimah, the Messenger of God, to Muhammad, the Messenger of God. Salutations to you. I have been given a share with you in this matter. Half the earth belongs to us and half to the Quraysh. But the Quraysh are a transgressing people."

The Prophet responded, "From Muhammad, the Messenger of God, to Musaylimah, the arch-liar. Peace be upon him who follows (God's) guidance. Surely the earth belongs to God, who bequeaths it to whom He will among His servants. The ultimate good end is for the God-fearing."[324]

This was exactly what Allaah had revealed to his Prophet in the Qur'aan: "Verily, the earth is Allaah's. He gives it as a heritage to whom He wills of His servants; and the (blessed) end is for the righteous."[325]

Companion Abu Sa'eed Al-Khudri said, "I heard the Apostle of Allaah as he was addressing the people from his pulpit, saying, 'I saw the night of *Al-Qadr* (decree), and then I was made to forget it; and I saw on my arms two bracelets of gold that I disliked, so I blew on them, and they flew away. I interpreted them to mean these two liars, the man from Al-Yamamah and the man from Al-Yaman (Yemen).'"

The Prophet also said, "The hour will not come until thirty imposters come forth, each claiming to be a prophet." Musaylimah had married a woman from the Banu Tamim named Sajah bint Al-Haarith, who also claimed to be a prophetess.

324 History of Tabari; also, Safiur Rahman Mubarakpuri, The Sealed Nectar.

325 Aa'raaf 7:128.

Two other imposters had claimed prophethood soon after the death of the Prophet: Tulayhah, the chief of the Banu Asad, and Aswad bin Ka'ab of Yemen. The Yemenite had a brief success and rapidly gained control over a wide area, but his pride soon turned many of his followers against him. He was assassinated shortly thereafter. Tulayhah was defeated by Khaalid bin Waleed, after which he renounced all claims to prophethood. As for Musaylimah, he was killed in the Battle of Yamamah, which was led by Khaalid during the caliphate of Abu Bakr. His death came from a javelin thrown by Wahshi, who was now a Muslim, and from a sword blow by Abdullaah, the son of Nusaybah.

Another Plan to Assassinate the Prophet

Among the delegations that came was one from the Banu Amr bin Sa'saa that included Aamir bin Tufayl and his half brother Arbad bin Qays. Some years earlier, Aamir had orchestrated the killing of Muslim missionaries at the Wells of Ma'unah. He was still unrepentant, and his motive for coming to Madinah was to assassinate the Prophet with help from Arbad. They reached Madinah, and Aamir kept talking to the Prophet while Arbad turned aside to draw his sword. No sooner had Arbad drawn his sword the length of a hand than Allaah froze his hand in its place. The Prophet had been informed of their nefarious plot and had invoked Allaah against them. So when they returned, Allaah sent down a thunderbolt unto Arbad, and he was burned to death. As for Aamir, he was afflicted with an extremely painful gland, which caused his death. In the moment he cried out, "What am I like? I have a gland similar to a camel's. And here I am dying in the house of the woman from Bani Salul."

The Farewell Hajj

People often ask, How many times did the Prophet perform *Hajj*? The historians and scholars are unanimous that the Prophet went for only one *Hajj* after he migrated to Madinah. As for the period before migration, some say the Prophet performed Hajj once or twice. How many *Umrahs* did he perform? Al-Waaqidi said three *Umrahs* before *Hajj*—*Umrat al-Hudaybiyah* after the treaty, *Umrat al-Qadiyah* in Dhul Qa'dah of the seventh year, and *Umrat Al-Ji'raanah* in Dhul Qa'dah of the eighth year. As has been recorded, the Prophet also performed *Umrah* during the Farewell *Hajj*.[326]

The Prophet had spent almost the entire tenth year of Hijrah (631/632 CE) in Madinah, and on the twenty-fifth of Dhul Qa'dah of that year, he began to prepare for *Hajj* and asked the people to do the same. Some 30,000 people answered the call, and Muslim tribes from far and wide kept pouring in, to the extent that an unprecedented 124,000 people joined the *Hajj*. People were xcited for the opportunity to share the company of the Messenger of Allaah on the entire journey and learn the rituals of *Hajj* directly from him. All of the Prophet's wives joined him as well.

No doubt, this was a pilgrimage unlike any other that had taken place in many centuries. For the first time since idol worship had been introduced to this holy city, the pilgrims would all be worshippers of the One God, and no idolater would perform *Hajj* and desecrate the Ka'bah with their heathen rites.

A Premonition of the End

In the tenth year of his migration (631/632 CE), the Prophet began to notice things outwardly and perhaps within himself that told him his earthly life was going to end soon. He made a point of mentioning this to people close to him. For instance, he told his daughter, Faatimah, that that year during Ramadan, Gabriel had had him read the entire Qur'aan (most of which was already revealed by that time) twice. "Gabriel recited the Qur'aan unto me and I unto him once every year, but this year he has recited it with me twice. I cannot but think that my time has come," the Prophet told his daughter.

326 Al-Waaqidi, Muhammad bin Umar, Kitab Al-Maghazi, translated as The Life of Muhammad by Rizwi Faizer, Oxon, Canada, Routledge, 2013, 533

That Ramadan he also went into seclusion (*I'tikaaf*) for twenty days to worship God, in contrast to ten in previous years. Then on another occasion he spoke to Mu'aadh bin Jabal as the latter was getting ready to be sent off to Yemen on a mission. "O Mu'aadh! You may not see me after this year. You may even pass by this very mosque of mine and my tomb." Hearing that, Mu'aadh began to cry. The thought of the Prophet's passing away was too painful for him.

More Signs Were Yet to Come

On the day of the *Hajj* journey, the Prophet put on his garment and combed his hair, and his wife Aayeshah applied some perfume on him. His sacrificial animals were with him. He then saddled his camel and set off in the afternoon, arriving at Dhul Hulayfah before the afternoon prayer. He performed two units of the shortened prayer of a traveler and spent the night there. When it was morning, he told his Companions that Gabriel had called on him and said, "Pray in this blessed valley and say, 'I intend *Umrah* combined with *Hajj*.'"

Upon arriving in Makkah, the Prophet shortened his four units of prayer to two and asked the local residents to pray four. "Complete your prayer, O people of Makkah; we are travelers." When he came within sight of the Ka'bah, he raised his hands in reverence, letting fall the rein of his camel, which he then took up in his left hand, and with his right hand held out in supplication, he prayed, "O God, increase this House in the honor and magnification and bounty and reverence and piety that it receives from mankind!" It was a sight reminiscent of the supplication of Prophets Abraham and Ishmael when they were building the Ka'bah: "And (remember) when Ibraahim said, 'My Lord, make this city (Makkah) a place of security and provide its people with fruits, such of them as believe in Allaah and the Last Day.'"[327]

327 Baqarah 2:126.

A Profound Sermon

On the eighth day of *Dhul-Hijjah*, the Prophet left for Mina, where he performed the noon, the afternoon, the sunset, the evening, and the dawn prayers of the next day. When the sun rose up on the ninth, he left for the Plains of Arafah, where there was a tent built for him at Namirah. He sat inside till the sun went down. Then he rode his she-camel Al-Qaswa and came down to the valley, where 124,000 people had gathered.

The Prophet began by praising Allaah and then said:

"O people! Listen to what I say. I do not know whether I will ever meet you at this place again after this. It is unlawful for you to shed the blood of one another or take (unlawfully) the fortunes of one another. They are as unlawful, (*haraam*) as shedding blood on such a day as today, and in such a month as this sacred month and in such a sanctified city as this sacred city (Makkah and the surrounding areas). Behold! All practices of paganism and ignorance are now under my feet. The blood revenge of the Days of Ignorance (pre-Islamic time) are remitted. The first claim on blood I abolish is that of Ibn Rabi' bin Haarith, who was nursed in the tribe of Sa'ad and whom Hudhayl killed. Usury is forbidden, and I begin by remitting the interest that Abbaas bin Abdul Muttalib is owed. Verily, it is remitted entirely.

"O people! Fear Allaah concerning women. Verily you have taken them on the security of Allaah and have made their persons lawful unto you by Words of Allaah! It is incumbent upon them to honor their conjugal rights and not to commit acts of impropriety, which, if they do, you have authority to chastise them, yet not severely. If your wives refrain from impropriety and are faithful to you, clothe and feed them suitably. Verily, I have left among you the Book of Allaah and the *Sunnah* (Traditions) of His Messenger, which if you hold fast, you shall never go astray. O people, I am not succeeded by a Prophet, and you are not succeeded by any nation. So I recommend you to worship your Lord, to pray the five prayers, to fast Ramadan, and to offer the *zakaat* (mandatory charity) of your provision willingly. I recommend you to do the pilgrimage to the Sacred House of your Lord and to obey those who are in charge of you; then you will be awarded to enter the Paradise of your Lord."

The Prophet also said, "Beware of Satan. He has lost all hope that he will ever be able to lead you astray in big things, so beware of following him in small things. All mankind is from Adam and Eve; an Arab has no superiority over a non-Arab or a non-Arab over an Arab; similarly, a white person has no superiority over a black or a black person over a white person, except by piety (*taqwa*) and good action. Know that every Muslim is a brother to another Muslim and that the Muslims constitute one brotherhood. Nothing shall be legitimate to a Muslim that belongs to a fellow Muslim unless it was given freely and willingly. Do not, therefore, do injustice to yourselves."

On the tenth of Dhul-Hijjah, the Day of Sacrifice (*Yaum An-Nahr*), the Prophet conveyed another message: "Time has returned to the same state as when Allaah created the heavens and the earth. A year is twelve months, four of which are Sacred Months (*Hurum*). Three of the four months are successive. They are Dhul-Qa'dah, Dhul-Hijjah, and Muharram. The fourth month is Rajab of Mudar, which comes between Jumaadah and Sha'baan." Then he said, "What month is this?"

They replied, "A sacred month."

Then he said, "What city is this?"

They replied, "A sacred city."

He said, "Allaah has made your blood and your property and your honor as sacred as this day of yours, in this month of yours, in this city of yours. Have I conveyed the message?"

They replied, "You have conveyed it, O Messenger of Allaah!"

He said, "Let whomever is present convey it to whomever is absent." The Prophet then raised his forefinger heavenward and moved it down toward people while repeating thrice: "O Allaah, bear witness."

Soon after the Prophet had finished his speech, Allaah sent down the following verses in a perfect finale of his sermon: "This day I have perfected your religion for you, completed My favors upon you, and have approved Islam as your religion."[328]

Upon hearing this verse, Umar cried. "What makes you cry?" the Prophet asked.

In his wisdom and foresight, Umar said, "I am crying because I know that nothing succeeds perfection except imperfection." Umar clearly understood that when the era of the Prophet passed, it would never be surpassed in its quality.

While the Prophet was still in Mina, one of the shortest chapters of the Qur'aan, and its last, was revealed, and it was addressed to the Prophet:

> *When there comes the help of Allaah and the Conquest. And you see that the people enter Allaah's religion in crowds. So, glorify the praises of your Lord, and ask His forgiveness. Verily, He is the One Who accepts the repentance and Who forgives.*[329]

Abu Bakr, a deeply perceptive man, understood the hidden message in the surah and cried, saying that it meant the Prophet would soon leave this world. Surely, somewhat later the Prophet confirmed Abu Bakr's conclusion, saying, "My death has been announced to me."

---

328 Maa'idah 5:3.

329 Nasr 10.

After the ritual stoning of the Satan in Mina, the Prophet sacrificed the animals and called for a man to shave his head. The pilgrims gathered around him in the hopes of obtaining some locks of his hair. Abu Bakr remarked afterward how amazed he was while looking at Khaalid bin Waleed in that moment. There was a world of contrast between the Khaalid of Uhud and the Trench, and the Khaalid of now, who was pleading with the Prophet, "O Messenger of God, your forelock! Give it to no one but me; may my father and mother be your ransom!" And when the Prophet gave it to him, he pressed it reverently against his eyes and lips.

Ali and the Troops Return from Yemen

Ali had been sent to invite the people of Yemen to Islam after Khaalid's mission had not borne fruit. With his Yemen campaign successful, Ali returned to Makkah ahead of his troops. He had received a large quantity of spoils. His troops had requested new clothes, but Ali had declined, saying he was deferring the matter to the Prophet. Moreover, he had instructed the person whom he had left in charge not to distribute the garments, but that man went ahead and did it anyway. So when the soldiers trickled into Makkah a short while after Ali, they had new clothes on. On being questioned, the commander said, "I gave them the garments so that their appearance might be more seemly when they entered among the people."

Ali became upset and ordered them to return the clothes. That caused a great deal of anger among the troops, and it reached the Prophet, who said, "O people! Do not blame Ali, for he is too scrupulous in the path of God to be blamed."[330]

But that did not assuage everyone, and on the way to Madinah, a soldier bitterly complained about Ali to the Prophet, which angered the Prophet, and his face showed signs of displeasure. "Am I not nearer to the believers than their own selves?" he asked the man. When the man said yes, the

330 Lings, *Muhammad: His Life Based on the Earliest Sources*, Rochester, Inner Traditions, 351

Prophet continued. "Whoso I am nearest to, Ali is his nearest." And to further explain the point, he held Ali's hand and prayed, "O Allaah, be the friend of him who is his friend and the foe of him who is his foe." People got the message, and the bitterness subsided.[331]

Another Mu'tah Expedition

The Prophet headed back to Makkah on or about the fourteenth of Dhul-Hijjah. The journey was full of reflections and portents. His own pronouncements and some of the final verses that had been sent down signified that the Prophet's mission had been fulfilled and that he might not remain in this earthly life much longer.

Having returned to Madinah, the Prophet took stock of the state of affairs. The deaths of Zayd bin Al-Haarithah, Jaa'far bin Abi Taalib, Abdullaah bin Rawaahah, and their Companions in the Battle of Mu'tah against the Romans and their allies a few years earlier were still painfully fresh in his mind. To make things worse, the news had come that the Romans were behaving very arrogantly in Shaam and were harassing those from their vassal tribes who had embraced Islam. The final straw was their killing of Farwah Bani Amr Al-Judhami. Farwah was an Arab leader who, like many Arabs living in the lands of Shaam, had allied himself with the Byzantine Empire in order to protect himself. He was known as a Byzantine agent. His home was in Mu'tah, where he had earlier seen the courageous fight of a small group of Muslims against a massive Roman army about three years before. He had entered Islam and sent a white mule as a gift to the Prophet Muhammad to inform him of his new faith. When the Byzantines learned of his embracing of Islam, they sent him to prison. At first they gave him an opportunity to choose one of two options: leave Islam or face death. When he refused to leave Islam, the Romans crucified and then beheaded him.

331 Ibid, 352

So in the month of Safar of the eleventh year of *Hijrah* (632/633 CE), the Prophet decided to send a large force back to Mu'tah led by none other than Usaamah bin Zayd bin Haarithah, whose father's martyrdom in Mu'tah three years earlier had deeply grieved him. He ordered Usaamah to lead the Muslims to the lands bordering Balqaa and Darum of Palestine and let them cast terror in the heart of the Byzantine Empire and instill confidence among the Arabs who lived along the borders of the Roman colonial holdings. This would give a clear message to the Romans that they could no longer harass new Muslims or Arab tribes with impunity.

Usaamah was still in is his teens and the force that he had been ordered to lead included some of the most senior Companions, like Umar bin Al-Khattaab and Abu Ubaydah bin Al-Jarraah. Some people showed unhappiness at Usaamah's appointment as the commander of this important army, and when Umar heard about it, he rejected the people's criticism.

The matter, however, reached the Prophet, who climbed into the pulpit while a band was tied around his head to treat a headache, and he said, "What are these words that I hear from some of you regarding my appointment of Usaamah bin Zayd as the commander? By God, if you doubt my appointment of Usaamah, surely you doubted my appointment of his father before him. By God, he was surely one worthy of authority, just as his son after him is worthy of authority. Indeed, he was one of the most beloved people to me, and this is one of the most beloved people to me. Indeed, they are both worthy of every goodness. Take care of him, for indeed he is one of your best."

The Prophet told Usaamah, "Go in the name of God, and with His blessings, until you reach the place where your father was killed, and attack them with the horses, for I have appointed you over this army. Attack the people of Ubna in the morning and be aggressive."

While the army was still equipping itself, the Prophet called Usaamah again and emphasized a certain code of conduct during war. He said, "Attack, but do not act treacherously. Do not kill a newborn or a woman...Indeed they (the enemy army) will confront you with screams, and may God-inspired tranquility and quiet come upon you. Do not fight each other nor be cowardly, for your strength will depart, but say, 'O God, we are Your slaves, and they are Your slaves. Our fate and their fate are in Your Hands. Surely you will conquer them.' Know that Paradise is under the flashing gleam of the sword."

Finally the army left. The Prophet had instructed Usaamah to camp at Al-Jurf, a place four miles from Madinah. There were so many people that the troops formed a seemingly endless line streaming out of the city. Umm Ayman, who was aware of the Prophet's illness, asked him to allow Usaamah, her son, to stay until he recovered. But the Prophet said, "Let Usaamah go."

Usaamah went to see the Prophet one last time before he left and kissed him in the forehead. The Messenger of Allaah did not speak, but he raised his hands to heaven and then placed them on Usaamah, who later said, "I knew the Prophet was praying for me."

The next day, the Prophet's condition improved, and the Muslims rejoiced. The army left. However, before the army could go much farther, the news came that the Prophet's condition had worsened. Usaamah ordered the troops to halt until things became better.

The Final Moments

When two days remained in the month of Safar, in the middle of the night, the Prophet called for Abu Muwayhibah, a former slave whom he had freed, to take him to Baqiyatul Gharqad (the cemetery near his mosque, which today is known as Jannatul Baqi') to pray for the dead, especially the martyrs of Uhud. Abu Muwayhibah said that while there, the Prophet prayed, "Peace be upon you, O people of the graves! Happy are you that you are so much better off than men here. Dissensions have come like waves of darkness one after the other, the last being worse than the first." Abu Muwayhibah said that then the Prophet turned to him and said, "I have been given the option to choose between the keys of the treasures of this world and long life here followed by Paradise, and meeting my Lord and Paradise (right away)."[332] Abu Muwayhibah quickly advised the Prophet to choose the former, but the Prophet replied he had already chosen the latter.

Reflections: Many thinking and conscientious people in our own time want to move to a solitary place where they do not have to deal with the selfishness and greed, politics and conniving, plotting and scheming, oppression and lies, and rebellion and aggression of the worldly people. What is amazing is that more than fourteen centuries ago, when the Prophet was at the apex of his political power, he preferred to leave this world to meet with his Lord. Imam Bukhari, when he had become distressed about the mischief of his opponents, wished to be called back to Allaah, and a few days later he passed away. It must be kept in mind, though, that Islam forbids Muslims from asking for death, with some exceptions, such as Umar's request for death as a martyr in Madinah or a Muslim's asking Allaah to give him or her death if that is good for him or her.

Aayeshah, the Prophet's wife, narrated, "The Prophet returned from the cemetery to find me suffering from a severe headache, and I was saying, 'Oh my head!' He said, 'No, Aayeshah, rather it is oh *my* head.' Then he said, 'Would it distress you if you were to die before me so that I might wrap you in a shroud and pray over you and bury you?'" Aayeshah was surprised by the Prophet's statement. This was not anything she had heard from him before.

Despite his severe headache, the Prophet led the dawn prayer the next day, and after he had finished, he mounted the pulpit and invoked Allaah's blessings on the martyrs of Uhud for a long time, as if this were his last opportunity to do so. Then he broke the previous night's news to the

332 Ibn Isshaaq, *Sirat Rasul Allah.*

congregation. "Allaah has given one of His servants the choice between this world and that which is with Allaah, and he has chosen the latter."

Hearing that, Abu Bakr burst into tears, as he understood that the servant the Prophet was alluding to was none other than himself. He said, "No, we and our children will be your ransom."

The Prophet consoled him, saying, "Gently, O Abu Bakr." Then he praised Abu Bakr in these memorable words: "The most beneficent of men unto me in his Companionship is Abu Bakr; Allaah has taken me as a *Khaleel* (an intimate friend) like he had taken Ibraahim as a *Khaleel*, and if I were to take from all of mankind an intimate friend, he would be Abu Bakr, but Companionship and brotherhood of faith is ours until Allaah unites us in His Presence." Then the Prophet ordered that all the doors of the houses that opened into the mosque be closed, except that of Abu Bakr's house. This was a singular honor for Abu Bakr and a hint for succession. Before leaving the pulpit he said, "I go before you, and I am your witness. Your meeting with me is at the Pool (*Al-Kawthar*), which indeed I behold from here where now I stand. I do not fear that you will set up gods beside Allaah, but I fear that you will compete with each other for the things of this world."[333]

From there he went to the residence of his wife Maymunah, whose turn it was to house the Prophet. But soon he was overcome with a high fever. In that state he asked whose turn it would be to house him the next day, and his wives, who were all there, informed him. But he kept asking where he would be next until they all realized that he longed to be in the house of Aayeshah, and they at once agreed to give up their nights with the Prophet so he could be with Aayeshah.

333 Al-Kawthar is a river in Paradise that Allaah has granted to the Prophet Muhammad. According to a Hadith, the Prophet will hand out drinks from that river to the righteous on the Day of Judgment. Whoever drinks from it will not be thirsty again on that scorching day.

Sensing that the Prophet could hardly walk on his own, his uncle Abbaas, and Ali, helped him to Aayeshah's house. His fever continued, but with great difficulty he managed to lead the prayers, sometimes in a sitting position. Later the same day or the next, Bilaal came to the Prophet to inform him it was time for prayer. The Prophet was suffering from a high fever, and when he tried to get up, he fell down and fainted.

When he regained consciousness, he asked, "Have the people prayed?" He was informed that they were waiting for him. So he tried to get up again and fell down again. This scenario repeated itself several times, and then finally the Prophet asked Aayeshah to tell Abu Bakr to lead the congregation. Aayeshah, however, felt that it would anguish her father to take the place of the Prophet. She also knew that her father used to cry when he recited the Qur'aan, so she said, "O Messenger of Allaah, Abu Bakr is a very soft-hearted man, not strong of voice, and given to much weeping when he recites the Qur'aan." The Prophet ignored her imploring and repeated his order to call Abu Bakr.

This time Aayeshah suggested Umar's name to lead the prayer, and she looked at Hafsah, Umar's daughter, for support. When Hafsah tried to speak, the Prophet silenced them both, saying, "You are like the women of Joseph (meaning they were plotting against his wish). Tell Abu Bakr to lead the people in prayer. Allaah and His Messenger will not have otherwise." This was yet another indication as to whom the Prophet wanted to succeed him.

During the severe illness, the Prophet praised the Ansaar (Helpers) for their help and sincere advice, and he commanded the Emigrants to take care of them. This was highly symbolic, as it signified a higher status for the Emigrants and the Ansaar as their advisors and facilitators. And that is what happened. The future rulers came from the Emigrants, and the Helpers played highly important roles in their government.

While the Prophet lay propped against Aayeshah's chest, his daughter Faatimah came to see him. Faatimah had visited her father frequently during his illness, and on one occasion Aayeshah noticed that the Prophet whispered something in Faatimah's ears that made her cry, but then he said something that made her laugh. Aayeshah tried to find out, but Faatimah declined to tell her what he had said. It was only after the Prophet's death that Faatimah revealed her father's secret. She said she had cried when the Prophet had told her that that illness would culminate in his death, but then she had laughed when he told her she would be the first from his surviving family to join him in the other world. That indeed came true when Faatimah died barely six months after the Prophet's demise.

The Prophet's prolonged high fever and pain made everyone distraught, especially his wives. Safiyyah, for one, could not bear this, and she said, "O Prophet, I wish it were I who suffered rather than you."

A day before the Prophet departed this world, his fever had somewhat abated, and he asked to be carried to the mosque. Abbaas's son, Al-Fadl, and Thawbaan, a freed slave, helped him to the mosque while his feet were dragging on the ground and his head was wrapped in cloth. Abu Bakr was leading the morning prayer, and when the Prophet approached the congregation, they were diverted away from prayer. Abu Bakr surmised that the worshippers would not be distracted unless it was the Prophet, so he withdrew from his place.

According to a narration in Bukhari, the Prophet motioned Abu Bakr to stay in his place while he sat on his left and led the prayer while sitting. So the people could hear, Abu Bakr said *Allaahu Akbar* with the Prophet's movements. After the prayer, the Prophet turned to the people and spoke to them in a voice that was loud enough to be heard outside of the mosque. "O people, the fire is kindled, and rebellions come like the darkness of the night. By God, you cannot blame me for anything. I allowed you only what the Qur'aan allows and forbade you only what the Qur'aan forbids." The Prophet's condition had somewhat improved, and noticing that, Abu Bakr asked for permission to visit his wife, Habibah bint Khaarijah, in Sunh.

When the request was granted, Abu Bakr left for the outskirts of Madinah to visit his family.

That day the Prophet asked how much money he had in his possession. When told he had seven silver *dinar* (currency), he exclaimed, "What do I have to do with this?" and he ordered that they be given away in charity. In another narration, he said, "What have I to do with this world? I and this world are like a rider and a tree under which he takes shelter. Then he goes his way, and leaves it behind him."

The Prophet asked that Hasan and Hussain, his grandchildren from Faatimah, be brought to him. He kissed them and recommended that they be looked after. He asked to see his wives. They were brought to him. He preached to them and told them to remember Allaah. When the pain grew, he said he could feel the effects of the poisoning at Khayber. He ordered the people to perform the prayers and be attentive to their slaves. He repeated it several times.

On the fourteenth day of his illness, which was Monday, the twelfth of Rabi Al-Awwal, the Prophet lifted the curtain of Aayeshah's apartment while people were offering the morning prayer. Then the door was opened, and the Prophet stood there wearing an expression of immense joy to see people being led in prayer by one of their pious Companions. Those who saw him reported that they had not seen him with a nobler smile. The Prophet motioned them to proceed with their prayer and went back in the house, leaving the people to think that he had recovered.

Back in Aayeshah's apartment, the Prophet's condition quickly worsened, as if his Creator had given him the momentary respite so that he could speak some memorable words to his Companions for the last time. When Abbaas came out of Aayeshah's house with Ali, he was convinced that the Prophet was in the last moments of his life, so he took Ali by the hand and said, "I swear I have seen death in the face of God's Messenger as I have before in the faces of our family members. So let us go and ask him if the authority is going to be vested in us, and if not, then at least he can advise people to treat us well."

Ali did not think it was a good idea. "By God, I will not," said Ali, "for if he withholds the authority from us, none after him will ever give it to us."

As the Prophet lay suffering from the agony of death, Aayeshah's brother Abdur Rahmaan entered the room with a tooth-stick in his hand. Aayeshah noticed that the Prophet looked at the tooth-stick as if he wanted it, so she took it from her brother's hand, chewed upon it to soften it, and then gave it to the Prophet, who thoroughly brushed his teeth with it. Even in this condition the Prophet managed to advise the people, saying, "You should have good thoughts of Allaah when you are dying. Guard your prayer and fear Allaah with regards to the slaves, women, and the weakest of the society."

Aayeshah said there was a water container in front of the Prophet, and he started dipping his hand in the water and rubbing his face with it. He said, "None has the right to be worshipped but Allaah. Indeed, death has its agonies." At one point he moved his lips, and when Aayeshah moved closer to listen, she heard him say, "With those on whom You have bestowed Your Grace, with the Prophets and the Truthful, the martyrs and the good doers. O Allaah, forgive me and have mercy upon me and join me with the Companionship on high." It was as if was trying to recite what Allaah had revealed in the Qur'aan about the righteous people: "And whoever obeys Allaah and the Messenger, then they will be in the company of those on whom Allaah has bestowed His grace, of the Prophets, the truthful, the martyrs, and the righteous. And how excellent are these Companions!"[334]

The Prophet then lifted his hands toward the sky and started saying, "Indeed, with the highest Companion in Paradise," till he expired and his hand dropped. We belong to Allaah and to Him is our return. He was

334 Nisaa 4:69.

sixty-three years and four days old when he left this world on Monday, 12 Rabi Al-Awwal, 11 AH (8 June 632 CE).

At the time of his death, the Prophet's possessions consisted of some mats, blankets, jugs, a bowl from which he ate, and other simple things even though he was the ruler of Arabia. He left nothing to be inherited except a white mule, a gift from Muqawqis, some arms, and a piece of land that he had already given away in charity. As he was about to depart, he had told his followers, "We the community of the prophets are not inherited. Whatever we leave is for charity." In another narration, he said, "We do not leave behind dirham and dinar but the knowledge of the prophethood." The Prophet's wives, like the rest of the citizens, received stipends from the state.

What Followed the Prophet's Death?

The news of the Prophet's death had left the people in shock. Umar refused to believe that the Prophet had died and threatened to harm anyone who said so. He said the Prophet had gone to see his Lord like Moses and would return, like Moses did. The Prophet's departure was much harder for his family, which tried to nurse its grief in seclusion.

Companion Anas bin Maalik said, "The day the Prophet came to Madinah was the happiest day, and the day he died was the saddest." The Prophet himself had once said that the greatest tragedy that would befall the Muslims would be his death. Besides the loss of his Companionship, the people suffered rebellions, infighting, and chaos soon after the Prophet's death.

When the news of the Prophet's death reached Abu Bakr in Sunh, he immediately returned to Madinah. Upon arrival he saw Umar talking to the people, but he did not pay attention to him and instead proceeded to his daughter's house, where the Prophet's body was. He uncovered the Prophet's face and kissed him, saying, "You are dearer to me than my father and mother. You have tasted the death that God had decreed for you; a second death will never happen to you." As he came out of the room, Abu Bakr saw Umar still talking, and he asked him to be quiet, but Umar ignored him and kept talking. So Abu Bakr left him and went to the people, who now began to gather around him, the Prophet's closest friend and confidant.

After thanking and praising Allaah, Abu Bakr said, "If anyone among you worshipped Muhammad, then Muhammad has died, but if anyone worshipped Allaah, then Allaah is alive and shall never die." Then he recited a verse from the Qur'aan: "Muhammad is no more than a messenger and indeed (many) messengers have passed away before him. If he dies or is killed, will you then turn upon your heels? Whoso turns upon his heels will not harm God; and God will reward the thankful."[335]

It was as if the people had not read this verse before, and when Abu Bakr recited it, they all remembered and began to chant it. Bukhari reported the following reaction from Umar: "By Allaah, when I heard Abu Bakr reciting it, my legs could not support me anymore, and I fell down, knowing that the Prophet had indeed died."

Abu Bakr's composed state, even though he was among the most hurt at the Prophet's death, seems to suggest that in that critical moment in time, he was divinely inspired. The few historic words he spoke kept the people from falling in utter confusion and despair.

While the Prophet's family was mourning in seclusion and the people were trying to absorb the shocking reality, the news came to Abu Bakr and Umar that some of the Helpers (Ansaar) had gathered around Sa'ad bin Ubaadah in the courtyard known as *Thaqifah Banu Saa'idah.* The bearer of the news emphasized, "If you want to take control, then act before their action becomes too serious."

335 Aal Imraan 3:144.

It was a delicate situation. The Prophet's body was still in the house where he had died, and the funeral arrangements had not yet been discussed. His close family had closed the door to mourn privately. But the news of the gathering in *Thaqifah Banu Saa'idah* was not something they could ignore. So Umar suggested to Abu Bakr and Abu Ubaydah bin Al-Jarraah, who also happened to be there, that they all should go and check things out. Usayd bin Hudhayr, a Helper who was with them, also came along.

When they reached the courtyard, they found Sa'ad sitting in the middle wrapped up in a sheet because of illness. Before their arrival, the Aws and Khazraj had been pondering over the question of succession, and they seemed to be of the view that a Helper should rule over them because of their contribution to the establishment of Islam. They had almost settled on Sa'ad, who, although he was the leader of the Khazraj, was also acceptable to the Aws.

It was at that point that an Ansaari man stood up, praised Allaah, and spoke. "We are the Helpers of God and the fighting force of Islam, and you, O Emigrants, are of us, for a group of your people has settled among us." The speaker extolled the virtues of the Helpers and at times acknowledged the Emigrants' contributions.

Umar, who narrated the whole incident, said that it seemed that the Helpers wanted to wrest authority away from the Emigrants. So when the Ansaari man was done, Umar wanted to speak, for he had prepared a nice speech, but Abu Bakr said to him, "Gently, O Umar!" Understanding that Abu Bakr wanted to say something, Umar deferred the matter to him.

Abu Bakr began his address by thanking and praising God and then said to the Helpers, "The good things you have said about yourselves are deserved. But the Arabs will not accept anyone other than this clan of the Quraysh as their leader because they are the best of the Arabs in blood and country and because they were the first ones to enter Islam and emigrate for the sake of Allaah, while you are the Helpers." He also recited verse 100 of Surah Tawbah (chapter 9) to remind them that Allaah had mentioned the Emigrants before the Helpers whenever both were mentioned in the same verse: "The foremost—the first of the Emigrants and the Helpers—and those who have followed them in doing good: Allaah is pleased with them and they are pleased with Him. He has prepared Gardens for them with rivers flowing therein, remaining in them timelessly, for ever and ever. That is the great victory."

Then Abu Bakr took hold of the hands of Abu Ubaydah and Umar and said, "I offer one of these two men as the leader; choose either as you please." Umar said he felt very distressed at Abu Bakr's proposal, as he would rather accept death than rule over a people when Abu Bakr was one of them. Someone from the Helpers proposed a shared leadership, one from the Helpers and one from the Emigrants. That led to voices being raised, and the situation seemed to get out of hand. It was then that Umar said to Abu Bakr, "Stretch out your hand." When Abu Bakr did so, Umar took his hand and immediately pledged allegiance to him. The Emigrants followed, and so did the Helpers. It all happened very quickly, and a potentially serious dispute was averted.

What happened in the courtyard had included only a small number of people, so the following morning when Abu Bakr had led the prayer, Umar got up and spoke about the virtues of Abu Bakr, saying, "O men, Abu Bakr is the best of you, the Companion of God's Messenger, the second of two when they were both in the cave, and the one whom the Prophet appointed to lead the prayer during his illness." They all agreed with what had been said about Abu Bakr and enthusiastically pledged allegiance to him, except Ali, who did so a few months later.

Abu Bakr's acceptance speech was as remarkable for its humility and conviction of faith as it was for its brevity. He said, "I have been given authority over you, but I am not the best of you. Help me if I do well, and set me right if I do wrong. Truth is in loyalty and falsehood in treachery. The weak among you will be strong by me until I secure his right, God willing, and the strong among you will be weak by me until I wrest the rights of the weak from him. If a people refrain from fighting in the way of God, God will disgrace them. Never is wickedness widespread among people except God sends calamity upon them all. Obey me as long as I obey God and His Messenger, and if I disobey them, then you owe no obedience to me. Arise for prayer; may God have mercy upon you."

Washing, Funeral Prayer, and Burial

The Companions had washed many bodies, offered numerous funeral prayers, and buried a large number of Muslims. But the Messenger of Allaah was not like anyone they had ever dealt with. He was special, so questions arose as to how Muslims should conduct the final rites of the Prophet. Should he be washed with his clothes on or off? Should there be a funeral prayer for him, and if so, who should lead it? And where should he be buried?

Aayeshah reported that as people were arguing whether the Prophet should be washed with or without the clothes he was wearing, Allaah caused a deep sleep upon them. Then a voice came from the direction of the house, saying, "Wash the Messenger with his clothes on." They heard the voice, but none knew where it came from. Those who washed the Messenger of Allaah included Ali; Abbaas and his sons Fadl and Qutham; and Usaamah bin Zayd and Shuqraan, the freedman of the Prophet. It is said that Aws bin Khawli, a Companion of the Prophet who was with him in the Battle of Badr, pleaded with Ali to be included, and so he was.

Ali was the only one who moved his hands over the Prophet's body above his garment to wash it, while others helped turn it. At one point Ali said, "Dearer than my father and mother, how excellent you are in life and in death!" After the bath, the Prophet's body was wrapped in three garments, at least one of which was from Yemen. Some say there was also an Egyptian sheet.

The Prophet's body was now placed on his bed. People differed as to the place of burial; some suggested that he should be buried in the mosque, while others wanted to bury him in Baqiyatul Gharqad alongside his Companions and family. Abu Bakr rose to the occasion and settled the matter, saying that he had heard the Prophet say, "A prophet is buried where he dies."

The Prophet's uncle, Abbaas, sent for Abu Ubaydah bin Al-Jarraah and Abu Talhah Zayd bin Sahl. Both men were known for their skills at digging graves: Abu Ubaydah in the Makkan style and Abu Talhah in Madinan style, with a niche on the side. Abu Ubaydah could not be found, whereas Abu Talhah was, so he dug the grave in the style of the Muslims of Madinah. In light of the Hadith that Abu Bakr had narrated, the Prophet's grave was dug in the house of Aayeshah underneath his bed.

There were still some unsettled questions. How should the Prophet's funeral prayer be performed? Who should be the imam? Should the people pray for Allaah's forgiveness for him, knowing that Allaah had already forgiven him for all his mistakes?

Muhammad ibn Sa'ad reported in his Tabaqaat that Ali said to the people, "Let no one stand over him as an imam. He is your leader in life and in death." So the people entered in small groups and prayed for the Prophet without an imam while Ali stood beside the Prophet's body, saying, "Peace be upon you, O Prophet," and the people would simply say, "Aameen! Aameen!" Similar supplications and blessings are recorded from Abu Bakr and Umar. Approximately thirty thousand men and women came from far and wide to pray for the Prophet. They came in small groups, and each group prayed the funeral prayer—firstly the men, then after them the women, and after them the children. The lack of an imam over the Prophet showed the highest form of respect to someone who had led all God's messengers and prophets in prayer in Jerusalem before *Mai'raaj* (Ascension to the Heavens).

Ali, Fadl, Qutham, and Shuqraan placed the Prophet's body in the grave on Wednesday night, 14 Rabi Al-Awwal, 11 AH (10 June 632 CE). Aayeshah said they learned about the burial of the Prophet upon hearing the sound of pickaxes in the night. Some days later when Faatimah came to the house of Aayeshah and saw the Prophet's grave where his bed used to be, she told Anas bin Maalik, the servant of the Prophet, "How could you have allowed yourselves to throw dust at the Messenger of Allaah?" It is said that the Companions hesitated to fill the grave of the Prophet with the earth after his body was lowered, as the thought of it was too hard for them.

Madinah was plunged into deep sadness. The Companions consoled each other and counseled patience but wept themselves. When Umm Ayman was consoled, she said, "I do not weep because the Prophet has died, as I know he has gone to that which is better than this world; I weep because revelation has stopped."

Ali Pledges Allegiance to Abu Bakr

As the Prophet had prophesied, Faatimah fell ill and died about six months after her father. Sometime after her passing, Ali requested a meeting with Abu Bakr. Until that time he had withheld his pledge of allegiance from Abu Bakr, who had succeeded the Prophet as the leader of the Muslims. When Abu Bakr came, Ali said, "We know your preeminence and Allaah's bounty upon you, and we are not jealous of you on account of what He has given you, but you did it (accepted leadership position) without consulting us, and we thought that we had a right because of our kinship with the Messenger of Allaah."

Hearing that, Abu Bakr burst into tears and said, "By Him in Whose Hand is my soul, I would rather have good relations with the kindred of God's Messenger than with my own kindred." According to Imam An-Nawawi, Abu Bakr apologized to Ali for the lack of consultation with him. At that moment Abu Bakr publicly announced that he held no grudge against Ali for having withheld his allegiance. That same day Ali pledged his fealty to Abu Bakr.[336]

The Prophet's Legacy: From Here to Where?

Indeed the Prophet died, but his legacy lives on. More than 1.8 billion people on earth call themselves Muslims today. As the last Messenger and Prophet of God, he was sent to all of mankind, and for that reason the book that was revealed to him (the Qur'aan) and his teachings (the Sunnah) will be preserved as long as the sun rises from the east.

The questions that require serious reflection from Muslims are as follows: How much of the Prophet's legacy are today's Muslims implementing in their lives? And why is it that a people who claim to follow the Qur'aan and Sunnah are mired in backwardness, infighting, and corruption? One may say that the legacy of Muhammad the Messenger of Allaah is too difficult to emulate because he set the bar too high. In that case a Muslim might do well to look at the legacy of Muhammad the man, as described by Khadijah bint Khuwaylid, his first wife.

When he came back shaken from the Cave of Hira after the first encounter with Gabriel, he said, "Cover me up, cover me up; I am afraid that something terrible is about to befall me."

Khadijah replied, "Never! By Allaah, Allaah will never disgrace you. You keep good relations with your family, you help the poor and the

336 Bukhari, Hadith #3998; Muslim, Hadith #1759.

destitute, you serve your guests generously, and you assist those afflicted by calamities."

The Prophet said that one of the biggest reasons for his coming was to "perfect the good character" of people. And he personified the best of it. Allaah said about him: "And verily, you are on an exalted standard of character."[337]

Does our character today mirror his? Allaah revealed that He made us a "justly balanced and moderate nation,"[338] and the Prophet exemplified that moderation through his life for us to follow. When the Prophet was given a choice in religion, he always chose what would be easy for the people. He discouraged his Companions from going to extremes in worshipping Allaah, saying that although Allaah would not tire of rewarding them, they would not be able to continue worshipping Him in the extreme manner.

Bukhari reported that three Companions once made an unusual vow. One of them said he would pray all night, every night; another said he would fast every day; and yet another said he would never marry. When the Prophet heard about their extreme pledges, he told them, "By Allaah, I fear Allaah more than you do, and I am the most obedient and dutiful among you to Him, yet I fast some days, and I don't fast other days; I pray at night, and I also sleep a part of the night; and I married, and whoever does not follow my *Sunnah* (way of life) does not belong to me."[339]

The Prophet also forbade excessive praise of him, saying, "Do not exaggerate in praising me as the Christians praised the son of Mary (i.e. Jesus), for I am only [Allaah's] slave. So, call me the slave of Allaah and His messenger." [*Saheeh al-Bukhari*: 654]

337 Qalam 68:4.

338 Baqarah 2:143.

339 Bukhari, Volume 7, Book 62, Hadith # 1

In a Hadith collected by Muslim, the Prophet said, "Ruined are those who insist on hardship in matters of religion."

Is it not a great tragedy that, despite clear admonition from Allaah and His Messenger, some fringe groups of Muslims have taken the path of extremism? Today, not a day goes by without us hearing about murder and mayhem in a Muslim land. Nations of the world are calling us extremists and worse. We are traumatized by such pejorative labeling, knowing that the vast majority of Muslims have nothing to do with extremism.

As we yearn for the restoration of Islam's glory, it is imperative that we bring back moderation in our individual and collective lives. Our current predicament requires a serious reappraisal. We need a reformation, not of Islam, but of our own selves. Although extremists are a tiny minority among us, they are speaking the loudest, and their brutal actions are holding all of us hostage. It is time for the silent majority to stand up and be heard. True, many Muslim scholars have spoken against the scourge of extremism, but the denunciation needs to be in a persistent, methodical, and practical way. Coupled with that, the Muslim rulers need to address social injustice and political corruption in their societies.

The positive change and brighter future we seek for Muslims will not be possible without the youth playing a major role in our own renaissance.

Someone once asked a Muslim scholar, "What is the future of Islam in America?"

The wise man pondered for a moment and countered, "What is the state of the Muslim youth in America?" The scholar's wisdom spared him a long lecture on the subject. Those past the youthful years know what it means to be a youth: the explosion of hormones, the overpowering attraction to the opposite sex, and the sudden impulse to commit sin.

The question is, if the puberty blues are part of being a youth, can we really guard against them? Can we really think of the distant future when the present is so captivating?

The answer is, yes, we can if we are sincere.

One of the most powerful examples of the youth in the Qur'aan is that of the People of the Cave. To the Christian world they are known as the Seven Sleepers of Ephesus. The Qur'aan does not specify their exact number but says: "They were young men who believed in their Lord, and We increased them in guidance."[340]

The People of the Cave were some young believers in Allaah who lived in a land of disbelief under a tyrant ruler. They are thought to be followers of the Prophet Jesus. To escape religious persecution and protect their faith, they decided to leave the society and took shelter in a cave where they prayed: "Our Lord! Bestow on us mercy from Yourself, and facilitate for us our affairs in the right way!"[341]

Allaah not only answered their prayer but also made their story an enduring inspiration by telling it in the Qur'aan. The People of the Cave believed in Allaah and His promise of Paradise. They put their faith into action. That is the real image of a Muslim youth: strong in faith, dynamic, and active. He or she has courage, sincerity, and self-sacrifice. We find these qualities in young prophets like Abraham, his son Ishmael, his great-grandson Joseph, in John the Baptist (Yahya), and in Jesus (Eesa).

We also find these virtues in the youthful followers of the Prophet Muhammad, such as Ali, Faatimah, Asmaa, Sumayyah, Aayeshah, Abdullaah bin Umar, Abdullaah bin Abbaas, Sa'ad bin Abi Waqqaas,

340 Kahf 18:13.

341 Kahf 18:10.

Talhah bin Ubaydullah, Zubayr bin Al-Awwaam, Usama bin Zayd, and many others.

The youth in the time before Islam were an unutilized resource. They spent much of their time chilling. Under Islam, the youth became supercharged and super good. Through these Muslim youth, Allaah gave glory to His religion and humiliated His enemies.

In our time, while many Muslim youth are struggling to survive in the onslaught of pop culture, a segment has its gaze set beyond the coolest video games and fastest cars. They are the future leaders of the community. We draw inspiration from these young men and women who are serving on the boards of Islamic centers, running youth programs, participating in the political process and interfaith dialogue, and campaigning to eradicate homelessness, domestic violence, and injustice in the society.

The ultimate goal of Islam is not to have a bunch of pious Muslims praying five times a day, fasting during Ramadan, paying alms, and going for Hajj, but to have Muslims who care about their societies and fix what is broken. A big reason for the Islamophobia in the West today is ignorance about Islam, for which Muslims are responsible. Often times, non-Muslims see the beauty of Islam through the beautiful actions of a Muslim. Research has shown that when people know a Muslim, they are less likely to have a negative opinion of Islam.

Muslims were once leaders of the world in science, medicine, and education. Their advancement and progressive thinking helped give Europe its Renaissance. Today, they are in a sorry state. Let Muslims take heed of a reminder from the Qur'aan: "Allaah does not change the condition of a people until they change what is in themselves."[342]

342 Ra'd 13:11.

To my Christian and Jewish brethren, I say, let us build the brotherhood and sisterhood of our shared faiths together, reject the extremists among us who want a clash of civilizations, denounce the vilification of Islam and the Prophet Muhammad, and love each other as children of common ancestors. And finally, let us be reminded by our own teachings:

> *You shall not take vengeance or bear a grudge against the sons of your own people, but you shall love your neighbor as yourself: I am the Lord.*[343]

> *So whatever you wish that others would do to you, do also to them, for this is the Law and the Prophets.*[344]

> *None of you will truly believe until he wishes for his brother what he wishes for himself.*[345]

---

343 Leviticus 19:18, ESV.

344 Matthew 7:12.

345 Imam An-Nawawi, Forty Hadith, Hadith #13.

Appendix

The Articles of the Madinah Charter

In the name of God, the Compassionate, the Merciful.

(1) This is a document from Muhammad, the Prophet governing the relations between the believers and the Muslims of the Quraysh and Madinah, and those who followed them and joined them and labored with them.

(2) They are one Ummah (community) to the exclusion of all men.

(3) The Quraysh emigrants, according to their present custom, shall pay the blood wit within their number and shall redeem their prisoners with the kindness and justice common among believers.

(4–8) The Banu Awf, according to their present custom, shall pay the blood wit they paid before Islam; every section shall redeem its prisoners with the kindness and justice common among believers. The Banu Saa'idah, the Banu Al-Harith, the Banu Jusham, and the Banu Al-Najjaar likewise.

(9–11) The Banu Amr Banu Awf, the Banu Al-Naabit, and the Banu Al-Aws likewise.

(12)(a) Believers shall not leave anyone destitute among them by not paying his redemption money or blood wit in kindness.

(12)(b) A believer shall not take as an ally the freedman of another Muslim against him.

(13) The God-fearing believers shall be against the rebellious or him who seeks to spread injustice, or sin or animosity, or corruption between believers; the hand of every man shall be against him even if he be a son of one of them.

(14) A believer shall not slay a believer for the sake of an unbeliever, nor shall he aid an unbeliever against a believer.
(15) God's protection is one; the least of them may give protection to a stranger on their behalf. Believers are friends one to the other to the exclusion of outsiders.
(16) To the Jew who follows us belongs help and equality. He shall not be wronged nor shall his enemies be aided.
(17) The peace of the believers is indivisible. No separate peace shall be made when believers are fighting in the way of God. Conditions must be fair and equitable to all.
(18) In every foray a rider must take another behind him.
(19) The believers must avenge the blood of one another shed in the way of God.
(20)(a) The God-fearing believers enjoy the best and most upright guidance.
(20)(b) No polytheist shall take the property of a person of Quraysh under his protection, nor shall he intervene against a believer.
(21) Whoever is convicted of killing a believer without good reason shall be subject to retaliation unless the next of kin is satisfied (with blood money), and the believers shall be against him as one man, and they are bound to take action against him.
(22) It shall not be lawful to a believer who holds by what is in this document and believes in God and the last day to help an evil-doer or to shelter him. The curse of God and His anger on the day of resurrection will be upon him if he does, and neither repentance nor ransom will be received from him.
(23) Whenever you differ about a matter, it must be referred to God and to Muhammad.
(24) The Jews shall contribute to the cost of war so long as they are fighting alongside the believers.
(25) The Jews of the Banu Awf are one community with the believers (the Jews have their religion, and the Muslims have theirs), their freedmen and their persons except those who behave unjustly and sinfully, for they hurt but themselves and their families.

(26–35) The same applies to the Jews of the Banu Al-Najjaar, Banu Al-Harith, Banu Saa'idah, Banu Jusham, Banu al-Aws, Banu Tha'labah, and the Jafna, a clan of the Tha'labah and the Banu al-Shutaybah. Loyalty is a protection against treachery. The freedmen of Tha'labah are as themselves. The close friends of the Jews are as themselves.

(36) None of them shall go out to war save with the permission of Muhammad, but he shall not be prevented from taking revenge for a wound. He who slays a man without warning slays himself and his household, unless it be one who has wronged him, for God will accept that.

(37) The Jews must bear their expenses and the Muslims their expenses. Each must help the other against anyone who attacks the people of this document. They must seek mutual advice and consultation, and loyalty is a protection against treachery. A man is not liable for his ally's misdeeds. The wronged must be helped.

(38) The Jews must pay with the believers so long as war lasts.

(39) Yathrib shall be a sanctuary for the people of this document.

(40) A stranger under protection shall be as his host, doing no harm and committing no crime.

(41) A woman shall only be given protection with the consent of her family.

(42) If any dispute or controversy likely to cause trouble should arise, it must be referred to God and to Muhammad the Apostle of God. God accepts what is nearest to piety and goodness in this document.

(43) The Quraysh and their helpers shall not be given protection.

(44) The contracting parties are bound to help one another against any attack on Yathrib.

(45)(a) If they are called to make peace and maintain it, they must do so; and if they make a similar demand on the Muslims, it must be carried out, except in the case of a holy war.

(45)(b) Everyone shall have his portion from the side to which he belongs.

(46) The Jews of Al-Aws, their freedmen and themselves, have the same standing with the people of this document. Loyalty is a protection against treachery. He who acquires it should acquire it for himself. God approves of this document.

(47) This deed will not protect the unjust and the sinner. The man who goes forth to fight and the man who stays at home in the city are safe unless he has been unjust and sinned. God is the protector of the good and God-fearing man, and Muhammad is the apostle of God.[346]

Names of *As-haab As-Suffah*

1. Abbaad bin Khaalid al-Ghifaari
2. Abdullaah Dhul Bujaadayn
3. Abdullaah bin Abd Al-As'ad
4. Abdullaah bin Al-Haarith
5. Abdullaah bin Amr bin Hiraam
6. Abdullaah bin Habashi Al-Khash'ami
7. Abdullaah bin Hawaala Al-Azdi
8. Abdullaah bin Mas'ud
9. Abdullaah bin Umar bin Al-Khattaab
10. Abdullaah bin Umm Maktoom
11. Abdullaah bin Unays Al-Juhani
12. Abdullaah bin Zayd Al-Juhani
13. Abdur Rahmaan bin Jabr bin Amr
14. Abdur Rahmaan bin Qirt
15. Abu Ayyub Al-Ansaari
16. Abu Dharr Al-Ghifaari
17. Abu Firaas Al-Aslami
18. Abu Hurayrah Abdur Rahmaan bin Sakhr
19. Abu Kabshah (freed slave of the Prophet)
20. Abu Lubaabah bin Abd Al-Mundhir Al-Ansaari
21. Abu Razin
22. Abu Sa'id Al-Khudri
23. Al-Arbad bin Saariya
24. Al-Agharr Al-Muzani

346 Ibn Isshaaq, *Sirat Rasul Allah.*

25. Al-Baraa bin Maalik Al-Ansaari
26. Al-Hakam bin Umayr
27. Amr bin Anbasah As-Sulami
28. Amr bin Awf Al-Muzani
29. Amr bin Taghlab
30. Asmaa' bin Haarithah al-Aslami
31. As-Saaib bin Khallaad
32. At-Tafaawi Ad-Dawsi
33. Aws bin Aws Al-Thaqafi
34. Bilaal bin Rabaah
35. Dukayn bin Sa'id Al-Muzani
36. Faraat bin Hayyaan Al-Ajli
37. Fudaalah bin Ubayd Al-Ansaari
38. Haarithah bin An-Nu'maan Al-Ansaari
39. Haazim bin Harmala Al-Aslami
40. Habib bin Zayd bin Aasim Al-Ansaari
41. Hajjaaj bin Amr al-Aslami
42. Hanzalah bin Abi Aamir Ar-Raahib Al-Ansaari
43. Harmala bin Iyaas
44. Hilaal (Freed slave of Mugheerah bin Shi'bah)
45. Hudhayfah bin Al-Yamaan
46. Hudhayfah bin Aseed
47. Iyaad bin Himaar Al-Mujaasha'i
48. Jaariya bin Humayl
49. Jarhaad bin Khuwaylid Al-Aslami
50. Ju'ayl bin Suraaqah Ad-Damri
51. Ka'ab bin Amr Abul Yasaar Al-Ansaari
52. Kannaaz bin Al-Husayn Abu Marthad
53. Khabbaab bin Al-Aratt
54. Khubayb bin Yasaaf bin Utbah
55. Khunays bin Hudhaafa As-Sahmi
56. Khuraym bin Aws At-Taai
57. Khuraym bin Faatik Al-Asadi

58. Mas'ud bin Ar-Rabi' Al-Qaari
59. Mistaah bin Uthaathah
60. Mu'aadh Abu Halimah Al-Qaari
61. Qurrah bin Iyaas Abu Mu'aawiyah Al-Muzani
62. Sa'ad bin Abi Waqqaas
63. Saalim (freed slave of Abu Hudhayfah)
64. Saalim bin Ubayd Al-Ashjaa'i
65. Safina Abu Abdur Rahmaan (freed slave of the Prophet)
66. Safwaan bin Baydaa'
67. Said bin Aamir Al-Jamhi
68. Salim bin Umayr
69. Salmaan al-Faarisi
70. Shaddaad bin Asid
71. Shaqran (freed slave of the Prophet)
72. Suhayb bin Sinaan
73. Takhfa bin Qays Al-Ghifaari
74. Talhah bin Amr Al-Basri
75. Thaabit bin Ad-Dahhaak al-Ansaari
76. Thaabit bin Wadi'a Al-Ansaari
77. Thaqif bin Amr
78. Thawbaan bin Yajdud (freed slave of Rasul Allaah)
79. Ubaadah bin Qars (also known as Ubaadah bin Qart)
80. Ubayd (freed slave of the Prophet)
81. Ukkaashah bin Mihsan Al-Asadi
82. Uqbah bin Aamir Al-Juhani
83. Utbah bin Abdullaah as-Sulami
84. Utbah bin An-Nadr As-Sulami
85. Uwaym bin Saa'ida Al-Ansaari
86. Waabisah bin Ma'bad Al-Juhani
87. Waathilah bin Al-Asqaa'
88. Yasaar Abu Fakihah (Freed slave of Safwaan bin Umayyah)
89. Zayd bin Al-Khattaab

BIBLIOGRAPHY

Qur'aan, Muslim Holy Book, Arabic Text, Several Translations.

Hadith, The Prophetic Traditions, Several Collections.

Ibn Isshaaq, Muhammad. *Sirat Rasul Allah.* Translated by A. Guillaume as *The Life of Muhammad.* 27th Ed. Karachi: Oxford University Press, 2014.

Ibn Hishaam, Muhammad Abdul Malik. *Seerat An-Nabi.* Beirut: Daar Al-Fikr, 1981.

Ibn Sa'ad, Muhammad, *Tabaqaat Ibn Sa'ad*, Urdu. Karachi: Nafis Academy, 1966.

Tabari, Mohibuddin. *The Mothers of the Believers.* Karachi: Darul-Ishaat, 2010.

Ibn Kathir, Muhammad, and Tafsir Ibn Kathir. *Under the Supervision of Safiur-Rahmaan Mubarakpuri.* English translation. Riyadh: 2000.

Al-Jawziyah, Ibn Qayyim. *Zaad-ul-Ma'aad, Provisions for the Hereafter.* Translated by Jalal Abualrub. Orlando: Islamic Earning Media Publications, 2003.

As-Sallaabee, Ali Muhammad. *The Noble Life of the Prophet.* Translation by Faisal Shafeeq. Riyadh: Darussalam, 2005.

Mubarakpuri, Safur-Rahman. *The Sealed Nectar.* Riyadh: Darussalam, 2002.

Lings, Martin. *Muhammad: His Life Based on the Earliest Sources.* Rochester, VT: Inner Traditions, 2006.

Salahi, Adil. *Muhammad: His Character and Conduct.* Leicestershire, UK: The Islamic Foundation, 2013.

Qadhi, Yasir. *Seerah of the Prophet Muhammad.* Audio Lectures.

Yusuf, Hamza. *The Life of the Prophet Muhammad, An Audio Rendition of Martin Lings's Book, Muhammad: His Life Based on the Earliest Sources, with His Own Commentary.*

Jumaah, Ahmad Khaleel, Nisaa Min Asr Al-Nabiy, Damascus, Daar Ibn Kathir (2003)

Hamid, Abdul Wahid, *Companions of the Prophet*, UK, Muslim Education and Literary Services, vol. 1

Various Articles from Numerous Sources.